Reviewers' Praise for *The Manufactured Crisis*

"For anyone interested in the true story of how our schools are doing, *The Manufactured Crisis* is must reading."　　　*—Mesa Tribune*

"It should be force-fed to every elected official, news reporter, and business executive in America, simply because it offers another perspective on the quality of public schools."　　　*—Denver Post*

"Though they defend public schools vigorously, the authors are hardly wedded to the status quo. They examine what they consider the real problems of education today and suggest a long list of changes."
　　　—Arizona Republic

"A welcome antidote to the gloom and doom that one constantly reads about the state of public education in America. The authors see the public schools as the essential cornerstone of American education and a central element in the social fabric. . . . *The Manufactured Crisis* is a sophisticated critique of school-bashing."　　　*—Commonweal*

"It is invigorating to have liberals such as Berliner and Biddle hitting back effectively with the kind of hard-hearted statistical analysis for which conservatives are famous."　　　*—The New Republic*

"Berliner and Biddle's new book examines those myths extensively, discusses the sources of those myths, and offers some solutions to the genuine problems that face this country's schools."　　　*—Education Digest*

"A gutsy, cogent, and well-documented book that both defends public education and offers ways to improve it."　　　*—Kirkus Reviews*

"With cogent facts and straightforward logic, they debunk the carefully nurtured conventional wisdom on American students' aptitude and achievement, school funding, and the effectiveness of U.S. schools versus those of other industrial nations. . . . A thorough but accessible analysis of an appalling campaign of disinformation."　　　*—Booklist*

Readers' Praise for *The Manufactured Crisis*

"This is one of the most important books we've had in education in a long time."
> —John Goodlad, Director, Center for Educational Renewal, University of Washington

"A very important book. A crucial antidote to the recklessness of the right-wing voucher advocates. Wise, insightful, politically charged."
> —Jonathan Kozol, author of *Savage Inequalities*

"This book makes it clear that the opponents of public education have manufactured an educational crisis, and the authors have effectively cut through the rhetoric to debunk anti-public school disinformation. A powerful piece of truth-telling."
> —Keith Geiger, former President, National Education Association

"Berliner and Biddle have made a significant contribution to the knowledge base by reinterpreting educational statistics which have painted a dire picture of the state of American public education. They challenge the notion that American schools are failing and are inferior to European schools. Whether you agree with their interpretations or not, I think *The Manufactured Crisis* should be required reading for all educators and policy makers."
> —Dr. Jane Stallings, former President, American Educational Research Association

"They got the story right, and they should be listened to."
> —Robert J. Shavelson, Dean, School of Education, Stanford University

"It's a wonderful correction to the imbalance in the national discourse."
> —Thomas Sobol, former Commissioner of Education, State of New York

The
Manufactured
Crisis

◆

The Manufactured Crisis

◆

Myths, Fraud, and the

Attack on America's Public Schools

David C. Berliner • Bruce J. Biddle

BASIC
BOOKS

A Member of the Perseus Books Group
New York

All acknowledgments for permission to reprint previously published material can be found on pages 413–414.

Library of Congress Cataloging-in-Publication Data

Berliner, David C.
    The manufactured crisis : myths, fraud, and the attack on America's
public schools / David C. Berliner, Bruce J. Biddle.
      p. cm.
    Includes bibliographical references and index.
    ISBN 0-201-40957-7
    ISBN 0-201-44196-9 (pbk)
    1. Public schools—United States.   2. Educational change—United
States.   I. Biddle, Bruce J. (Bruce Jesse), 1928–   . II. Title.
LA217.2.B46   1995
371′.01′0973—dc20   95-3271
                                                    CIP

Cover design by Suzanne Heiser
Text design by David F. Kelley
Set in 10.5-point Minion by Maryland Composition Co., Inc.

Perseus Books is a member of the Perseus Books Group

Previously published by Perseus Publishing
Published by Basic Books, A Member of the Perseus Books Group

Books published by the Perseus Books Group are available at
special discounts for bulk purchases in the United States by
corporations, institutions, and other organizations. For more
information, please contact the Special Markets Department at
the Perseus Books Group, 11 Cambridge Center, Cambridge, MA
02142, or call (617) 252-5298, (800) 255-1514 or e-mail
special.markets@perseusbooks.com.

Dedication

◆

To
Ursula Casanova
and
Barbara Bank

*for their intelligence,
creativity, and colleagueship;
moral commitments and humanity;
and unending support,
affection, and companionship.*

Contents

$\blacklozenge$

Preface

◆

This book was written in outrage.

Throughout much of recent history, our federal government seemed to be willing to promote the interests of public education. Advocates who favored public schools appeared regularly in both the White House and Congress; various programs to support the needs of our schools passed into law over the years; and although we knew that those schools continued to face many problems, our political leaders seemed to be aware of those problems and to be willing to respect the results of research on education in their pronouncements. Thus, like many other Americans, we came to believe that in their discussions of education, our federal leaders were, within limits, well-intentioned and honest people.

Events in the last decade have certainly challenged these beliefs. In 1983 the Reagan White House began to make sweeping claims attacking the conduct and achievements of America's public schools—claims that were contradicted by evidence we knew about. We thought at first this might have been a mistake, but these and related hostile and untrue claims were soon to be repeated by many leaders of the Reagan and Bush administrations. The claims were also embraced in many documents issued by industrialists and business leaders and were endlessly repeated and embroidered on by the press. And, as time passed even leading members of the education community—including a number of people whom we knew personally—began to state these lies as facts.

Slowly, then, we began to suspect that something was not quite right, that organized malevolence might actually be underway. We were, however, busy people, and it took us a while to begin to act on our suspicions. Though we had been friends for some years, our first acts were independent ones. David began to make speeches in which he challenged some of the false claims that were being made about schools and their effects, and Bruce began to write essays about the various ways in which federal politicians and their allies were throttling research and misusing evidence about education.

Eventually, we discovered that we were worried about the same things, and we decided to do a book together; then our education truly began. The more we poked into our story, the more nasty lies about education we unearthed; the more we learned about how government officials and their allies were ignoring, suppressing, and distorting evidence; and the more we discovered how Americans were being misled about schools and their accomplishments. This, then, has been the source of our outrage. We also began to wonder why this was happening—why were some people in Washington so anxious to scapegoat educators, what were they really up to, what problems were they trying to hide, what actions did they want to promote or prevent?

We also learned that the answers to these questions are not simple. Some of those who have accepted hostile myths about education have been genuinely worried about our schools, some have misunderstood evidence, some have been duped, and some have had other understandable reasons for their actions. But many of the myths seem also to have been told by powerful people who—despite their protestations—were pursuing a political agenda designed to weaken the nation's public shools, redistribute support for those schools so that privileged students are favored over needy students, or even abolish those schools altogether. To this end they have been prepared to tell lies, suppress evidence, scapegoat educators, and sow endless confusion. We consider this conduct particularly despicable.

This book, then, is designed to set the record straight about these events; to examine the evidence and correct the hostile myths that have been told about our schools; to explore why they were told and what the myth-tellers were up to; to examine the real problems of education that have too often been masked; and to explore what might be done about those problems.

In the process of writing the book, we also discovered that many good-hearted people shared our concerns, and we have benefited greatly from their insights and help. To begin with, we have learned from and owe thanks to those who have publicly challenged some of the myths and lies recently told about education—particularly Gerald Bracey, Eleanor Chelimsky, David Clark, William Cooley, Harold Hodgkinson, Richard Jaeger, George Kaplan, Jonathan Kozol, Edith Rasell and Lawrence Mishel, Iris Rotberg, Richard Rothstein, Joe Schneider and Paul Houston, Daniel Tanner, Howard Wolpe, and the brave scholars at the Sandia National Laboratories, who wrote and then had to defend a report that dramatically contradicted the untrue claims of the federal administration that had funded them. (We tell this last story in more detail later.) It is never easy to accuse powerful persons of deceit, but some of those we've noted above have dared to do just that—and all Americans owe them a debt of gratitude.

Many professional friends and colleagues have also assisted our work in various ways. In some cases, we note this help in our references by listing personal communications from specific individuals. In addition, we want to thank the following people for their encouragement and help: Don Anderson, N. L. Gage, Tom Good, Ivor Goodson, Mary McCaslin, Thomas McGowan, Fred Pincus, James Powell, Gary Smith, and Arthur Wirth.

Finally, we owe debts of thanks to the following people and institutions for specific types of assistance:

- Gary Fenstermacher and the American Association of Colleges for Teacher Education, for providing David the first opportunity to speak about these issues publicly

- The College of Education at Arizona State University and particularly Consuelo Kolbec, Karen Schultz, Chrys Gagopoulos, and Mary Sue Garganta, for services and help provided to David

- The Research Council and Graduate School at the University of Missouri, for awarding Bruce a research leave, thus facilitating a good deal of writing

- Kind souls who provided tangible help while Bruce was writing overseas, including Malcolm Clarkson of Falmer Press in London; and Frank Jones, Chair, and the faculty and staff of the Sociology Programme, Research School of Social Sciences, Australian National University

- And, above all, the Center for Research in Social Behavior at the University of Missouri—particularly Patricia Shanks, for endless hours of work with manuscripts and communications; Kathy Craighead, for expert preparation of exhibits; and Amy Wiard, for dedicated help with references for more than two years.

None of these kind people is responsible for the details of what we have written, of course, let alone the errors we may have made, but our book certainly could not have been completed without their very real help. We are much in their debt. Our work on this book owes no debts, however, to any foundation, professional association, educational group, or funding agency; for none of these organizations supported the writing of this work, and we alone are responsible for the judgments expressed in it.

In the meantime, we profoundly hope that this effort will help to dispel clouds of ignorance and confusion and that it will encourage the reemergence of more humane and honest dialogues concerning American education.

D. C. Berliner, Phoenix, AZ
B. J. Biddle, Columbia, MO
October 1994

The
Manufactured
Crisis

◆

Chapter One

Thinking About Education in a Different Way

◆

Headlines, news articles, and television news reports have recently portrayed a grim picture of children and their schools, a picture consistent enough to frighten thoughtful and caring people into concern for the future of their nation. Take, for example, the following news reports:

- In a typical year during the 1980s, minors aged fourteen to nineteen accounted for 43.4 percent of all criminal offenses. Fifty-four percent of all murder cases in the nation involved jobless youth.[1]
- A junior-high-school gang of six extorts $2,500 from 120 classmates.[2]
- Forty-four high school students go wilding and raid five shops for merchandise.[3]
- High school girls turn to prostitution for entertainment, curiosity, and as a source of revenue—police report their rate up 262 percent.[4]
- Fourteen-year-old student, repeatedly tormented and beaten by school thugs, hangs himself.[5]
- Teen tortured by two gang members. Victim burned by cigarettes on hands and back.[6]
- Group of students report feeling "refreshed" after beating up another child.[7]
- Ten percent of the nation's middle schools request police guards for their graduation ceremonies.[8]

With reports like these so commonplace, it is easy to understand why so many people worry so much about schooling and youth. But in this case, the people who have the worrying to do are not Americans. These are all reports from the *Japanese* media about the awful world of *Japanese* youth and the terrible failure of *Japanese* public schooling!

Were you surprised? We suspect that most American readers would automatically think that these statements concerned *American* youth and *American* schools. After all, every week our media seem to supply us with yet another frightening story about the dreadful state of education in our country.

In contrast, Americans regularly read and hear glowing reports of Japanese schools and their students' performance on international tests of achievement. Negative stories about Japanese schools are rarely found in our press or on our TV screens. Thus, Americans have been prevented from learning that the Japanese educational system also has enormous problems. In fact, if one judges by American values and standards, Japanese schools are often brutal, overly competitive places.

Perhaps you find this hard to believe. This may be because, like many other Americans, you have not been told about the thousands of elementary and junior high school students in Japan who refuse to attend school because of persistent problems of bullying—often directed against those with a foreign upbringing or against those who get outstanding grades or who have physical disabilities. Nor have Americans been made aware of the coercive overregulation of students and their families by many Japanese schools. For example, one Japanese school has a policy about the number of pleats permitted in a girl's skirt, violation of which results in the suspension of the child unless the mother comes to the school to beg forgiveness. Another school's policy on hair color and curls requires those who do not have straight black hair to obtain a note from a physician stating that they have a genetic problem. Other schools have policies that encourage cruelty by teachers; students have been given electric shocks for low grades, have died because they were locked in unventilated sheds as punishment for smoking, or have been beaten for using a hair dryer "illegally."[9] Americans are also not often told about the gifts of money that Japanese parents frequently pay to teachers to ensure good grades and good letters of recommendation for their children.

You may think our judgments are harsh, but we are not alone in condemning Japanese schools for brutality and for promoting overachievement. A decade ago, a select committee of *Japanese* educators reported to their own prime minister and his council of advisors that,

> Bullying, suicides among school children, dropping out from school, increasing delinquency, violence both at home and at school, heated entrance exam races, over-emphasis on scholastic ratings, and torture of children by some teachers are the result of the pathological mechanisms that have become established in Japan's education system.[10]

Manufacturing a Crisis in Education

> Seldom in the course of policymaking in the U.S. have so many firm convictions held by so many been based on so little convincing proof.
> —Clark Kerr, President Emeritus of the University of California (1991)

Given the serious problems of Japanese education, why have so many Americans come to believe that *American* education is so deficient and that we should look to the Japanese to find out how to run our schools! The answer is that for more than a dozen years this groundless and damaging message has been proclaimed by major leaders of our government and industry and has been repeated endlessly by a compliant press. Good-hearted Americans have come to believe that the public schools of their nation are in a crisis state because they have so often been given this false message by supposedly credible sources.

To illustrate, in 1983, amid much fanfare, the White House released an incendiary document highly critical of American education. Entitled *A Nation at Risk*,[11] this work was prepared by a prestigious committee under the direction of then Secretary of Education Terrel Bell and was endorsed in a speech by President Ronald Reagan. It made many claims about the "failures" of American education, how those "failures" were confirmed by "evidence," and how this would inevitably damage the nation. (Unfortunately, none of the supposedly supportive "evidence" actually appeared in *A Nation at Risk*, nor did this work provide citations to tell Americans where that "evidence" might be found.)

But leaders of this disinformation campaign were not content merely to attack American schools. *A Nation at Risk* charged that American students never excelled in international comparisons of student achievement and that this failure reflected systematic weaknesses in our school programs and lack of talent and motivation among American educators. Thus, it came as little surprise when the White House soon sent a team of Americans to Japan to discover and report on why Japanese education was so "successful." Following this visit, the then Assistant Secretary of Education, Chester Finn, a leader of the team, said of the Japanese,

> They've demonstrated that you can have a coherent curriculum, high standards, good discipline, parental support, a professional teaching force and a well-run school. They have shown that the average student can learn a whole lot more.[12]

This enthusiasm was echoed by others on the team. According to team member Herbert Walberg, an educational researcher, features of the Japanese system could be adopted in America and would help to solve the many "problems" of American education. Walberg suggested, "I think it's portable. Gumption and willpower, that's the key."[13]

This was far from the end of White House criticisms of American education. Indeed, the next decade witnessed a veritable explosion of documents and pronouncements from government leaders—two American presidents, Ronald Reagan and George Bush, secretaries of education, assistant secretaries, and chiefs and staff members in federal agencies—telling Americans about the many "problems" of their public schools. As in *A Nation at Risk*, most of these claims were said to reflect "evidence," although the "evidence" in question either was not presented or appeared in the form of simplistic, misleading generalizations.

During the same years many leaders in industry claimed in documents and public statements that American education was in deep trouble, that as a result our country was falling behind foreign competitors, and that these various charges were all confirmed by "evidence" (which somehow was rarely presented or appeared in simple misleading formats). And these many charges, documents, and pronouncements from leaders of government and industry, often seconded by prominent members of the educational community, were dutifully reported and endlessly elaborated upon by an unquestioning press.

So it is small wonder that many Americans have come to believe that education in our country is now in a deplorable state. Indeed, how could they have concluded anything else, given such an energetic and widely reported campaign of criticism, from such prestigious sources, attacking America's public schools? To the best of our knowledge, no campaign of this sort had ever before appeared in American history. Never before had an American government been so critical of the public schools, and never had so many false claims been made about education in the name of "evidence." We shall refer to this campaign of criticism as the Manufactured Crisis.

The Manufactured Crisis was not an accidental event. Rather, it appeared within a specific historical context and was led by identifiable critics whose political goals could be furthered by scapegoating educators. It was also supported from its inception by an assortment of questionable techniques—including misleading methods for analyzing data, distorting reports of findings, and suppressing contradictory evidence. Moreover, it was tied to misguided schemes for "reforming" education—schemes that would, if adopted, seriously damage American schools.

Unfortunately, the Manufactured Crisis has had a good deal of influence—thus, too many well-meaning, bright, and knowledgeable Americans have come to believe some of its major myths, and this has generated serious mischief. Damaging programs for educational reform have been adopted, a great deal of money has been wasted, effective school programs have been harmed, and morale has declined among educators.

But myths need not remain unchallenged; in fact, they become shaky when they are exposed to the light of reason and evidence. When one actually *looks* at the evidence, one discovers that most of the claims of the Manufactured Crisis are, indeed, myths, half-truths, and sometimes outright lies. Thus, as our first major task, we undertake, through reason and displays of relevant evidence, to dispel some of the mischief of the Manufactured Crisis—to place the crisis in context, to counter its myths, to explain why its associated agenda will not work, to set the record straight.

But accomplishing only this first task would leave many questions unanswered. One of the worst effects of the Manufactured Crisis has been to divert attention away from the *real* problems faced by American education—problems that are serious and that are escalating in today's world. To illustrate, although many Americans do not realize it, family incomes and financial support for schools are *much* more poorly distributed in our country than in other industrialized nations. This means that in the United States, very privileged students attend some of the world's best private and public schools, but it also means that large numbers of students who are truly disadvantaged attend public schools whose support is far below that permitted in other Western democracies. Thus, opportunities are *not* equal in America's schools. As a result, the achievements of students in schools that cater to the rich and the poor in our country are also far from equal.

In addition, America's school system has expanded enormously since World War II and now serves the needs of a huge range of students. This increased diversity has created many opportunities—but also many dilemmas—and debates now rage over how to distribute resources and design curricula to meet the needs of students from diverse backgrounds, with many different skills and interests. Problems such as these *must* be addressed if Americans are to design a school system that truly provides high standards and equal opportunities for all students.

Our second major task, then, is to direct attention away from the fictions of the Manufactured Crisis and toward the real problems of American schools.

Our Strategy

Facts are stubborn things; and whatever may be our wishes, our inclinations, or the dictates of our passions, they cannot alter the state of facts and evidence.

—John Adams (1770)

In order to accomplish the tasks we have set for ourselves in writing this book, we must take up some complex and controversial issues. In countering the myths and lies of the Manufactured Crisis, we must discuss and display the evidence that has so often been misrepresented by the critics. But when we do this, readers may get lost in the details of some of our arguments. To guard against such confusions, we present here an outline of the issues on which we focus.

In Chapter 2, we counter the myths about achievement and aptitude that have been spread by those who claim that American schools are in deep trouble. These myths include the following:

- Student achievement in American primary schools has recently declined
- The performance of American college students has also fallen recently
- The intellectual abilities and abstract problem-solving skills of America's young people have declined, although—paradoxically—it

is also believed that their intelligence and the skills that indicate "giftedness" are fixed and identifiable at an early age

- America's schools always come up short when compared with schools in other countries, indicating that our educational procedures are deficient and that our educators are feckless

As shall be shown, *none* of these charges can be supported. When one actually examines the evidence, one discovers that it simply will not support the fiction that America has a generally failing system of education. This claim is nonsense.

In Chapter 3, we take up other myths invented by the critics that tarnish the image of America's public schools. Among them are these:

- America spends a lot more money on its schools than other nations do

- Investing in the schools has not bought success—indeed, money is unrelated to school performance

- Recent increases in expenditures for education have been wasted or have gone merely into unneeded raises for teachers and administrators

- The productivity of American workers is deficient, and this reflects the inadequate training they receive in American schools

- America produces far too few scientists, mathematicians, and engineers; as a result, the country is losing its industrial leadership

- Our schools are not staffed by qualified teachers, the textbooks they use promote immorality, and most American parents are dissatisfied with their local schools

- Because they are subject to market forces, private schools are inherently better than public schools

Again, *none* of these myths can be supported. Although the critics have conceived a marvelous array of additional charges to lay against public schools, the evidence makes it clear that most of these charges are unfounded nonsense.

In Chapter 4, we look at the context for these charges. Why was the Manufactured Crisis invented in the early 1980s? Why was this unprecedented attack on public education unleashed at that particular time? Who was involved in it? What strategies were used by those responsible for the attack? Why did it have such striking effects?

Our answers touch on various matters: unresolved problems for education that escalated in the 1970s; reactionary voices that were given unprecedented legitimacy in the Reagan and Bush administrations; beliefs of American industrialists who were worried about overseas competition; long-established traditions of school-bashing in America; desires to scapegoat educators as a way of diverting attention from America's deepening social problems; self-interest on the part of some government officials; Americans' long-held beliefs in individualism and the powers of education; the misuse, abuse, and suppression of evidence by the critics; and irresponsible actions of the media. These factors help one to appreciate why the Manufactured Crisis appeared, but they do not make it admirable.

Myths lead to poor ideas for educational reform. Chapter 5 considers the likely outcomes if Americans foolishly allowed themselves to adopt some of the major reform proposals put forward by those responsible for the Manufactured Crisis. We look, for example, at proposals for voucher programs that would divert public funds to support private schools; intensification efforts (such as lengthening the school day or year); the use of monitoring and external reward systems with students or teachers; accountability programs, in which schools compete with one another for status or funding; immersion programs for bilingual education; and programs that provide enriched education for "gifted" students.

Evidence suggests that many of these proposals are not merely foolish. If enacted, most would seriously damage America's students, educators, or school programs. The chapter ends with a brief discussion of the educational programs of the Clinton administration.

In Chapters 6 and 7, we turn to issues in education that have been difficult to think about as long as Americans have had to contend with the myths of the Manufactured Crisis. Chapter 6 explores major social problems that afflict our country—problems that are often worse here than in other advanced democracies, that are often escalating, and that affect our schools directly. These problems include income and wealth inequality; recent stagnation of the economy; racial, ethnic, religious, and linguistic diversity in America; prejudice toward Americans of color; the ghettoization of America's cities; violence and drugs; the aging of the population; the restructuring of work. Everyday features of American education also generate problems for schools—features such as age-graded classrooms; heavy stress on public competitions; tracking systems; bureaucratization of large school systems; America's unique system of quasi-autonomous local school districts; problems generated by private schools; and the acceptance of too many tasks for public education. In addition, American education faces three extraordinary problems: our traditional willingness to tolerate *huge* differences in funding for public schools; the dilemmas created by our radically expanded education system; and the fact that more and more disadvantaged children will be entering our schools. Realistic plans for improving America's schools must *begin* by taking problems such as these seriously.

Chapter 7 takes up some principles for educational improvement. Among other things, we argue that improvements are more likely to come about if the following occur:

- Families have dignity and children have hope
- Extra funding for schools goes where needs are greatest
- Equalization of school funding takes place within states
- Average school size is reduced
- Traditional conceptions of the goals of education are modified and enlarged
- Teaching methods are changed in such a way that they emphasize more collaborative learning
- Curricular changes that foster the skills actually needed for employment and citizenship in the twenty-first century are introduced
- New evaluation systems are evolved in such a way that they reflect the new curricula, methods, and actual achievements of educators
- Age-graded classrooms and ability tracking are abandoned
- Local communities are more involved with efforts to improve their schools
- Teachers and other educators are treated as intelligent professionals

In Chapter 8 we make a plea for more research and more compassion. We point out that our review has drawn extensively from research evidence; research, however, has not yet addressed many of the crucial issues facing education today. This is hardly surprising since America spends only a pittance on educational research. In addition, effective reforms cannot follow from premises that are based on myths and lies, that scapegoat American educators, that blame American students, or that heap indignities on minorities and the poor. Effective educational reforms must begin with compassion for America's neediest students and for the many educators who give so much, so often. Indeed, the ultimate test of a society is not how well it takes care of its rich and powerful, but how well it attends to the needs of its poorest and weakest citizens.

Battling Disbelief

It is always easier to believe than to deny. Our minds are naturally affirmative.
   —John Burroughs (1900)

The great masses of the people . . . will more easily fall victims to a big lie than to a small one.
   —Adolf Hitler (*Mein Kampf,* 1933, Chapter 10)

Lots of intelligent people believe things that aren't true. Many people believe, for example, that more babies are born during the full moon, and tourists are often frightened about the alligators that are thought to live in the sewers of New York City. Belief in such fictions seems to be remarkably durable and resists contradicting evidence or energetic campaigns to ease the fears that such fictions cause. Indeed, widespread belief in some things that are untrue seems to be part of the human condition.

Many of the myths promoted in the Manufactured Crisis are now so widely believed that we suspect that some people will find it hard to accept what we write here. Some will find it difficult to stop believing in these myths because they were endorsed by so many "important" people in government and industry—including two American presidents! Others may suspect that the two of us are politically motivated and that we are distorting or even fabricating our reports of evidence. Still others—good people, energetic people, people devoted to education—may be so committed to educational reforms based on the myths we cite that they cannot abandon them. And still others may choose to cling to those myths in the hope that they can be used to promote needed reforms or encourage more funding for education.

Some readers may have difficulty with our ideas because they have long held suspicions about problems in America's public schools, and they find it hard to abandon myths which support those suspicions. Indeed, complaining about public education has long been a popular American indoor sport.

But beyond these reasons, several factors may make it especially difficult for some readers to accept our arguments. We review four of these here.

Fraud and Its Victims. Some readers may be reluctant because they don't want to acknowledge that they had bought into fraudulent ideas, that they were victimized by a massive "con game." To appreciate their plight, one must come to understand that the Manufactured Crisis was not merely an accidental set of events or a product of impersonal social forces. It also involved a serious campaign by identifiable persons to sell Americans the false idea that their public schools were failing and that because of this failure the nation was at peril. This campaign involved a great deal of effort, chicanery, playing on people's worries, pandering to prejudices, and misreporting and misrepresenting evidence. In short, to use terms that were popular when discussing World War II propaganda, this campaign constituted a Big Lie—and a lot of people were gulled by its claims.

It is never easy to acknowledge that one was gullible—that one has swallowed deceptions sold by charlatans—and this is particularly hard when those deceptions are massive. And yet many good-hearted Americans have been victimized in just this way. As we challenge the myths and fictions of the Manufactured Crisis, some people will find it difficult to acknowledge that they were so often duped.

Distorted and Hostile Reporting. Others may question our arguments because they have so often been besieged by negative and distorted media reports about our educational system. A recent incident illustrates this point nicely. In mid-September of 1993, many newspapers in the country carried headlines announcing the results of a big federal study of literacy in America.[14] On September 9 the front page of the *New York Times* reported that "half of adults in the U.S. lack reading and mathematics abilities," while the *Washington Post* headlined, "Literacy of 90 Million Is Deficient."[15] And for a week thereafter reporters wrote countless stories about the supposed illiteracy of the American public that were to be *read* by the millions of people who collectively made up that public.

Most of these stories were based on a *press conference* called by the U.S. Department of Education to announce the study they had sponsored rather than on the *actual report* in which the study was summarized. Thus, the reporters failed to note or to inform Americans that the researchers had classified people as "illiterate" merely because they did not score well on a test of reading comprehension. This sounds reasonable until one begins to think about some startling characteristics of the so-called illiterate group that the report detailed. For example, nearly 40 percent of these "illiterate" persons were employed full-time; nearly 70 percent were reported to be "not poor"; over 80 percent did not receive food stamps; and approximately one-third were receiving regular interest from their own savings accounts. About four out of five "illiterates" also declared that they read "well" or "very well." Only a few said they needed to rely on family or friends to interpret prose material, and nearly half reported reading a newspaper every day! Worse, some truly startling categories of people turned out to have been classified as among the most illiterate: 26 percent had debilitating physical or mental conditions, 19 percent had difficulties reading print because they were visually impaired, and 25 percent were immigrants whose native language was not English—the language of the test.

This means that reporters failed to note details of the study that seriously challenged the major conclusions announced at the press conference. (In fact, one wonders who were actually illiterate, the visually impaired and non-English-speaking Americans who could not pass the study's test or the reporters who failed to read or understand its report!) Moreover, no news analyst seems to have questioned the basic premise put forth by the Department of Education at that conference; namely, that illiteracy causes poverty. Somehow, no one seems to have thought that the relationship between poverty and illiteracy might go the other way—indeed that good research had already been done indicating that *poverty causes low levels of literacy.*[16] This is a difference that matters. If poverty is a major *cause* of illiteracy, then it is time indeed that Americans take seriously the fact that poverty rates are *far* worse in our country than in other Western democracies.

Unfortunately, this episode is all too typical of recent, ignorant, highly critical media portrayals of American education and its effects. Hardly a week passes without one or more inflammatory press accounts detailing the "rotten" state of America's schools. (In later chapters we provide other examples of such accounts.) Given that the press regularly trumpets "evidence" purporting to confirm the failures of American education, is it any wonder that many Americans have accepted this message? And given such incessant media irresponsibility, who would be surprised if some readers had difficulty believing *us?*

The Legacy of Socrates. Other readers may question our arguments because they believe that many things, including education and the manners of young people, were better in the past than in the present. Such beliefs are not new. Consider the legacy of Socrates. Ever since Socrates roamed the streets of Athens 2,500 years ago, muttering about the lack of discipline and knowledge among Athenian youth, countless older people have believed their offspring to be inferior to themselves.

We suspect that Socrates' Syndrome shows up most often among adults when their culture is changing rapidly, as was happening in ancient Athens and as is happening in America today. When cultures change rapidly, younger people do not know the same things their parents know. For example, in a farm family in Nebraska in the 1890s, adults and children probably shared a good deal of knowledge and values. With the nation's rapid pace of change, however, Nebraskan youths of the 1990s are presumably *much* less likely to think and act like their parents. (They probably know a lot less about how to stoke a coal furnace or how to use a wringer washer and a great deal more about programming personal computers and rock music!) And this almost always makes parents nervous.

Parents and other adults, however, may not stop to think that children may know *different* things than they do, a natural consequence of living in a rapidly changing culture with an exploding knowledge base. Their problem, like Socrates', is that they see differences as deficiencies, but such reasoning is questionable. Each generation must determine which bits of knowledge from the past to retain and which to abandon in favor of new knowledge. Some people find this a threatening state of affairs and may well decide to blame the schools for their discomfort. Such people may question our arguments that the schools have been maligned.

Confusing Reality With Desire. Other people confuse what schools *are* with what they *would like* schools to be. They condemn the schools of today because they are afraid that the graduates they produce will not be ready for the twenty-first century, will find they are not able to compete in the global marketplace, or will not be able to respond to the needs of corporations in the future. Such worries are difficult to address, since it is not easy to predict the future clearly.

But it is *not* necessary to destroy faith in the public schools because some people believe that schools are not doing all that is necessary to prepare for the next century. Directing the schools toward a different set of goals would certainly be appropriate—*if* we were truly wise enough to predict the future. But we need not condemn the schools of today in order to engage in debates about what the schools of the future should be like.

Be that as it may, those who seriously confuse reality with desire are unlikely to be satisfied with schools in today's America, no matter how impressive the performance of those institutions. Such people may also have difficulty with our words of comfort.

Suspending Judgment. Although all of these people may have reasons for disbelieving what we write here, we urge them to set aside those reasons for the present. There is something marvelously persuasive about *evidence,* and—as readers will discover—whenever possible we present evidence to back the claims we will make about the myths of the Manufactured Crisis and about the real problems of American education. Moreover, we've tried to provide citations for all of our claims, and readers are urged to check our original sources whenever they have questions about what we present here.

Of course, it is hard to find any single study that will convince someone who is sure of beliefs that those beliefs are wrong. It is also very difficult to find evidence that is easy to interpret and that is unambiguous and convincing enough to settle issues as complex as the ones we address here. Further, evidence from social research rarely comes in easy-to-use formats. For this reason, we have tried, where possible, to convert tabular data, obscure statistics, and technical jargon into common-language words and visual images that readers can more easily follow.

But the arguments we make do not rest on single studies, nor do they hang or fall on obscure and technical points. On the contrary, in most cases the evidence we display comes from many studies and makes simple and straightforward points. And collectively that evidence leads to two simple and straightforward conclusions: (1) on the whole, the American school system is in far better shape than the critics would have us believe; (2) where American schools fail, those failures are largely caused by problems that are imposed on those schools, problems that the critics have been only too happy to ignore. American education *can* be restructured, improved, and strengthened—but to build realistic programs for achieving these goals, we must explode the myths of the Manufactured Crisis and confront the real problems of American education.

Chapter Two

Myths About Achievement and Aptitude

◆

This chapter is concerned with a key tenet of the Manufactured Crisis. Critics of American schools have argued that student achievement has declined sharply, that American students now lag seriously behind students in other Western countries, and that these facts are confirmed by massive evidence. America's teachers and schools are failing the nation, they say, and America is in danger of falling into the ash can of history. As we shall show, these assertions are errant nonsense.

Americans are, of course, concerned about the performance of their schools. Such concerns are legitimate and should be encouraged. However, concerns about education and plans for its improvement should be based on an honest and informed evaluation of available evidence. In this chapter we shall use many data sources that lead to clear but perhaps surprising conclusions—that, on average, today's students are at least as well informed as students were in previous generations and that education in America compares favorably with education elsewhere.

What makes these conclusions surprising is that the critics have so often stated otherwise. But repetition of false claims does not make those claims true. Let us therefore restate the major myths about achievement and aptitude that critics have used and look carefully at the evidence that refutes those myths.

MYTH . . . Student Achievement Has Recently Fallen Across the Nation

For the first time in the history of our country, the educational skills of one generation will not surpass, will not equal, will not even approach those of their parents.

— Paul Copperman (cited in *A Nation At Risk*, National Commission on Excellence in Education, 1983, p. 11)

Average achievement of high school students on most standardized tests is now lower than 26 years ago when Sputnik was launched.

— *A Nation At Risk* (1983, p. 8)

> [From 1950 to 1989] we probably experienced the worst educational decline in our history. Between 1963 and 1980, for example, combined average Scholastic Aptitude Test (SAT) scores—scores which test students' verbal and math abilities—fell 90 points, from 980 to 890.
>
> —William Bennett (*The Devaluing of America,* 1992, p. 55)

Shortly after he became secretary of education in the Reagan administration, William Bennett held a televised news conference. Fortified with impressive visual aids, he claimed that student achievement had declined greatly in the nation. Evidence from objective tests supported this claim, he said. A CRISIS was at hand. Our schools were failing, our youth were becoming ignoramuses, our industries were losing their competitive edge, our country was in *danger.* And given that Secretary Bennett spoke from the "pulpit" of the White House, the press dutifully reported his claims as if they were gospel. Moreover, Secretary Bennett was not alone in making these claims. They were also made in *A Nation At Risk* and other reports that were then being commissioned by government and industry. Reading each other's flawed reports, a host of critics have since chorused that student achievement has declined "massively" and that this decline is confirmed by "many" different standardized test records.

Although we are not sure how appropriate it is to use standardized test data to judge the performance of schools, such tests *do* provide hard, objective evidence that seems relevant to claims about achievement. Standardized tests appear to be rocks of stability in a sea of unanchored opinions, and it is small wonder that people worry when critics make alarming assertions about "massive" declines in student achievement.

We confront these assertions with a novel approach; we review here the actual *evidence* generated by standardized tests. From that evidence, readers will learn that standardized test data reveal *no* recent drop in student achievement; indeed, many of the tests indicate modest recent *gains* in students' knowledge. In fact, we know of only *one* standardized test that ever generated falling aggregate test scores—the Scholastic Aptitude Test (SAT)—but, as we shall show, that decline had nothing to do with average student achievement. In fact, when analyzed correctly, the SAT data also reveal a pattern of achievement *growth!* In short, the real evidence indicates that the myth of achievement decline is not only false—it is a hysterical fraud.

The Scholastic Aptitude Test. We begin with the SAT story. To be sure, *aggregate* total SAT scores obtained by the nation's high school seniors fell between about 1963 and 1975 (see Exhibit 2.1). Moreover, that decline came about because aggregate scores fell for both parts of the SAT—the parts that measure, respectively, verbal and mathematics achievement.

This decline has been cited as evidence that our schools were failing by many people—such as William Bennett—who were either ignorant or

Exhibit 2.1   Average SAT Scores by Year

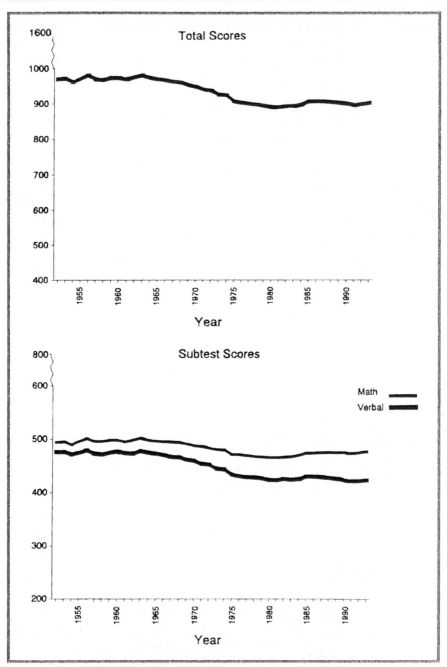

—Sources: Donlon (1984) and The College Entrance Examination Board (1993).

wanted to rubbish public education. These doomsayers argue that such a "huge" decline in SAT scores—ranging from 60 to 90 points, depending on the years used to compute the figure—was sure proof that the nation was in trouble. And to this day the press continues to report annual figures for aggregate national SAT scores (sometimes citing shifts of one or two point‍ in those scores) as if they were a report card that can tell Americans something about the effectiveness of their schools.

This is all nonsense. Such small shifts in SAT scores are not meaningful, and by themselves aggregate SAT scores provide no information about the performance of American schools. To understand this, one must learn a bit about the SAT and its limitations.

First, how are SAT scores generated, and what does an SAT score truly mean? The SAT is taken by high school seniors and for some years has required those students to answer 138 multiple-choice questions, 78 concerned with verbal materials, 60 focused on mathematics. (It has *not* examined student knowledge of history, the sciences, the arts, the humanities, foreign languages, the social sciences, or other important subjects that high schools also teach.) Although new questions are developed for the SAT each year, those questions have been carefully checked so that each new edition of the SAT has been presumed to be equivalent to the first "standardized" form of the test, which appeared *in April of 1941.* If we believe the critics, then, the quality of the entire twelve or more years of schooling to which American students are exposed could be judged by means of a 138-item test requiring only a few hours to complete, and composed of questions designed to assess only a narrow range of student knowledge against the standards of fifty years ago!

Second, scores for the SAT are not reported as numbers of right answers but are "converted" (through obscure rules) in such a way that the scale scores earned by each student for each subtest range from 200 to 800 points. This means that the total SAT score for an individual can range from 400 to 1600 points, but this huge range of scale points actually represents a much smaller range of correct or incorrect answers. Thus, in the middle of the SAT range, a difference of one correct or incorrect answer will generate about *ten* points of difference in the SAT scale score. You may think this is absurd, but there is actually more confusion. The relation between number of correct SAT answers and scale scores also varies, depending on the number of right answers. In fact, the very talented student who correctly answers all but one of the questions on the verbal part of the SAT loses *fifty* scale points for that one error, earning a score of 750 rather than 800.

What does this mean for the interpretation of aggregate SAT scores? Such aggregates are computed by averaging the individual scale scores of many thousands of students. Since the scale scores summed in those averages come from students representing the entire talent range, it is literally impossible to compute exactly what a difference in aggregate SAT scores means in terms of average numbers of questions answered correctly on the test. But if we assume that most students answered a middling number of questions correctly, then a decline of "from 60 to 90 points" in aggregate SAT scale scores probably means that the average student answered from six to nine fewer questions correctly. Since students had to answer 138 questions in all, this means that the "terrible" decline in SAT scores was in reality a drop of perhaps 5 percent in the number of questions answered correctly. Put this way, the decline in aggregate SAT scores that began about 1963 seems a good deal less "massive." Moreover, the drop that did occur in aggregate SAT scores ceased in the mid-1970s, and there has been no evidence of a decline since then. Recent annual shifts in aggregate national scores have been minute, often amounting to only one or two scale points, which probably means that the students of America have answered, or failed to answer, one or two *tenths* of an additional SAT question.

Third, problems are also generated when one tries to figure out the meaning of *aggregate* SAT scores. The SAT was designed to predict the grade point averages of individual college freshmen and has demonstrated real, if limited, value when used for this purpose. SAT scores were never intended to be aggregated for evaluating the achievements of teachers, schools, school districts, or states, and such scores have *no* validity when used for such evaluations. The reason is that the SAT is a *voluntary* test and is typically taken only by those high school seniors interested in going to college. Moreover, the proportion of students choosing to take the SAT varies sharply across the country. For example, in 1993 the percentage of students taking the SAT varied from *less than 10 percent* in Alabama, Arkansas, Iowa, Kansas, Louisiana, Mississippi, North Dakota, Oklahoma, South Dakota, and Utah to *more than 70 percent* in Connecticut, the District of Columbia, Massachusetts, New Hampshire, New Jersey, New York, and Rhode Island.[1]

Does this matter? Absolutely. When only a few students take the SAT, those students are likely to be people with strong high school records, who are trying to get into "the best" colleges. In contrast, when a larger proportion of students take the SAT, that proportion will include more students with weak high school records, who are merely hoping to qualify for some kind of higher education. This means, of course, that the aggregate SAT score earned by a school, school district, or state is not valid for judging the educational quality of that unit unless all, or a *representative* sample, of its students take the test. This may sound like a harsh judgment, but we are only echoing a warning that has already been circulated by the College Entrance Examination Board, which publishes the SAT (see Exhibit 2.2).

Now, let us apply this principle to the problem of interpreting aggregate SAT scores for the nation. Widespread adoption of the SAT came about gradually, but since the mid-1960s, only about half of all eligible high school seniors in the country have taken the test each year.[2] Aggregate national SAT scores, therefore, have never represented the nation as a whole but have

■ EXHIBIT 2.2
Cautions on the Use of Aggregate
SAT Scores

As measures of developed verbal and mathematical abilities important for success in college, SAT scores are useful in making decisions about individual students and assessing their academic preparation. Using these scores in aggregate form as a single measure to rank or rate teachers, educational institutions, districts, or states is invalid because it does not include all students. In being incomplete, this use is inherently unfair.

The most significant factor in interpreting SAT scores is the proportion of eligible students taking the exam—the participation rate. . . . Thus, to make useful comparisons of students' performance between states [or among teachers, schools, or districts], a common test given to all students would be required. Because the percentage of SAT takers varies widely. . . , and because the test takers are self-selected, the SAT is inappropriate for this purpose.

—Source: Excerpted from *Guidelines on the Uses of College Board Test Scores and Related Data* (The College Entrance Examination Board, 1988).

always been generated by a self-selected pool of students who wanted to attend college and thought they could improve their chances by taking the test.

Moreover, the composition of students who take the SAT has varied over time. Data on the characteristics of test takers have been distributed by the College Entrance Examination Board since 1976, and these suggest how student composition has changed over the past eighteen years. The accompanying graph (Exhibit 2.3) displays the percentages of students from each of the five high school achievement ranks who chose to take the test in 1976 and 1993. As you can see, more students from the lower achievement ranks have recently opted to take the SAT. This would not matter if students from each achievement rank were equal in their abilities, but this is obviously not the case. Students who earn top high school grades also are much more likely to earn high SAT scores than students who earn mediocre high school grades. This means that even if the ability of schools to educate students remains constant across the nation, aggregate national SAT scores will fall when more students from the lower achievement ranks choose to take the test.

The proportion of students representing minority groups and differing levels of family income has also changed over time, and this has also affected aggregate SAT scores. As we noted above, the SAT was standardized to predict the college grades of students interested in entering college *in 1941*—at a time when these students were predominantly from white, Anglo-Saxon,

Exhibit 2.3   Percentage of Students Taking SAT by Class Rank

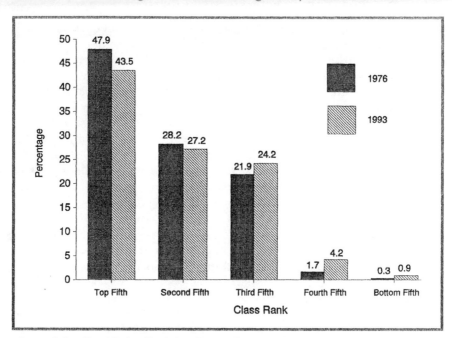

—Source: *College Bound Seniors* (The College Entrance Examination Board, various dates).

middle- or upper-middle-class, Protestant homes where English was spoken. We should not be surprised, therefore, to learn that minority and immigrant students tend to have lower scores than the group that first took the SAT fifty years ago. (In fact, so striking is this problem that James Crouse and Dale Trusheim have recently argued that whenever decisions about college admission are based on SAT results, those decisions are *always* biased against impoverished, minority students.[3]) Even if schools across the nation retain their abilities to educate students, aggregate national SAT scores will also fall when more students from impoverished, minority backgrounds choose to take the test.

Finally, SAT results are also closely tied to the income earned by students' families. In fact, at present the average SAT score earned by students goes down by *fifteen points* for each decrease of $10,000 in family income.[4] This means, of course, that whenever colleges use the SAT for making admissions decisions, they are also discriminating against students from poorer homes. And it means that aggregate SAT scores will also fall when more students from poorer families choose to take the test.

How does this help us to understand the small decline in aggregate SAT scores during the late 1960s and early 1970s? If nothing else, this decade was a period of exploding interest in higher education among groups in the population that had not aspired to college before then. Sharply larger numbers of students from the lower-achievement ranks in high schools, from minority groups, and from poorer families began to take the SAT during those years—and these decisions alone were sufficient to generate the decline in aggregate national SAT scores during these decades. Thus, the brief decline in SAT scores a generation ago provided no information whatever about the performance of American schools but was, instead, a signal that interest in higher education was spreading throughout the nation. Surely this should have been a matter for rejoicing, not alarm.

In larger terms, since the SAT is voluntary and is only taken by roughly one-half of high school seniors across the nation, aggregate national SAT scores will *always* reflect the characteristics of students who choose to take the test. And since those characteristics change over time, aggregate national scores simply *cannot* be used for making valid judgments about the performance of the nation's schools. Despite repeated claims by the critics and alarmist reports in the press, shifts in national *aggregate* SAT scores tell us nothing at all about the performance or problems in American education.

So much for *aggregate* SAT scores. But isn't it possible to discover something about the nation's educational achievements by looking at *disaggregated* SAT data? Yes, it is possible, and it can be done in various ways. For example, we can look at disaggregated SAT scores for students with stronger and weaker high school records, and we can ask, how have these different student groups fared recently in SAT scores?

Exhibit 2.4 displays average scores for the verbal and mathematics subtests of the SAT for students from each high-school rank for the past eighteen years. As this exhibit shows, over this period verbal SAT scores remained quite constant, but scores for the mathematics subtest increased slightly for each of the five achievement ranks. (Granted, these increases were small, but they were consistent. The increase for the top rank was ten points, and for the remaining ranks the increases were thirteen, thirteen, seven, and four points respectively.) Thus, students with both strong and weak achievement records have recently been holding their own on the verbal SAT and doing slightly better in mathematics. Moreover, the top fifth of high school seniors have continued to score at a healthy level on both subtests of the SAT and still earn an aggregate score that exceeds 1000.

In addition, data have been available since 1976 concerning the race and ethnicity of students taking the SAT. As Exhibit 2.5 shows, average SAT scores were nearly constant for white students, but the scores *increased* for every minority group during this period. (The slight decline for white students merely reflects the larger numbers of those students with weaker academic backgrounds who are now taking the test—look again at Exhibit 2.3.)

When one looks at *disaggregated* SAT data, then, one discovers the following: (1) scores for verbal achievement have been holding steady; (2) scores for mathematics achievement have shown modest recent increases; (3) white

Exhibit 2.4   Average SAT Scores by High School Class Rank

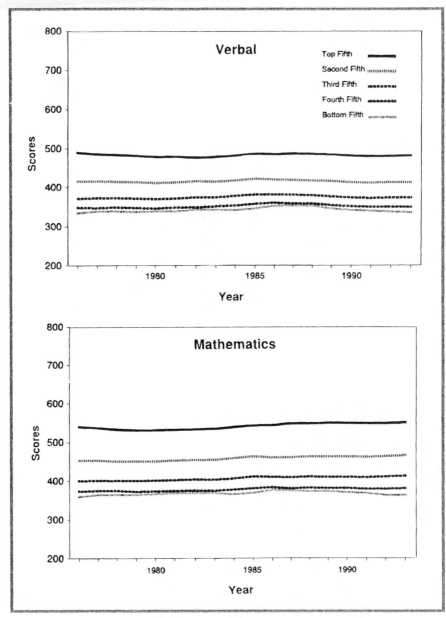

—Source: *College Bound Seniors* (The College Entrance Examination Board, various dates).

Exhibit 2.5   Average SAT Subpopulation Scores

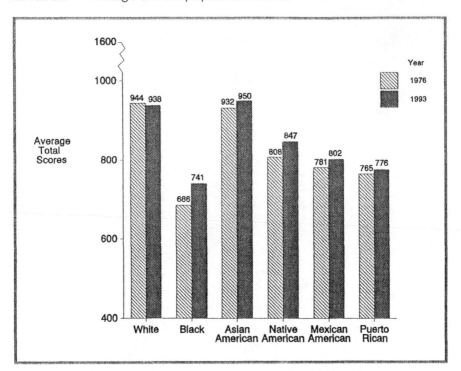

—Source: *College Bound Seniors* (The College Entrance Examination Board, 1993, p. 10).

students have been holding their own; (4) students from minority homes are now earning higher average scores. The last two findings, in particular, are truly startling when compared with incessant charges leveled by the critics. How on earth can America's teachers and schools be failing the nation when SAT scores for white students have recently been stable, the average SAT score for Native Americans has increased thirty-nine points, and average scores for blacks has gone up a whopping fifty-five points? Citizens should rejoice at this marvelous news.

A summary of the SAT story:

- The SAT is a one shot, multiple-choice test that is taken by high school seniors; the test assesses only students' knowledge of a fixed set of topics in mathematics and English against the performance standards of a group of high status, mostly male, mostly Northeastern students who wanted to enter highly selective colleges in 1941.

- SAT scale scores are not meaningful in and of themselves; large shifts in scale scores represent only small shifts in the number of SAT test questions answered correctly.

- Since the SAT is taken by only those students interested in going to college, *aggregate* SAT scores should not be used for judging the performance of schools, school districts, states, or the nation as a whole.

- *Disaggregated* SAT scores suggest that student achievement in the nation has either been steady or has been climbing over the past eighteen years.

So although critics have trumpeted the "alarming" news that aggregate national SAT scores fell during the late 1960s and the early 1970s, this decline indicates nothing about the performance of American schools. Rather, it signals that students from a broader range of backgrounds were then getting interested in college, which should have been cause for celebration, not alarm.

The American College Testing Program. Before turning to other data sources, we should also discuss briefly the other major test that is taken by high school seniors who hope to go to college. The American College Testing Program (ACT) was founded in 1959. Many students now take the twelfth-grade ACT test instead of the SAT, and some critics have claimed that ACT scores also confirm a recent "decline" in the performance of American schools. At first, this claim seems to make sense, since the ACT test is similar to the SAT in several ways. Like the SAT, it covers more than one subject (before 1989, English, Mathematics, Social Studies, and Natural Science). Like the SAT, the ACT test is voluntary. And though it uses a different scaling procedure, like the SAT it uses a fixed process, with obscure rules, for converting number of right answers to scaled scores. Shouldn't we, then, also look at ACT test scores over the years to check whether they confirm a national achievement decline?

Actually, we shouldn't do this at all. The reason is that the ACT test does *not* have a fixed set of content topics but, rather, is revised each year by panels of consultants. Each year these experts propose new items to test the *evolving* curricula at American colleges and universities for the subjects tested, and since those curricula change over time, so does the coverage of the ACT test.[5] This means that average ACT test scores for any given year should *not* be compared with those of other years because the tests they came from were measuring somewhat different things.

Thus, one can safely ignore claims by critics about recent shifts in average ACT test score results. Like the rumors of Mark Twain's death, the meaningfulness of such shifts (if any) is greatly exaggerated.

The Preliminary Scholastic Aptitude Test. Given problems with the SAT, it is useful to look also at other test data that may reflect the performance of students in American schools. We turn first to the Preliminary Scholastic

Exhibit 2.6   Average PSAT Mathematics and Verbal Scores

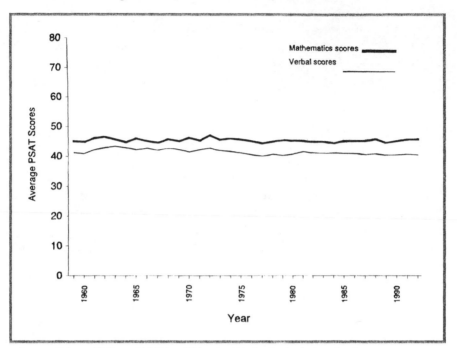

—Sources: Solomon (1983, pp. 24 & 27) and Educational Testing Service (various dates).

Aptitude Test (PSAT). A short version of the SAT, this test is designed to try out new questions and is given annually to national samples of high school juniors. Since the PSAT is given to *representative* samples, rather than to volunteers only, aggregate PSAT scores are more useful than aggregate SAT scores for assessing national achievement.

PSAT data are available for each year since 1959. As Exhibit 2.6 shows, they do *not* suggest any fall in the performance of American schools. In the words of Gerald Bracey, "The lines on a graph of average student scores on the PSAT are as flat as the surface of a frozen lake. Nowhere is there any hint of a decline."[6] In other words, evidence from the PSAT provides *no* support for the myth of a decline in the academic achievement of American students.

The National Assessment of Educational Progress. An even better source of data about academic achievement comes from the National Assessment of Educational Progress (NAEP). This testing program is conducted by the National Center for Education Statistics of the U.S. Department of Education and is designed to be "The nation's report card" when it comes to assessing educational progress. NAEP tests are given to national samples of

Exhibit 2.7   National Trends in Proficiency by Year (NAEP Data)

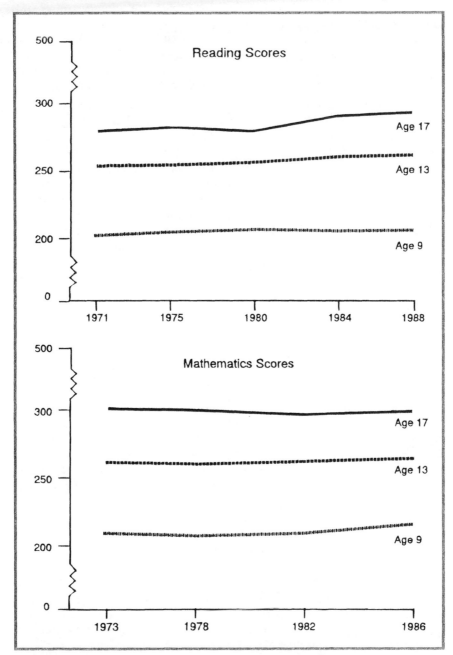

—Source: *Accelerating Academic Achievement* (Educational Testing Service, 1990, p. 32).

students aged nine, thirteen, and seventeen. The students are tested about every two years in mathematics, science, reading, writing, geography, and computer skills. These tests include items that assess reasoning ability and are not intended to be mere tests of memory. What have these tests shown over recent years with regard to student achievement?

In general, the NAEP tests have shown very little change over the past two decades. Exhibit 2.7 shows that average NAEP scores earned by students across the nation in reading and mathematics for various years between the early 1970s and late 1980s have hardly changed during this period.

This is not our judgment alone. In 1990 the Educational Testing Service reviewed findings from twenty years of the NAEP and concluded, "there have been various declines and improvements from assessment to assessment, but over the long term, achievement levels are quite stable."[7] Even such prominent critics of the schools as former Secretary of Education Lamar Alexander and former Assistant Secretary Diane Ravitch were forced to agree with this judgment. Following release of 1991 NAEP scores, Secretary Alexander opined that "today's children seem to know about as much math and about as much science and read about as well as their parents did at that age about 20 years ago"; and Assistant Secretary Ravitch asserted that "the achievement trend lines are essentially flat over the last 20 years."[8]

These general findings hide, however, some interesting NAEP results for subgroups. For example, some NAEP data confirm the recent growth in achievement for minority groups that are reflected in SAT scores. As Exhibit 2.8 shows, the NAEP data indicate that white students have recently held their own in mathematics and that black and Hispanic students have gained significantly.

A second NAEP result suggests a new effect that is difficult to confirm with data from the SAT. Exhibit 2.9 displays average NAEP scores for reading proficiency earned, respectively, by students in Advantaged Metro/Suburban, Rural, and Disadvantaged/Metro schools for various years from the early 1970s through the late 1980s. Over this period, students' scores from advantaged schools were relatively unchanged, while the achievement of rural and disadvantaged/metro schools showed small gains.

(We have reprinted these two graphs from *The Sandia Report,* a major review of evidence concerning the performance of American schools that was originally prepared in 1990 by officials of the Sandia National Laboratories, a branch of the Department of Energy.[9] Unlike so many recent works that have discussed American education, *The Sandia Report* actually *looked at evidence.* Not surprisingly, its findings contradicted the erroneous claims that were then being made by education critics in the Bush administration, and as a result the report was suppressed until George Bush was no longer in office. Chapter 4 provides details of this sad story.)

In brief then, evidence from the NAEP also does *not* confirm the myth of a recent decline in American student achievement. Instead, it indicates a

Exhibit 2.8 Percentage of Students with Basic Math Proficiency 17 Year Olds (NAEP Data)

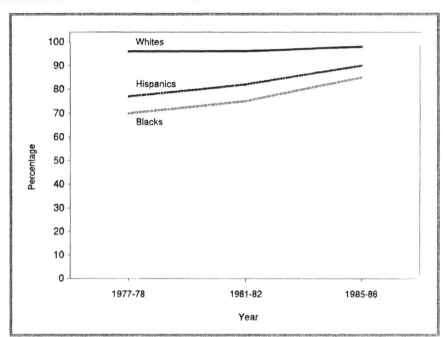

—Source: *The Sandia Report* (Carson et al., 1991, p. 35).

general pattern of stable achievement combined with modest growth in achievement among students from minority groups and from "less advantaged" backgrounds.

Interpretive "Spin." The "embarrassing" facts just discussed have not stopped the critics, however. Indeed, when it became clear that NAEP data did not confirm the mythic decline of American student achievement, the critics began to shift their ground. If achievement scores were not declining, they were certainly not sufficient for the future. According to Lamar Alexander, stable NAEP scores were "not nearly good enough for the 1990s," and Diane Ravitch declared that, "what was good enough 20 years ago is not good enough anymore."[10] As far as the Educational Testing Service was concerned, "students' current achievement levels [as measured by NAEP scores] are far below those that might indicate competency in challenging subject matter in English, mathematics, science, history and geography."[11] And from the National Center for Education Statistics we learned, "these figures show that many students appear to be graduating from high school with little of the mathematics understanding required by the fastest growing occupations or for college work."[12]

Exhibit 2.9   Reading Proficiency—Community Types
                   17-Year-Olds (NAEP Data)

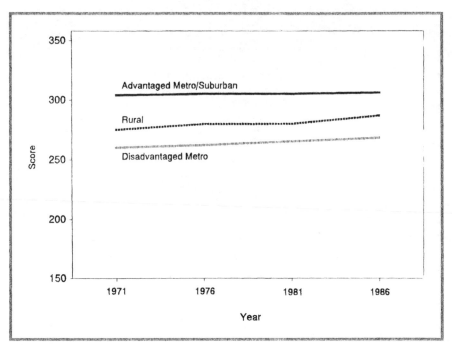

—Source: *The Sandia Report* (Carson et al., 1991, p. 37).

Maybe. It is hard to refute such claims except to note that *they cannot be substantiated* because they are based on unanchored perceptions of national need and on predictions that are not necessarily sound. For example, the jobs of the future may actually require fewer, not more, high-level skills. In an unusual display of agreement, dozens of economists have predicted that growth is likely in the *service* sector of employment—and this means more jobs for janitors, limousine drivers, word processors, sales clerks, and the like. We've also seen estimates that the hospitality industry—e.g., tourism—is now employing more people than any other and that the Wal–Mart chain will soon be the largest single employer in America. But most jobs in hospitality and retail sales do not require high-level mathematical skills. So if schools do not prepare everyone to perform high-level mathematics, perhaps it is because students and their teachers are responding sensibly to the looming job market.

Such musings may also be off the mark, however. What is important to point out here is that some critics confuse what education has accomplished with what one might want it to accomplish. As we suggested in Chapter 1, they muddle reality with desire. Although we would enjoy debating what skills America might need in the next decade, we claim no more prescience than the average seer. We have little sympathy, however, for critics who run down America's schools for their putative failures when the ongoing accomplishments of those schools are manifest and the society they serve is deteriorating. When school achievements are steady or even improve in a society that is falling apart, we think that educators have pulled off a miracle. It is time to celebrate the public schools of the nation, not to blame them.

Recent interpretations of NAEP data also illustrate another "spin" tactic used by some critics. Like other achievement batteries, the NAEP tests include some items that are easy and others that are very difficult, that require complex reasoning and problem-solving skills. Indeed, those who created the NAEP tests deliberately included both easy and difficult items so that the tests could measure student achievement across the full range of nongifted and gifted students. But this means, of course, that the average student earns only an average score on such tests. *Never* has the average student done well on the hardest items in NAEP tests of mathematics, science, and the other subjects assessed, and this fact offers wonderful opportunities for critics to inveigh against the schools for failing to educate students adequately.

To illustrate, we quote from the recent review of NAEP data prepared by the Educational Testing Service.

> Performance by high school students was even more unsettling. Although students graduating from high school seem to be able to add, subtract, multiply, and divide, this level of achievement is hardly in the spirit of our country's goal, which is grounded in competency with challenging subject matter. Only half of the 17-year-olds assessed in 1986 demonstrated a grasp of even moderately challenging mathematical procedures and reasoning (i.e., decimals, fractions, and percents; simple equations), and only 6 percent reached the highest level of proficiency defined—a level characterized by a high rate of success on questions measuring multi-step problem solving and algebra.[13]

Such judgments are nonsense. Like all well-designed tests, those of the NAEP were structured so that only the truly talented student could answer its most difficult questions, and the results cited by the ETS only indicate that the test is doing its job.

We are not the only ones to notice this flaw in reasoning. The General Accounting Office (GAO) is a watchdog agency designed to provide nonpolitical and nonpartisan evaluations of government programs. In 1992 the GAO examined standards set by the NAEP governing board. The GAO pointed out that the Bush administration had claimed that America's students are deficient in mathematics because fewer than 5 percent reach the "advanced" level on NAEP exams. But that same "advanced" level was also used in an international assessment of educational progress in many different countries, and Eleanor Chelimsky, head of the GAO noted,

> Fewer than 5 percent of the 9-year-olds in any nation . . . demonstrated advanced achievement. . . . For the 13-year-olds, 10 percent of the students in Taiwan and

at least 5 percent of [a restricted sample from] China . . . met this standard; in no other nation tested did as many as 5 percent meet the advanced threshold. This comparison indicates that the advanced level is extreme even by world class standards.[14]

As professors, we have made up hundreds of tests, and we have learned how easy it is to design tests on which nobody can achieve a high score. It is much easier, actually, to assess what people do *not* know than what they do know because the former far exceeds the latter. And being aware of this, we suspect that some of the NAEP effort focuses more on lack of knowledge than on educational progress.

In their zeal to bash American education some critics have also confused test performance with problem solving in the real world. Until recently, major testing organizations in the United States have largely relied on multiple-choice test items to assess what people know and can do—and such items have traditionally appeared in the SAT, NAEP, and related instruments. Testing of this kind simply does not assess the level of real-world thinking possessed by our young people. It confuses in-school problem solving with out-of-school problem solving, two different processes.

We know of one student who is considered quite ignorant in school, particularly in mathematics, but who has recently hired an investment counselor to handle the hundreds of thousands of dollars he made from illegal financial operations when he was a teenager. We do not condone his activities but point out that "school smarts" and "real-world smarts" are not the same thing.

Research supports this claim. Studies have appeared concerning second graders who sell chewing gum on the streets of lesser-developed countries.[15] These children estimate their market, determine markup, factor in inflation rates, determine sales prices, compute discount rates for big purchases, and make change for big bills. But the same children fail in standard tests because they do not know how to solve the in-school problems with approved in-school algorithms. Students with "street smart" mathematical skills often do poorly with some NAEP questions.

Let us look at a sample NAEP item designed to assess competency in mathematics:

> Suppose you have 10 coins and have at least one each of a quarter, a dime, a nickel, and a penny. What is the LEAST amount of money you could have? a) 41 cents b) 47 cents c) 50 cents d) 82 cents.[16]

Because most students find it difficult to answer such questions, critics conclude that they will have difficulty with real-world mathematics. But is this reasonable? In the real world, who actually cares about the *least* amount of money one might have from a set of coins? The young people whom we know care more about how coins add up, and those who have "street smarts" have learned to add their coins well.

Why are some adults so eager to find young people dysfunctional? Some adults simply fail to acknowledge what our young actually know and are able to do, and instead focus on what youths do *not* know and how they fail at arbitrary tasks. To illustrate, when the 1990 NAEP data on mathematics were released, they showed growth in average scores over *every* previous administration of the test. One would have thought this an occasion for rejoicing. Instead, the National Center for Education Statistics intoned, "The mathematical skills of our nation's children are generally insufficient to cope with either on-the-job demands for problem solving or college expectations for mathematical literacy."[17] We think it's appalling that a government agency would engage in such education bashing on the basis of tests that do not measure real-world skills and have unknown abilities to predict performance in the jobs of the future.

Commercial Tests of Achievement. Commercial tests of achievement provide yet another source of evidence concerning school performance in America. Each year, millions of students all over the country take tests that are prepared by commercial firms. One informant estimates that in the state of New York, a student in a college bound, academic track will have taken twenty-nine state-mandated tests between kindergarten and the twelfth grade.[18] Local districts may impose many more assessments. So lots of additional data are available to examine whether schools have, as the critics would have it, recently been "failing."

These commercial tests are associated with an interesting effect that is not widely known. According to Robert Linn, M. Elizabeth Graue, and Nancy M. Sanders, each year students tend to score higher on these various tests.[19] For example, on average, students in the 1980s gained roughly 2.10 percentile ranks for reading and 2.04 percentile ranks for mathematics, per year, on the California Achievement Test (CAT). These are large gains. Similarly, the Iowa Test of Basic Skills (ITBS) showed large annual gains, leading the test developer to write that "composite achievement in 1984–85 was at an all-time high in nearly all test areas."[20] (This statement appeared one year after the country was informed in *A Nation at Risk* that student achievement had declined in virtually every curriculum area!)

The same rising trends were also exhibited by the Stanford Achievement Test (SAT), the Metropolitan Achievement Test (MAT), and the Comprehensive Tests of Basic Skills (CTBS). As shown in Exhibit 2.10, each year students scored higher on both reading and mathematics on all of these commercial tests. Why then is this effect not more widely known? The answer seems to be that all these tests are recalibrated about every seven years, and when this is done, the test developers take pains to make certain that in all cases the typical student again scores at the fiftieth percentile rank for each subject assessed by the tests. In other words, whenever the tests are recalibrated, the achievement gains that students had earned over the past few years are wiped

Exhibit 2.10   Average Yearly Changes in Median Percentile Rank for
Well-Known Commercial Achievement Tests

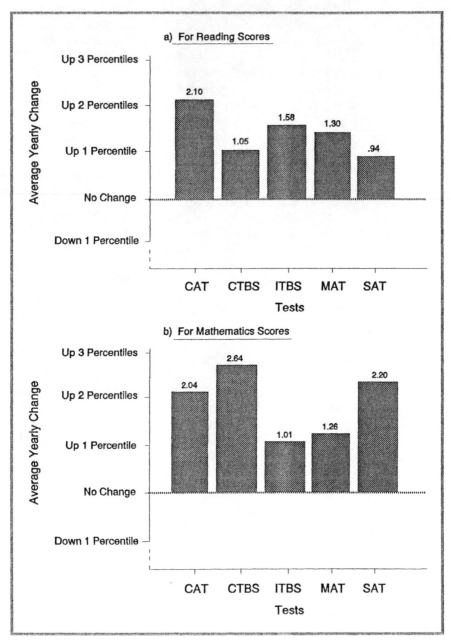

—Source: Linn, Graue, & Sanders (1990, p. 12).

out in the process. So, if commercial tests were not recalibrated, virtually all of them would show that today's students are out-achieving their parents substantially.

Given these data, we wonder where the columnist James J. Kilpatrick, writing in *The Nation's Business,* got his information when he asserted, "The average achievement of high school students on most standardized tests is now lower than it was 26 years ago when Sputnik was launched."[21] Mr. Kilpatrick, like so many of the critics, seems to have been unencumbered by the facts. In contrast, the evidence from commercial tests indicates that student achievement has been steadily improving over the years.

Tests of History and Literature. Finally, we offer evidence concerning a specialized study that has often been cited by the critics in their zeal to attack public education. During the Reagan and Bush years, Chester Finn and Diane Ravitch each held the post of Director of the Office of Educational Research and Improvement. Together they ran a special study in the mid-1980s, using NAEP techniques and test-item types, to assess how much high school students knew about history and literature. In 1987 they released a gloomy book, *What Our 17-Year-Olds Know,* which claimed that students' knowledge was shockingly thin.[22] Their conclusions were, of course, part of a barrage of similar arguments being made at the time by authors such as E. D. Hirsch in *Cultural Literacy,* Allan Bloom in *The Closing of the American Mind,* and William Bennett in *To Reclaim a Legacy;* and the press dutifully reported these charges as if they were gospel.[23]

Regarding Ravitch and Finn's claim that today's students know little history or literature, it suffices to point out that these investigators had also designed their test so that it included some truly tough questions, and they then complained when the average student could not answer them. For example, less than 50 percent of 17-year-olds seemed to know

- what made Samuel Gompers, Andrew Carnegie, and Jane Addams famous;
- what the Seneca Falls Declaration concerned;
- what the issue of "nullification" referred to;
- where Eudora Welty and Flannery O'Connor often set their stories;
- what John Bunyan's *Pilgrim's Progress* is about; and
- who wrote, "Things fall apart; the center cannot hold."

(Ask yourself whether *you* know the answers to all of these questions!) Such evidence certainly reveals lack of knowledge, but one wonders whether such a lack makes American youths unfit for citizenship, as Ravitch and Finn suggest, or whether it is relatively minor in a world where knowledge has exploded and children cannot know everything that historians and classicists would like them to know.

The Ravitch and Finn study was associated with a second charge, namely, that today's students know less history and literature than did students in previous generations. Although Ravitch and Finn did not make this claim, the press interpreted their study to mean that public schools were on the decline. (Perhaps this occurred because Ravitch and Finn suggested that the present generation of seventeen-year-olds are "at risk" because they lack historical and literary knowledge, thus implying that earlier generations might not have been "at risk.") In any case, it is useful to examine evidence concerning this second charge.

In a creative research project, Dale Whittington recently examined students' knowledge of history and social studies across the decades. Whittington carefully sought out tests administered from 1915 until recent years and equated them to the extent possible.[24] She then compared content covered, item difficulty, scoring procedures, types of students taking these exams, and so forth. (Among other things, she reports that students seem *never* to have known as much social studies material as the test developers wanted them to know. Like others suffering from Socrates' Syndrome, test developers in each generation have had a tendency to find the next generation wanting. Ravitch and Finn fit well into this sour tradition.)

It is crucial to note, however, that Whittington was able to find forty-three items on the Ravitch and Finn test that corresponded to items given in tests from earlier eras; so claims about the "decline" of student knowledge could be checked. On about a third of these crucial items today's students were less knowledgeable, on about a third they scored equally with students from the past, and on about a third they scored better than students from past generations. So much for the charge that today's students know less history. Whittington concludes,

> The perception of decline in the "results" of American education is open to question. Indeed, given the reduced drop-out rate and less elitist composition of the 17-year-old student body today, one could argue that students today know more American history than did their age peers of the past.
>
> Advocates for reform of education and excellence in public schooling should refrain from harkening to a halcyon past (or allowing the perception of a halcyon past) to garner support for their views. Such action . . . is dishonest and unnecessary. Indeed, excellence is a goal that should be advocated on its own merits.[25]

Amen.

Summary. Standardized tests provide *no evidence whatever* that supports the myth of a recent decline in the school achievement of the average American student. Achievement in mathematics has not declined—nor has that for science, English-language competency, or any other academic subject that we know of. Moreover, support for the myth of achievement decline has *always* been weak. Indeed, the two of us know of only *one* test, the SAT, that ever suggested such a decline—and, as readers know by now, the SAT is a voluntary test and each year is taken by differing types of students, which means that its aggregate results are not valid for judging the performance of American schools. Instead, the evidence suggests that average school achievement has either been stable or has increased modestly for a generation or more. And, although top-ranked students and those from "advantaged" homes have tended to hold their ground, those from "less advantaged" homes have recently shown achievement gains.

What, then, should we conclude about the critics' repeated, hysterical claims that student achievement has declined "massively" and hence that America is "at risk"? Somehow, in this case, the critics' behaviors bring to mind the tale of Chicken Little. Readers may remember that Chicken Little, when thumped by an acorn, began to rush around declaiming "The sky is falling! The sky is falling!" and managed to sell this alarming and unsubstantiated message to Turkey Lurkey and many other barnyard creatures before sanity was finally restored. But if this was truly a Chicken Little episode, what should we conclude about former Secretary William Bennett and others who played key roles in selling the hysteria? As far as we know, Secretary Bennett and company did not invent the myth of achievement decline but were only early and enthusiastic converts. Bennett and his colleagues were not, then, Chicken Littles but merely Turkey Lurkeys.

Although evidence does *not* support the myth of achievement decline, we doubt that belief in this myth will disappear overnight. Critics who have repeatedly asserted the myth may have difficulty abandoning it. Others, who wish the public schools well, may also endorse the myth in hopes of using it to encourage increased public funding. And citizens of good will may find it difficult to abandon the myth because they have heard it so often and cannot believe that so many important people—including presidents of the United States—could have prattled nonsense for so long.

But endless repetition of a myth does not make it true. On the contrary, the evidence makes it clear that student achievement in America has actually been growing in specific, if modest, ways. Remarkably, this growth has occurred when many measures—particularly those for poverty, violence, TV viewing, overworked and absent parents, and the like—indicate that more of our children are leading difficult lives.

MYTH . . . *College-Student Performance Has Recently Declined in America*

Today's select students know so much less, are so much more cut off from the tradition, are so much slacker intellectually, that they make their predecessors look like prodigies of culture. The soil is ever thinner, and I doubt whether it can now sustain the taller growths.

—Allan Bloom (*The Closing of the American Mind,* 1987, p. 51)

Most Americans and their policymakers, concerned about the quality of pre-collegiate education, take heart in the large numbers of Americans who receive associate's and bachelor's degrees every year. The harsh truth is that a significant minority of these graduates enter or reenter the world with little more than the knowledge, competence, and skill we would have expected in a high school graduate scarcely a generation ago.

—Wingspread Group on Higher Education (*An American Imperative,* 1993, p. 2)

Education at the college and university level has also come under attack from the critics, with a lot of the same charges leveled against it that are leveled against schools from kindergarten to high school. Critics of higher education worry about many things: the enrollment of too many "unqualified" students in colleges and universities; reports of decline in academic standards; the appearance of nontraditional students in college courses and their need for remedial work; the rise of courses on black history or feminist concerns, which are reputedly keeping students away from science and the "classics"; the reported promotion of homosexual values or of irresponsible heterosexual relationships on campuses; the number of students who now must work while attending college and therefore may not be able to concentrate on serious academic pursuits; and so forth.

It is not easy to refute these many unanchored worries, and we will not do so directly. We note, however, that if Americans are truly committed to a higher-education system that serves the needs of *many* students, then the fact that those students bring differing strengths and weaknesses to colleges and universities is not very important. What *is* important is that our colleges and universities teach those students well.

Indeed, we shouldn't forget the reaction of some university faculty and graduates to the enormous numbers of veterans who entered colleges after World War II. Some alarmists considered this an onslaught by the unwashed masses, particularly certain ethnic groups who had previously been kept out of higher education—Italians, Eastern Europeans, the Irish, the Jews, and the like. Since the G.I. Bill gave *all* veterans fiscal support to attend college, many children from poor families decided that they too wanted a college education. Allowing many people who did not meet traditional standards an entrance into higher education was declared a disaster by some who already had university degrees and by faculty who had earlier taught only the privileged and "well-mannered."

Not surprisingly, cries about the destruction of higher education were more likely to come from prestigious campuses that served affluent students. For example, the president of the University of Chicago, Robert Maynard Hutchins, suggested that if the G.I. Bill were not amended, it would convert America's colleges and universities into "educational hobo jungles." Instead,

■ EXHIBIT 2.11
The THREAT to American Education

Education institutions, as the big-time football racket shows, cannot resist money. The G.I. Bill of Rights gives them a chance to get more money than they have ever dreamed of, and to do it in the name of patriotism. They will not want to keep out unqualified veterans; they will not want to expel those who fail. Even if they should want to, they will not be allowed to, for the public and the veterans' organizations will not stand for it. Colleges and universities will find themselves converted into educational hobo jungles. . . .

The remedy lies in requiring the administrator to ascertain through a series of national examinations whether the veteran applying for the educational benefits has a reasonable chance of succeeding in and profiting by his proposed educational program. The government would pay only half the tuition and other fees of the veteran; the balance would have to be paid by the educational institutions themselves. Thus these institutions would exercise some discrimination in the selection of their students and co-operate with the administrator by admitting only those veterans who could use what the institutions had to offer. . . . These amendments would mean, of course, that fewer veterans would attend colleges and universities; for only those would attend who wanted and could get an education. . . . For these the G.I. Bill of Rights should provide support during their education. Other agencies, in other ways, must tackle and solve the problem of mass unemployment.

—Source: Robert M. Hutchins (1944, p. 21).

Hutchins proposed restricting college entry to those few students who could pass stiff national examinations—see Exhibit 2.11!

In retrospect, we realize that such worries from the privileged campuses were absurd. When post-war veterans flooded into America's colleges, most did very well indeed. Knowledge and values associated with higher education were spread in unprecedented fashion, and Americans' views about the need for widespread higher education changed forever. Some of those veterans required remedial help and special attention to get through college, of course, but in general they were highly successful.

Criticism of colleges and universities seems unlikely to disappear, however. Those who possess an advantage, say a college degree, often like to limit others' access to that advantage, and people who remember a higher education system that once catered largely to the sons of white, Anglo-Saxon privilege may be disturbed when college classrooms include many more students who are female, ethnic, of color, or less affluent. We certainly believe that universities should maintain high standards and teach well. But we also believe that universities should not serve just the sons and daughters of the well educated and well off. And if American universities need to make special accommodations for those who are motivated to learn but who do not have all the background skills needed, those accommodations should surely be made. That is what education in a democracy is all about.

One charge made against higher education can be assessed by looking at evidence, however. Critics have asserted that those who are now graduating from America's universities know less than earlier graduates, although the data available to assess this charge suggest that it is groundless. Indeed, students now graduating from colleges and universities may know *more* than those who graduated in previous years.

Here we review four sources of evidence that bear on this issue: (1) the Graduate Record Examination, (2) the Graduate Management Admissions Test, (3) the Law School Admission Test, and (4) the Medical College Admissions Test. These four tests are given annually to college seniors who seek entrance to some form of postgraduate or professional education. At least one-third, perhaps one-half, of all college seniors eventually take one or more of these tests, and records from them have been available for many years.

The Graduate Record Examination. The Graduate Record Examination (GRE) is a broad-spectrum test taken by seniors interested in studying for advanced degrees in academic fields. Average GRE scores for all students taking the test are available for each year since 1965—see Exhibit 2.12. Like SAT scores, GRE scores are computed for both verbal and quantitative subtests. As with the SAT, each computation involves obscure rules and yields scores that can range from a low of 200 to a high of 800. Thus, a total GRE score can range from 400 to 1600. And, as with the SAT, percentages of students taking the GRE can differ from year to year; thus, aggregate GRE scores reflect not only student knowledge but also the percentage of students taking the test. Since this is so, we have drawn Exhibit 2.12 so that it provides information about the total aggregate GRE scores and the percentages of students who opted to take the test each year.

As the Exhibit shows, aggregate GRE scores fell slightly from 1965 through the early 1970s, but this was also a period when the percentage of students taking the test *doubled.* Since 1971 the percentage of students taking the GRE has not varied greatly, but *average GRE scores have gradually risen.* What this means is that average total GRE scores are now roughly the same as they were in the 1960s—despite the fact that the percentage of students taking the GRE now is more than twice what it was a generation ago.

Moreover, the GRE story continues. In 1982 the GRE added a third subtest to its battery concerned with analytic ability. The latter instrument is designed to measure "higher-level" thinking skills; i.e., those associated with reasoning rather than factual knowledge. Aggregate GRE scores for the analytic-ability subscale have also climbed over the past decade and are now about thirty scale points higher than they were in 1982.[26]

Exhibit 2.12   Average GRE Scores and Percentage of Students Taking the GRE

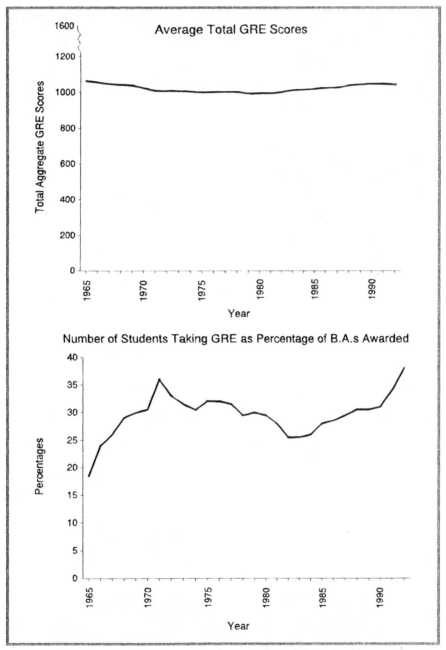

—Source: *The Condition of Education, 1993* (National Center for Education Statistics, 1993b, p. 56).

All of this is indeed good news. Critics have claimed that as more "unqualified" students have been allowed to enroll in America's colleges and universities, the standards of those universities have gone down. GRE evidence suggests that this claim is groundless. True, more students are now enrolled in America's colleges and universities, and a larger proportion of those students are now taking the GRE in the hope of going on to postgraduate education. Despite these greater numbers, college seniors of today are doing just about as well on the GRE as their parents did a generation ago, and evidence from the GRE analytic-ability subscale suggests that their ability to reason is climbing.

Specialized Tests. Results similar to those for the GRE are also available for three specialized tests that are taken by college students who want to enroll in professional schools. The Graduate Management Admissions Test (GMAT) is taken by seniors who want to enter Colleges of Business Administration.[27] In 1966 the GMAT was taken by 40,153 students, who earned an average score of 485. Over the next few years, GMAT scores fell slightly, while the numbers of students taking the test soared, but scores have risen appreciably since the early 1970s. In 1992 the GMAT was taken by 231,356 students, who earned an average score of 494. Thus, *five* times as many students are now taking the GMAT, and today's students display just about the same amount of business-relevant knowledge as did those of 25 years ago.

In the case of the Law School Admission Test (LSAT), the average scores earned by college seniors actually *rose* from the early 1960s to the early 1970s—despite the fact that the numbers of students taking the test increased fourfold.[28] (For example, average scores for the LSAT were 483 in 1962 and 521 in 1972, while student participation rose from 25,660 to 119,391.) Since then, average LSAT scores have continued to rise, although it is difficult to give comparable figures for more recent test results because different scoring systems were adopted for the test in 1983 and again in 1992.

Over the years, the Medical College Admissions Test (MCAT) has appeared in three different versions, each with altered scoring systems.[29] Before 1978 the MCAT consisted of four subtests—measures of Verbal Ability, Quantitative Ability, General Information, and Science Knowledge. Each of these was scored, as are subtests of the SAT, on a scale ranging from 200 to 800. Evidence from this version of the test confirms the same pattern we have seen. Between 1966 and 1975, the number of students taking the MCAT increased from 19,700 to 57,627, but the average scores earned by students increased for three of the four subscales. (Verbal Ability rose from 519 to 541, Quantitative Ability rose from 548 to 583, and Science Knowledge rose from 515 to 567. Only General Information fell—modestly—from 541 to 527.) Since 1978, when the first new scoring system was adopted, MCAT scores have remained relatively constant.

Summary. Given these four parallel sources of evidence—the GRE, the GMAT, the LSAT, and the MCAT—it is difficult to understand why critics continue to charge that student achievement in American higher education has declined. It is possible, of course, that the tests we have reviewed do not fully tap the types of knowledge that the critics want undergraduates to learn, and we would certainly agree that higher education faces challenges that are daunting. But we suspect that in this case the critics have not been motivated by any great respect for—or even awareness of—the evidence. Instead, it seems likely that in their zeal to express their fears and to motivate reform, the critics have been willing to throw around charges that sound plausible but are actually fabrications.

But whether this explanation is correct or not, the evidence again contradicts a myth about the putative decline of American education. The data we have just reviewed suggest that interest and participation in higher education have expanded greatly in the past generation. This is surely a matter for rejoicing. Moreover, despite this expansion, today's college seniors seem to know, on average, either as much as or a bit more than the seniors of earlier years. Americans should take pride in this evidence of the broad strengths of their colleges and universities.

MYTHS . . . About Intelligence:

- *Students are dumber today than they used to be.*
- *Student intelligence is determined only by inheritance.*
- *Student intelligence is largely fixed before students enter school.*

I've been watching and listening to you guys, and I can tell you that none of you are as smart as school kids were when I was in high school. You have it so easy today, you just don't work at learning enough.

   —Emanuel Berliner, to his high-school age son, David, and his friends (c. 1953)

The common opinion that the child from a cultured home does better in tests solely by reason of his superior home advantages is an entirely gratuitous assumption. . . . The children of successful and cultured parents test higher than children from wretched and ignorant homes for the simple reason that their heredity is better.

   —Lewis M. Terman (*The Measurement of Intelligence,* 1916, p. 115; cited in Gould, 1981, p. 183)

[The data] make it clear that intelligence is a developing function and that the stability of measured intelligence increases with age. . . . In terms of intelligence measured at age 17, about 50% of the development takes place between conception and age 4, about 30% between ages 4 and 8, and about 20% between ages 8 and 17.

   —Benjamin Bloom (*Stability and Change in Human Characteristics,* 1964, p. 88)

We turn next to three myths about intelligence that are common in America. In fairness, these myths have not often been voiced in recent criticisms of education, but each of these myths has its believers, and that has helped to generate both educational policies and arguments made by the critics of American education. As we shall see, evidence contradicts all three of these myths.

The first myth asserts that young people today are dumber than they used to be. Many untutored Americans, especially those who call in to radio talk shows, voice the idea that youths of the present generation know less than those of bygone days. Nor are these new charges. In perfect imitation of Socrates, our own parents or their friends sometimes asserted that, when they were young, students were a lot smarter, could think straighter, and had learned more valuable skills than we had. We responded then, of course, by saying that our generation was the brightest that the United States had ever produced. This was merely defensive puffery, but much to our surprise (now that *we* are the adults), we have learned that our defensive words were actually correct. When we were youths, ours *was* the smartest generation that America had yet spawned. Our delight with this information has been short lived, however, for we have also since learned that the generation of our own children is smarter yet.

The evidence confirming all of this comes from various sources. We begin with a 1987 study by a researcher from New Zealand, James R. Flynn, who analyzed data from fourteen countries.[30] When the publishers of the best-known IQ tests—notably the Stanford-Binet and the Wechsler—bring out new editions, which they do every so often, they check to make sure that the new versions generate the same IQ scores as the older tests did. This means that every few years survey data are generated concerning measured IQ scores for the populations of various nations. Exhibit 2.13 presents data from these surveys of IQs among Americans for the years when a new version of either the Stanford-Binet or the Wechsler was developed. As the Exhibit makes clear, whenever a survey was conducted, it found that the average measured intelligence of Americans had increased.

Now this is truly surprising. IQ scores are assumed to be stable throughout a person's adult lifetime, so *growth* in the average measured IQs of Americans presumably means that young people who are coming into the population are brighter, on average, than older people. To be sure, some people believe that these types of IQ tests do a poor job of measuring practical intelligence. It may also be argued that such tests are too narrowly conceived and leave out all sorts of other kinds of intelligence that should be measured—for example, musical ability or visual-spatial capacities. In addition, evidence suggests that standard IQ tests are biased against some groups in the population, particularly minorities and those whose native language is not the language of the test.

Exhibit 2.13   Average Wechsler and Stanford-Binet IQ Scores for White
Americans Aged 2–75 Years by Year of Retesting

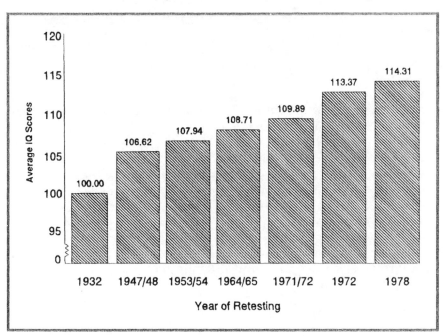

—Source: Flynn (1987, p. 177, Table 7).

We concur with these criticisms, but IQ tests do measure something like what is ordinarily meant by intelligence, and scores on these tests have been shown to relate to success and failure in subsequent education and in various kinds of jobs.[31] Also, school authorities and school psychologists seem to believe in the validity of these tests since they give hundreds of thousands of such tests each year, spending millions of dollars as they do so, and making important decisions about children on the basis of the scores these tests generate. So let us take Flynn's data seriously.

As Exhibit 2.13 shows, since 1932 the mean IQ for white Americans aged two to seventy-five has risen about .3 points per year. Although it is white Americans for whom the most complete data are available, there is no reason to believe that the pattern is different for other Americans. In fact, Flynn shows that the data from most other industrialized nations show similar results. In all of these nations, people seem to be getting smarter over the years, on average, at least as measured by IQ tests. In the United States, today's youth probably average about 15 IQ points higher than did their grandparents and 7.5 points higher than did their parents on the Stanford-Binet and Wechsler tests. (As with the children in Garrison Keillor's mythical home town of Lake Woebegone, today's students are, indeed, "all above average.") Or to put this another way, the number of students expected to have IQs of 130 or higher—a typical cut-off point for defining giftedness in many school districts throughout the nation—is now about *seven* times greater than it was for the generation now retiring from leadership positions in the country and often complaining about the poor performance of today's youth. Now *that* is something to contemplate.

Why Are the Young Smarter? With youth throughout the industrialized world showing huge increases in measured IQ, it seems likely that some similar influence is affecting them all. Could it be that young people everywhere are eating better, breathing cleaner air, or drinking cleaner water, and that this has generated the effect? This seems unlikely. The rise in measured intelligence is also correlated with increases in the consumption of fast foods, but we also find it hard to believe that this would cause growth in IQs throughout the world. Instead, we suspect that intelligence, as it is measured by IQ tests, is growing simply because *schools* are doing a better job of promoting the kind of intelligent thinking needed in academic settings. To understand how this has happened, we must briefly discuss IQ tests, heredity, home environment, and the effects of education.

We begin with a simple question: what is meant by *intelligence?* What do people mean when they say that Sally is "smart" and Susan is "dumb"? Such statements usually reflect judgments about a general ability to learn, understand, or solve problems, which is presumed to characterize Sally, Susan, or other people. This definition seems simple, but it also raises two issues. First, unlike height, weight, or eye color, intelligence is a *hypothetical* entity and cannot be observed directly. Thus, intelligence is like the quark or other subatomic particles in physics. It is convenient to think that intelligence is real, but we cannot be certain that it actually exists. Second, intelligence is thought of as a *general* ability, and this means that if Sally is "smart," she can easily learn, understand, or solve problems in various kinds of domains. This last assumption is controversial. Most people are able to accomplish at least some types of tasks—verbal, social, mathematical, mechanical, athletic—more easily than others, and psychologists have debated for years whether to think of intelligence as a single, general ability, or as a set of differing competencies.

In any case, most people today think of intelligence as a single, general ability which, though it cannot be observed, can nevertheless be estimated through appropriate tests. Thus, IQ tests are constructed to assess several types of skills thought to be *generally* useful—memory, reasoning, judgment, and the like. People who take those tests are asked to answer questions or to accomplish tasks measuring these skills, and the tester then computes a single total representing the number of questions answered or tasks the person accomplished correctly.

But how do we know whether such a total indicates a "high" or "low" level of intelligence? To make this last judgment, the total for the person is compared with the average of totals that others have earned on the test in the past, and an IQ score is assigned to indicate how that person stacks up against those others. (By convention, the person whose total matches the past average is given an IQ score of 100. Should that person's total exceed those of 97.5 percent of people from the past, he or she is given an IQ score of 130, and so on.) Since the ability to answer questions and to solve problems generally increases with age, at least among children, the total for each person is always compared with average scores that were earned by people their own age. To summarize, then, IQ tests generate a single score for each person that presumably represents his or her general ability to learn, to understand, or to solve problems when compared with the average abilities of people of similar ages from the past.

But what does the IQ test score imply? Whence cometh this unobservable characteristic, intelligence? Answers to these questions have varied sharply over time. A French scholar, Alfred Binet, created the first standardized IQ test in 1905.[32] Binet had been asked to solve a practical problem—to predict which children would have difficulty with standard classroom teaching—and he designed a test to accomplish this task. Binet seems never to have believed, however, that IQ tests measured an inherited, fixed capacity. Rather, he argued that intelligence is malleable and that children who earn low initial IQ-test scores can be given remedial education that will increase their subsequent scores and improve their performance in school. Binet wrote in 1913, "the intelligence of an individual is [not] a fixed quantity, a quantity that one cannot augment. . . . We must protest and react against this brutal pessimism."[33]

Unfortunately, such generous arguments were not echoed by early advocates for IQ testing in the United States. Instead, influential Americans such as Henry Goddard, Lewis Terman, and Robert M. Yerkes promulgated the myth that intelligence is strictly a product of inheritance and, as such, is largely fixed at conception.[34] In doing so they were responding to the writings of Francis Galton, who had urged that selective breeding be used to improve the human genetic pool; and in the hands of Goddard, Terman, and Yerkes, the myth of inherited intelligence became an excuse for arguments favoring the forced sterilization of "idiots" and immigration laws designed to keep "poor genetic stock" out of the country. Needless to say, these arguments were an expression of xenophobia as well as ethnic and racial bigotry.

Moreover, if intelligence is actually strictly inherited, early measurement of intelligence should enable one to predict completely who will and will not benefit from schooling. To illustrate, the infamous British psychologist, Cyril Burt, also believed in inherited intelligence. In 1947 he wrote,

> [Intelligence] will enter into everything the child says, thinks, does or attempts, both while he is at school and later on. . . . If intelligence is innate, the child's

degree of intelligence is permanently limited. No amount of teaching will turn the child who is genuinely defective in general intelligence into a normal pupil.[35]

Such an overly determined thesis seems absurd today, of course, and the myth that intelligence is determined solely or "largely" by inheritance is espoused today only in works that reveal bigotry and ignorance.

This year's leading candidate for the Bigoted Ignorant Annual Sham (BIAS) award must surely be *The Bell Curve* by Richard Herrnstein and Charles Murray.[36] The authors of this widely ballyhooed work argue that intelligence is "largely" inherited, that inheritance alone is sufficient to "explain" average differences in the measured IQs of people who also differ by race, ethnicity, and income, and that federal programs designed to help minorities and impoverished people should be scrapped because they will only encourage such dumb people to breed more rapidly. As we indicated above, these arguments have been around for at least seventy-five years, but in defending them today, Herrnstein and Murray not only had to misinterpret research but were also forced to ignore literally hundreds of studies demonstrating the sizable effects of social environment on measured IQ. These studies are widely known and understood in the large community of social researchers interested in intelligence. Given this widespread knowledge, one wonders why so many media figures have been willing to tout the stale and biased claims of *The Bell Curve.*

Such aberrations aside, by the middle of the twentieth century, most knowledgeable psychologists had come to believe that intelligence reflects both inheritance and the child's home environment. In this they were responding to many studies that had found relations between intelligence and early childhood experiences—particularly parental encouragement, availability of good reading materials, and emphasis on language use in the child's home. For example, in his influential 1964 review, Benjamin Bloom was able to write, "there is little doubt that intelligence development is [also] in part a function of the environment in which the individual lives."[37]

For decades now, "enlightened" thought has assumed that IQ-test scores will reflect both genetic inheritance and early childhood experience and that all children in the country, therefore, should have an equal right to home and preschool experiences that will help their different intelligences grow. The only trouble with this notion is that it is focused exclusively on *early* childhood experience. In effect, it suggests that whereas intelligence may reflect both heredity and the child's early environment, by the time the child enters school, those influences have played out; thereafter, intelligence is largely fixed. Thus, many people in this country believe that when children enter school they bring with them a relatively fixed capacity for learning, called *intelligence* (which reflects inheritance, home background, or both), and this plays a large part in their subsequent school achievement.

Where did the idea that intelligence was fixed before the early grades come from? Belief in this notion seems to have begun with the early-developmental theories of psychometricians such as R. L. Thorndike and Florence Goodenough. This belief was reinforced by influential reviewers such as Benjamin Bloom, who also concluded that "the effect of the environment . . . appears to be greatest in the early (and more rapid) periods of intelligence development."[38] In retrospect, we can see that this conclusion was based on faulty reasoning. Bloom made an assumption that intelligence was more or less fixed by age seventeen. He observed that correlations between early IQ measures and those for seventeen-year-olds varied widely in the early years but tended to stabilize when children entered school, and he concluded that this meant that most of the "development" of intelligence took place before age eight. (It seems not to have occurred to Bloom that the same effect could have been generated by consistencies in the educational experiences to which children are subjected during their school years.) This kind of thinking coincided with the national push for a "war on poverty" and the creation of the Head Start program for disadvantaged preschool children. So Bloom's belief that intelligence is fixed quite early helped provide justification for early-intervention programs.

Belief in the myth that intelligence must be largely fixed at an early age was already well entrenched in America by the early 1970s. And, given this myth, it hardly seems surprising that since then many American schools have measured children's IQs in the early grades assuming that the general ability such tests measure should be assessed in order to plan best for each child's education, perhaps through tracking or by assigning the child either to remedial or to enrichment programs.

So what's wrong with doing this? Actually, there are many things wrong with such policies, but we take on only one issue here. Let's suppose that environmental influences are not confined to the home alone. Suppose instead that the *school* can also affect the intelligence of children. What would this imply for educational policy? It clearly implies that *schools* should also be thought of as a significant source of intelligence and that all children in the country have an equal right to *educational* experiences that will help their intelligences grow. And this means, in turn, that if one denies those experiences to some children—because they are forced to attend underfunded schools, because they are assigned to low-status educational tracks, or because they receive substandard curricula—one is also condemning those children to stunted mental growth.

A Matter of Evidence. But what does the evidence say? Do schools indeed modify students' intelligence? A study by two Israeli psychologists, Sorel Cahen and Nora Cohen, sheds light on this question.[39] These researchers asked, as you grow from year to year, does your measured intelligence determine your achievement at school, or does what you achieve in school determine your measured intelligence? In other words, do you have to be intelligent to profit from schooling (as is widely believed in "enlightened" America), or do you have to have schooling to become intelligent?

Although Cahen and Cohen used complex statistical methods, their findings were straightforward. They found that school achievement was a *major* factor in the prediction of intelligence-test performance. In contrast, measured intelligence was only a *weak* predictor of school achievement. Thus, measured intelligence is strongly influenced by opportunity to learn in school. Over the past fifty years, high quality public education has been offered to larger and larger numbers of students in the industrialized world, and this fact explains why the average person today is measurably smarter than the average person was in the past.

Other evidence supports this idea. Torsten Husén and Albert Tuijnman, distinguished educational researchers from Sweden and Holland, also studied relations between school achievement and measured IQ.[40] These scholars reexamined data from an older study, originally conducted in Mälmo, Sweden, that looked at the IQs of 671 Swedish males over a ten-year period, from childhood to adulthood. Using complex statistical techniques unavailable at the time of the original study, the authors checked whether changes in measured IQ had occurred, and if so what might explain these changes. Their conclusion was unequivocal. Measured IQs *had* changed for many of the persons studied, and those who had experienced more schooling had also grown more in measured intelligence.

Thus, the characteristic that we call *intelligence* is not only dependent on inheritance and home background but is also influenced by schooling. Intelligence during the educative years is not a static and immutable characteristic. It actually appears to be quite dynamic and continues to be affected by environmental factors, particularly by access to high-quality schooling. Husén and Tuijnman concluded,

> schools not only confer knowledge and instrumental qualifications but also train and develop students' intellectual capacity. The results [of this study suggest] . . . that IQ as measured by group intelligence tests is not stable but changes significantly between 10 and 20 years of age. . . . [Apparently] schooling co-varies with and produces positive changes in adult IQ.[41]

Similar findings were also reported by an American psychologist, Stephen Ceci.[42] As a result of his research, Ceci concluded that the specific skills measured on intelligence tests and the processes underlying intelligence-test performance are taught and learned *in school.* Ceci also estimated that these influences are substantial. A child could lose as many as six IQ points for each year in which he or she misses high-quality education—from birth onward!

Consider briefly the implication of these studies for typical kindergarten-enrollment policies. If, for example, a school district declares that a child must be five years old by November 30 to enter kindergarten, then a child born in early December misses out on an entire year of schooling — though that child may be only a day or two younger than children born in late November. Suppose, then, that in this school district we look at the IQs of children born in adjacent months of the same year. With one month difference in dates of birth, we would expect to see little IQ difference among children of roughly the same age—and that is exactly what we find when we examine the IQs of the children born in March and April, for example, or in October and November of the same year. But when we look at the IQs of children born in November and December of the same year, we find these two groups substantially *different* in measured IQ, with the difference favoring the children born in November! Providing schooling at a younger age, then, gives children a small but significant advantage in the form of higher IQs over those who start schooling later.

In brief, schooling matters. Genes and home environment are not the only contributors to intelligence. A society that chooses to nurture and develop high levels of intelligence among its youth must also provide high-quality education for them. Poor schools, like poor home environments, have negative lasting consequences.

Intelligence, Schooling, and Wealth. The implications of this revelation are disturbing. Consider, for example, the effects of wealth on intelligence. Rich parents in America often provide early experiences for their children that will make them smarter. Wealth allows those parents to purchase high-quality day care and to enroll their children in private preschools. It also permits them to purchase instructional toys, encyclopedias, computers, and first-rate health care—all of which are likely to improve a child's measured intelligence. This means that the sons and daughters of wealthy parents are likely to enter school with higher measured intelligence than that of the children of poor parents.

This sounds bad if we believe in the ideal of equal opportunity for children, but there is worse. Since good schooling also leads to gains in intelligence, it follows that those children who attend "the best" schools will also gain the most. But since the quality of schools also varies greatly across the land, the growth of intelligence is not equal in America's schools. And in our country, children from rich families are much more likely than are children from poor families to attend "the best" schools—either because rich children are sent to private academies or because they attend well-funded public schools in affluent suburbs—and this means they will gain more in intelligence than will the sons and daughters of middle- or working-class families. (Such inequities in school funding appear less often in other Western countries, where private schools are fewer and public schools more often receive equal funding based on student enrollment.) Thus, in America we also allow the rich to "buy" intelligence-test points for their children through unequal school funding.

What are the implications for educational policy? In recent years, for example, the Bush and Clinton administrations both urged the states to adopt programs that would provide enriched educational experiences for students who are "truly gifted," and various states have obliged by passing laws setting up such programs. But intelligence tests are widely used to select students who are "truly gifted," and this means that children of the rich are far more likely to participate in such programs than are children of the poor. Many children from poor families could also profit from enrichment programs, but they cannot enter those programs because of the mistake they made at birth—they "chose" to be born to parents who were not wealthy!

This is a problem for our democracy because we continue to preach that all people should have equal opportunities to rise through public schooling. Unfortunately, rising-through-schooling is probably happening *less* frequently in the present decade, in part because so many states have now instituted programs for the "truly gifted." The tests used to select students for these programs measure intelligence or other traits that reflect advantages that only wealthy parents can buy for their children. *Such programs are inherently unfair.*

Other scholars have also made this point, of course, and we will have more to say later about special programs for "gifted" children. Here, we merely repeat that when high scores on intelligence tests are used to select students for enrichment programs, in the United States those programs always confer an unfair advantage on wealthy children.

Our reasoning about wealth and intelligence also suggests that as the number of children living in poverty grows, as it did in the 1980s,[43] the continuous rise in intelligence-test scores in this country is likely to stop. The cause for this will not be found in schools but in a society that imposes poverty on growing numbers of its young people. We would be willing to bet, however, that some critics will try to blame public schools for the coming IQ decline.

Summary. What, then, can we conclude from these studies of measured intelligence? First, today's children are smarter, not dumber, than their parents. Furthermore, the parents of today's children were also more intelligent than were their own parents, the grandparents of today's youth.

Second, intelligence is affected not only by inheritance and early childhood experiences; *schooling* also affects IQ test performance. More and better schooling in the U.S. and in other industrialized nations is the most likely reason for those nations' increases in IQ scores. High-quality instructional environments for toddlers, primary-school children, teenagers, and college students all seem to raise scores on IQ tests.

Third, if wealthy people have better access than do poor people to high-quality education, as is the case so often in this country, then some children will do poorly and some will do well on IQ tests because of their parents' wealth rather than because of their genetic makeup or home environment.

And if some educational programs provide advantages for "gifted" students—but if admittance to them requires a high IQ score—then those programs are systematically biased against poor children. Such programs are inherently unfair.

Access to schooling in this country and elsewhere has made people a lot more intelligent, at least as intelligence is normally measured. But if high-quality schooling is rationed in such a way that some have access to it and others don't, then millions of students will be shortchanged, and America will be deprived of the wonderful discoveries, inventions, art and music, innovative businesses, and political leadership those people will never be able to contribute to the country.

MYTH . . . *American Schools Fail in Comparative Studies of Student Achievement*

International comparisons of student achievement, completed a decade ago, reveal that on 19 academic tests American students were never first or second and, in comparison with other industrialized nations, were last seven times.

— *A Nation at Risk* (1983, p. 8)

The poor performance of American schools is now so well known that it makes the front page of the daily newspaper and is a source of public humiliation.

—John Murphy and Jeffry Schiller (*Transforming America's Schools,* 1992, p. 1)

In 1967 a new organization, the International Association for the Evaluation of Educational Achievement (IEA) brought out a two-volume work that compared average mathematics achievements for secondary students of the same age in twelve countries.[44] This was the first time that comparable achievement tests had ever been administered to large samples of students in so many countries, and the work attracted a lot of attention. The IEA had not finished its labors, however, for in short order it generated other comparative studies reporting average student achievements for such subjects as science, reading, literature, native-language instruction, and the like. Much to the surprise of many people, the United States generally did *poorly* in these comparisons. In general, American students' average achievement scores lagged behind those of students in comparable countries—particularly Japan, Korea, and Western Europe—and sometimes American students' scores were in last place!

The IEA studies were mainly written for professionals, but eventually they began to attract wider attention. Then in the early 1980s, the studies were highlighted in *A Nation At Risk* and other critical documents claiming that America faced an educational CRISIS. These sources argued that the IEA studies indicated serious deficiencies in American public education and that those deficiencies were responsible for America's inability to keep up with other nations in industrial competition.

This was heady stuff, of course. As at the Olympics, national pride was involved, and the media rose to the occasion. They began to report that American schools and teachers were failing badly by international standards. Those who wanted to discredit public schools were given new ammunition, columnists provided endless commentary on the "sad" state of American education, and even educators and supporters of public schools began to cringe and to seek ways to explain away the apparent "weaknesses" of American education revealed by comparative research.

Unfortunately, most people who have claimed that American education lags behind education elsewhere have never bothered to *look* at the evidence, and few authors have taken the time to *think* about the assumptions involved when one compares aggregate achievement scores among countries. If one actually looks at and thinks about the comparative evidence, however, one discovers that it does *not* confirm the myth of American educational failure. Indeed, it suggests that in many ways American education stands head and shoulders above education in other countries. Let us, then, look at and think about the evidence of comparative research.

Different Visions. We begin by noting that countries vary greatly in their notions about childhood and how to conduct education. This sounds like a truism, but it is also a fact that generates serious problems for comparative studies of achievement. For example, countries in continental Europe have traditionally used stiff national exams to sort out students at the end of primary or junior-high education, and only those who pass such exams are allowed to enter specialized high schools, *gymnasia,* that prepare them for university entrance. Many Asian countries also use such examinations today, but the United States does not. Does it make any sense, then, to compare the average, national achievements of high school students in mathematics, science, or literature from countries with such disparate systems of education?

This issue becomes crucial when one ponders the unique values reflected in American education. To begin with, Americans think that children should have a wide variety of experiences. Our middle-class neighbors seem to agree that their children should participate in organized sports such as Little League, basketball, and soccer; engage in after-school activities such as piano lessons and dance; watch a good deal of TV; spend weekends in leisure pursuits; have their own cars and begin to date while in high school; and so forth. This means, of course, that many American parents do *not* favor an educational system that assigns vast amounts of homework or that encourages students to become high-achieving drudges. By comparison then, American teenagers probably have more nonacademic interests and a wider knowledge base than do students from countries that stress narrow academic concerns.

As a nation, we apparently also believe that it's worthwhile for young people to gain work experience and to learn how to handle their own money. Thus, we promote employment for our teenagers; as a result, our young people are more economically active than is the youth of comparable nations—Japan, for example.[45] (Given some of the critics' desires to promote growth in the nation's economy, why have they so consistently ignored this potential strength of America's young people?)

Again, Americans like their children to be creative, to be spontaneous, to be socially responsive and friendly, and to challenge unreasonable authority. Visitors to our country often comment with pleasure on these qualities in America's young people. But if school experiences in this country are designed to promote these qualities, it may also be that the schools downplay stress on the subservient conformity that generates high levels of subject-matter achievement in some other countries.

Americans are also profoundly committed to breadth of education. Primary students in our country not only study the three Rs, but they also paint, play musical instruments, debate, and compete in chess tournaments in their schools. American high schools offer a huge range of courses, and students are encouraged to sample these courses as electives and to participate in a host of extracurricular activities. This commitment to breadth shows up also in the concept of a four-year, liberal-arts undergraduate education, a concept unique to the United States; students elsewhere begin their professional training as doctors, lawyers, or licensed psychologists when they *enter* the university at age 18. Our system works well because students stay in school longer than they do in other countries. By comparison then, at any given age American students are likely to be more broadly educated than are students elsewhere though they may not yet have as much detailed knowledge of specific academic subjects. They will acquire this knowledge over time, of course; and they should, on average, end up with a knowledge base that is uniquely broad as well as deep.

What this means is that if Americans are truly interested in learning how their schools stack up comparatively, they should insist that at least *some* comparative studies focus on the values that *Americans* hold for their children and on the unique strengths of *American* schools. To the best of our knowledge, comparative studies to date have all examined student knowledge of specific academic subjects, and nearly all have compared the achievements of equivalent-age junior high or high school students. None of the studies seems yet to have investigated breadth of student interests or knowledge; none has yet examined student creativity, initiative, social responsibility, or independence of thought; and few have studied knowledge among undergraduates or young people who have completed their educations. In fact, comparative studies to date seem almost to have deliberately avoided looking at the strengths of American schools!

Problems with the Studies. The critics and the press seem also to have ignored crucial reasons why comparative evidence can be shaky. Many countries have large ethnic minorities that do not speak the dominant language of the country. Schools serving those minorities often do not conduct education in the dominant language and are excluded from comparative research. In contrast, comparative-study samples from America usually include students from families that *do* and *do not* speak English. Many other countries also operate educational systems in which only selected students are allowed to enter high-status high schools, and comparative data from those countries may be collected only from those high-status schools. In contrast, the typical high school in America serves the full range of students, and comparative evidence from this country usually represents all students attending those schools. Such differences mean that American student-achievement scores may look bad simply because they are gathered from the full range of students in the country, whereas scores from other countries are gathered from biased samples.[46]

Further, countries may differ in the conditions that exist when comparative data are gathered. For example, a Quality Control Observer reported the following conditions for testing in South Korea (a nation famous for its high overall achievement scores):

> The math teacher . . . calls the names of the 13-year-olds in the room who have been selected as part of the IAEP sample. As each name is called, the student stands at attention at his or her desk until the list is complete. Then, to the supportive and encouraging applause of their colleagues, the chosen ones leave to [take the assessment test].[47]

As Gerald Bracey has noted, these students were apparently taking the test for the honor of their country![48] This is surely not likely to occur in America, where our overtested students are accustomed to competing regularly for individual rewards and are likely to view the tests used in comparative studies as an inconvenience offering no obvious personal advantage. Thus, American students may have fewer reasons to perform well in comparative studies.

The point is that in many comparative studies the aggregate scores reported for different countries are not strictly comparable. Such studies are not useless, of course. Indeed, one can learn from them by looking at disaggregated data for subsamples in various countries. But the differences in aggregate national-achievement scores reported by those studies—differences so often relished by hostile critics and the compliant press—may reflect little more than biases in samples and differences in testing procedures.

Opportunity to Learn. A third issue to think about when examining comparative evidence is whether opportunity to learn is the same for different nations. Such opportunities may vary for several reasons. Some countries require that all of their students study key academic subjects—such as advanced algebra or specific foreign languages—whereas in other countries those subjects are optional, and some countries (and poorer school districts in America) may lack resources to offer those subjects at all. In some nations key subjects are taught in the early grades, but elsewhere they are delayed until the high school years. Factors such as these make an enormous difference in the aggregate level of student knowledge at a given age. In fact, if we had to identify a single factor that best predicts student knowledge of specific subjects, that factor would certainly be opportunity to learn. This principle is so important, and is so often ignored by those who misuse evidence to criticize American schools, that we restate it here as our *Student Achievement Law* (see Exhibit 2.14).

■ Exhibit 2.14
Berliner and Biddle's
Student Achievement Law

Regardless of what anyone claims about student and school characteristics, *opportunity to learn* is the single most powerful predictor of student achievement.

A good example of the Student Achievement Law at work appears in studies of gender and mathematics achievement. Many good-hearted people have wondered why the mathematics achievement of American girls is roughly equal to that of boys throughout the primary and junior high school years, but suddenly drops off in senior high school. Actually, there is no mystery here. Higher-level mathematics courses are optional in most American high schools, and since more boys choose to take those courses, the boys have more opportunity to learn advanced mathematics, and they learn it!

The same process affects comparative studies of mathematics achievement. The Second International Mathematics Study from the IEA was conducted from 1980 to 1982. It looked at the achievement of both thirteen-year-olds (i.e., eighth-graders) and high school seniors. Among other things, the study found that the aggregate achievement of eighth-grade American students lagged behind that of students in many other countries, notably Japan.[49] This fact was immediately pounced on by critics and by a dutiful press, which enthusiastically vilified American schools for fecklessness.

Nobody at the time seemed to notice that Japanese schools were then *requiring* eighth-grade students to take mathematics courses that stressed algebra, whereas such courses were typically offered to American students a year or two later. However, this fact *was* noted by Ian Westbury, a scholar at the University of Illinois who knew the IEA study well. And when Westbury reexamined the IEA data—looking at the achievement of American students who had and had not taken algebra—he found striking differences in American student achievement. Westbury identified four contrasting math curricula to which eighth-grade American students had been exposed: (1) remedial classes (30 cases); (2) typical nonalgebra classes (174 cases); (3) enriched prealgebra classes (31 cases); and (4) algebra classes (38 cases).[50] Only the latter two types of classes were comparable to those offered to Japanese students, and when Westbury examined student achievement for those classes, he found records that matched or exceeded those of students in the Japanese schools (see Exhibit 2.15).

Thus, what the critics had interpreted as a failure of American schools turned out to be merely a reflection of the age at which algebra instruction is typically begun in Japan and America. One may choose to debate whether algebra should or should not be taught at an earlier age, and Americans might want ultimately to change the ways in which instruction is scheduled in our schools. We might wonder, too, what prealgebra is. No other nation seems to have it, and it sounds odd to us. If American schools have students who can do prealgebra, perhaps they should give them algebra instead.

One can debate such curricular issues forever, but what is clear is that the IEA data displayed by Westbury do not suggest that American teachers or schools are deficient compared with those in Japan. Instead, the data reveal merely that the two nations differ in the typical ways in which they structure opportunities to learn. And, if Americans should truly decide that they want their high school students to be "first" in high-level mathematics achievement, all they need do is to fund, offer, and encourage students to take high-level mathematics courses at an early age, in all schools. Is this wise? Ah, that is another question, to which we return later in this book.

Another example of the impact of opportunity to learn also concerns Japanese and American student achievement. From upper elementary through high school, most Japanese students go to private academies called *Juku* schools. Such schools offer additional instruction in academic subjects after regular school hours and on weekends, helping students prepare for entrance exams. Given the time spent in instruction in regular and *Juku* schools combined, the typical Japanese sixteen-year-old will have accrued something like two more years of formal schooling than his or her American counterpart. What is newsworthy if occasionally a comparative study finds that one group of high school students with two more years of instruction happens to outperform another group, which has not had that opportunity to learn?

In general then, *aggregate* comparative evidence provides no convincing support for the myth that American students fail in mathematics achievement—or achievement in any other subject—compared with students in other countries. Instead, much of that evidence merely reflects differences in opportunities to learn, and when controls for those opportunities are used

Exhibit 2.15 Japanese and American Achievement Scores for Students Age 13—from The Second International Mathematics Study of the IEA

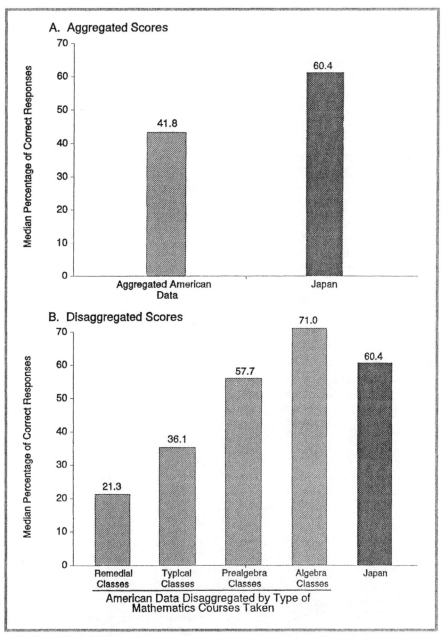

A. Aggregated Scores

B. Disaggregated Scores

—Source: Ian Westbury (1992, 1994).

with the data, American students' school achievement looks quite similar to that of students from other countries.

Variability and Test Performance. Yet another issue plagues attempts to compare aggregate scores for student achievement in the U.S. with that of other countries. To state this issue succinctly, the achievement of students from American schools is a *lot* more variable than is student achievement from elsewhere. Thus, any simple attempt to aggregate American students' school achievements may be thought of as akin to reporting the average weight for a group of mice and elephants.

Two serious problems help to generate huge differences in achievement among American students. First, the American population exhibits more extremes of wealth and poverty than does that of comparable nations; the problem of income disparity falls largely on young people; and children from rich and poor families are unlikely to attend the same schools. By comparison, then, the United States has both more extremely rich children and a *much* larger population of poor children than do other Western countries. (By 1980 about one-fifth of all children were living in impoverished families in the United States, and the numbers have gotten worse in subsequent years.[51]) This means that vast numbers of poor, ill-clothed, undernourished children from distressed homes with few educational resources now flood our inner-city and poorer rural schools. This extreme problem is simply *not* faced by schools in other Western countries, where rates of childhood poverty are a fraction of those in America[52] and residential ghettoization is less prevalent. (Readers may think we are exaggerating this problem. The frightening data that confirm it are summarized in Chapter 6.)

Second, Americans tolerate enormous inequities in funding for schools that serve the rich and the poor. Rich people in the United States are able to buy some of the world's finest education for their children, either in private academies or in well-financed, suburban, public-school districts. In contrast, children of the poor are often crowded into miserable rural or inner-city schools whose annual per-student support may be one-fifth or less of that in nearby, suburban public schools. This means, of course, that students in the suburbs have smaller classes, teachers with higher salaries and morale, and more computers and other facilities—whereas schools in slum neighborhoods must contend with dangerous and decaying buildings, gross overcrowding, violence, and inadequate funding for even basic instruction. This problem is also not faced in other Western countries, where equal basic support is normally provided to each student in all public schools.

Together these two problems mean that scholastic achievements will vary far more in the United States than in other countries. To put it baldly, America now has some of the finest, highest-achieving schools in the world—and some of the most miserable, threatened, underfunded educational travesties, which would fail by any achievement standard. This means that any attempt to aggregate the achievements of American schools into a single score is bound to misrepresent the true picture.

How, then, might one use comparative evidence to gain a valid understanding of how American schools stack up against schools elsewhere? Perhaps the best way to do this would be to isolate the independent effects of student poverty, per-student support of the school, and national context when analyzing school achievement data. This analysis could be done either through complex statistical techniques or by disaggregating the achievement of schools that differ in student poverty or per-student support. Unfortunately, we know of *no* comparative study that has provided either of these types of analysis.

We do know of one analysis, however, that generated disaggregated data comparing the average mathematics achievements of eighth-graders from public schools in various American states with age-equivalent students from other countries. (Such data have value because poverty and annual per-student support for schools also vary among the states.) This analysis was provided by the National Center for Education Statistics and drew from a recent comparative study.[53] As Exhibit 2.16 shows, the average scores of eighth-graders in public schools in some high-achieving states (Iowa, North Dakota, and Minnesota) are actually just about the same today as those of the highest-achieving foreign countries included in the study (Taiwan and Korea). In contrast, poorly achieving American states (Louisiana and Mississippi) stand just about with Jordan—a struggling, not yet developed nation.

Thus, the performance of American public schools ranges from the truly remarkable to the unforgivably miserable. With a range of this magnitude, it seems fruitless to make proclamations about the "average" achievement of American schools. Instead, aggregate statistics hide more than they reveal about student achievement in our country. The real task facing America is to find ways to improve the education and lives of America's poorest and most neglected citizens.

The Unreported News. Finally, we note with sadness that when comparative research appears in which American education looks good, somehow the press seems not to notice. As far as we know, the press paid no attention to the studies of Ian Westbury and the National Center for Education Statistics summarized in Exhibits 2.15 and 2.16. Similarly, in one of the few international comparisons ever done at the college level, John Cogan, Judith Torney-Purta, and Douglas Anderson recently found that American students know less than Japanese students about global issues when both groups enter college but that by graduation that gap has disappeared.[54] (American students tend to grow in knowledge of international affairs between their freshman and senior years, but Japanese students do not.) The press seems also to have ignored these findings.

In 1992 the IEA released a report of findings from a comparative study of reading achievement involving two hundred thousand students in thirty-

Exhibit 2.16   Average Mathematics Proficiency Scores for Public School 8th-Graders (in America) and 13-Year-Olds (in Other Countries): 1991 or 1992

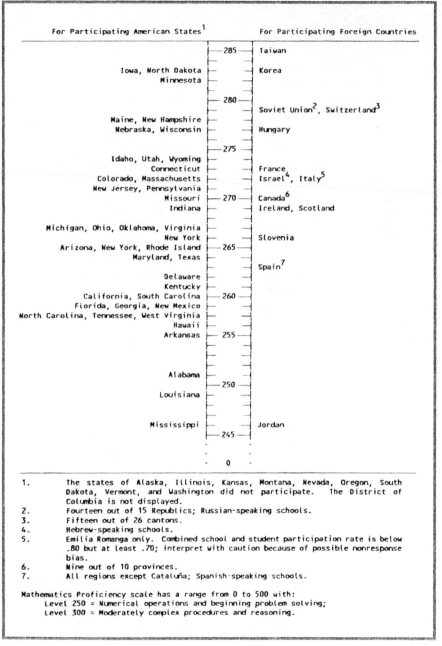

1.   The states of Alaska, Illinois, Kansas, Montana, Nevada, Oregon, South Dakota, Vermont, and Washington did not participate.   The District of Columbia is not displayed.
2.   Fourteen out of 15 Republics; Russian-speaking schools.
3.   Fifteen out of 26 cantons.
4.   Hebrew-speaking schools.
5.   Emilia Romanga only. Combined school and student participation rate is below .80 but at least .70; interpret with caution because of possible nonresponse bias.
6.   Nine out of 10 provinces.
7.   All regions except Cataluña; Spanish-speaking schools.

Mathematics Proficiency scale has a range from 0 to 500 with:
    Level 250 = Numerical operations and beginning problem solving;
    Level 300 = Moderately complex procedures and reasoning.

—Source: *Education in the States and Nations* (National Center for Education Statistics, 1993a, pp. 56–57).

one nations.[55] In this study, American nine-year-olds placed second in the world—while our fourteen-year-olds finished ninth, which was well above average and only a few points off the top. According to Gerald Bracey, the IEA put out a major press release concerning the study—but not one newspaper, radio station, or television outlet in the United States chose to cover the announcement of this study and its results. Americans learned about it only after *European* newspapers reported it and some wire services had picked up the story of high American students' achievement in reading that had appeared in the European press.[56]

In a recent study, Richard Mayer, Hidetsugu Tajika, and Caryn Stanley compared two types of mathematical knowledge between samples of Japanese and American fifth-graders.[57] By comparison, Japanese students are exposed to curricula that stress more *computational* mathematics, so the researchers predicted and found greater computational achievements among Japanese students. In contrast, American fifth-grade classes stress more *problem solving* in mathematics, so the authors predicted and found greater problem-solving skills among American students. (The Americans excelled at constructing conceptual models for mathematical problems, selecting and combining information about those problems, and breaking the problems down into manageable steps.) But this study also seemed to hold no interest for the press.

If those stories do not make the case, how about the following? Evidence confirms that Americans are *far* more likely to complete higher education than are people in other Western countries. In 1993 the National Center for Education Statistics released data about the percentages of people who have graduated from colleges and universities by age twenty-two in the United States and other countries from the Organisation for Economic Co-operation and Development (OECD).[58] These data also provided comparisons among the American states (see Exhibit 2.17). Rates of college graduation also vary enormously among the states, but look at the rates for other Western countries. More than half of all American states are graduating 27 percent or more of their twenty-two-year-olds, but the *highest* percentage for a foreign country (Japan) is 26 percent. Even the lowest-ranking American states—Nevada (with 13 percent) and Alaska (with 10 percent)—are graduating roughly the same proportion of twenty-two-year-olds as are major Western European nations that are so often touted as models for American education to emulate. But have these data provoked noisy debate? They have not; indeed, as far as we can tell, media silence concerning them has been complete.

In the spring of 1993, the press *did* carry the good news that worker productivity in the United States had just hit a twenty-year high and was, as it had been for years, greatly ahead of worker productivity in countries that are our international rivals. But without questioning the incongruity of its stories, the same press thereafter continued to report on America's "uneducated," "ill-prepared," and "poorly motivated" workforce. Thus, while the

Exhibit 2.17   Percentage of Persons Age 22 in American States and Other
OECD Countries Who Were University and College Graduates
in 1988

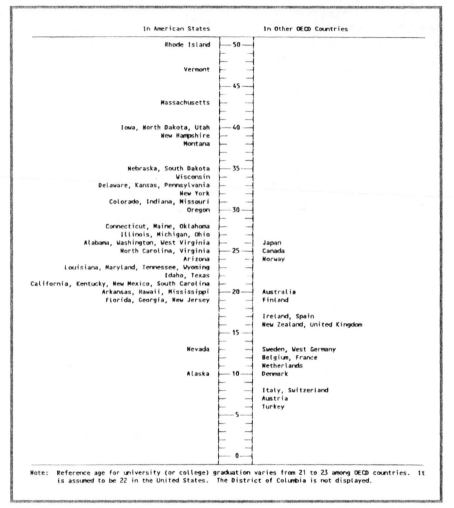

Note: Reference age for university (or college) graduation varies from 21 to 23 among OECD countries. It
is assumed to be 22 in the United States. The District of Columbia is not displayed.

—Source: *Education in the States and Nations* (National Center for Education Statistics, 1993a, pp. 60–61).

media seem quite willing to report bad news about our schools, they are
much less willing to report news about the strengths of American education.[59]

One wonders, Why? Is it possible that bad news about education is thought
to be more newsworthy? Or have reporters by now been so brainwashed by
the critics that they cannot believe good news? Are too many of the reporters'
employers close friends of powerful people who wish the public schools no

good? We don't know the answer to these questions, but America's public schools have certainly been getting a bad reputation from the media.

Summary. The myth that American schools fail badly by comparison with schools in other industrialized countries is also not supported by the evidence. Instead, when we analyze that evidence responsibly and think carefully about its implications, we discover that American schools stack up very well. And although the United States looks bad when aggregate scores from some comparative studies are examined, we should understand the following:

- Few of those studies have yet focused on the unique values and strengths of American education.
- Many of the studies' results have obviously been affected by sampling biases and inconsistent methods for gathering data.
- Many, perhaps most, of the studies' results were generated by differences in curricula—in opportunities to learn—in the countries studied.
- Aggregate results for American schools are misleading because of the huge range of school quality in this country—ranging from marvelous to terrible.
- The press has managed to ignore most comparative studies in which the United States has done well.

Thus, despite what you may have been led to believe by the critics and the press, and even though the comparative evidence to date is weak, the evidence that does exist suggests that American education has important strengths which do *not* appear in other countries. This does not mean that American education is without flaws. Indeed, achievement levels of American schools vary greatly, and that variation is a product of serious and growing problems in our society and of unconscionable differences in the funding of American schools. But, as with the other myths we have reviewed in this chapter, the myth that American education fails generally in international comparisons is balderdash.

Recapitulation

From one source after another, for the past decade we've been receiving evidence that American education is doing a mediocre job, one that ill-serves this country and our children. What is most alarming is that after a sustained period of valiant reform effort—and no small investment of resources—in the 1980s, we have so little to show for our labors and our money.

>   —Chester E. Finn, Jr. and Theodor Rebarber (*Education Reform in the '90s*, 1992, p. xi)

Since the early 1980s, Americans have been subjected to a massive campaign of criticism directed at their public schools and colleges. We have been told that student achievement in those institutions has slipped badly, that our achievement now lags behind that of students in other industrialized countries, and that these judgments are confirmed by numerous studies. As a result, the critics charge, American students are now being shortchanged and the nation is "at risk." Unfortunately, these charges have often been made by the White House and other prestigious sources, and they have been picked up and endlessly elaborated on in the media.

These charges are errant nonsense. If we go by the evidence, despite greatly expanded student enrollment, the average American high school and college student is now doing as well as, or perhaps slightly better than, that student did in previous years. Indeed, not only is student achievement remaining steady or rising slowly across the land, but so also is student intelligence. And when comparative-study evidence is examined carefully, that evidence also confirms impressive strengths of American education.

Unfortunately, the press, the public, and often educators themselves have not understood the evidentiary shortcomings of this massive, critical attack against American public education. So our message will come as a surprise to many people. This does not mean that all American schools do well or that the educational system in this country does not have shortcomings. Indeed, America suffers serious problems that threaten our schools, and some of those schools are miserably funded and do poorly indeed. But on average, American schools and colleges do a lot better than the critics have been claiming. As we shall see in later chapters, where those schools do fail, they usually fail because of problems imposed on them—problems that the critics have blissfully ignored.

Chapter Three

Other Myths About American Schools

◆

The picture we uncovered in the previous chapter was far different from the dismal portrait peddled by the critics who, through ignorance and ideological commitment, have promoted endless tales about how poorly American schools are doing. But myths told by the critics have concerned more than just achievement and aptitude. Other aspects of our nation's educational system have also been maligned, and many Americans have also been deceived by these myths as well. This gullibility continues to surprise us, since public education is such a large part of the American experience, and since it requires such a huge investment of public funding. Still, despite the prominence of education in the life of the American people, many citizens today seem to have accepted various notions about our schools that just aren't true.

Most of the myths we discuss in this chapter seem to have been designed to debase the image of *public* education. It is convenient to sort these myths into three groups.

1. Myths concerned with the costs of education—which seem designed to persuade Americans that spending tax dollars on education is wasteful

2. Myths concerned with relations between schools and industry— which blame education for problems and challenges faced by American business corporations

3. Myths concerned with specific features of public schools—features that are alleged to be offensive or to indicate widespread dissatisfaction with public education

In making these charges, the critics have used various tactics to discredit ·public schools in our country. And, in their zeal, the critics have again made a host of claims that fly in the face of evidence. As we look at that evidence, we will learn that the average public school in our country is a lot less costly and a lot more effective than the public has been led to believe.

This does not mean, of course, that *all* American teachers, schools, and school systems are effective. We know of school systems, for example, that spend money in wasteful ways, and each of us has met individual teachers and school administrators we wanted to strangle. Nor does it mean that

American education is without problems or that it serves all American students well. On the contrary, because of huge differences in the funding of America's schools, some of America's most impoverished students are served miserably. Therefore, generalizations about the characteristics or problems of education in our country are often meaningless. But such shortcomings bear little resemblance to charges that America's public schools are *generally* profligate or feckless, and that is exactly the sort of nonsense the critics have been trying to sell to the American people.

MYTH . . . *America Spends a Lot More Money on Education Than Other Countries*

We spend twice as much [on education] as the Japanese and almost 40 percent more than all the other major industrialized countries of the world.

—John Sununu, then chief of staff in the Bush administration (1989)

Some years ago critics began to claim that America was spending a lot more for public education than other Western countries, and this idea has since been repeated endlessly. During his presidency, George Bush received a good deal of economic advice from the chair of his Council of Economic Advisors, Michael Boskin. Perhaps the reason the economy of the U.S. took a turn for the worse toward the end of the Bush years was that Mr. Boskin did not always have his facts straight. On education, he was quoted as saying that we spend more per pupil than most of the other industrialized economies.[1] Nor was this claim made by Boskin alone. Two former secretaries of education, Lauro Cavazos and Lamar Alexander, also claimed that America spends more on education than do our industrial rivals, Germany and Japan. And former Assistant Secretary of Education, Chester Finn, wrote in the *New York Times* that we "spend more per pupil than any other nation," an opinion echoed by John Sununu in the quotation with which we began this section.

In 1990 two members of the Economic Policy Institute of Washington, D.C., Edith Rasell and Lawrence Mishel, decided to check out the truth of these claims.[2] They found that, like former Budget Director David Stockman a decade earlier, the people who had issued these claims seem to have made up the numbers as they went along.

Although these officials claimed that American educational costs were "excessive," according to data from UNESCO, the branch of the United Nations that conducts research on education, the United States was actually tied with Canada and the Netherlands, and all three nations fell *behind* Sweden in the amount spent per student for all levels of education.[3] But even this position as one of the "big spenders" was distorted, because higher education was included in the per-student costs reported by UNESCO. Compared with other countries, a much larger proportion of Americans are enrolled in colleges and universities; thus, we spend a lot more than other nations on our higher-education system.

When it comes to primary and secondary education, the United States actually spends *less* than the *average* industrialized nation. Exhibit 3.1 presents the appropriate evidence—which, of course, flatly contradicts what was said by leaders of the Bush administration. As the exhibit shows, if one uses the exchange rates prevalent in 1988, the United States ranked only *ninth* among sixteen industrialized nations in per-pupil expenditures for grades K through 12, spending 14 percent *less* than Germany, 30 percent *less* than Japan, and 51 percent *less* than Switzerland.

On the surface, then, the U.S. appears to be near the middle of the pack among industrialized nations in expenditures for schooling. But the real shame of our rich nation is hidden in these aggregate data. If we examine the numbers more closely, we find that 1985 expenditures per student in Norway and the United States were about $5,000 and $3,500 per year, respectively. But these are *average* figures that have quite different meanings in the two countries. Like most countries, Norway operates a national education system that tries to distribute educational support equally throughout the country, and this means that in 1985 each child in Norway received the Norwegian Kroner equivalent of roughly $5,000 for his or her education.

Exhibit 3.1 K-12 Per Pupil Expenditures for Education in 16 Nations in 1985 (Based on Exchange Rates in 1988)

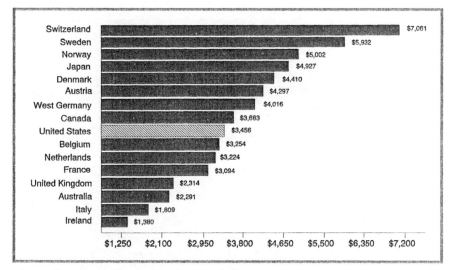

—Source: *Shortchanging Education* (Rasell & Mishel, 1990).
—Statistical Sources: *Statistical Yearbook* (UNESCO, 1988); *Digest of Educational Statistics* (National Center for Education Statistics, 1988).

In contrast, because of the local taxation system unique to the U.S., funding for schools is dramatically unequal in our nation. This means that some American students received a great deal more, and many—tragically—received a lot less than $3,500 for their schooling. How much more and less? In the late 1980s some American school districts spent more than *$11,000 per pupil per year* whereas others spent less than *$2,000 per pupil per year!* No wonder Jonathan Kozol described our education system as one of "savage inequalities."[4]

But the comparisons go on. It is also possible to examine how students fare in each country in terms of the portion of per capita income spent on primary and secondary education. This is one way to measure how a society values its young—a crude yet meaningful estimate of how much a nation is willing to spend in caring for and preparing the next generation. Since citizens of the United States have always prided themselves on their huge investment in public education, the data in Exhibit 3.2 may come as a shock to you.

When we compare ourselves with other industrialized nations, we find that in 1985 most of them spent a *greater* percentage of their per capita income on primary and secondary education than we did. If America were to come up to merely the *average* percentage of per capita income that the other displayed industrialized nations spent on education, in 1985 we would

Exhibit 3.2   K-12 Per Pupil Expenditures for Education as a Percent of Per Capita Income in 16 Nations in 1985

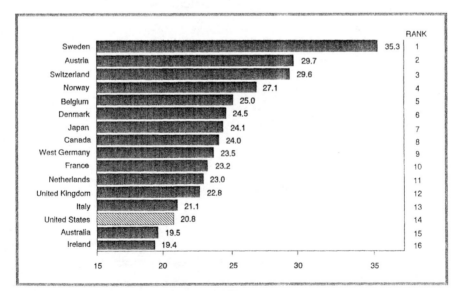

—Source: *Shortchanging Education* (Rasell & Mishel, 1990).
—Statistical Sources: *Statistical Yearbook* (UNESCO, 1988); *Digest of Education Statistics* (National Center for Education Statistics, 1988).

have needed to spend about $20 billion *more per year* on K through 12 educa-
tion.

This sounds like a lot of money, but it pales by comparison with other national expenditures. As we write, Congress is once again conducting its annual debate over whether to waste yet more money on "stealth" bombers. Each of these useless aircraft costs a little over one billion dollars, so we are only talking about the cost of 20 bombers! We sometimes wonder, why are Americans so much less willing to invest in the education of their children than are people in other advanced countries? Might it be that people in our country spend so much more of their tax dollars on the costs of defense, medical care, violence, and debt-servicing that, by comparison, they can no longer afford even average support for their public schools?

We must not leave this topic without also noting that quibbles can be raised about the data we present in Exhibits 3.1 and 3.2. Various methods can be used for comparing educational expenditures among nations, and the data we display in these exhibits were challenged by the Bush administration in a 1992 report from the National Center for Education Statistics (NCES).[5] The NCES analysis did not use simple exchange rates but rather "purchasing power parity rates" to determine the value of money in each nation. (Such "parity rates" are based on how much common items cost in each country.) In the NCES analysis, our nation's expenditures were slightly greater when compared with other nations'. But still we were *not* first in per-pupil expenditures—Canada was. Moreover, when the percent of Gross Domestic Product (GDP) spent on primary and secondary education only was computed, we ranked third out of six nations.

Another set of data was published in 1992 by the Organisation for Economic Co-operation and Development (OECD).[6] Although it also used purchasing power parity rates, the OECD report painted a bleaker picture of American educational expenditures than did our government's own report. The OECD analysis estimated that the public dollars expended in education for grades K through 12 in 1988 led us to rank seventh out of twenty countries. Expressed as a percent of GDP, the same figures gave us a rank of thirteen out of this pool of twenty industrialized nations. Or, to rephrase this finding, according to the OECD, in the late 1980s twelve other nations found ways to spend more of their Gross Domestic Product on schooling than we did.

The OECD report also went on to shatter other myths. It informed readers that in comparison with nineteen other countries, the U.S. was tenth in capital expenditures for education. And out of seventeen nations, five others managed to have lower pupil-teacher ratios in the primary grades than did America, and nine others had lower pupil-teacher ratios than we did in the secondary grades.

Thus, regardless of the technique used to compare educational expenditures for primary and secondary schools, the United States *never* comes out first. It is always somewhere in the middle of the pack when compared with other industrialized nations.[7] Given these facts, one wonders what Mr. Boskin, Mr. Sununu, Professor Finn, and the two secretaries of education under George Bush were talking about when they decried our nation's "excessive" expenditures for education. Perhaps they were merely repeating cant, perhaps they did not know how to interpret evidence, perhaps they were ignorant of the facts, or perhaps—could it be?—they were conducting a deliberate disinformation campaign.

In summary, given the picture of expenditures on primary and secondary education revealed by evidence, we can only conclude that George Bush, "The Education President," was not telling the truth at the big education conference his administration organized in 1989. At that much ballyhooed meeting his lips were read, and he was quoted as saying that the United States "lavishes unsurpassed resources on [our children's] schooling."[8] Actually, he should have said that the United States has amazingly high levels of achievement when compared with other nations—especially given the fact that Americans devote only *average* resources to their schools—and that those resources are distributed in uniquely unfair and unequal ways.

MYTH . . . *Money is Not Related to School Achievement*

I live in a manufacturing town. . . .We are going to spend over a million dollars for a high school to teach the children of the working people of that town white collar, starched collar jobs. . . .The expenditure that is now being made [for the public school system], and the laws that are being passed for its expenditure are as absolutely a waste as though it were thrown into the gutter.

　　—The Treasurer of the National Association of Manufacturers, speaking before its
　　annual convention in 1920 (cited by S. Alexander Rippa, 1988)[9]

Virtually all studies of school performance, in fact, reveal that spending has little bearing on student achievement. . . .Research demonstrates that [concentrating on performance assessment] will be far more successful than [reforms] that concentrate on salary levels and class size.

　　—The Heritage Foundation (1989, pp. 1–2)

Critics leading the Manufactured Crisis have also promoted a second myth about school finance, namely, that the level of school funding does not matter—that educators always complain they need more money, but in fact spending on education is unrelated to productivity in the schools. It doesn't take much thought to realize that this charge is absurd. Extra funding usually means that schools can improve their facilities, cut class sizes, and hire teachers with better qualifications; and surely these steps should help to improve student performance. Nevertheless, this myth has circulated since at least the turn of the century and has too often been accepted as truth by uninformed people. Let's look at the recent history of this myth and the evidence that now refutes it.

The Coleman Report. Contemporary beliefs that school funding does not matter seem to have had their origin in a 1966 study by James Coleman and others entitled *Equality of Educational Opportunity*.[10] Commonly called the Coleman Report, this study was based on a massive survey of school achievement among students in first, third, sixth, ninth, and twelfth grades in several thousand schools from across the nation. Various kinds of data were collected for the survey, and complex statistical controls were used by the researchers in their analysis.

The Coleman Report had been commissioned by the National Center for Education Statistics in response to the Civil Rights Act of 1964, and many of its results concerned issues of equity for students from different racial and ethnic groups. Its third section focused on the determinants of student achievement, however, and came to a surprising conclusion. In brief, the Report found that characteristics of students' own home backgrounds and those of other students in their schools were the major determinants of the students' achievement and that school characteristics—and, by implication, school funding—had only a small effect once home and peer factors were taken into account. Thus, the investigators wrote,

> Schools bring little influence to bear on a child's achievement that is independent of his [*sic*] background and general social context; and that this very lack of an independent effect means that the inequalities imposed on children by their home, neighborhood, and peer environment are carried along to become the inequalities with which they confront adult life at the end of school.[11]

Simply put then, the Coleman Report concluded that schools have no important effects on children, while family and neighborhood do. The most important predictor of academic success for children seems to be the choice they made of their parents at birth.

The Coleman Report itself was lengthy, its statistics were complex, its text was murky, and it had not been subjected to prior peer review. It was released with great fanfare, however, and its surprising conclusion about the weak effect of schooling was widely trumpeted in the press. Critics quickly embraced this conclusion and used it to inveigh against funds for public education. Conversely, supporters of public education were worried, and arguments about implications of the Report ensued. Thus, the public was led to believe that reputable research had "proved" that schools (and school funding) had but weak effects, and the fat was in the fire.

Problems With the Report. Why did the Coleman Report come to this odd conclusion? Although most people did not understand it at the time, major problems afflicted the Report, and these helped to generate its weak findings for the effect of schools on student achievement. Here, we look at four of these problems.

First, in its analyses the Coleman Report distinguished four categories for measures thought to be related to student achievement: (1) *factors related to the student's home background,* (2) *characteristics of the student body,* (3) *characteristics of the teachers,* and (4) *school facilities and curriculum.* The conclusion about school impact on student achievement was based on the size of effect for only the last of these four categories. But is this reasonable? Clearly, student-home-background factors are *not* measures of school quality, but what about the student body or the characteristics of the teachers? Among student body characteristics, the investigators included measures of "number of student transfers," "attendance rates," and "average hours of homework." These certainly sound like indicators of school quality. Worse, measures of teacher characteristics included "average years of [teachers'] experience" and "average level of [teachers'] education." Surely *these* are indicators of school quality. Thus, the investigators had made poor decisions when they assigned the measures they used to their analysis categories. They would have generated larger estimates for the effect of schools had they included *all* available measures of school quality in their crucial fourth category.

Second, measures used in the Coleman Report were chosen largely for administrative convenience rather than for their relevance to student achievement. For example, what teacher qualities would *you* look for if you wanted to maximize student learning? Perhaps you would search for teachers who have high instructional ability, or perhaps you would want to find teachers who are good classroom managers; but, alas, no measures of instructional ability or classroom-management skills appeared in the Coleman Report. None! Similarly, measures chosen to represent school facilities and curriculum concerned such issues as "school size" and "volumes per student in the school library," rather than, let us say, the school's academic demands or its disciplinary standards. (Interestingly, Coleman has recently argued that the latter are, in fact, *major* determinants of student achievement.[12]) All this means that estimates for the effect of schools were also minimized in the Report because the investigators chose the wrong measures. They seem to have studied easy-to-obtain information rather than measures truly relevant to student achievement, perhaps because the latter were more difficult to gather. This reminds us of the proverbial drunk who, having lost his watch elsewhere, looked for it under the lamp post because "the light is better there."

Third, data from the Coleman Report were cross-sectional rather than longitudinal. That is, the Report looked at student achievement only *once* and thus could not assess the *gains* in student achievement that are a more accurate indicator of successful schooling. Which would you judge a better indicator of school success, the achievement scores that students presently earn, or the achievement scores they have gained over the years they attend school? Surely the former reflect the impact of students' home backgrounds as well as that of their schools, but gains in scores are better indicators if we want to focus on the impact that school attendance has on children. Thus, estimates of the effect of schools were also minimized in the Report because the investigators used a weak measure for the outcomes of schooling.

Fourth, the Coleman Report also used a poor method for analyzing data, and this method generated distorted estimates for the effect of each of the four categories into which it had sorted the measures that they used. In brief, analyses in the Report proceeded in several steps. In the first step, the investigators estimated the effects of home background factors while imposing no controls for the other categories. Then, in subsequent steps, they estimated the net effects for student body characteristics, teacher characteristics, and school characteristics while also controlling for students' home backgrounds. The trouble with this procedure is that measures from these four categories are all correlated with each other. Surely, at least in America, students from affluent homes are also likely to be found in schools where other students are also affluent, teachers have high qualifications, and the school's facilities are good. And this means that if one estimates the simple effects of any one of these four categories, that estimate will inadvertently include some of the effects of the other three. Since the Coleman Report began its analyses by estimating the simple effects of home background, without using controls, those estimates were *inflated* because they included the unexamined effects of the other three categories. And since the Report controlled for the effects of home background when estimating the effects of each of the other categories, the latter estimates were *depressed* because the effects they shared with home background factors had already been taken out of the analysis. The upshot was that the analysis strategy gave inaccurately inflated estimates for the effects of home background and unfairly depressed estimates for the effects of school characteristics.

A better way to analyze survey data is to consider all measures at once, in a single step of analysis, and to use an analysis technique that estimates the net effect of each measure while controlling for the effects of the other measures. Various techniques are available for doing this, of which "regression analysis" is currently the most popular. Moreover, six years after the Report appeared, Coleman himself published reanalyses of its data using "regression" procedures.[13] As would be expected, these reanalyses generated *smaller* estimates for the size of the effects of home background and *larger* estimates for the size of the effects of student body, teacher characteristics, and school characteristics. But Coleman did not stress this fact in his later text, and by the time that work was published, it was too late. Mischief had already been done, and Coleman's reanalyses were generally ignored.

The Coleman Report had serious problems, then, and these helped to generate its mistaken conclusion that schools (and school funding) do not affect student achievement. Most people did not know about these problems at the time, however, and the Report's erroneous claims were widely and uncritically reported by the press. And critics who wanted to believe that giving additional aid to public schools would be useless found great solace in these reports.

Other Studies. Public interest in the issue of the effects of schooling on achievement remained high, of course, and review works soon appeared that summarized other early studies whose findings were thought to bear on the topic.[14] Most of these other studies had designs that were even weaker than that of the Coleman Report. But the Report had set the terms of the debate, and reviewers did not then understand that findings of apparently weak effects of schooling could be generated by poor research designs. Thus, when reviewers also found weak effects for schools in other studies, they tended to ignore design issues and merely assumed that those effects "confirmed" the Coleman Report's dismal conclusion. It is hardly surprising, then, that by the early 1980s many people had come to believe that student achievement was "largely a product of the attitudes and characteristics students brought with them into the classroom, with the schools little able to alter the influence of these background factors"[15] and that this conclusion was supported by massive evidence.

Much of this has now changed, of course. Although ignorant people—and leaders of the Heritage Foundation—may still believe that "research proves" that student outcomes are unaffected by school characteristics and levels of funding, thoughtful reviewers have now explained how findings supporting this false conclusion can be generated by poor research designs.[16] Moreover, *careful* reviews now conclude that even evidence from the early, poorly designed studies implied sizable relations among funding, school characteristics, and student achievement.

To illustrate, Larry Hedges and others recently reported a careful reanalysis of data from a sample of early studies on school effects that E. A. Hanushek had reviewed a few years earlier.[17] Hanushek had based his early analysis on simple "vote-counting" procedures and had concluded, "there is no strong or systematic relationship between school expenditures and student performance."[18] In contrast, Hedges et al. used newer and more accurate meta-analytic procedures and concluded not only that early studies provided overwhelming evidence for the positive school effects of funding but estimated that if a typical school district increased annual per-pupil expenditure by $500 and used those funds wisely, students in that district would gain an average of 25 percentile points on tests of school achievement.[19]

Moreover, recent studies, with better designs, have now appeared that confirm the positive effects of good school characteristics and better funding. Let's look at three of the newer studies.

Academic Climate and Student Achievement. Our first example appeared in a recent (and notorious) book by John Chubb and Terry Moe entitled *Politics, Markets, and America's Schools.*[20] As we will detail later in this chapter, much of Chubb and Moe's book presents an ideologically driven argument against public education, but in it they also offer analyses of selected data from "High School and Beyond" (HSB), a major, longitudinal set of data concerned with student achievement, funded by the National Center for Education Statistics. The full HSB study sampled achievement records from nearly sixty thousand students who were enrolled in roughly one thousand public and private high schools from across the nation in the early 1980s, but supplementary data concerning school characteristics were available for only a portion of those schools. Thus, the Chubb and Moe analyses involved "only" twenty thousand students from roughly four hundred high schools. Data for the study included both the achievement records of students and questionnaires that were administered to students, their teachers, and the principals of their schools. Achievement-record information was gathered twice—once in 1980 when students were in the tenth grade, and again in 1982, when they were seniors. Thus, the study could examine gains in achievement.

In analyzing their data, Chubb and Moe assembled questionnaire responses into scales and then used those scales as measures of conditions that might affect student achievement. Several analyses were reported, but these generally revealed that four conditions had significant net effects on the twelfth-grade achievement of high school students. These were students' tenth-grade achievements, the socioeconomic status (SES) of students' parents, the average SES of all parents for the students' schools, and a factor that Chubb and Moe called "school organization." What this means is that students who had higher achievement records when they were seniors were also more likely to have had higher achievement records when they were sophomores. (So far, no surprise.) They were also more likely to have come from wealthier families and to have come from schools serving wealthier neighborhoods (thus confirming the claim made in the Coleman Report about the effects of home and neighborhood). Finally, these students were more likely to have experienced better "school organization."

This sounds promising, but what did Chubb and Moe's "school organization" scale really measure? According to the authors, this scale included measures of graduation requirements, priority given to academic excellence by educators in the school, the principal's motivation and dedication to teaching, estimated excellence and professionalism of teachers, staff harmony, percentage of students in an academic track, homework assignments, classroom administrative routines, and disciplinary fairness and effectiveness. In short, this scale had little to do with "school organization" but should have been called *academic climate* (or some such). Thus, Chubb and Moe's real finding was that, net of other effects—and particularly the SES of the student's family and the average SES of students in the school—*schools with better academic climates had higher levels of student achievement.* Chubb and Moe had discovered that school characteristics do, indeed, have a net effect on gains in student achievement. Moreover, the effect they reported was not small. Chubb and Moe estimated that, over the two-plus years of the HSB study, schools in the highest quartile of academic climate (*a.k.a.* "school organization") created nearly half a year of additional achievement for their students when compared with schools in the lowest quartile.

This finding challenged the dismal conclusion of the Coleman Report that schools had little influence, of course, and one would have thought that Chubb and Moe would discuss this fact in their text. Unfortunately, they did not do so, nor did reviewers of their book generally tumble to the fact that one of its major findings flatly contradicted the infamous Coleman Report. Pity. As we shall see shortly, Chubb and Moe's empirical efforts were largely driven by a desire to show why public schools are (allegedly) ineffective, and to this end they offered other findings that were at best questionable. Their evidence confirming the positive effect of school academic climate was far more persuasive.[21]

Funding, Teacher Quality, and Class Size. One cannot tell from Chubb and Moe's analyses whether *funding* affects school characteristics or student achievement. Fortunately, findings concerning these latter issues are provided in a persuasive article by Ronald Ferguson.[22] This work reports a massive study concerned with the determinants of achievement in most of the public-school districts of Texas. Data for the study included information on teachers' years of experience and academic achievement (measured with a standardized test), average class size in each school district, school funding and demographic characteristics for all of the school districts in the study, and student achievement for various grade levels for each year from 1986 to 1990. Roughly 90 percent of all Texas school districts were included in the sample, meaning that millions of students, tens of thousands of teachers and nearly a thousand public-school districts were involved.

Ferguson's findings were generated in two stages of analysis, each involving many statistical controls. In the first stage, he found that when student achievement levels were high in some school districts, those districts not only had more supportive home environments but also had significantly fewer pupils per teacher, had teachers with more years of experience, and had recruited teachers with higher scores on tests of academic ability. Moreover, the effects of these district characteristics were not small. Average class size, years of teacher experience, and teacher academic ability accounted for "between one quarter and one third of the variation among Texas school districts in students' scores on statewide standardized reading exams."[23] Then, in a second stage of analysis, Ferguson established that smaller class size and teachers with more qualifications were more likely to be found in school districts with better home environments and, in addition, *higher levels of funding.*

In Texas, then, richer school districts *do* have higher net student achievement, and this net achievement edge is accomplished, in part, because those districts are able to reduce average class size and hire teachers with better qualifications. It seems likely that effects such as these also appear elsewhere in America.

Ferguson's study also suggests that districts that are able to pay higher salaries hire talented teachers away from poorer neighboring districts and that the richer districts eventually get the best teachers in the region. Other evidence also confirms that teachers with better qualifications drift to more affluent schools.[24] Thus, in a nation like ours, where salary competition is not restrained, rich districts will use their greater funding to attract teachers with better qualifications, and this will improve the achievement levels of students in those districts. But those improvements come about at the expense of districts unable to pay the price. This inherently undemocratic condition is but one of the many harmful effects of unequal public-school funding. (We will say more about the pernicious effects of unequal funding in Chapters 6 and 7.)

School Quality and the Subsequent Earnings of Students. So far we've reviewed studies concerned with the effects of funding and school quality on academic achievement, but what about long-term consequences for students? This question was addressed in research reported by two prominent economists, David Card and Alan Krueger.[25] In a clever study that used data from the Bureau of the Census and from the *Biennial Survey of Education* published by the then U.S. Office of Education (more recently, the *Digest of Education Statistics*), the authors examined the net effects of public-school characteristics on the subsequent earnings of white men who had been students in the decades of the 1920s, 1930s, and 1940s. Data were assembled for each of the forty-eight contiguous states and the District of Columbia. Major analyses of the research focused on the effects of school characteristics that are clearly associated with the funding of the schools—for example, the pupil-teacher ratio, the length of the school year, the average teacher salary, and the average number of years of education teachers had completed. Controls were also entered for other nonschool variables often thought to generate effects on schooling such as parental income, years of parental education, state and regional affluence, and the like.

Confirming common assumptions about the value of education, the authors found that, in all states, students' net subsequent earnings tended to increase with each additional year of completed schooling. However, this effect was *much more pronounced* for students from states that had lower pupil-teacher ratios, longer school years, and teachers who were better educated and better paid. In other words, states that had invested in smaller classes, more days in the school year, and higher salaries for more-talented teachers during the '20s, '30s, and '40s were found to have generated *larger* incomes in later life for white male students. Moreover, in related research the authors found similar but even stronger effects for black males. The authors commented,

> The estimates presented in this paper provide new evidence that the quality of schooling affects earnings. Men who are educated in states with higher-quality school systems earn higher economic returns for their years of schooling. Although the evidence is necessarily nonexperimental, we believe that our findings are consistent with a causal interpretation of the role of school quality. . . .At a minimum, [they] should give pause to those who argue that investments in the public school system have no benefits for students.[26]

Summary. Taken together, then, the evidence is clear. The Coleman Report was *right* when it alerted Americans to the effects of home background on student achievement, but it was *wrong* when it concluded that school characteristics and funding have no effects on student achievement. And earlier reviewers were also *wrong* when they thought that other studies supported such conclusions. Good research now confirms that higher levels of school funding are associated with gains in school quality and higher levels of student achievement, on average, and that these effects persist even when controls are entered for the impact of home background. Moreover, other studies suggest that higher levels of school funding help to generate other desired effects, such as increases in subsequent earning power for students.

It is time to put to rest the foolish notion that it would make no difference if Americans provided extra funds for their schools. We doubt, however, that critics truly hostile to the public sector—such as the Heritage Foundation—are likely to welcome this advice. Extra funds for schools in a typical district would require more tax dollars, but if one goes by the evidence, that extra investment would enable those schools to hire and hold more talented teachers, decrease average class size, upgrade programs, and improve facilities—and these steps would pay off in higher average levels of student achievement, subsequent earnings, and contributions to the nation. Citizens may or may not want to provide additional funds for their schools, but let it be clear that *such decisions matter,* that they make *real* differences in the lives and future prospects of America's young people.

MYTH . . . *Costs in Education Have Recently Skyrocketed Wastefully*

We have roughly doubled per-pupil spending (after inflation) in public schools since 1965 . . . yet dropout rates remain distressingly high. . . . Overall, high school students today are posting lower SAT scores than a generation ago. The nation's investment in educational improvement has produced very little return.

—Benno Schmidt, former President of Yale University, attempting to justify a new national for-profit private school program (quoted in Rothstein, 1993, p. 24)

Other critics have claimed that costs for education have "soared" in recent years, that these additional tax dollars were "wasted" on large increases in salaries for educators or on the costs of bureaucracy, and that Americans have gained little or nothing from this investment. On the surface, this argument might seem plausible. In the decade from 1980–1981 to 1990–1991, for example, public-school expenditures per pupil rose thirty-six percent after adjustment for inflation,[27] and since American schools had declining enrollments in the late 1970s and early 1980s, this might, indeed, seem to indicate mismanagement or padded payrolls. (Besides which, it is a basic tenet of reactionary thought that increases in nonmilitary public expenditures are always a "waste.") However, when one examines the evidence carefully, an entirely different picture emerges.

Salaries and Bureaucracy. While it is true that teachers made real gains in salaries during the twelve years from 1960 to 1972, they have only done marginally well since then.[28] From 1972 to 1991, the average salary of elementary teachers in the nation rose slightly—from $30,775 to $32,448—in terms of constant 1991 dollars. During the same years, average constant-dollar salaries for secondary teachers also rose modestly—from $32,757 to $33,701—and average starting salaries in education inched ahead from $22,761 to $22,830. Given these figures, we see that recent sharp increases in the costs of education were *not* generated by exorbitant raises for teachers.

Perhaps it was the administrators? Critics often complain about the "fat" bureaucracies in education. But when one looks closely at the evidence, one sees that such complaints can't be supported for education as a whole. Across the country, central-office professionals constitute only 1.6 percent of the staffing of public school districts.[29] Thus, if the entire central-office professional staff of the nation were fired and their salaries put back into instruction, as some have argued should be done, teachers would receive, on average, *only* a 5 percent raise in salary, or average class size could be reduced by *one* student. Thus, with the exception of a few mammoth school districts, very little money could be realized by doing away with education's central-office budgets because on average those budgets are remarkably lean.

Principals, assistant principals, and other supervisors in the schools make up another 2.9 percent of the staff.[30] Nationally, then, the vaunted "bureaucrats of education" constitute a mere 4.5 percent of the total staffing of the public schools. By comparison with other sectors of the economy, this figure is remarkably *small*. Exhibit 3.3 presents data from the U.S. Bureau of Labor Statistics on the numbers of supervisors, executives, administrators, or man-

Exhibit 3.3   Number of Persons Employed Per Executive, Administrator, and/or Manager in Industries and Occupations

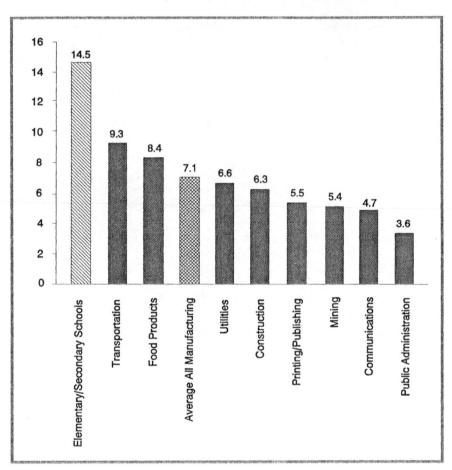

—Source: Robinson & Brandon (*Perceptions about American Education: Are They Based on Facts?*, 1992, p. 15).
—Statistical Source: Bureau of Labor Statistics (1991).

agers per employee in nine sectors of the economy. As indicated there, the average for all sectors displayed is 7.1 employees per administrator. In contrast, education has *twice* that rate—14.5 employees per supervisor or administrator—which means that it has fewer than half the average number of "bureaucrats."[31] Most *private* sectors of the economy are afflicted with far more bureaucracy than is *public* education.

It is also important to place the administration of schools in context. The *average* school superintendent in this country is responsible for 2,700 students, 291 staff members, and a budget of over 14 million dollars.[32] A few

superintendents in this nation actually manage annual budgets of more than
1 billion dollars. Enterprises of this size have to have high-quality management, or they will surely waste money. Just as in industry, it costs money to
recruit, train, and keep talented individuals on the job. Yet, when compared
with industry, the level of compensation for these positions of leadership and
responsibility in education is really quite modest. In 1990–91 the average
salary paid to central-office administrators and professional staff in the nation
amounted to only 2.2 percent of school-district operating budgets.[33] Contrast
this with major American industries whose CEOs often receive *multimillion-*
dollar salaries and annual bonuses ten times that amount.

Highly talented people who serve as leaders in education could often earn
a great deal more in the private sector, yet they accept more modest salaries
because they know they are dealing with public dollars and take seriously the
fiscal responsibility that they and their school boards share. Indeed, the nation
is blessed because so many of its leaders see education as a "calling." They
believe that serving children, their families, and the nation through education
is an honorable way of life and do not view school systems as businesses
from which they might extract the highest personal wages at the expense of
their colleagues or clients.

So neither teachers' salaries nor the size and remuneration of the bureaucracy can be the culprits in the recent rise in school costs. Teachers' salaries
or administrative costs may have risen greatly in a few districts, of course,
but the average rise in costs of schooling throughout the nation has *not* been
due to excessive teacher or administrator expenses.

Where, Then, Did Those Increased Costs Come From? We can
start answering this question by looking at federal laws passed a decade or
so ago that required public schools to provide programs and facilities for
special education. Exhibit 3.4 presents data showing approximately what it
cost, per student, for special and regular education in 1988–1989. In that
year, it cost about 2.3 times as much to educate a child in special education
as it did to educate a child who needed no special attention. (This ratio has
changed very little over the past few years.)

But how does this explain increases in the overall costs of education?
Have enrollments in special education recently climbed? The answer is an
unequivocal *yes!* Exhibit 3.5 presents the percentage changes in total enrollment and in special-education enrollment that occurred in the twelve years
from 1976–1977 to 1988–1989. While total enrollment went down, special-
education enrollment went up, and the latter created expenses that were more
than enough to offset the savings generated by the former.

Thus, as America became concerned for its special-education populations,
average costs for public schools climbed. In 1988–1989 the extra funding
needed to care for our 4.5 million special-education students was 22 billion
dollars.[34] Moreover, although special education is mandated by federal law,

Exhibit 3.4   Approximate Pupil Cost for Regular Education Students and
Special Education Students, 1988–1989

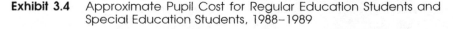

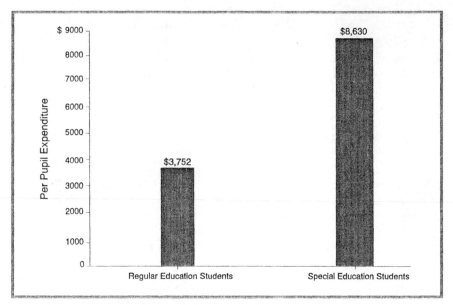

—Source: Robinson & Brandon (*Perceptions About American Education: Are They Based On Facts?*,
1992, p. 9).
—Statistical Source: U.S. Department of Education.

few of its costs are funded by federal dollars. Thus, local school districts and
the states have had to meet most of these expenses. And that is a major reason
why local school budgets have risen.

Richard Rothstein estimates that nearly *30 percent* of the new money recently allocated for education went for special-education programs, which
now serve 12 percent of all public school children.[35] Rothstein further notes
that it makes no sense at all to argue that extra funds needed for *special*
education programs should produce gains in achievement scores for *regular*
students—but this is exactly what the arguments of some critics have implied.

Because of recent increases in immigration to this country, many local
districts now also find themselves serving Vietnamese, Korean, Hispanic, Haitian, Cambodian, and Hmong children. These and other foreign-born youngsters are entitled to bilingual education, another federal mandate that costs
local schools more money than that required to educate the average native-
born American. In addition, poverty has risen dramatically over the last two
decades, particularly for children. This necessitates additional costs for
school-nutrition programs. Rothstein estimates that 35 percent of children
in today's schools get free or subsidized meals, costing the nation over 6

Exhibit 3.5   Percentage Changes in Special Education Enrollment and in Total Enrollment Using 1976–1977 As a Base Year

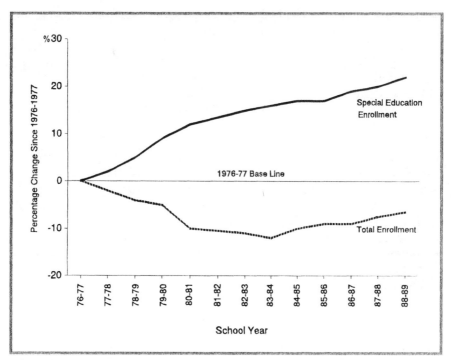

—Source: Robinson & Brandon (*Perceptions About American Education: Are They Based on Facts?*, 1992, p. 11).
—Statistical Source: U.S. Department of Education.

billion dollars a year, and that such costs have been responsible for about 10 percent of recent increases in school costs.[36]

Finally, during the last two decades, concerned citizens in America have demanded: (1) the removal of asbestos in the schools (costing in New York State alone 800 million dollars)[37]; (2) the improvement of school safety (costing in New York City alone 65 million dollars); (3) the expansion of the school day to meet the needs of working two-parent and single-parent families; and (4) medical care and day-care programs for children and *their* children. (We could add many other items to this list.) And increased costs of medical insurance for teachers and their families have also had to be provided. Such services, programs, and benefits all cost money—money that was not needed a decade or two ago, money *not* directly related to student achievement scores for basic subjects.

Missing Tax Revenues.   Yet another factor also supports the perception that costs for schooling have soared—a factor we shall call "the great Ameri-

can tax giveaway."[38] Over the last decade or two, many large corporations
in our country have moved or have threatened to relocate their administration
buildings or production plants. This threat has given them marvelous opportunities to bargain for relief from responsibility for paying state or local taxes,
and as a result those corporations now pay a *far* lower share of school taxes
than they did a generation ago. Ironically, some of those corporations also
regularly proclaim their enthusiasm for public schools in glowing terms.

A good example of how "the great American tax giveaway" works comes
from the state of Louisiana.[39] Before 1970, corporations in Louisiana were
taxed through property assessments, and they paid a reasonable share of taxes
collected in the local parishes (counties) in that state. In 1974, however, the
state adopted constitutional provisions that granted a ten-year exemption
from paying property taxes to all "new," or "additions" to, "manufacturing
plants." Exhibit 3.6 summarizes the results of this action.

As a result of this law, a total of 5,037 Louisiana companies were able to
escape paying property taxes during the 1980s. Over this decade, the value
of the taxes those corporations did *not* pay totaled 2.5 billion dollars. Ninety
percent of this "giveaway" went to the fifty largest corporations in Louisiana,
thirty-four of which were in the Fortune 500 list and among the most profita-
ble companies in America. Moreover, during this ten-year exemption, these
corporations were also able to depreciate much of the facilities and equipment
they use, so when they finally came off the ten-year waiver, they were able
to pay local taxes at a much reduced rate. The total estimated costs of these
waivers to the local educational systems of Louisiana was almost 1 billion
dollars for the decade—that is, about 100 million dollars per year, or more
than a half million dollars per school day! For the public schools in each of
the sixty-four parishes of the state, this worked out to an average loss of tax
revenues of about 1.5 million dollars per year.

Did Louisiana need this money for their public schools? We think so.
Louisiana is ranked *last* among the fifty states in its number of high school
graduates, forty-ninth in its poverty rate, forty-seventh in its rate of adult

---

Exhibit 3.6   Selected Statistics, State of Louisiana, 1980–1989

Number of exemptions to forego paying local property taxes	5,037
Total value of industrial plants paying no local taxes	$25.6 billion
Uncollected revenues by parish taxpayers	$2.55 billion
Tax revenues not collected for public services	$1.33 billion
Tax revenues not collected for roads	$71 million
Tax revenues not collected for levees and drainage	$201 million
Tax revenues not collected for public schools	$942 million

—Source: Louisiana Coalition for Tax Justice (*The Great Louisiana Tax Giveaway*, 1993).

illiteracy, and forty-sixth in its rate of teen pregnancy. Moreover, the rip-off story goes on. The tax breaks awarded to Louisiana corporations also meant a loss of about 1.5 billion dollars for public services for the decade of the 1980s. And this in a state that is rated fourth in the nation for hazardous waste generation, seventh in crime rate, ninth in rate of bridges that need repair, and forty-fifth for health coverage. Furthermore, because the corporations that received the most in tax relief were among the biggest polluters in the state, and because these corporations employed more people in jobs where injury rates are high, state and local governments have had to finance additional, uncompensated costs for pollution control and disability payments —costs that would not have been incurred had those corporations moved elsewhere.

The Louisiana story is particularly outrageous, but it exemplifies a process that has been happening across the nation. (We recently learned, for example, that the state of South Carolina awarded the BMW Corporation $150,000,000 in tax breaks and other incentives in order to secure the construction of its new production plant within the state.) So throughout the land, local taxpayers are being robbed of corporate tax revenues at a time when school costs are rising to meet additional needs. As a result, those taxpayers have come to feel that something is wrong, that costs for education (and other local services) must be out of control. And they *are* out of control—but this situation has resulted, in part, because large corporations have found such an effective way to duck their responsibilities for paying local taxes. Robert Reich, now Secretary of Labor in the Clinton Administration, recently estimated that the overall corporate share of local property tax revenues declined "from 45% in 1957 to around 16%" in 1990. As Reich suggests, "the inescapable conclusion is that American business isn't really worried about the future of the American work force."[40] Moreover, the cities which have suffered most from this loss are industrial communities where people are often very poor and have little ability to fund the schools their children so badly need. The result of this horror story is illustrated by East St. Louis, Illinois, where huge industrial corporations pay little or no taxes, the schools are in desperate shape, and the city government is so bankrupt that it recently had to auction off city hall.[41]

Additional Thoughts. Critics have tried to scapegoat educators and the public schools, blaming them for the feeling that state and local tax spending are out of control. But the reality is that society is spending much of its strained state and local tax dollars elsewhere—on corporate giveaways, construction of new prisons, medical aid and other services for the homeless and elderly, and so forth. With so many other demands for public dollars, schools are being starved for resources to support their core programs at the very time they are being asked to take on additional responsibilities. This is clearly unreasonable, but it seems likely that public-school budgets will continue to be the subject of fierce debate for the foreseeable future. Those budgets will continue to be pressured, and many competing public agencies, special-interest groups, ideologues, and curmudgeons will be tempted, again and again, to distort data on school funding to promote their own purposes.

In this continuing debate over the costs of education, we should remember that it is a mark of our humaneness as a nation that we provide programs for our special students and agreed-upon services and benefits for the students, staff, and parents served by our schools. We cannot expect these programs, services, and benefits to be free of cost.

Furthermore, some increases in the costs of public education occur because our society asks its schools to make up for missing social services that are commonly found in other Western countries. American schools are asked to cover soaring health-insurance costs for its teachers because our nation has no national health-care system. Our schools are asked to extend their hours because the society does not provide support services for working parents. Our education system must provide for many students with disabilities, in part because of the appalling state of prenatal health care in the country. Needs of this sort must be met in some way, and when our nation is unwilling to meet them with services common in other "civilized" countries, those needs spill over into our schools.

It is easy, therefore, to understand why taxpayers think that costs of public education have soared. In part the taxpayers are right; costs of education *have* increased, but this is so because the schools have been required to take on more services. In part, however, concerned citizens are responding to "the great American tax giveaway," which has allowed corporations to shift their responsibilities to the states and local communities.

Nobody likes to pay taxes, but what is the alternative when it comes to education? Either we must fund our schools adequately, or the nation will have to spend *far more* tax dollars on the welfare systems, prisons, hospital emergency rooms, and drug-rehabilitation programs needed to deal with the broken lives of those whom our underfunded education system has failed. Surely, if given valid information, most Americans would prefer to fund a truly adequate education system.

Industrial Myths About Public Schools

A crisis exists today in American kindergarten-through-12th grade (K-12) education, and the situation is getting worse. Almost 4,000 young people drop out of high school each day in this country. Achievements of students continue to decline despite large increases in funding for education. The American work force is rapidly losing its world-class status. If America becomes a third-ranked nation, behind Japan and Europe, as some people forecast, every individual in this country will lose. The obsolescence of the American school system is a major factor in that potential decline.

—Opening lines of a booklet sent to every employee of Motorola by Gary L. Tooker, president and CEO of the company (no date)[42]

Myths about public schools have been promoted not only by politicians, but also by some industrialists in our country. Although these myths have sometimes been voiced by business leaders who were confused or genuinely worried about education, most seem to have been motivated by the desire to persuade Americans that our public schools are somehow responsible for a host of problems or challenges faced by American industry.

Myth: American Schools Are Generally Incompetent.

We begin with a general complaint expressed by certain business leaders, namely that our schools are *broadly* inadequate, that they fail on many different grounds, and that this threatens American business and industry. Some business leaders have been asserting this kind of nonsense for over a century. In each decade some industrialists have complained about the shortcomings of public education, but our nation and its industries have somehow managed to survive, even thrive, during most of this period.

In fact, many foreign-owned corporations have recently been flocking to the United States to take advantage of our work force (which, if we believe the public-education critics, is "losing its world-class status"). To illustrate, two large German automobile manufacturers, BMW and Mercedes-Benz, recently chose to invest hundreds of millions of dollars in new plants in this country. They did so for lots of reasons: tax abatements, low likelihood of unionization, weak environmental protection laws, and other "advantages" of the American industrial scene. But they also chose this country for another reason—because, they said, the American work force is skilled, and the education programs in each state are responsive to the industries in their region. Either these German companies are run by fools, or they have come to different conclusions about American education than have the critics.

Why might the perspective of foreign companies differ? Recently, Joel Kotkin wrote in the *Washington Post* about the problems of European workers—sloth, ignorance, and xenophobia—that are hindering economic recovery. In contrast, he suggested,

the U.S. education system provides college-level instruction to roughly three-fifths of all young people between 20 and 24. In France and Germany, fewer than one in three youths go to college; in Great Britain and Italy fewer than one in four. . . . [Not surprisingly, the] recent world competitiveness report issued by the Swiss-based IMEDE business school ranked the U.S. workforce ahead of every European country, with particularly huge leads over such countries as Italy, France, and the United Kingdom.[43]

Perhaps, then, the leaders of BMW and Mercedes-Benz knew exactly what they were doing when they chose to build their newest production plants in our country.

In addition, evidence suggests that the critical opinion with which we began this section is *not* shared by everyone in American industry. A report by the Commission on the Skills of the American Workforce noted that *only* 15 percent of employers in our country said it was difficult to find workers with appropriate skills for the jobs they want to fill.[44] And the commission found that 80 percent of employers were satisfied with the education of new hires they brought into their companies. These percentages are sharply at odds with incessant claims that American education is generally inadequate and is failing American business.

Myth: American Schools Do Not Produce Workers with Good Technical Skills.

Critics in the business community do not always complain about schools in general terms; some also have specific complaints. For example, some CEOs of major corporations argue that American schools do not produce enough workers with the technical skills for today's (or tomorrow's) jobs. At the Clinton economic summit of December 1992, John Sculley, then CEO of Apple Computers, asserted that America is "trapped in a K–12 education system preparing our young people for jobs that don't exist anymore."[45]

Although CEOs from major industries may make this charge, personnel directors from those same industries do not back them up. Two recent surveys of personnel directors asked them to rate the five most important skills and the five least important skills currently needed by employers, and their responses were summarized in *The Sandia Report*[46] (from which we've prepared Exhibit 3.7). As these surveys suggest, personnel directors believe it is the *habits* and the *motivation* of workers that are of greatest concern to employers. Businesses depend on workers to show up on time, to get along with others, and to care about doing well on the job. They seem not to worry about the technical skills of their workers. Personnel directors believe that needed technical skills can easily be taught to workers. One personnel director recently told us that what his firm really looks for in an employee is someone who will show up sober on Monday mornings and is willing to give a fair day's work for the pay they offer.

Additional evidence suggests that personnel directors are quite correct when they claim that technical skills can be learned on the job. For example, a decade ago the Ford Motor Company set up a new engine plant in Chihuahua, Mexico, that employed workers with few technical skills—indeed, many of them were high school dropouts. The plant set up its own skills-training program and provided good job security; and it now leads the world in automotive-engine productivity (see Exhibit 3.8).

■ EXHIBIT 3.7
The Five Most Important Attributes For Employment

Michigan Survey	Rochester, N.Y. Survey
Doesn't abuse substances	Doesn't abuse substances
Honesty, integrity	Follows directions
Follows directions	Reads instructions
Respects others	Follows safety rules
Punctual, regular attendance	Respects others

The Five Least Important Attributes For Employment

Michigan Survey	Rochester, N.Y. Survey
Mathematics	Natural sciences
Social sciences	Calculus
Natural sciences	Computers
Computer programming	Art
Foreign language	Foreign language

—Source: *The Sandia Report* (Carson et al., 1991, p. 131).
—Statistical Sources: The Michigan Department of Education; The Rochester, N.Y. School District.

If schools are truly to serve the needs of business, it appears they should concentrate less on skill training and more on the values that students will need when they enter the workplace. Schools should be preparing workers who believe in striving for quality, who possess a willingness to work hard, who give loyalty to their employers, who understand why punctuality and high rates of attendance are necessary, who can treat customers and fellow workers with respect, and who can work cooperatively in teams.

This argument was also laid out in detail in a book by David Kearns and Denis Doyle, who wrote about how to make our schools and businesses more competitive.[47] Their argument is cogent, but it does not tell the whole story. Kearns and Doyle neglected to note that these values cannot be taught and sustained for long unless *employers* treat their workers with respect—unless they supply jobs that give people a chance to have some dignity in their lives. Such is not always the case, of course, and this lack of respect for employees surely underlies some of the unhappiness that business has with youth in America today.

A study by Carol Axtell Ray and Roslyn Arlin Mickelson illustrates the problem. These authors asked questions of a group of business people meeting as a local Chamber of Commerce task force to study education and jobs.[48] The business people agreed that they wanted disciplined, motivated, and

---

■ EXHIBIT 3.8
The Story of One High-Performance
Workplace

Ten years ago, Harley Shaiken began to study Ford Motor Company's new engine plant in Chihuahua, Mexico. Initially he believed that Ford's gamble to save on labor costs in Mexico (where six years of school is the norm) would fail. Manufacturing engines is a sophisticated operation, with machine tolerances of one-ten-thousandth of an inch. Coordination between production workers and technicians is essential. Yet while Ford required only 9 years of education for new hires in its Chihuahua facility, it has become the world's most productive engine plant and is now Ford's sole North American engine source.

Ford enrolled Mexican school-dropouts in a 4–12 week technology-institute program covering gasoline engines, mechanical drawing, and mathematics. New hires learned to tear down and reassemble an engine. Once on the job, they were rotated every 3 to 6 months to new tasks, so skills would be broadened further.

As the Chihuahua plant matured, Ford hired workers with less schooling and relied even more on its own training. As skilled technicians left, Ford replaced them with production workers promoted from within, as required by Ford's Mexican union contract.

It is not evident that our schools fail to produce workers qualified to staff such a system. . . .Most American corporations, however, make few training investments, so their claim that public schools can't provide qualified workers rings hollow.

—Source: Richard Rothstein (1993, p. 23).

---

trainable workers. They said many new workers wouldn't do what people told them to do, didn't respect authority, lacked motivation, and only thought they should get rich quickly. And they blamed the schools for these problems with their new workers. Then educators were called in to confront the needs of business, and they claimed that the real problem lay not in the schools but, rather, with *parents* who would not, or could not, socialize their children appropriately. Low-income parents, who sometimes had their own set of problems, including lack of employment, unstable living arrangements, illiteracy, and drug use, were seen as the primary cause of the problems of businesses.

So business blamed the schools, and the schools blamed the parents, but no one on the task force thought to link these problems of youth "with the kinds of jobs that companies have eliminated and created over the past several years."[49] Not one of these well-intentioned people thought to ask whether the jobs available for these young people would allow them actually *to achieve* success in life if they were, in fact, disciplined and motivated.

In fact, jobs with such prospects have recently become much scarcer in America. Many entry-level positions advertised today are for part-time, insecure, low-wage positions that provide few if any health or retirement benefits and lack opportunities for advancement. Labor-intensive, unionized industries are being replaced by others whose "work forces" consist of robots and part-time attendants. And many organizations are replacing full-time workers with contract labor, consultants, and independent contractors; and by so doing, they distance themselves from employees.

One estimate by the Department of Labor is that positions for casual employees doubled from 1982 to 1992 and now constitute about half of all new jobs created.[50] This arrangement allows management to employ "disposable workers," to cut or add hours as needed, to fire individuals as soon as the work load shrinks, and to avoid making payments for health or retirement plans. Not surprisingly, workers in such positions tend to lack "motivation" and "commitment" to the firm, but not all managers seem willing to accept responsibility for these outcomes (see Exhibit 3.9).

In brief then, those critics among business leaders who have claimed that American schools harm industry because they do not produce workers with appropriate technical skills are talking nonsense. The evidence suggests that technical skills can be trained on the job and that most industries worry more about the attitudes, motivation, and discipline of their workers. Moreover,

---

■ EXHIBIT 3.9
A Different Version of a Story About The
Poorly Prepared Workers of America

Pacific Telesis Chairman Sam Ginn complained to a 1991 press conference that his company gave a seventh-grade-level reading test to 6,400 "operator" job applicants, and more than half failed, proof of the need for improved education to provide "workers with skills that will allow us to be competitive into the next century."

But Ginn failed to mention that for the 2,700 who passed his test, there were only 700 openings, paying wages of less than $7.00 per hour. A more telling conclusion would have been that the schools provided PacTel with nearly four times the number of qualified operator-candidates it needed, even at low wages. If the company offered wages above the poverty line, even more successful test takers might have applied.

—Source: Richard Rothstein (1993, p. 23).

at least some recent problems with America's work force seem to reflect deteriorating conditions in the work place. No one condones poor work habits—indeed, they drive us to despair when we find them among students, colleagues and administrators, bureaucrats, or salespeople. However, punctuality, loyalty, commitment, cheerfulness, and other attributes that all of us value in workers seem not to be encouraged in many of the jobs that today's young people must take to earn a living.

Myth: American Workers Are Not Productive, and the Schools Are at Fault. Other critics in the business community have tried to blame American workers and the schools that educated them for declines in American competitiveness. They have claimed that our industrial productivity is falling behind productivity elsewhere, that our workers are lazy, and that schools are to blame for this supposed state of affairs. This myth was also promoted by the Reagan White House in *A Nation at Risk,* the incendiary report, highly critical of education, that was released by the White House in 1983. This report pointed with alarm at the nation's supposed impending loss of world industrial leadership. It noted that "history is not kind to idlers" and suggested that our country was now losing its competitive edge because of inadequacies in our work force. Schools were to blame for this sad state of affairs, and only improved education could save our nation.

But when we look at the evidence, we discover once again that these claims are utter nonsense. For years, American workers have been performing at spectacularly high levels, and they continue to do so today. It is *our* work force that provides the benchmark for the world, not the other way around. The *American* worker has long been the most productive worker in the world, and if it could ever be shown that there is a strong link between the quality of the schools and the productivity of the labor force, then the public schools of America would indeed have a lot to be proud of.

This does *not* mean that American businesses have always been competitive. Indeed, those businesses were having a hard time of it in the late 1970s, when American firms in many fields—among them electronics, steel making, and automobile production—were losing out to foreign competitors. In the mid-1980s, however, the dollar began to sag in value against foreign currencies, and this helped American competitiveness greatly. By 1992 the dollar had fallen by 45 percent (as measured against the yen), and that year American industry also registered its largest gain in productivity in two decades.[51] A major condition hurting our industries in previous years had been an overvalued dollar, making our goods too expensive to buy overseas. But it cannot be argued that this had anything to do with worker productivity. What about the latter?

Evidence indicates not only that American worker productivity leads the world but also that it has been growing. Worker productivity was recently studied by McKinsey and Company, a knowledgeable and prestigious man-

Exhibit 3.10 Worker Productivity (U.S. Productivity Set As Standard)

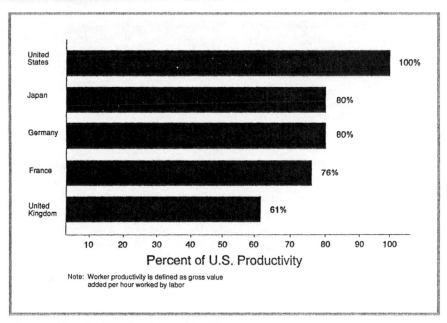

Percent of U.S. Productivity

Note: Worker productivity is defined as gross value
added per hour worked by labor

—Source: McKinsey Global Institute (1992, Table 1-11).

agement consulting firm. Their researchers were truly surprised to find out how remarkably productive Americans were. Their story was told in a report issued by the McKinsey Global Institute in 1992, and we reproduce a figure from that report as Exhibit 3.10.[52] This exhibit displays worker productivity for various countries computed as gross value added at manufacturing plants per hour worked by labor. To make comparisons easy, the researchers set American worker productivity at 100 percent and computed productivity elsewhere as a proportion of the American percentage. As can be seen, American worker productivity holds a substantial *lead* over productivity in other major countries with which we compete. Moreover, the McKinsey report showed that this aggregate result was not a fluke; American worker productivity leads the world in *nearly all* sectors of the economy.

The McKinsey analysts were also particularly interested in the service economy (including such industries as banking, merchandising, restaurants, and telecommunications), and they therefore examined factors that might be related to worker productivity in that sector in each of the countries they studied. Among other factors examined, they looked at rules governing labor and the degree and nature of unionization, capital available for business, market conditions in the country, laws regulating competition, degree of government ownership, behaviors of managers, and the skills of the labor force. In *no* case were skills of the labor force a factor in the productivity of an industry, while *in every case* the behavior of managers was a major factor determining industry's productivity. (So much for the argument that worker skills are crucial. Actually, the evidence suggests that *managerial* skills make the most difference.)

Moreover, the tale of American productivity goes on. According to *Newsweek,* in 1991, a recession year for the United States, 18 million workers in our country produced *twice* as much in manufactured goods as 19.2 million workers did in 1966.[53] Since 1982 the per-unit costs of factory output have *fallen* in our nation while they *rose* by 48 percent in France, 67 percent in Japan, and 76 percent in Germany. And in 1993 Harvard economist Dale Jorgenson estimated that American productivity was 10 to 15 percent higher than productivity in Japan and that it was growing just as fast as the latter.[54]

Thus, a decade ago, industrial critics were arguing that American industry was in trouble because our workers were nonproductive, and they claimed that the schools were responsible because they were turning out such deficient workers. Neither notion has ever been backed by a shred of evidence. Now that American business productivity is shooting ahead, we would like to see the critics who made these arguments turn around and compliment American workers and their schools. But we won't hold our breaths.

Curiously, the amazing productivity of America's highly skilled work force has also caused our country to lose a number of high-wage jobs. High levels of worker efficiency also appear to be a major factor holding back job growth in our country.[55] We are eliminating our own sources of livelihood by our extraordinary increases in productivity. How on earth would those who expect high-level skills to translate into high-wage jobs interpret this phenomenon?

Myth: Because of Inadequate Schooling, American Industries Must Spend Vast Amounts for Remedial Training of their Workers. *A Nation at Risk* also asserted that business leaders "are required to spend millions of dollars on costly remedial education and training programs in such basic skills as reading, writing, spelling and computation,"[56] and that claim was subsequently repeated by various business leaders. This myth also flies in the face of evidence.

The facts are quite simple. Industry does, indeed, spend billions of dollars on training. By one estimate, the industrial-training bill for 1990 was a staggering 45 billion dollars. Other estimates place the bill at somewhere between 30 to 60 billion dollars and suggest that actual expenditures could easily be twice that amount if informal on-the-job training were taken into account.[57] But these huge sums are typically *not* spent for the remediation of deficient skills among an unprepared work force. *The Sandia Report* noted that *two-thirds* of industrial training dollars go to college-educated employees—salespeople, first-line supervisors, professionals, white-collar managers, and the like.[58] Most of the rest of the training dollars go to upgrade the skills of technicians and craftspeople—tool makers and machine operators, for exam ple. Less than *ten* percent of all dollars that business spends on training goes to blue-collar, entry-level people, and even then most of that money is not spent on remediation of deficient skills but on orientation to the firm or on motivational training programs.

How much, then, does industry actually spend on remediation? Sandia analysts estimated that remedial training, the stuff of which the myth is made, accounts for only two to four percent of training dollars. And, they reported that remedial training in the three Rs is virtually nonexistent among the eighty million or so workers employed in businesses with less than 100 employees. So much for the myth that American industry must provide remedial training for hordes of uneducated, incompetent workers!

Summary. We've now examined several myths that are promoted by critics who would like to blame education for problems that are supposedly faced by or are looming for American industry. And we have learned that not one scintilla of evidence supports these myths. Indeed, most of the supposed problems cited in the myths turn out to be fictions, while the few problems that are real have been generated by poor federal policies and managerial incompetence. No evidence can be found that would tie *any* of these (supposed) problems to America's schools.

All of which raises interesting questions. Why have Americans been so willing to embrace these myths? Why have they not greeted the nonsense these myths represent with disbelief and laughter? We suspect that the answers to these questions reflect Americans' long-standing acceptance of the ideas that education *can* and *should* serve the needs of industry, that businesses must have an educated work force, and that investments in public education are needed to fuel the American economy. These ideas may reflect grains of truth, but they are too often oversold. In their worst form, they suggest the philistine notion that the existence of public schools is *only* justified because of their contributions to industry. But even when Americans recognize that education contributes in other ways to quality of life, they often think that industrial concerns take precedence when making policy decisions about schools.

It is time to embrace a more balanced view of the contributions of public education. Schools in our country serve *many* needs and institutions, and their contributions to industry are only part of the picture. Indeed, as our work force is restructured and the population is provided more leisure, *other* contributions of education become more and more important.

MYTH . . . *American Education Doesn't Produce Enough Scientists, Mathematicians, and Engineers*

Education in America is broadly viewed as a system in crisis. Helping students to develop competence in mathematics and science is of particular concern because of the predicted catastrophic shortfalls by the turn of the century with regard to the number of scientists, engineers, and technicians needed to "run the country" and keep America economically competitive.

—Charles Spielberger, writing as Former President of the American Psychological Association (1993, p. xi)

Of all the nonsense associated with the Manufactured Crisis, the notion that America doesn't produce enough scientists, mathematicians, and engineers seems to have created the most mischief among academics and politicians. The myth has been asserted, repeated, and elaborated on in countless scholarly articles, professional books, and speeches by leaders of the academic community. Moreover, it has stimulated actions in Congress that have increased substantially the production of technically trained persons and is often cited today by educational leaders who want to cozy up to industry or to improve mathematics and science education.

Why has this myth proved so popular? To begin with, it feeds on a broader set of ideas that Americans have embraced since World War II; Americans view science as a form of magic that can "save" not only our society but Western civilization. The myth also fits with one of the core commitments of higher education—that American society will be better off if we educate more and more of our citizens to high standards in core subjects. Further, it serves specific business concerns, since key industrialists have argued for at least a decade that America needs more scientific leadership if it is to remain competitive in the world market. (Moreover, as a cynic would see it, when the supply of scientists, mathematicians, and engineers is increased, industry benefits because it can hire people with these skills for lower wages.)

These reasons help us to understand why the myth is so readily embraced, but they don't explain why belief in it flowered so strikingly a decade ago. Actually, this is no mystery. The myth was SOLD to the American people by a major federal agency that normally prides itself on its honesty and respect for evidence.

In 1985 the National Science Foundation (NSF), no less, began an energetic campaign to sell the myth, basing its actions on a seriously flawed study that had been conducted by one of its own staff members. The study in question argued that *supplies* of scientists and engineers would shortly decline in America and that this meant we had to increase production of people with these skills. This thesis was dubious at best, but, worse, the study made no estimates of job-market *demands* for scientists and engineers. Thus, the researcher completely forgot to worry about whether these people were likely to find jobs.

Endless versions of this flawed study were prepared and distributed by the NSF, outside peer reviews of the issue were avoided, and contradicting data were ignored or suppressed. Many, many speeches on the topic were delivered by the Director of the NSF, Erich Bloch, who argued that the nation faced a serious "crisis" and *had* to step up its production of scientists and engineers. This myth-selling campaign lasted for at least five years. Indeed, the NSF efforts were not completely squelched until April of 1992, when they were whistled to a stop by an angry Congressional committee.

Supply. The trouble with this myth is that it is contradicted by *all* available evidence. Despite claims from the NSF, evidence indicates that the *supply* of young scientists and engineers is *not* declining in America. *The Sandia Report*[59] summarized data from the National Center for Education Statistics that showed not only that America leads the world in the percentage of its college graduates who obtain degrees in science and engineering, but that since 1970 this percentage has been climbing steadily (see Exhibit 3.11).

Additional evidence from the National Center for Education Statistics extends the Sandia case. In the two decades from 1971 to 1991, America either maintained or enlarged its production of young people with bachelor's, master's, and doctor's degrees in most fields of science and engineering.[60] We should note, too, that in 1990 alone, 120,000 students received Associate of Arts degrees in science and technology from junior and technical colleges.[61]

Exhibit 3.11   Percentage of 22-Year-Olds Obtaining a Bachelor's Degree in Science or Engineering

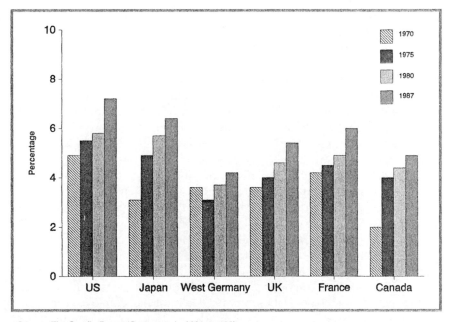

—Source: *The Sandia Report* (Carson et al., 1991, p. 103).
—Statistical Source: National Center for Education Statistics.

Moreover, it appears that the number of minority and women students who take bachelor's, master's, and doctor's degrees in these technical areas is climbing. For example, in America 35 percent of new scientists are women, as compared with only 10 percent in Japan.[62] Apart from the greater equity this comparison reveals, if such trends continue, America will be drawing from a *much* larger pool of talent for its next generation of scientists. (We can only hope that these trends will not be reversed by recent reductions in federal support of higher education for poor and minority students. That support has withered while costs for post-secondary education have increased sharply all over America.)

Demand. So much for supply. What about the *demand* for scientists, mathematicians, and engineers? The evidence indicates that supply is *far exceeding* demand. First of all, America now exceeds or is at parity with *all* of our economic competitors in terms of the technical competence of our work force—as measured, for example, in the number of engineers and physical scientists in the work force per hundred workers.[63] So if America is actually losing its economic edge in the world marketplace, as some industrialists claim, this is certainly *not* due to the lack of a technically skilled work force.

Characteristics of our present work force aside, the fact is many young scientists and engineers who are now trying to enter the job market *cannot* find work. Pascal Zachary, writing in the *Wall Street Journal,* notes that *hundreds* of America's young scientists and engineers cannot find jobs for which they are trained and describes their plight as a "black hole."[64] Similarly, the *New York Times* reports that a mere *813* scientists recently applied for one junior-faculty position in physics advertised by Amherst College (see Exhibit 3.12).

This is not a transitory problem. *The Sandia Report* estimated that even with *no* increase in the rate of supply of scientists and engineers, America will accumulate a surplus of about *1 million* of these trained professionals by the year 2010.[65] But this may actually underestimate the problem. Given further reduction in military spending in America, the failure of senior academics to retire as early as predicted, and an influx of scientists from Eastern Europe and the former Soviet Union, the glut of trained scientists is likely to be even worse than that estimated in *The Sandia Report.*

Yet another problem plagues young scientists who are looking for jobs. The 1980s were a decade of federal irresponsibility, corporate greed and quick profits, business takeovers, and junk bonds. These activities generated huge debts for many of America's major corporations, and one tragic way those corporations have met their debts is by the closing of their research departments. An illustrative story appeared recently in the *New York Times.*[66] The Phillips petroleum research laboratory in Oklahoma had employed more than one thousand research workers in the early 1980s, generating more patents for Phillips than for any other oil company in our country. The laboratory

■ EXHIBIT 3.12
On the Need for Scientists

Even as leading scientists warn that America's educational system is failing to produce scientists fast enough to fill a glaring projected shortage, many young physicists contend that universities are already turning out far more physicists than there are permanent jobs.

Permanent research jobs for young physicists have virtually dried up, partly because the recession has dramatically undercut the resources of universities and commercial research institutions. In addition, physicists in senior faculty and research positions who had been expected to retire in large numbers . . . have not done so. At the same time, a growing tide of physicists emigrating from the former Soviet Union and Eastern Europe has begun to exacerbate the glut of American physicists.

The situation was underscored last month when [the] chairman of the physics department at Amherst College disclosed that 813 physicists had applied for a single job on the college's faculty. About three-quarters were recent recipients of doctoral degrees. . . .

In 1990 . . . 12 percent of all physicists with recent doctorates seeking positions received no job offers at all, and fifty percent received only one.

—Source: Browne (1992).

studied how to develop new products from gas and oil and explored the uses of new technologies, such as the use of nuclear fusion for the production of electricity. In 1984, however, a corporate raider, T. Boone Pickens, mounted a hostile takeover on Phillips. To protect itself the company went billions of dollars into debt to buy back its own stock. When the scare was over, they cut their research facility in half—they could no longer afford it. (The *Times* article also described how, when the General Electric Corporation (GE) bought out the Radio Corporation of America (RCA), one of the first things it did was to jettison RCA's prestigious David Sarnoff Research Center.)

As America's industrial research closed down, it not only threw thousands of scientists and engineers out of work, it also cut into the production of new inventions in our country. As a result, patents awarded to American companies have also declined sharply. Believe it or not, in 1991, the three companies awarded the most patents in the *United States* were Japanese: Toshiba, with 1,014, Mitsubishi, with 936, and Hitachi, with 927. Eastman Kodak ranked fourth, Canon (also a Japanese company) placed fifth, and General Electric, which once was number one in the world, had moved to sixth place. Some critics have cited this loss in the patent race as yet another example of the failure of our schools to provide technically able people who can create jobs for the future. But blame for this loss in the patent race should not be laid at the doors of America's schools; rather, it belongs at the doors of the federal government and of the board rooms of American industry. Unwise governmental policies and industrial shortsightedness have combined to create low demands for industrial research and workers trained in science and technology.

Shifts in the Job Market. Finally, demands for scientists and other highly educated people are also declining because of evolving shifts in the job market. Lawrence Mishel and Ruy Teixeira of the Economic Policy Institute estimate that the occupations requiring the most highly skilled workers will make up only 6 percent of the job pool by the year 2000.[67] On the other hand, service jobs, requiring the least technical skill, will grow rapidly in the next few years and should constitute about *17* percent of the job pool by the year 2000.

Robert Reich also recently reviewed the job market.[68] Reich estimated that one-fourth of new jobs in the last decade fell into "routine production services," which can be successfully filled by individuals with only basic literacy and numeracy. A second set of new jobs constituted "in-person services" such as clerking in retail stores, waiting on tables, and clerking in banks. These jobs require a high school diploma, some vocational training, and a good demeanor since they involve contact with the public. Reich estimated that 30 percent of new jobs in 1990 fell into this category, and that the proportion was growing rapidly. A third type of new job consisted of "symbolic analysts," the computer designers and programmers, financial planners and architects, marketing managers and chemists of America. Jobs in this last category command the highest salaries, status, and power, of course, and require four or more years of college; but Reich estimated that they constituted only 20 percent of the total number of new jobs available in 1990. (By way of contrast, America is now awarding bachelor's degrees to about *30* percent of its young people!)

In a recent article, Richard Rothstein noted that "the Bureau of Labor Statistics expects 'paralegals' to be the nation's fastest-growing occupation, with employment increasing from the years 1988 to 2000 by 75 percent. But this growth means just 62,000 new jobs."[69] By way of contrast, the growth rate for jobs as custodians and housekeepers will only be 19 percent, but that will generate 556,000 new jobs over the same time period, and 4 percent of *all* job growth in the U.S. by the year 2000 should be in one category—retail sales.[70] Further, columnist Edward Fiske noted that in 1989 the economy was creating *nine* new cashier jobs for every computer-programming job.[71] Moreover, the United States now has 1.5 times as many janitors as it has lawyers, accountants, investment bankers, stockbrokers, and computer programmers combined.[72]

What the country's job market needs most, then, are not physicists, mathematicians, engineers, and other people with high-level technical skills but

rather a whole lot of people to work at jobs that are not intellectually challenging—driving vehicles of various types; doing typing, word processing, and
data entry; cleaning; selling in retail stores; waiting on tables; and providing
services for others in need. However, most of these jobs do not pay well. So
if these low-level jobs are to constitute, let us say, 80 percent of the job market
in the near future, America must also find ways to pay decent wages to those
who hold these jobs. If not, and if more and more people with college degrees
must take on these jobs, we can expect a good deal of turmoil in our country.

What, then, is the future for the many technically trained, ambitious college
graduates whom parents, politicians, the press, and business leaders want us
to have? There are those who say we need not worry about this problem,
that higher average levels of education will help to generate high-status, high-
paying jobs. That is the thesis of Marc Tucker and Ray Marshall, who argue
that the reform of schooling should lead to the production of many more
people capable of high-level symbolic analysis, and that those people can help
to create the sophisticated jobs of the future.[73] Some people in the Clinton
administration also appear to have this same mind-set, promoting federally
supported training programs as a way to insure that America will have a
highly educated populace and therefore a high-status work force.

But evidence suggests that we already have *too many* college graduates for
the high-status jobs that are available. Richard Rothstein claimed that 20
percent of those earning a college degree in 1990 took work in jobs that did
not require such a degree or found no work at all. And that rate is up sharply
from 1968, when it was 11 percent.[74] Thus, when American education produced more people with high levels of qualification, this did *not* lead to
equivalent numbers of high-wage jobs. Moreover, Rothstein noted that there
are now 644,000 college graduates working as retail sales clerks, 83,000 laboring as housekeepers or custodians, and 166,000 driving trucks and buses.
Blue-collar workers now include among their number some 1.3 million college graduates, which is double the rate of fifteen years ago. And despite their
college degrees, four hundred thousand college graduates were unemployed
before the 1989–1992 recession began.

Thus, the evidence does *not* suggest that high levels of education automatically translate into high-status jobs. Rather, it seems more likely that the
creation of more high-status jobs would translate into greater demands for
education. All of which implies that at least one educational commitment of
the Clinton administration is seriously flawed.

Perhaps, in our collective zeal to promote higher education, Americans
have overstressed the tie between qualifications and employment. It is one
thing to point out that undergraduate and postgraduate degrees increase the
individual's chances of landing a good job; it is another thing entirely to
claim that good jobs are guaranteed for all those with high-level qualifications.
In an era of increasing unemployment and high demand for low-status work,
perhaps we should be stressing the other benefits of higher education—its

ability to develop an appreciation of the arts and humanities, to encourage awareness of social problems and the need for moral political conduct, to instill fascination with the mysteries of the biological and physical world, to promote the joy of learning for its own sake. Such benefits can enrich the lives of both those who do and those who do not succeed in finding high-status jobs.

Summary. Despite claims you may have heard or read, America today does *not* have a shortfall of scientists, mathematicians, and engineers. Instead, our country currently has a *surplus* of people with high-level technical qualifications. Moreover, it seems unlikely that the economy of the future will require large increases in the numbers of jobs for these and other highly qualified people. But that does *not* mean that America should shut down its production of highly educated, able people. Far from it! Our nation *needs* a highly educated population. We *need* a citizenry that knows enough mathematics and science, history and philosophy, psychology, sociology, political science, and economics to understand and evaluate solutions that are proposed for the complicated problems of our perplexing world. And we need a citizenry that appreciates and participates in many types of artistic, creative, and recreational enterprises, for these are the tools from which meaningful lives can be built—whether or not one holds a high-status job.

Building broad competency in science and other fields of higher education is absolutely necessary if our nation is to thrive and if our citizens are to lead meaningful lives. In saying this, we are again noting that education is associated with important goals that extend far beyond the work place. Americans have too often justified higher education by its association with high-status jobs. Such associations are not only philistine but are also becoming less tenable in a world where qualifications no longer guarantee employment. It is time to remember that there are *many* reasons for higher education, among them those associated with the complex demands of democratic citizenship and with learning how to live a good and fulfilling life. These benefits have always been there, of course, but they should now be looming larger in debates about the future of education in a post-industrial society.

MYTH . . . *Those Who Enter Teaching Have Little Ability and Receive a Poor Academic Education*

The worst of the ed schools are certification mills where the minimally qualified instruct the barely literate in a parody of learning.

—Rita Kramer (Reciting the sins of a "professional education industry," 1991)

For many years some critics have argued that the average teacher in America is hopeless. Those who choose to teach are portrayed as representing the bottom of the academic barrel. In addition, colleges of education are considered to be at best mediocre and at worst hopelessly inadequate institutions. As we shall see, the truth is far more complex and flattering to education than the myth would have it.

Our country places high value on the possession of material goods and social status, and thoughtful high school students surely know that teaching is not the royal road to high income and prestige. Moreover, the prospect for teachers has worsened in the past generation, an issue discussed cogently by Derek Bok, former president of Harvard University (see Exhibit 3.13). As Bok notes, "while our leading private-sector professionals and managers receive *several times* the compensation of their counterparts in other leading democracies, schoolteachers and government officials are modestly paid by international standards." At least in part as a result, teaching is *not* the chosen occupation for many of our most talented and ambitious students. In fact, the 1991 SAT scores of high school seniors who intended to be teachers were, on average, forty-nine points below the national average for total SAT scores.[75] This is surely not desirable.

In the United States, teachers make roughly 1.67 times the average per capita income of the nation, while people working in other professions requiring a college degree make considerably more than that. In Japan, teachers make 2.43 times the average per capita income of their country.[76] The average teacher in Japan earns just about the same as the average engineer, while in our country the average teacher earns only about 60 percent as much. Donna Kerr eloquently explains how this poses a problem for our nation.

> [By] design and by default, this society has chosen to promote pathology-based medicine, to encourage litigious forms of conflict resolution, and to engineer technologies for an ever increasing military capability. The relatively lucrative, upward-bound professional careers in medicine, law, and engineering clearly reflect these values. That is, by design and by default this country has chosen to turn disease, disputes, and war into profitable career fields. At the same time, it has made most unattractive the activity of educating our young. The question is not whether resources should be dedicated to the maintenance of health, domestic tranquility and international peace. Rather, the question is whether any society can afford to make their opposites profitable and to do so at the expense of education. . . . Health and tranquility depend at least as much upon education of the general populace as upon expertise in medicine, law and engineering. The task is to attract a reasonable portion of our brightest, most capable young people into teaching careers.[77]

It is hardly surprising, then, that the average SAT scores of those who intend to teach are less than the best. Indeed, this is likely to be the case for *any* field perceived to be low in salary and prestige. Moreover, the problem has recently become worse. In earlier years teaching was often the *most* prestigious profession open to young women. Now women have access to many other professions, and education has lost its ability to attract the most talented women with but modest salaries.

This does not mean, however, that education now attracts only "the dregs." Between 1981 and 1991 the average SAT verbal score for those intending to teach went up thirteen points and the average mathematics score climbed twenty-four points, suggesting that the caliber of high school seniors thinking

---

■ EXHIBIT 3.13
Salaries and Career Choices

When I graduated from law school 40 years ago, I could go to work for a Wall Street firm for $4,200 a year, take a job with the Justice Department for about the same pay or change careers and begin teaching in a public school for just a few hundred dollars less. By the end of the 1980s, the outlook for graduating Harvard law students had changed drastically. Now, they could teach at a public school for $18,000 to $20,000, begin work in the Justice Department for $28,000 or accept a position with a major Wall Street law firm for $83,000.

For young people, many with heavy educational loans to repay, career choices must seem very different from those I faced in 1954. Of course, *lifetime* earnings for professionals have always been much greater in the private sector than for public servants and schoolteachers. But the differences have grown much more significant in the last 20 years.

During the 1970s and 1980s, Federal civil servants saw their pay decline by 25 percent, while schoolteachers barely held their own. In contrast, the earnings of leading managers and professionals soared. By 1990, chief executives of the top 200 companies were receiving almost $3 million each in total compensation, while partners in elite law firms and cardiovascular surgeons averaged several hundred thousand dollars apiece.

Some of these changes may be driven by competitive forces, but most are not. In fact, there is little real price competition for top professional talent. No one shops around for the lowest-priced brain surgeon or the cheapest chief executive. . . .

Public officials and schoolteachers face a radically different situation. Unlike their counterparts in the private sector, they have little control over their pay. Instead, their salaries are limited by political forces generated by voters hostile to new taxes. As a result, while our leading private-sector professionals and managers receive *several times* the compensation of their counterparts in other leading democracies, schoolteachers and government officials are modestly paid by international standards.

What is wrong with all this?

To begin with, it is hard to justify the pay earned by leading American lawyers, doctors, and executives, since market competition does not account

about careers in education has climbed over the last decade.[78] In other words, while the average total SAT score for those planning to teach was seventy-seven points below the national average in 1981, the gap is now twenty-eight points less. In addition, these figures for "average" SAT scores mask an interesting effect. As in past years, those intending to teach represent a *wide* range of both gifted and less-gifted students. Over 10 percent of those entering teacher-education programs come from the highest fifth of the SAT

for their compensation or explain why they are paid so much more than their opposite numbers overseas. . . . Growing differences in pay between the public and private sectors are cutting into the fair share of talent needed by our government agencies and public schools. No longer can we expand the nation's supply of exceptional talent simply by building new universities and increasing student loans; almost all of our intellectually ablest young people are already graduating from college. As the need for such talent continues to grow, therefore, the way in which it is distributed among sectors and professions will become more and more important.

While money is not the only factor determining students' career choices, it is an important consideration. Small wonder, then, that as the gap in pay between the public and private sectors has widened, the number of Phi Beta Kappas entering teaching and public service has declined sharply. And all this is happening just as the nation has become vitally concerned about improving the effectiveness of public education and government. . . .

It is naive to hope that society can ever devise a system that will automatically produce justifiable levels of compensation for its most educated, successful members. That is why compensation must ultimately represent an issue of personal values, a moral challenge for all who determine or receive the compensation given to the most talented people in the society. It is no accident that the pay of top executives rose substantially faster than the earnings of workers as a whole only in two decades since World War I—the 1920s and the 1980s. Both of these decades were periods in which America's values moved sharply toward the celebration of material rewards. Fortunately, this is not the inevitable state of affairs. From 1940 to 1965, for example, the after-tax earnings of top executives rose less rapidly than average blue-collar earnings even though our economy moved upward quite briskly.

It is not too much to hope, therefore, that society will shift back again to a more mature, responsible view of appropriate compensation. Such a change could bolster the quality of public education and government, strengthen social morale and cause private enterprise and the leading professions to rise in public esteem. Who knows? It could even help some highly paid professionals and executives. After all, as an old saying goes, "it behooves us to be careful of what we are worshipping, for what we are worshipping, we are becoming."

—Source: Derek Bok, Former President of Harvard University, writing in the *New York Times* (1993).

distribution; these students have aptitude scores that would presumably allow them to succeed in many other fields of study at the college or university level. Thus, a good many people with strong academic qualifications are continuing to opt for careers as teachers.

But, as our earlier arguments suggest, one should not use SAT scores as the sole indicator of competency for America's teachers. As Linda Darling-Hammond puts it:

> Test scores are not clear evidence of quality. What we mean by teacher quality should be more influenced by what teacher candidates learn after they enter college than by the entrance examination scores they presented at matriculation. The likeliest interpretation of the test score trends during the 1970s is that teaching became a less attractive career option to many college students facing alternative opportunities.[79]

It turns out that SAT scores are extremely weak predictors for success in teaching. SAT scores actually predict job success poorly for *most* fields, but the problem is worse for teaching. In fact, neither test scores—such as those from the SAT, the ACT, or the National Teachers Exam—nor grade-point averages in college are useful for predicting on-the-job ratings of success as a teacher.[80] So let's look at other characteristics of America's teachers.

To begin, if one hundred children start first grade, about thirty of them will ultimately obtain a four-year college degree. But such a degree is now *required* of most people who will enter teaching. Thus, teachers represent an educated *elite*, since about 70 percent of their agemates have not completed college. Moreover, the proportion of teachers holding advanced qualifications is climbing. In 1961 about 15 percent of the teaching force held less than a four-year degree, but by 1991 this figure had dropped to only 0.6 percent.[81] And during the past thirty years, the percentage of teachers holding a master's or a doctoral degree increased dramatically and now hovers at about 50 percent (see Exhibit 3.14). Moreover, women are gaining parity with men in the attainment of these advanced degrees. Given that teaching represents by far the largest profession in the nation, this is a remarkable record.

In 1991 about 35 percent of teachers in the U.S. had to take academic competency tests to be certified to teach, and throughout their student teaching their moral character was assessed as well. (We sometimes wonder how our country would fare if its legislators and politicians had to meet the same kinds of standards for competency and moral character that these same legislators now impose on America's teachers.)

The point of all this is that teachers, as a group, have impressive academic credentials and are increasingly subjected to quality-control standards. Does this mean that teachers are well educated? Some critics would continue to say "no," would claim that teacher-education programs are a "joke." Such claims might actually be tenable *if* teacher-trainees actually took the bulk of

Exhibit 3.14  Percentage of Male and Female Teachers Holding M.A. Degree or Higher, 1961–1991

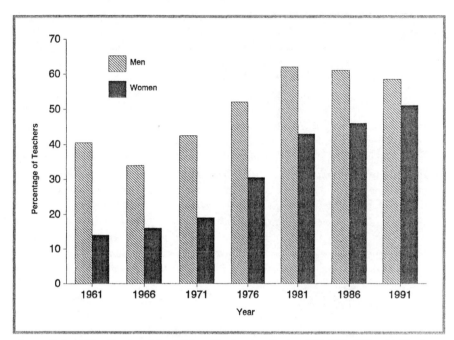

—Source: National Education Association (*Status of the American Teacher 1990–1991*, 1992, p. 24, Fig. 1).

their course work in colleges of education and if the offerings of those colleges were seriously deficient. But neither of these charges is true.

First, teachers do not train exclusively in colleges of education. In fact, students typically declare an education major only *after* successfully completing about two years of course work in other colleges on the campus, and most continue to take courses in other fields while completing their requirements in education. The typical candidate for elementary teaching takes about 70 percent of his or her course work *outside* the school or college of education, and candidates for high school teaching take about 80 percent of their work in other colleges.[82] Furthermore, an increasing percentage of those who start to teach do so after having already completed a bachelor's or master's degree in a subject other than education.[83]

But what about that remaining 20 or 30 percent of courses that are taken in schools of education? The quality of these programs is more difficult to assess. Although we suspect that some of it was once quite mediocre, informal evidence suggests that the quality of education programs has been improving in recent decades. First, about 70 percent of all teacher-education programs now have minimum grade requirements that must be met before a student is admitted to the program, and those minimum grade requirements seem to be going up across the nation. In addition, about 50 percent of all students in teacher education now have to pass a proficiency exam in order to get their degrees.[84] Second, teacher-education curricula have improved substantially in recent years. Most students in education colleges are required, for example, to complete a course in educational psychology. A generation ago these courses provided very little content that was directly relevant to teaching. In recent years, however, significant research has been completed on classroom teaching and its effects. As a result, textbooks and other curricular materials for courses on educational psychology now draw extensively from this research base, and the focus of the course has shifted dramatically.

It should be clear, then, that the teaching force of America does *not* consist of bottom-of-the-barrel people who are deficient in intellectual ability and poorly trained by their colleges and universities. Despite the enormous size of the teaching force, evidence suggests that the average teacher in America is talented, high achieving, and well educated. To be sure, dull and poorly trained teachers may be found, and it would be good to get them out of the classroom. But untalented and poorly trained physicians, CPAs, clerics, insurance counselors, engineers, lawyers, and the like may also be found—although they are often not highlighted in the press. By contrast, education takes place in a *public* arena, and therefore its personnel problems are more often visible.

To illustrate this issue, the public does not ordinarily hear about the incompetence of the medical profession, yet a 1991 Harvard University medical-practice study group found that roughly 80,000 people die every year—and at least 150,000 more are injured annually—from medical negligence in hospitals. This makes medical malpractice the third leading cause of preventable death in the U.S., right after cigarettes and alcohol, causing more deaths per year than automobiles and firearms combined.[85] In addition, the vast majority of the 10,289 physicians disciplined by state or federal agencies in 1992 are still practicing, and the damage they do each year is, *literally*, killing Americans.[86]

In short, incompetence, and the removal of incompetents, are problems every profession faces. Few professions (including education) handle that problem well. But we know of *no* persuasive evidence that would confirm the charge that America's teachers are particularly incompetent, untalented, or poorly trained by comparison with other professions.

MYTH . . . *American Public Schools and Textbooks No Longer Promote Moral Values*

Up until 1962, the values [of the Judeo-Christian ethic] were unquestioned as a positive influence in public education. Kids were taught to recognize the moral and historical value of their inalienable rights. The precepts embodied in the Ten Commandments were the mortar that held our laws together, gave them weight, and that fueled individual self-government ... [but this is no longer true.] We have allowed moral values and a creator to be kicked out of public schools, and because most kids attend public school, we are paying a high price.

—Rep. William E. Dannemeyer (remarks to the U.S. House of Representatives, 1991)

Public school textbooks commonly exclude the history, heritage, beliefs, and values of millions of Americans. Those who believe in the traditional family are not represented. Those who believe in free enterprise are not represented. Those whose politics are conservative are almost unrepresented. Above all, those who are committed to their religious tradition—at the very least as an important part of the historical record—are not represented. Even those who uphold the classic or republican virtues of discipline, public duty, hard work, patriotism, and concern for others are scarcely represented.

—Paul Vitz (*Censorship: Evidence of Bias in Our Nation's Textbooks,* 1986, p. 77)

Some critics charge that today's public schools and textbooks are amoral, that they no longer promote (appropriate) values for students. Frankly, it is difficult to tell whether today's schools are less concerned with moral values than at other times in history. To assess this charge would require conducting a difficult study, one that compares evidence showing how values are presented in today's classrooms with how values were presented in classrooms of earlier years. We know of no study that has taken on this task.

We suspect, however, that this charge is groundless. Most teachers in our country subscribe to mainstream, middle-class, American values—sharing and caring, neatness and punctuality, rewards for effort, sanctions against bragging, punishment for fighting, the legitimacy of pursuing money, and the like—and these commitments are often expressed in their classroom practices. Recent criticism by those who do not want the schools to teach values explicitly have probably made more teachers cautious about what they say and do, but studies of classroom teaching suggest that these values are communicated nevertheless.

Various critics have also claimed that today's textbooks display a lack of traditional American values,[87] and this charge can easily be assessed with evidence. Patricia Sharp and Randy Wood, of the Baylor University Center for Christian Education, examined this charge by conducting a content analysis of reading and social studies texts that are approved for third- and fifth-grade classrooms in Texas.[88] Their sample of textbooks included twenty-four different basal readers, grade-level texts, and texts that were parts of a series from leading publishers. The books they studied are commonly used throughout the nation.

In their study the authors examined whether these texts expressed three kinds of values: (1) *religious values* (religious conformity, belief in God, traditional beliefs associated with religion, respect for religious symbols, questions on the meaning, purpose, and value of life); (2) *individual values* (independent decision making, attitudes toward nonstereotypical life styles, virtuous behavior, accountability for one's own actions, and the need to take action); and (3) *social-secular values* (reflection on societal standards, focus on positive family values, vicarious experience of societal mores, alternative moral perspectives, explicit statements of personal moral values).

What these authors found flatly contradicted charges that had been made by the critics. For example, the average third-grade social studies text expressed over *80* percent of the values that the authors sought. The average fifth-grade social studies text displayed over *90* percent of the values believed by the authors to be desirable. The authors commented,

> social studies texts were replete with commentary on religious freedom, the fact that the church has been the center of community life in many nations, that people from many different backgrounds came to the U.S. and had to establish friendships to survive in this new land, that freedom has to be fought for, that courage is needed by our citizens, and so forth.[89]

Reading texts had fewer expressions of values, but even these were not value-free. The authors found that the typical third- and fifth-grade text reflected over 55 percent of the values they had sought. For reading texts, the authors noted,

> Many examples of honesty, courage, compassion, persistence, bravery, and other positive values were [found]. . . . Literature chosen for these textbooks is replete with characters who embody . . . moral values, . . . and the books provide models that children can understand and accept.[90]

The authors conclude that "charges of lack of positive values presented in social studies and reading textbooks would appear to be unfounded."[91] So, when expressing charges about amoral textbooks, the critics seem to have been more concerned with attacking America's public schools than with the facts of the matter. From McGuffey's Reader to today's texts, our school books have been repositories of moral messages that encourage unity in our nation.

Surprisingly, some critics of textbooks seem to be less concerned with moral values than with the promotion of docility and ignorance. One well-known leader of the religious right, Norma Gabler, whose words the press has regularly reported, seemed to see nothing wrong in saying,

> Too many of today's textbooks leave students to make up their own minds. Now, that's just not fair to our children. What some textbooks are doing is giving students ideas, and ideas will never do them as much good as facts.[92]

(We find it marvelously amusing to learn that texts should be "guilty" of giving students "ideas." God help America if its citizens should ever begin to get "ideas" from books such as the one you are now reading!) Perhaps Mrs. Gabler would like to model our schools after *Jeopardy!* on television or the game of *Trivial Pursuit*, for both are filled with undigested "facts." In contrast, most Americans seem to conceive of public schools as places where students learn to think about challenging notions such as evolution, relativity, social class, moral behavior, the unconscious, Marxism, Big Bang theory, environmental degradation, manifest destiny, isolationism, consumerism, and a thousand other "ideas" that Mrs. Gabler cannot see any value in discussing. Textbook publishers need to hear that most Americans prefer meaty, interesting, idea-filled books that stretch our children's intellect, rather than simple-minded, fact-filled texts that bore our young people and tax only their memory.

In summary then, we know of no evidence to support the myth that values have disappeared from America's public schools or from textbooks. Instead, the evidence available suggests just the opposite. America's public schools were originally conceived, in part, as institutions where social integration was promoted by introducing students to shared moral values. It appears that they still perform this function.

MYTH . . . *American Citizens Are Unhappy With Their Schools*

There is . . . nearly universal agreement that our schools are in desperate trouble and must be "restructured"—which is to say, redesigned from the ground up.
—Denis P. Doyle (*Voices From the Field,* 1991, pp. 5–6)

We . . . know from numerous surveys on education that most Americans, and especially parents, were misinformed and self-satisfied [about their schools].
—Diane Ravitch, Former Assistant Secretary of Education (Launching a revolution in standards and assessment, 1993)

Many critics have stated that Americans, particularly American parents, are now dissatisfied with public schools. The press frequently quotes these statements, and they are regularly cited on radio and television talk shows. In one sense, these charges seem actually to be supported by evidence. Recently, the National Opinion Research Center (NORC) at the University of Chicago reported that public confidence in education had declined significantly from 1973 to 1990,[93] so at first blush the critics' charge might seem realistic.

But there is more to the story. The same NORC study also examined confidence in other institutions and professions in society and found that *most* received less favorable ratings today than they did twenty years ago. For example, the number of people expressing "a good deal of confidence" in medicine had gone down 9 percentage points from 1973 to 1990. Over the same period, confidence in religion was down 12 percent, confidence in banking was down 15 percent, and confidence in the press was down 8 percent. Confidence in business, in the executive branch of government, in television, in Congress, and in labor was also down sharply. This suggests that we live

in a time of *broadly* eroding confidence in America's institutions and professions, so it is hardly surprising that confidence in education has also declined.

In addition, let us look in detail, however, at how opinions about education
fare in this time of general cynicism. In order to do this, we should make
two distinctions. First, we should distinguish between public opinion about
"schools in general" and public opinion concerning local public schools.
Opinion about the former are likely to be stereotypic, to reflect rumors and
portrayals of education in the popular press. And since American schools
have been under attack since the beginning of the Manufactured Crisis, it
should not surprise us to learn that our schools have also received a bad
portrayal in the press in recent years.[94] And this means that stereotypic opinion about public schools should be somewhat negative. In contrast, public
opinion about the public schools in our own, local communities are more
likely to reflect personal experience, direct observation, informed judgment,
and discussions with others who are familiar with the actual strengths and
weaknesses of those schools. So public opinion about those schools should
be more realistic and positive in tone.

Second, we should distinguish between two groups of adult citizens: parents of school-age children, and the rest of the population. The former are
more likely to have first-hand, direct knowledge of the schools that serve
their children. The latter may also include concerned people, but they are
less likely to have had recent, personal experience with schools. Thus, by
comparison, the opinions of parents are also more likely to reflect reality
rather than stereotypic judgment.

Now, let's see how these distinctions play out in opinions about America's
public schools. In 1993 the *Phi Delta Kappan,* a widely read journal in education, reported the twenty-fifth annual Gallup poll on the public's perception
of the public schools.[95] A representative sample of American adults were
asked to give letter grades (A, B, C, D, or F) to indicate their ratings of schools
(see Exhibit 3.15). Not surprisingly, when they were asked to give their general
opinion about "The Nation's Public Schools," respondents gave answers that
reflected the negative, stereotypic views recently promulgated by the critics
and the press. Only 19 percent of respondents gave the nation's schools a
grade of A or B, while 21 percent gave them grades of D or F. But when
these same people rated their local schools, a different picture emerged. Forty-
four percent of respondents gave their local schools a grade of A or B, and
only 14 percent gave them grades of D or F. Moreover, when *parents* were
asked about the local school that served their children, a whopping 72 percent
gave that school an A or B—while only 7 percent graded it D or F! These
last figures, in particular, seem amazing given the generally negative images
of public schools recently promulgated. And what is more amazing, this high
level of parental satisfaction with their local schools is growing and is actually
higher today than it was seven years ago. So much for the canard that American parents are generally dissatisfied with public schools.

Exhibit 3.15 Grades Given to Public Schools

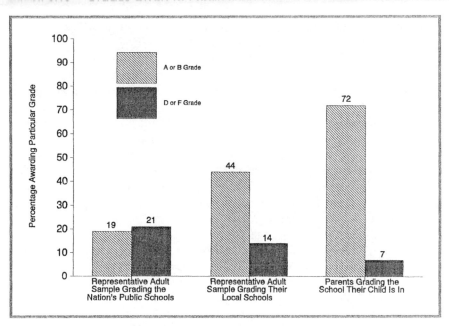

—Source: Elam, Rose, & Gallup (*The 25th Annual Phi Delta Kappa/Gallup Poll*, 1993).

How do the critics interpret this remarkable degree of consumer satisfaction? When Denis Doyle of the Hudson Institute, a leading advocate for private-school vouchers, attended a meeting where these data were presented, he remarked, "This is scientific proof that ignorance is bliss."[96] Diane Ravitch declared that Americans were "misinformed" about their schools. Similar views were expressed by Former Assistant Secretary of Education Chester Finn, who suggested that ordinary parents of the nation are not to be trusted with their opinions about public education. Since their standards are not rigorous, Finn suggested, their judgments about the quality of schools their children attend are suspect.[97] And Harold Stevenson, who studies schools in Asia, apparently regards American satisfaction with their local schools as a form of pathology. In one of his studies, Stevenson found that about three-quarters of American fifth-grade mothers were very satisfied with their local school, whereas only half of the mothers sampled in Taipei, Taiwan gave such high ratings to their local school, and in Sendai, Japan only about a third of mothers sampled were so satisfied. But Stevenson also found that students from the Taiwanese and Japanese schools out-performed those from America on comparative tests of subject-matter achievement, so he condemned the American mothers' opinions as "pathological."[98]

When critics such as Doyle, Ravitch, Finn, and Stevenson are confronted with evidence indicating that Americans hold their local schools in high regard, then, they decide that the public is unable to make intelligent judgments about public schools. This scares us. In effect, these critics have proclaimed themselves part of an elite who, for the good of the nation, will be pleased to tell other Americans what they are to believe and how they are to act.

We, on the other hand, would rather put our faith in the judgments of those Americans who are most familiar with their schools. If the majority of parents with children in school say that their local schools are pretty good, who are Doyle, Ravitch, Finn, and Stevenson to tell them they are wrong? The evidence we reviewed in Chapter 2 suggests that the typical American school generates a lot more student achievement than recent critics and the press would have us believe. Perhaps American parents are responding to this reality when they give high marks to their local schools. Perhaps, also, they are reflecting the many other strengths of American public education—strengths based on the ability of American schools to respond to needs expressed in their local communities. And perhaps, just perhaps, parents in Taiwan and Japan also know what they are doing when they give low marks to *their* local schools. Could it be that their schools are *less* responsive to the needs of the students and parents whom they are supposed to serve?

In summary, those who say that Americans are fed up with the public schools should qualify what they say. Public esteem for *many* institutions has declined recently, and those who know the least about the public schools—those whose knowledge about the schools has been gained largely from listening to the critics and from the mass media—do indeed give low marks to the schools. But those who know the most about public schools—parents who are in regular contact with and receive service from those institutions—rate them highly. In fact, the biggest complaint that American parents indicated in the 1993 Gallup poll was that their local schools were not supported adequately. This complaint took precedence over their concerns about drug abuse, lack of discipline, fighting, violence, gangs, and a host of other real and imagined problems. So not only are American parents well satisfied with their public schools, but they would presumably be willing to pay more for them than they do now. The major problem they face is trying to persuade those who do not have children in the schools to agree to pay their share of school taxes. But this seems unlikely to happen as long as Americans are bamboozled by the myths and lies of the Manufactured Crisis. Perhaps it is time for citizens without children to join parents and go into the schools to see for themselves what is actually happening there.

MYTH . . . *Private Schools Are Inherently Better Than Public Schools*

When all else is equal, autonomy, organization, and achievement are significantly better in private schools than in public. But while our research [was] the first to demonstrate just how far-reaching the differences between politics and markets can be, it [was] hardly the first to indicate that private schools outperform public schools academically when the two kinds of schools are working with similar students.

—John Chubb and Terry Moe (Educational choice: Why it is needed and how it will work, 1992, pp. 46–47)

Finally, we turn to one last myth that reflects the critics' hostility to public education—the myth that private schools are inherently superior to their public counterparts. For years many Americans have thought that private schools are generally superior to public schools and that this superiority is confirmed by studies showing the higher achievement of students who attend the former. Moreover, this belief is a major reason why those who can afford the tuition are willing to shell out extra money for private education.

But if it is true that private-school students outperform public-school students, why should such differences occur? Is it because those private schools offer stronger programs or because they recruit more advantaged students? This question clearly matters. If private schools have stronger programs, then either those programs should be examined for hints about how to improve *all* schools, or perhaps public schools are inherently flawed. But if private schools merely recruit "better" students, their supposed achievement advantage is ephemeral, and all we need to do to improve public schools is make sure that *they* enroll the "better" students too.

Given the importance of these questions, it is small wonder that in April 1981 newspapers across the country picked up the following story from the *Washington Post:*

> *Private High Schools Are Better Than Public, Study Concludes.* A major study by sociologist James S. Coleman concludes that Catholic and other private high schools provide a better education than public ones do. . . . [Supporters of public schools] fear that the findings could strengthen the case for tax credits to families paying tuition for private schools.[99]

The study reported in these stories had been conducted by the same James Coleman we met earlier in the chapter. In this new study he was assisted by Thomas Hoffer and Sally Kilgore, and the study itself would shortly appear in a report to the National Center for Education Statistics[100] and as a book entitled *High School Achievement: Public, Catholic, and Private Schools Compared.*[101] Moreover, for once the newspapers had it right. In their study Coleman and his colleagues *had* concluded that private high schools enjoy an edge in achievement over public high schools, that this edge is substantial, and that it persists even when controls are entered for student background characteristics—thus, by implication, private schools are *inherently* superior to public schools.

As had occurred earlier with the Coleman Report, these controversial conclusions were released with great fanfare and created a furor before details of the study that generated them became known. As a result, news stories reporting them became the first salvo in a public controversy that has recently beset public education. On one side of the debate, critics of public schools quickly embraced the conclusions of Coleman and company because they appeared to offer evidence confirming long-held suspicions that public schools were inherently flawed. On the other side, defenders of public schools were threatened by the conclusions and began defensive actions designed to blunt their impact. Unfortunately, much of this debate took place without examining the evidence offered by Coleman and his colleagues. That evidence has now been studied carefully, however, and the more one looks at it, the weaker that evidence appears to be. Let us unpack some of the issues.[102]

High School and Beyond. The study reported by Coleman, Hoffer, and Kilgore was, in fact, the first reported analysis of the "High School and Beyond" (HSB) data set we discussed earlier in the chapter. You may recall that HSB had been funded by the National Center for Education Statistics and that it concerned the achievement of roughly sixty thousand students in more than one thousand public and private high schools sampled across the nation. HSB data included achievement tests (composed of multiple-choice items) administered to students and questionnaires that students filled out reporting their personal and family characteristics.

HSB data were first collected in 1980 and dealt with the achievements of both sophomores and seniors from the sampled schools. The study reported by Coleman and colleagues in 1981 was based only on the 1980 data and thus used a *cross-sectional* (rather than a *longitudinal*) design. Nevertheless, this initial data set allowed Coleman et al. to compare the achievement of students in the sampled schools, and after conducting complex analyses, the authors concluded: (1) that average student achievement *was* greater in private schools; (2) that the average student in private schools *did* have a more advantaged background; and (3) that, when controls were entered for student background characteristics, achievement in private schools was still roughly "one grade level" above achievement in public schools.[103]

Only the last of these claims was truly controversial, of course, and in time other investigators also looked at the HSB data, using differing analysis strategies, to see whether this sensational last claim was justified.[104] In general, these other researchers have concluded that private schools either had a *much smaller net edge* or *no net edge at all* over public schools in the 1980 HSB data. But Coleman et al. had been first off the mark, and it was their conclusions that continued to generate press stories and public debate which assumed that inherent private school "superiority" had been confirmed by evidence.

Then, in 1982, additional HSB data were collected from those students who had been sophomores two years earlier, and subsequent analyses of HSB were able to examine the growth of student achievement in *longitudinal* designs. These analyses have also been subject to controversy. For example, in 1985 the research team of Hoffer, Greeley, and Coleman published analyses of student-achievement growth from HSB data which, they asserted, confirmed a "substantial" net edge for private schools. But two years later, two researchers, Karl Alexander and Aaron Pallas, and, separately, Douglas Willms, looked at the same growth data, and these authors found that the effects of private school were a lot smaller than those estimated by Coleman et al. In fact, they judged that the private-school net edge (if any) was "trivial."[105]

Problems with HSB. Why did these various people come to such different conclusions about HSB findings? In part, the investigators had used a variety of analysis strategies, and this helped to muddy the waters, but part of the issue reflected problems with the HSB data. First, only about 10 percent of the schools sampled in HSB came from the private sector. This means that HSB data provided better estimates for achievement in public schools than in private schools. Worse, only a tiny group of non-Catholic private schools appeared in HSB, so most reputable analyses of HSB data have made comparisons only between public and *Catholic* schools. (In their original 1981 and 1982 reports, Coleman and associates also reported findings for non-Catholic private schools but later conceded that such findings were questionable.) Comparisons between public and Catholic schools are valuable, of course, but Catholic schools are only a part of the private-school story. When many Americans talk about "private schools," they have in mind not only Catholic schools but also parochial schools representing other religions, specialty schools offering a specific curriculum (such as Montessori schools), schools that cater to students from a specific race or ethnic group, and elite academies that serve the rich. HSB data are *not* useful for studying any of these types of schools.

Second, in their 1981 analyses, Coleman and his colleagues used a single, composite index to estimate student achievement. This index summed responses from three subtests designed to measure reading, vocabulary, and general mathematics skills that were administered to both sophomores and seniors in 1980. When using this index, the investigators assumed that it was a valid measure of high school achievement and that its three subtests would reflect differences among schools in parallel ways. How reasonable were these assumptions?

Actually, subsequent events suggest that they *weren't* reasonable at all. In 1980 HSB had actually assessed sophomores' knowledge of *seven* different topics—reading, vocabulary, general mathematics, writing, civics, advanced mathematics, and science—and these same seven topics were reassessed with identical questions in 1982, when those students were seniors. Thus, later scholars were able to study responses to each of these seven achievement tests in subsequent longitudinal analyses. When this was done, they found that differences between Catholic and public schools in net achievement growth varied depending on the topic chosen! (In brief, after controlling for student characteristics, Catholic schools were found to have a *slight* net edge in achievement growth for vocabulary, general mathematics, and writing; but when it came to reading, civics, advanced mathematics, and science, neither type of school had a net edge.)[106]

Worse, serious questions were subsequently raised about the achievement tests that were used in HSB. Such questions arose when it was discovered that those tests revealed *very* little growth in student knowledge over the two years of the full study. Student scores from these tests varied a lot, but little of that variability was associated with achievement growth—or, for that matter, with differences between Catholic and public schools. Moreover, additional work with these tests has shown that students who dropped out of school at the end of their sophomore year *also* gained in measured achievement; in fact, they had gained about half as much as those who had remained in school.

What does one make of such findings? One possibility is that American students actually learn very little academic subject matter between their sophomore and senior years, and if this should be the case, then, as Alexander and Pallas suggested, "not only would it not matter which [school] sector one attended, it seemingly would not matter much whether one stayed in school at all!"[107] To provide some perspective for this point, Douglas Willms prepared estimates comparing the greater net achievement gains of Catholic schools in the HSB data with gains reported for other types of educational interventions.[108] According to these estimates, the typical American student attending a public school might gain slightly in achievement by transferring to a Catholic school, but he or she would gain *twenty-to-thirty times as much* by being exposed to cross-age tutoring or involvement in cooperative learning experiences! In short, if one decides that the HSB tests were actually valid for measuring student growth, one must also conclude that HSB differences in achievement between Catholic and public schools were minuscule.

Alternatively, it also seems possible that the HSB tests were simply poor tests for measuring what was taught, or at least what upper-division students learned, in American high schools between 1980 and 1982. And this would mean that HSB had erred in its measuring techniques or in what it chose to measure. Perhaps it should have used essay-type questions rather than multiple-choice items; or, instead of assessing broad academic topics that are largely taught in the lower grades, it should have assessed materials more relevant to *senior* high school—topics such as the evolving, specialized knowledge of high school students or aspects of their emotional and social growth. But if one concludes that the HSB tests were not valid measures for high school student growth, one must also question whether they can be used for judging differences in that growth between Catholic and public schools. Indeed, had HSB used other, more appropriate, indicators, it seems quite possible that public schools would have been given the edge.

Whichever way one interprets the HSB tests, then, it is difficult to under stand how evidence from those tests could possibly confirm a "substantial" net Catholic-public school difference in achievement growth. HSB data *do* suggest that the average Catholic high school generates slightly higher levels of student achievement in basic skills and that it enrolls more advantaged students than does the average public high school. However, when one controls for student characteristics, HSB evidence for a net Catholic school edge becomes weak, topic dependent, and questionable.

Thus, careful analyses of HSB evidence do *not* support the claim that private schools have a substantial, inherent edge over public schools. Moreover, we know of *no* other systematic evidence that supports such a claim. But lack of evidence has not troubled the critics, of course. Mischief had again been created when James Coleman (and colleagues) trumpeted a controversial conclusion with but flimsy evidence, and it may take some years for the general public to discover that, when it comes to claims about the inherent advantages of private schools in fostering academic achievement growth, *the emperor truly has no clothes.*

Chubb and Moe (Again). Unfortunately, beliefs about the putative advantages of private schools were recently bolstered by the appearance of Chubb and Moe's controversial book, *Politics, Markets, and America's Schools.*[109] We discussed this work earlier in the chapter, and you may recall that it was also based, in part, on HSB data. In their work, however, Chubb and Moe used not only HSB but also data from a supplementary survey that had been gathered from teachers and principals in a subsample of HSB schools in 1984. This meant that Chubb and Moe were able to study relations between student achievement and characteristics of schools' *programs,* and earlier in the chapter we praised their work for uncovering a net association between school academic climate and growth in student achievement.

Now come the questionable bits. Chubb and Moe's book was written to advance a controversial thesis. That thesis began by asserting that American public schools are now in deep trouble, that efforts to reform them have failed, and that the superiority of private-school programs had been well established by previous research. Why should public schools be so inferior to private schools? Clearly, according to Chubb and Moe, it has to do with the way these two types of schools are governed. They write,

America's public schools are governed by institutions of direct democratic control, and their organizations should be expected to bear the indelible stamp of those institutions. They should tend to be highly bureaucratic and systematically lacking in the requisites of effective performance. Private schools, on the other hand, operate in a very different institutional setting distinguished by the basic features of markets—decentralization, competition, and choice—and their organizations should be expected to bear a very different stamp as a result. They should tend to possess autonomy, clarity of mission, strong leadership, teacher professionalism, and team cooperation that public schools want but . . . are unlikely to have.[110]

Since the major premises of this thesis are factually in error, as we have shown, it is not surprising that Chubb and Moe had difficulty defending their argument. They covered their tracks quite well, however, with vigorous rhetoric, extensive but slanted reviews of historical and comparative materials, and—crucially—by drawing artful but questionable conclusions from analyses of HSB data. So well did they draw those conclusions, in fact, that most reviewers have not understood that Chubb and Moe's evidence did *not* support their argument. Let's see how they performed this trick.

As indicated earlier, Chubb and Moe began their analyses by demonstrating that school academic climate (which they called "school organization") had a positive net effect on growth in student achievement, even when controls were entered for the socioeconomic status (SES) of students' families and the average SES of students in the school. They then reasoned that schools high in academic climate ("school organization") were, ipso facto, "effective," and they set out to determine what made for "effective schools."

Chubb and Moe tackled this task in two steps. First, they sought to uncover the structural factors associated with good or poor academic climate. Since their thesis suggested that those factors would be associated with bureaucracy, they conceived three bureaucratic factors: (1) "administrative constraint," which was concerned with the authority of *central office* administrators; (2) "personnel constraint," which focused on *union* authority over personnel issues; and (3) "school board influence," which dealt with *school board* authority. They then conducted statistical analyses in which these factors and others concerned with school characteristics were used to predict school academic climate and found that "administrative constraint" and "personnel constraint" had negative net effects on academic climate. (They found no substantial effect for "school board influence.") This means that, net of the other school factors examined, schools subject to high levels of central office and union authority tended to have poorer academic climates.

Second, they conducted additional analyses that focused on the determinants of "administrative constraint" and "personnel constraint." They found that, net of other school factors examined, private schools and schools in suburban (rather than urban) settings were subject to less authority from central office administrators and unions.

The problem with this multistep analysis strategy is that nowhere did Chubb and Moe put all of these factors together. Their analyses showed that, with other factors controlled:

- public schools (A) are more subject to external authority (B);
- high levels of external authority (B) are associated with depressed academic climate (C); and

- good academic climate (C) is tied to growth in student achievement (D).

However, they provided no evidence indicating that public schools (A) are inherently associated with depressed academic climate (C) or that public school status and high levels of external authority (A and B) inherently depress student achievement (D). Although Chubb and Moe did not exactly claim they had tied all of these factors together in their text, they certainly claimed that their analyses supported their general thesis, and many reviewers and newspaper accounts jumped to the conclusion that their work "explains why private schools have better effects." This is nonsense.

Why didn't Chubb and Moe conduct and display the proper analysis, which would have nailed down their thesis? Could it be they did not know how to do the proper analysis or were afraid of what that analysis might reveal?

On balance, we are quite prepared to accept Chubb and Moe's evidence that, on average, public schools are more subject to external authority, excessive external authority is detrimental to academic climate in American schools, and American high schools with better academic climates have higher levels of student achievement. But this does *not* mean that these three propositions can be bundled together in a single, causal chain.

This issue has, in fact, recently been addressed in a clever study by Sandra Glass.[111] Glass studied relations between administrative style and student achievement in highly successful high schools from both the public and private sectors. She collected several kinds of data, among them lengthy interviews with administrators and others in those schools concerned with various topics, including the nature of constraints faced by those schools and the degree of their administrative autonomy. Her data indicated that schools from the public and private sectors actually experienced *quite similar* kinds of constraints. All the schools had to deal with the same state and federal laws, limited funds, the demands of parents, college admission requirements, the same College Board examinations, and so forth. Moreover, both the public and private schools exhibited high levels of administrative autonomy and high levels of student achievement.

At a minimum, then, this suggests that Chubb and Moe were writing nonsense when they claimed that private schools enjoy inherent freedom from external constraints and that high levels of administrative autonomy and student achievement are unlikely to co-occur in public schools. In addition, Chubb and Moe argued that administrative autonomy leads to high levels of student achievement, but Glass's data suggest that they may have confused the cart with the horse. Her interviews implied that these schools were granted autonomy *because* the students in these schools were high achievers. And if her informants were right, this might help to explain why so much constraint is imposed on poor urban schools where average student achievements are low.

In sum, Chubb and Moe's analyses do *not* confirm their thesis, nor do those analyses explain why private schools might possibly have programmatic advantages over public schools. Moreover, they do *not* confirm that private schools even *have* such an advantage. And it follows that their analyses do *not* support their recommendation that Americans should abolish public-school systems—a topic to which we return in the next chapter.

NAEP and the Public-Private Controversy. At this point, some readers may still be having difficulty with the public-private controversy. Despite what we have written, isn't it true that, all things considered, students in the typical private school outperform students in the typical public school in most subjects? Actually, as a general finding, it *isn't* true. To illustrate this point, let's examine recent data from the National Assessment of Educational Progress (NAEP). As we noted in chapter 2, the National Center for Education Statistics conducts regular NAEP surveys of student achievement in American high schools. In 1991 it released a report from such a study that was focused on mathematics.[112] These data were gathered in both public and private schools, and they offer opportunities to compare average student achievement for students in these two settings. Let's examine the results.

The graph we have reproduced as Exhibit 3.16 was assembled by Albert Shanker and Bella Rosenberg. It compares average mathematics proficiency scores from NAEP data for grade twelve students who had been exposed to various levels of mathematics instruction.[113] Not surprisingly, those students who had taken higher-level mathematics courses scored a lot higher in mathematics knowledge than those who had taken only lower-level courses—but note the results for public and private high schools. If anything, public high schools had a slight edge for students who had taken higher-level courses, while private high schools generated slightly greater scores for students who had taken only lower-level courses. But the basic pattern revealed *no sizable difference* in students' average mathematics achievement between the public and private sectors.

Nor are these the only data one can tap to assess gross differences between achievement levels of students in public and private schools. Shanker and Rosenberg also looked at recent NAEP data for science achievement and found the same pattern of findings.[114] Similarly, Chester Finn was at one time U.S. Assistant Secretary of Education and has been a strong advocate for private schools over the years. Nevertheless, when he looked at 1986 NAEP data, he found only *small* differences between public- and private-schools in students' achievements for reading, history, and literature. Surprised about these results, he commented, "it is conceivable that there is no private school effect showing up here at all."[115] Thus, evidence from the NAEP provides little support for the notion that private (or public) schools have a broad, substantial edge in average student achievement.

Exhibit 3.16   Average Overall Mathematics Proficiency of High School
Seniors Taking Similar Courses in Public and Private Schools

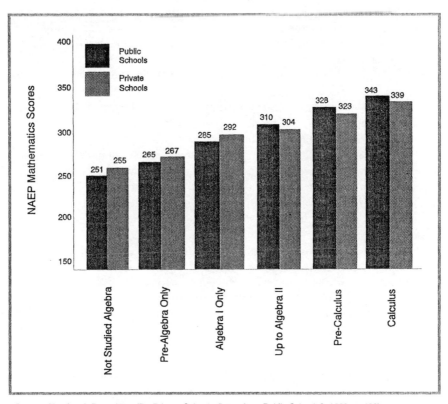

—Source: Shanker & Rosenberg (Do Private Schools Outperform Public Schools?, 1992, p. 136).
—Statistical Sources: National Center for Education Statistics (1991b) and American Federation of
Teachers.

All of which raises an interesting issue. Several reasons may be cited for
why students in private schools *ought* to outperform those in public schools,
on average, on tests of achievement in core subjects. Private schools are able
to select students whom they will enroll and expel; and this control should give
them more opportunity to choose talented students, to enforce disciplinary
standards, and to create a sense of "community." By contrast, public schools
must cope with all comers. In addition, private schools enroll mainly students
whose parents can afford to pay tuition, whereas public schools must enroll
students from impoverished families that cannot afford to provide home
support for education. And many private schools focus their academic efforts
on core subjects, whereas public-school curricula often reflect a broader range
of interests.

   Why, then, are average public-private differences in academic achievement
so *small?* We suspect that the answer to this question may also be found in

the preceding graph (Exhibit 3.16). As these results suggest, it seems to make little difference whether the student attends a public or private school. What matters in mathematics achievement is whether or not the student takes advanced courses in mathematics. Thus, the biggest factor determining mathematics achievement is *opportunity to learn*, and it matters little whether students have that opportunity in a public or private school. (*Berliner and Biddle's Student Achievement Law* strikes again!) To the extent, then, that some private schools generate high levels of achievement, they do this by providing better-than-average opportunities to learn. But such opportunities can also be provided in the public sector—indeed, they are provided today in America's best public high schools.

To summarize then, evidence from various sources suggests that *average* public-private differences in student achievement are minimal in America. This does not mean that certain types of private schools don't do well. HSB data suggested that students in Catholic schools have a slight achievement edge over those in public schools; but this seems largely due to the fact that Catholic schools restrict student enrollment, create a sense of "community," and stress slightly more rigorous course work.[116] Elite academies that serve rich students undoubtedly enjoy additional advantages. But other types of private schools offer programs that are *inferior* to those of the typical public school, and the best public schools in America generate truly magnificent achievement levels for their students. We know of *no* evidence that confirms a broad, inherent edge in student achievement for private schools, and it is time for the critics to stop pretending that such evidence exists.

Elite Schools and Their Effects. Although the *average* private school may provide little inherent advantage for students, elite academies certainly do, and we should also look at their programs. While such institutions constitute only a small minority of schools in America, they have an importance that far outweighs their numbers. This is because elite schools serve children of the rich and powerful. Attendance at such schools constitutes an important part of the process through which the upper class in our country reproduces itself, and this means that graduates of elite academies are likely to end up in positions of power. President Bush came from a wealthy family, of course, but he also attended Phillips Academy in Andover, Massachusetts, which, in turn, helped him to enter Yale. Studies of those who, like President Bush, attended the elite academies have also appeared, and we turn to these now.

Attendance at elite academies is associated with higher income in later life,[117] and most research on the effects of those schools has investigated the mechanisms generating this advantage. As a rule, it appears that those who graduate from elite schools are more likely than graduates of other high schools to gain entrance into high-status, highly selective, four-year undergraduate colleges (e.g., Ivy League colleges, Oberlin, Stanford, and the like). This, in turn, promotes subsequent entry into high-status graduate programs and into careers providing wealth and power.[118] Moreover, evidence for the greater ability of elite-academy graduates to enter high-status colleges persists, even when controls are entered for family background and students' senior-year SAT scores.[119] And although this elite private-school advantage in admissions declined somewhat in the early years of this century, it remains substantial to this day.[120]

Why should students who attend elite schools be more able to enter high-status colleges? In part, those students are exposed to programs that stress leadership and encourage them to apply to such colleges; in part, they are required to take a focused curriculum suitable for college entry; in part, the high-status colleges discriminate in their admissions decisions in favor of graduates from those elite schools; and in part, elite schools actively negotiate with high-status colleges for the admission of their graduates.[121] In short, students from elite academies are more often given both curricular and extra-curricular experiences, and they more often enjoy prejudicial assistance, which helps them "get ahead" in life.

Is this "fair"? The answer to this question depends on one's standard of fairness. Our own values suggest that *all* American students deserve equal encouragement and opportunities to "get ahead"; but Americans have always been willing to tolerate a lot of inequality, and allowing the rich to buy extra educational advantages for their children seems to be only an extension of this principle.

Summary. The evidence to date does *not* support the conclusion that, on average, private schools have an inherent programmatic edge over public schools. On the other hand, one group of private schools—the elite academies—clearly has such an edge, although it can be debated whether the public schools can or should emulate the techniques by which their advantages are gained.

Conclusion

We have no reason to be complacent about schools' performance. . . . But when schools are doing better than ever before, the best way to encourage continued improvement is not a concerted attack on school governance and organization. A more effective approach would be praise for accomplishment, provision of additional resources to programs whose results justify support, and reforms on the margin to correct programs and curricula shown to be ineffective.

—Richard Rothstein (The Myth of Public School Failure, 1993, p. 34)

This chapter completes a long journey. It began in Chapter 2, where we examined evidence about aptitude and achievement. Although critics central to the Manufactured Crisis have claimed repeatedly that America's schools have fallen on evil days, when we look at the evidence of student aptitude and achievement, we discover that America's schools have *not* recently declined. In fact, some evidence suggests that American schools are now generating *higher* levels of achievement than ever before and that such achievement is now spread *more widely* in the population. And though the critics have also claimed that American schools look terrible by comparison with schools from other industrialized countries, support for this claim has also proved to be illusory.

In this chapter we have taken on other charges the critics have made, many of them designed to degrade the image of America's public schools. Some of these charges have focused on money. Critics have said that America spends more than other countries on its schools, but this turns out to be untrue. Others have claimed that the level of financial support for schools is not related to student achievement, but this absurd notion is also contradicted by the evidence. And critics have railed against recent increases in the costs of education, but we now know that these increases were not associated with wasteful bureaucracy or rises in basic instructional costs but rather with expanding services for students with special needs, auxiliary programs, social problems originating in the larger society, and increased costs of keeping the schoolhouse door open.

Critics have also claimed that American schools are performing so poorly that they hurt business, but this claim also flies in the face of evidence. Nor can evidence be found supporting the charge that our schools do not produce enough technically trained workers. Indeed, what America's industries seem to need is more workers with supportive attitudes and good work habits, but these problems are more associated with changes in working environments than with education. And no evidence supports the charge that businesses are stuck for billions of dollars to train a work force that is deficient in basic skills. Despite what critics have claimed, America's schools are *not* generating unproductive workers; indeed, America's work force actually leads the world in productivity! And despite hysteria generated by the National Science Foundation and hundreds of academics and opinion leaders, American education is *not* generating too few scientists, mathematicians, and engineers for our nation's economy. Rather, the country now enjoys a *surplus* of well-educated and technically able workers.

Critics have also charged that America's teachers are untalented and poorly educated, but the vast majority of those teachers have completed undergraduate degrees, and about half of them now have postgraduate degrees. Moreover, academic standards are rising in colleges of education, and most of the course work taken by education majors is taken in other academic subjects. Despite charges to the contrary, it appears that American classrooms and texts still convey firm, conservative, moral values to students. And, contradicting what you may have heard from critics or read in the press, American parents are *not* dissatisfied with their local schools; rather their satisfaction seems to be greater than for parents in other countries. Finally—as if these charges weren't sufficient—critics have also argued that private schools have inherent advantages over public schools and that they are able to educate equivalently talented students to a higher standard than are public schools. But this charge is again unsupported by evidence.

Despite incessant claims to the contrary from critics and an ill-informed press, in aggregate the public schools of America look pretty good. And given the evidence we've reviewed, it appears that the reason so many American parents are satisfied with their schools is because, on average, those schools tend to meet their own and their children's needs. It's that simple.

This does not mean, of course, that American schools do not face serious problems, that educational opportunities are equitable in our country, or that our schools cannot be improved. Indeed, later in this book we take up some of these real, all-too-pressing problems and consider workable ideas for improving American education. But a major tenet of the Manufactured Crisis has always been that the average American school is failing our nation, and this tenet is clearly a fabrication. The idea that American schools are now failing the nation is a Big Lie. And like all Big Lies, it has created a great deal of mischief and unhappiness for hard-working citizens and educators who deserved better from America's political leaders, industrialists, media figures, and others responsible for creating and spreading the Manufactured Crisis.

Chapter Four

Why Now?

◆

We now turn to questions that are both fascinating and hard to answer. Why have so many flawed criticisms of American public schools recently appeared, and why have those criticisms had such an effect? What has been unique about the past few years? Why now?

Our answers to these questions will focus largely on social forces, on recent problems faced by American education, and on events in the society at large, rather than on the critics and their followers. We choose this focus deliberately. Most Americans are people of good will, and we believe that in many cases those criticizing education have simply misunderstood or are not aware of the actual problems faced by American schools. On the other hand, a few actions of the critics seem to have reflected less than total honesty and goodwill, and we shall alert readers when we believe this to be the case.

Mounting Problems

The popularization of American schools and colleges since the end of World War II has been nothing short of phenomenal, involving an unprecedented broadening of access, an unprecedented diversification of curricula, and an unprecedented extension of public control. In 1950, 34 percent of the American population twenty-five years of age or older had completed at least four years of high school, while 6 percent of that population had completed at least four years of college. By 1985, 74 percent of the American population twenty-five years of age or older had completed at least four years of high school, while 19 percent had completed at least four years of college. . . . It was in many ways a remarkable achievement, of which Americans could be justifiably proud. Yet it seemed to bring with it a pervasive sense of failure.

—Lawrence Cremin (*Popular Education and Its Discontents*, 1990, pp. 1–2)

The twenty-five years following World War II were unique in American history. These years generated not only a booming economy but also a huge expansion of public education. During this period enrollment in America's high schools increased by 50 percent or more, and American colleges and universities more than doubled their capacities. At the end of this period, the United States had an educational system that was the envy of the world for the opportunities it offered to a much-expanded range of Americans.

Unfortunately, the same decades also generated problems for education that Americans found difficult to solve or, in some cases, even to think about clearly. These problems increased sharply during the 1970s, and by the end of the decade, American education was facing a number of dilemmas that called for careful analysis and remedial action. Unfortunately, neither was to be provided. Most of these dilemmas have yet to be resolved, and many have become worse.

For one thing, by the 1970s Americans were beginning to suspect that public schools could not fulfill the many expectations that had been expressed for them in the 1950s and 1960s. Those earlier years were a period of great optimism in America. The expansion of education that took place then was often justified by claims about the ability of public schools to accomplish a huge range of tasks. In those years schools were seen not only as providers of knowledge and cultural uplift but also as centers for hobby and recreational interests, objects of ethnic or community pride, solvers of social problems, purveyors of services for individuals and their families, and engines of economic growth. In retrospect, many of these expectations were unrealistic, but this was not understood at the time. And when the economy soured and social problems soared in the 1970s, these expectations became standards against which schools were judged and found wanting.

This dilemma was compounded because American schools were not provided funds with which to finance their expanded programs. As a rule, expansions in the 1950s and 1960s were matched by increased funding, but as the economy turned sour in the 1970s, Americans became less willing to fund the expansions in education that they still wanted. As a result, funding for education became strained, per-capita expenditures for primary and secondary education began to fall, and eventually they came to lag behind those in other Western nations. American educators were not unaware of this problem, of course, and by the mid-1970s, they were issuing anguished calls for additional tax dollars to match the expanded programs they were still being asked to provide.

Unfortunately, those calls were not answered. Instead, the 1970s brought not only economic stagnation but also increases in other demands for tax dollars, particularly those associated with medical care, entitlement programs, public aid, and debt servicing. And if this were not enough, by the late 1970s, America was in the grip of a serious inflation, which meant that each year the public schools had to plead for increased tax support merely to keep abreast of their mounting costs. (Like the Red Queen in *Through the Looking Glass*, the schools had to run as hard as they could merely to stand still.) By the end of the decade, then, public education in America was facing not only a loss of confidence but also the annual need to beg for additional funds from an increasingly strained public purse.

The expansion of American education had also generated dilemmas concerning curricula and educational standards. Prior to World War II, about

50 percent of all students in the country dropped out of high school before graduation, and only 20 percent actually entered higher education. This meant that in those years it was thought appropriate that public high schools conducted tracking programs in which a quarter of their students were selected for "college preparation" and were required to take a tough, focused curriculum; "vocational" curricula were provided for another quarter; and "general education" was offered to the remainder (who would shortly leave school). Contrast this with today's high school, where any student who withdraws from school before graduation is stigmatized as a "dropout," *all* students are encouraged to consider at least some form of post-secondary education, and tracking programs are widely questioned.

As time passed, American high schools also made curricular adjustments to accommodate the wider range of students they were now to serve. Some schools began to offer a broader range of courses, many focused on "soft" subjects (such as civics, health, personal development, or recreation), and some changed the contents of core courses so as to make them more "interesting." Many also began to relax their requirements and academic standards to encourage students to remain in school as long as possible. Thus, in many schools students with potential interests in college were no longer required to take foreign language courses, four years of English, or three years of science and mathematics—which had been the norm for college-bound students in earlier years—and grading procedures were modified to make academic failure less likely.

These adjustments were controversial, of course. Parents with degrees in higher education could remember the tough, focused requirements and standards they had had to meet when preparing for college, and they became alarmed by new policies that were apparently "shortchanging" their children. Debates concerning curricula and standards had become common in school boards and state legislatures by the late 1970s. Moreover, some people began to reason that the "declining academic standards" of American high schools would inevitably generate a matching decline in academic achievement. (Such reasoning made untenable assumptions, of course. It ignored the fact that the earlier tough curricula had *never* been applied to the majority of students and assumed that high school students will only achieve if *forced* to do so by tough requirements. Repeated studies have shown that students are more likely to achieve when they are offered materials that are interesting and relevant to their needs than when they are coerced.)

As schools expanded their programs, they also came under pressure to provide better opportunities for blacks, Hispanics, women, students with disabilities, and other "minorities" who had been underrepresented among college-bound elites in earlier years. This was, of course, a threat to older people who had been members of those elites, since "social groups possessing a relatively rare and highly valued commodity that establishes their superiority over other groups are reluctant to see that commodity more widely distributed."[1] And if this weren't bad enough, in the 1970s these pressures were often generated by court decisions and the federal government, which had the effect of reducing the powers of local school boards or of challenging the prejudices of powerful groups in local communities. (Court decisions and federal programs designed to promote racial desegregation, for example, were often resented by prejudiced white school boards.) By the late 1970s, then, some traditional power-holders were being threatened by changes in the public schools that they felt they could no longer control.

Finally, for years America has suffered from serious social problems that place pressures on public schools. Several of these problems escalated significantly in the 1970s. Violence and drug use increased, the urban centers of American cities were decaying, and poverty among America's children was growing. As a result, educators forced to cope with these problems were coming under increased pressure, and since they were not provided with extra resources to help them cope, their schools and programs often deteriorated.

By the end of the 1970s, then, American education was suffering from many dilemmas—dilemmas perceived somewhat differently by educators, school boards, suburbanites and urban dwellers, legislators, minorities, elite groups, bigots, ideologues, and other sets of concerned citizens. Most would have agreed, however, that public schools were then suffering from problems that needed attention. Thus, many Americans were becoming worried about education, and this worry set the stage for the critics and their actions.

The Entitlement of Reactionary Voices

If the 1960s go down in history as the decade of liberal educational reform, the 1980s will most likely be known as the decade of conservative restoration. Although many reforms were eroding by the late 1970s, they came under direct assault in the 1980s, especially after the election of Ronald Reagan.

—Fred L. Pincus (The rebirth of educational conservatism, 1984, p. 152)

Surely a major reason for increased criticism of schools in the 1980s was that reactionary voices were given more credence in America during that decade. When Americans elected Ronald Reagan, and afterwards George Bush, to the presidency, they made the expression of right-wing ideologies fashionable. Ideologues on the right had long been critical of the public schools, and once avowed conservatives were in the White House, those criticisms were granted legitimacy and given prominence by the press. This was, indeed, a break with recent history.

It's useful to look at the events that encouraged these reactionary ideas. America has always supported conservative notions; indeed, for years political thought in the United States has generally been to the right of political thought in other advanced countries. Early in the 1970s, however, a number of wealthy people with sharply reactionary ideas began to work together to promote a right-wing agenda in America. Their major tools for this were a set of well-funded family foundations such as the Adolph Coors Foundation and the John M. Olin Foundation among others. For the past two decades, these foundations have undertaken various activities to "sell" reactionary views: funding right-wing student newspapers, internships, and endowed chairs for right-wing spokespersons on American campuses; supporting authors who write books hostile to American higher education; attempting to discredit social programs and other products of "liberal" thought; supporting conservative religious causes; lobbying for reactionary programs and ideologies in the federal Congress; and so forth.[2]

From the beginning, these same foundations have also invested heavily in think-tanks or institutes that can be counted on to express ideas—organizations such as the Heritage Foundation, the Hudson Institute, the American Enterprise Institute, the Hoover Institution, the Manhattan Institute, and the Madison Center for Educational Affairs. Over the past twenty years, these organizations have had a remarkable impact in America—in part, because they are well funded; in part, because they are able to make use of the press; and in part, because they have provided an alternative public forum for prominent people who had also served, or would later serve, in key federal posts. The rhetoric they produced certainly helped to propel Ronald Reagan into the presidency, and even today the propaganda they generate commands significant press attention.

Despite its successes, this reactionary movement is not a monolith but actually represents a variety of ideological strands. These include, for example: classical conservatism a la Edmund Burke; "economic rationalism"; defense of the rich; religious fundamentalism; suspicion of the federal government; hostility to public education and the academy (in general) and to social research (in particular); and racial, sexist, and ethnic bigotry. Most analysts have identified several groups within this movement, and we distinguish here among three of them that have expressed somewhat different views about education: the *Far Right*, the *Religious Right*, and *Neoconservatives*.

The Far Right.   A faction that had great influence during the early Reagan years is the Far Right (sometimes called the New Right, the Radical Right, or the Reactionary Right). One of the Far Right's major voices is the Heritage Foundation, and at earlier points we've quoted some of that Foundation's questionable opinions about education. Far Righters such as Edwin Meese and David Stockman were prominent within the early Reagan White House, Orrin Hatch and Jesse Helms can still be counted on to express Far Right ideas in the United States Senate, and some Far Right tenets have appeared in Rep. Newt Gingrich's "Contract with America."

In general, the Far Right blames the federal government for most of the problems facing American schools today. Fred Pincus, for example, quotes the following from the Heritage Foundation:

> The most damaging blows to science and mathematics education have come from Washington. For the past 20 years, federal mandates have favored "disadvantaged" pupils at the expense of those who have the highest potential to contribute positively to society. . . .By catering to the demands of special-interest groups—racial minorities, the handicapped, women, and non-English-speaking students—America's public schools have successfully competed for government funds, but have done so at the expense of education as a whole.[3]

Such views reveal hostility both to the public sector and to the interests of minorities in American society.

Given such beliefs, a major goal of the Far Right has been to decentralize education so that all federal involvement in education is abolished or "returned" to the states or local communities. At a minimum, this means abolishing the Department of Education, closing down federal support for educational research, eliminating funds for categorical grants in education that support minorities, and reducing the influence of federal courts.

In addition, some from the Far Right seem to believe that *all* public expenditures are inherently feckless or pernicious (pick one) and advocate reducing the entire public sector as a matter of policy. This has led to all sorts of proposals for privatization—e.g., of the post office, of the TVA, of state prisons, of welfare services, and the like—proposals that have become more strident since the demise of communist governments in the former Soviet Union, where central planning had been excessive. And if other citizen services are to be privatized, why exempt the schools, which consume such a large portion of public funds? In particular, economists of the Far Right (such as Milton Friedman) have argued that public-school districts should be replaced by a "free market" of competing private schools that are supported through tax credits or vouchers.[4]

Regarding the interests of "minorities," the Far Right argues that increased federal control has allowed powerful "vested interests" to have excessive influence in schools and that balance will not be restored until control over schools is "returned" to the states or local communities. (The vested interests they have cited include, for example, teachers' unions, educational associations, and federal bureaucrats; racial, religious, and ethnic minorities; women, the disabled, and homosexuals—indeed, presumably, anyone who is not WASP, male, and straight.)

To see how these ideas were expressed at the beginning of the Reagan years, we turn to a document designed to affect the president's early policies. In the second half of 1980, shortly before his election as president, Ronald Reagan appointed an Education Policy Advisory Committee that was to prepare a private set of recommendations for the new administration. This group was chaired by W. Glenn Campbell, director of the Hoover Institution, and we have been given a document dated October 22, 1980, that is labeled a "tentative draft" of the committee's report. We have been unable to locate a copy of the submitted report, but Glenn Campbell has assured us that it followed the "tentative draft" closely.[5] This "tentative draft" offers good insights into how the Far Right viewed education during this crucial period.

As one reads the "tentative draft," one is struck by how many of the myths and themes of the Manufactured Crisis it expresses. Educational achievement is reported to have declined sharply in America, and SAT and NAEP data are said to confirm this decline. Constant-dollar educational expenditures are said to have tripled in recent years. Discipline is said to have broken down in the schools. And these problems are seen as the product of federal interference that favors unruly minorities, bilingualism, and persons with disabilities; encourages mediocrity; and slights talented students. Public schools are called weak because they enjoy monopoly status, while private schools are stronger because they must compete in the marketplace. Educational research is "largely propaganda." Standards are falling and costs are rising in higher education because of federal harassment and because of the imposition of racial and ethnic quotas. And to solve these problems, the "tentative draft" suggests abolishing the Department of Education, restricting categorical grants in education, reining in the courts, and funding voucher plans to encourage private schools.

Members of the Education Policy Advisory Committee presumably had reason to expect good things from these recommendations. Candidate Ronald Reagan had already proposed to abolish the Department of Education and was known to favor school vouchers. As it turned out, however, the committee had less initial effect on administration policy than the Far Right had hoped. President Reagan's first secretary of education was Terrel Bell, former U.S. commissioner for education; and Terrel Bell did *not* favor abolishing the Department of Education. In addition, educational issues were not high on the president's early list of concerns. As a result, Bell was able to block some of the Far Right agenda.[6] Nevertheless, advocates for the Far Right remained prominent in the early Reagan White House, and they influenced education policy in various ways both during the Terrel Bell years and afterwards. Even today, some claims and beliefs of Far Right rhetoric may be detected in documents released by the Department of Education.

The Religious Right. A second reactionary faction, the Religious Right, also became prominent in the early Reagan years. The core of this movement seems to be represented by the Religious Roundtable, a network of leaders who help to coordinate its activities. Prominent figures associated with it include Jerry Falwell, Tim LeHay, Mel and Norma Gabler, and former presidential candidate Pat Robertson. Although the Religious Right did not secure "insider" positions in either the Reagan or Bush administrations, both administrations were beholden to it for political support and paid lip service to some of its ideas. The Religious Right also remains active today and wielded considerable influence at the 1992 Republican National Convention.

In general, the Religious Right argues that federal controls have been used to deny students the "right" to pray in schools; to restrict unfairly the teaching of "scientific creationism"; to encourage the appearance of "dirty," "anti-family," "pro-homosexual," and "anti-American" books in school curricula; and to enforce "cultural relativity" in courses on values and sex education. In the typical rhetoric of religious fundamentalists, these "evils" are bundled together as "secular humanism," a catch-all phrase that refers to educational philosophies that are "human-centered rather than God-centered."[7] Such "evils," they believe, can be countered only by doing away with federal controls in education or, paradoxically, by promoting federal laws or constitutional amendments that prohibit the government from imposing "secular humanism" on public schools.

In addition, advocates among the Religious Right argue that because public schools are *inevitably* used to promote "secular humanism," they are iniquitous and should be abolished completely! You might think that we're exaggerating this argument to make a point, but we aren't. According to one Religious Right advocate, Robert Thoburn,

> I imagine every Christian would agree that we need to remove the humanism from the public schools. There is only one way to accomplish this: to abolish the public schools. We need to get the government out of the education business. According to the Bible, education is a parental responsibility. It is not the place of the government to be running a school system.[8]

And how should "Christians" proceed to dismantle public education? They are urged to take all legitimate actions to hamper and discourage public schools, such as arguing against them in public debates and voting No in all school-bond elections. Moreover, "subversive" actions are also encouraged:

> Christians should run for the school board. This may sound like strange advice. After all, I have said that Christians should have nothing to do with the public schools. What I meant was that Christians should not allow their children to have anything to do with public schools. This does *not* mean that we should have nothing to do with them.... Our goal is not to make the schools better.... The goal is to hamper them, so they cannot grow.... Our goal as God-fearing, uncompromised ... Christians is *to shut down the public schools*, not in some revolutionary way, but step by step, school by school, district by district.[9]

So, apparently, running for the school board under false colors would also be an acceptable means, given that the end is "pure."

Recommendations of the latter type held little charm for Ronald Reagan or George Bush, but both tried to accommodate Religious Right educational interests in their policies. Both made speeches favoring school prayer and "family values." Moreover, both argued that federal funds should be used to

support religious schools through vouchers or other means. And the ideology
of the Religious Right has clearly promoted dissatisfaction with public education over the years, thus also helping set the stage for the Manufactured Crisis.

The Neoconservatives. By the mid-1980s, a third faction had begun
to emerge that claimed to represent "centrist" conservative thought, the
Neoconservatives. Many people associated with the Neoconservative movement have had ties to the American Enterprise Institute, another conservative
think tank, and their ideas often appear in *Public Interest, Commentary,* or
(more recently) *The New Republic.* In addition, a set of influential Neoconservatives—William Bennett, Chester Finn, Lamar Alexander, and Diane Ravitch—came to dominate federal education policy during the late Reagan years
and the Bush administration.

In general, Neoconservatives argue that American schools have suffered
from two serious problems: a history of social experiments concerned with
peripheral issues that made too many demands on schools and diverted them
from their basic missions, and excessive federal intervention to promote educational equity. As a result, they argue, academic standards and discipline
have eroded, and basic achievements in American schools have fallen and
now lag behind those of other countries. This threatens both the moral integration of the nation and its ability to compete with other industrialized
countries.

Neoconservatives also prescribe various steps that should be taken to meet
these problems: schools should recommit themselves to academic excellence
and require a larger number of basic-skills courses; higher academic standards
should be encouraged through tougher grading procedures and national tests
of student achievement; schools should maintain discipline and reassert their
rights to discharge students who cannot meet reasonable standards for behavior; stress should be given to competitiveness and other values thought to be
"traditional" in America; and greater effort on the part of teachers should
be encouraged through merit pay, competency testing, and stronger requirements for teacher certification. Above all, schools and educators should be
made "accountable"; they should be required to provide objective evidence
of their accomplishments.

Neoconservatives also generally oppose the concepts of educational or
hiring quotas for minorities as "reverse discrimination" and argue that the
federal government has already "taken care of" most problems of educational
equity. (This may come as surprising news to the many thousands of educators who today serve the needs of minority students in desperately underfunded schools in urban ghettos and isolated rural areas.) In contrast with
the Far Right, however, Neoconservatives favor a strong educational role for
the federal government to ensure that schools carry out their mission. In
addition, Neoconservatives have been ambivalent about private schools, some

(James Coleman, for example) urging that the federal government provide increased support for the private sector, others (such as the Twentieth Century Fund Task Force) arguing that "provision of free public education must continue to be a public responsibility of high priority, while support of nonpublic education should remain a private obligation."[10]

Neoconservative ideas were not new in the 1980s, but they emerged influentially during the later Reagan years and the Bush administration. A good deal of recent criticism of the schools reflects Neoconservative tenets.

Common Ideas. Despite their obvious differences, the three conservative ideologies we have reviewed share basic ideas about American education. All three are offended by recent changes in public schools and would like to return to mythic "golden years," when schools were more to their liking. All believe that public education has recently "deteriorated." All tend to be intolerant of the interests of minorities in education. All share a profound mistrust of both educators and students. (The former are never portrayed as trustworthy professionals; the latter are never thought to be capable of self-motivated learning.) And all blame "defects" in the public schools for problems in the larger society and propose changes in federal policy that will presumably cure those problems.

Moreover, spokespersons for both Far Right and Neoconservative positions argue that academic achievement has declined in recent years in American schools, and, given the dominance of these ideologies within the Reagan and Bush administrations, it is small wonder that those administrations promoted the myths that we tackle in this book. Ideologues committed to these beliefs have had little reason to challenge simplistic "evidence" that public education was in trouble, and in the Reagan and Bush years they were provided marvelous opportunities to sell these beliefs from the bully pulpit of the White House.

Since the defeat of George Bush in 1992, reactionary rhetorics about education have been given less attention. Nevertheless, many Americans (including leaders in the Clinton administration) have embraced some ideas from these rhetorics, and the congressional elections of 1994 resurrected many conservative tenets. So educators may have to contend with the debris of reactionary educational thought for some time to come. Thus, it is worthwhile pointing out that, since they reflect prejudices against minorities and tend to ignore or misunderstand the *real* problems of American schools, right-wing educational agenda are usually misguided and are often dangerous. To quote Fred Pincus:

> Like the more humane liberal policies of the 1960s and 1970s, [conservative] educational policies have their own contradictions. In a society characterized by racism, class conflict, and economic stagnation, there is little that the schools can do to help create a better society. Liberal policies can make things less bad and create limited avenues of upward mobility for a few individuals. Conservative

policies will simply lead to the reproduction of a blatantly inequitable social system.[11]

"A Nation at Risk," The Human Capital Ideology, and CRISIS Rhetorics

Since 1983 the United States has been besieged by a series of reports that severely criticize the nation's public school system. In prose befitting a public relations firm preparing the nation for war, the reports discover massive problems in the schools and recommend hundreds of solutions that, taken together, would cost about as much money as a major war.

> —Ron Haskins, Mark Lanier, and Duncan MacRae, Jr. (The commission reports and strategies of reform, 1988, p. 1)

As far as the public was concerned, the Manufactured Crisis began on April 26, 1983—the date when, amidst much fanfare, the Reagan White House released its critical report on the status of American schools, *A Nation at Risk*. In many ways this report was the "mother of all critiques" of American education. The bashing of public education has long been a popular indoor sport in America, but never before had criticism of education appeared that

- was sponsored by a secretary of education in our national government;
- was prepared by such a prestigious committee;
- was endorsed by a president of the United States;
- made such explicit charges about a supposed recent, tragic decline of American education—charges said to be confirmed by both longitudinal and comparative studies;
- asserted that because of this putative decline of education the nation was losing its leadership in industry, science, and innovation;
- assigned blame for said decline to inadequacies in teaching programs and inept educators; and
- packaged its messages in such flamboyant prose.

To illustrate merely the last of these wonders, on its first page the report asserted:

> Our Nation is at risk. Our once unchallenged preeminence in commerce, industry, science and technological innovation is being overtaken by competitors throughout the world. . . . The educational foundations of our society are presently being eroded by a rising tide of mediocrity that threatens our very future as a nation

and a people. . . . If an unfriendly foreign power had attempted to impose on America the mediocre educational performance that exists today, we might well have viewed it as an act of war. As it stands, we have allowed this to happen to ourselves. . . . We have, in effect, been committing an act of unthinking, unilateral educational disarmament.[12]

This was heady stuff. *Never* before had such trenchant rhetoric about education appeared from the White House. As a result, the press had a field day, tens of thousands of copies of *A Nation At Risk* were distributed, and many Americans thereafter read or heard, for the first time, that our public schools were "truly" failing.

Terrel Bell was then secretary of education. Bell had previously helped to prevent Reaganaughts from dismantling the federal Department of Education. Why, then, did he sponsor the committee that prepared this alarming report? At an individual level, it appears that Bell sincerely believed in the simple idea that "declining academic standards" in American high schools inevitably meant that achievement had also declined, and he felt he had to do "something" to awaken concern for education within the White House.[13] At a deeper level, however, *A Nation At Risk* merely gave public voice to charges about education that right-wing ideologues had already been telling one another. Thus, it served to publicize tenets of conservative educational thought and was, as a result, embraced with enthusiasm by right-wing troops in the Reagan White House. (Actually, their enthusiasm was tempered. *A Nation At Risk* also called for raising the salaries of teachers and for increased federal funding of education, but these recommendations were conveniently ignored by the White House.)

The White House was not alone, however, in sponsoring critiques of public schools in the early 1980s. The same years also produced an explosion of independently generated books and commission reports about American education, some well meaning and scholarly, some not, *all critical*. Consider just the titles of some of these documents:

- *High School: A Report on Secondary Education in America*
- *A Place Called School: Prospects for the Future*
- *America's Competitive Challenge: The Need for a National Response*
- *Action for Excellence: A Comprehensive Plan to Improve our Nation's Schools*
- *Making the Grade*
- *Business and Education: Partners for the Future*
- *Horace's Compromise: The Dilemma of the American High School*
- *Investing in our Children: Business and the Public Schools.*[14,15]

Why did so many highly critical reports about American education suddenly appear in the early 1980s? In part, these works expressed legitimate concerns. But they also reflected the blossoming of conservative ideologies then underway. In addition, many of these works revealed concerns about an economic crisis thought to be pending for American business, coupled with a belief that this crisis was linked to changes needed in education.[16]

In the early 1980s, concern began to be expressed by business leaders that the American economy was not keeping pace. Analysts began to refer to the "deindustrialization of America" and to observe that the United States had lost its once-competitive advantage in labor-intensive industries.[17] This suggested that America needed to develop a new industrial policy in order to "transfer labor-intensive, low-skill production to Third World developing countries, at the same time maintaining control over the entire world production process in ways that ensure the future competitive supremacy of the United States."[18] Such a need, in turn, implied that American schools should be training their students for somewhat different jobs—but what might those jobs be?

Answers to this question involved assumptions about the likely effects of automation, computers, robotics, lasers, telecommunications, and other new technologies on the labor market. Conventional wisdom had it that these technological innovations would gradually make manual labor obsolete but that America could enjoy a new burst of technological growth and development—with associated increases in productivity and standard of living—if only its labor system generated skilled workers able to plan and implement that kind of growth.[19] Thus, our educational system should stress skills appropriate to the new technologies—technological visualization; abstract reasoning; mathematical, scientific, and computer expertise; knowledge of specific technologies and production techniques; individual initiative; and so forth—because the evolving job market will need more workers with these skills.

This argument was actually an offshoot of yet another ideology that had evolved in the nineteenth century but that flowered in the late 1950s concerning "Human Capital."[20] Human Capital theorists argued that education should be thought of as "investing" in human resources and that appropriate investments in education can benefit industry and fuel the national economy. In early years this argument had been seized by canny industrialists, who realized they could reduce costs if the public schools could only be persuaded to provide the specialized training their firms would otherwise have to fund in apprenticeship programs. In addition, Human Capital arguments became a strong catalyst for the growth of educational systems in underdeveloped countries.

Although it remains popular today, Human Capital theory has never been supported by much evidence. In addition, analysts have raised questions about whether the new technologies will actually create or destroy more jobs.[21] They have pointed out that "unlike other technologies which increase the productivity of the worker, the robot actually replaces the worker. That indeed is one of the prime tasks for which robots are built"[22] and that it takes only a small number of highly trained people to design the robots, computers, and machinery that will replace large numbers of dangerous and boring jobs. Such arguments suggest that conventional industrial thinking about education was flawed, that the proposals it advocated would not have worked in any case. Indeed, recent employment statistics suggest that job growth is appearing not in "high tech" industries, but rather in *service* occupations and in the skilled crafts.

Nevertheless, conventional wisdom largely held sway. And as the business community came to think that deindustrialization was indeed a looming problem, and that this problem required changes in American schools, it began to sponsor reform reports that sought to remold education in "appropriate" ways. These reports argued that schools should:

- Revise their curricula to give more stress to information-age subjects and to science and mathematics;

- "Intensify" their programs by lengthening the school day or year, by raising academic standards, and by increasing core curricular requirements;

- Assist students with school-to-work transition problems;

- Stock classrooms with "the latest" instructional materials and computers;

- Stress achievement, individual initiative, free enterprise, and other values thought to help students become information-age leaders;

- Require upgraded levels of technical competency among teachers and provide programs to increase teachers' skills;

- Identify talented students at an early age and provide them with "enriched" educational experiences (and thus adopt or strengthen ability-grouping programs).

Some of these proposals would have generated changes that could benefit *any* student in the school. Others, however, such as the last we listed above, would have turned back the clock and recommitted America to an elitist model for education. In fairness, concern for the elitist implications of some of their recommendations often appeared in the reform reports, and most of the reports paid at least lip service to both "excellence" and "equity." Despite such protestations, however, most of the reports did not make clear how the twin goals of excellence and equity could be achieved while adjusting school programs to meet "the problem of deindustrialization." In addition, many of the recommendations made in the reports would have required additional funds for schools, and enthusiasm for providing these funds has not been great in recent years.

Although most of their recommendations were not funded, the reform reports certainly have had an effect on education. First, some of their proposals are still being debated as ways of "improving" American schools. Proposals for "intensifying" school programs, for example, by increasing hours in the school day or days in the school year, by assigning more homework, by covering more subject matter during lessons, and so forth, have proved popular among politicians—possibly because they appear to offer more bang for the same educational bucks. And some of the proposals the reports made to "strengthen" curricula in the sciences and mathematics eventually found their way into George Bush's America 2000 agenda and Bill Clinton's recent Goals 2000 legislation.

Second, the reports led to calls for greater contact between educators and industrial leaders. Such contact was needed, the argument went, to make education relevant to industrial needs, to increase the employability of graduates, and to improve productivity—thus enhancing America's ability to compete successfully in the global economy.[23] In response to these calls, many school districts set up "Adopt a School" programs or other arrangements that allowed members of the business community to exert more influence on their local schools.

Unfortunately, such programs also bring problems. For one thing, they can lead to overemphasizing the needs of business or industry when making decisions about education. They may lead, for example, to overstressing technological curricula rather than curricula concerned with moral, social, or aesthetic concerns. The latter, we would argue, are not only necessary for a well-rounded education but also may do more, finally, to preserve our democracy than a curriculum that focuses largely on business needs. In addition, when industrial leaders are given unique leadership roles in education, it is assumed, in effect, that they are peculiarly able to estimate the future educational needs of American society. This seems a dubious assumption; industrialists are often very bright people, but we know of no evidence to suggest that they are more prescient than other thoughtful leaders in the community.

Above all, the reform reports reinforced the belief, first announced in *A Nation at Risk,* that American education is in deep CRISIS. Moreover, the education crisis message has since been repeated endlessly by leaders in both government and industry and has been embraced by a host of journalists, legislators, educators, and other concerned Americans. Thus, in a September 1991 address by President Bush: "The ringing school bell sounds an alarm, a warning to all of us who care about the state of American education. . . . Every day brings new evidence of crisis." And from a September 1991 article in *Time* magazine entitled "Can this man [Lamar Alexander, the newly appointed secretary of education] save our schools?":

> By almost every measure, the nation's schools are mired in mediocrity—and most
> Americans know it. Whether it is an inner-city high school with as many security

checkpoints as a Third World airport, or a suburban middle school where only the "geeks" bother to do their homework, the school too often has become a place in which to serve time rather than to learn. The results are grimly apparent: clerks at fast-food restaurants who need computerized cash registers to show them how to make change; Americans who can drive but cannot read the road signs; a democracy in which an informed voter is a statistical oddity.[24]

The trouble with such messages is that they can lead to quick-fix or damaging "solutions" for minor distresses and to ignoring the truly serious problems of education and American society that need long-term effort. People can become blasé when critics cry educational "wolf" too often.

Americans need to keep two ideas about education clearly separated. The first is the notion that American schools are *generally* "mediocre." As we have shown repeatedly, the evidence simply does *not* support this claim. The second is that *some* American schools are terrible places. This is certainly true, but it is largely true because those schools lack resources and must contend with some of society's worst social problems. Thus, hysterical utterances about a broad, fictive crisis in American education are not only lies; when they are believed, *they are likely to confuse and derail efforts that are badly needed to help our neediest schools.* The Sandia Report expressed it thus:

> Although we have shown that there are indeed some serious problems at all levels of education, we believe that much of the current rhetoric goes well beyond assisting reform, and actually hinders it. Much of the "crisis" commentary today professes total system-wide failure in education. Our research shows that this is simply not true. Many claim that the purpose of the rhetoric is to garner funding for reform; but, if these funds are used to alleviate a nonexisting "crisis," education and educators will suffer in the long run.[25]

School-Bashing and Governmental Scapegoating

School-bashing enjoys a long and rich tradition in this country. It appeals to the public, it grabs attention, and it doesn't cost anything.

—Richard M. Jaeger (World class standards, choice, and privatization, 1992, p. 124)

As far as we're concerned, many of our political and corporate leaders are using educational reform as a scapegoat for problems schools didn't cause and can't fix. We believe many of these elected leaders and their corporate sponsors are engaging in a conspiracy—a conspiracy against candor with the American people.

—Joe Schneider and Paul Houston (*Exploding the Myths,* 1993, p. 3)

We turn now to more subtle reasons for the Manufactured Crisis. At least some recent attacks on schools have come from elitists who are against the

whole idea of public education. Such elitism is not new, of course.[26] There
have always been those—such as Richard Herrnstein and Charles Murray—who refuse to believe in the intelligence of the poor or who never want
to share the advantages of education with "common people."

Some criticisms of education are simple scapegoating, however. It is no
longer fashionable in most American settings to blame the economic and
social tragedies of contemporary life on an "international Jewish conspiracy"
or on the "lack of motivation or talent" of Irish American, African American,
Polish American, or Mexican American workers. "Greedy union bosses" cannot be blamed anymore, since the country no longer has strong unions. Right-
wing politicians still hurl charges against welfare "cheaters," but these charges
pale because the amounts spent on welfare are small potatoes compared with
the amounts recently used to bail out the savings and loan companies. (Moreover, the savings and loan robbery of the American people was perpetrated
by nice, upper-class, well-educated, religious white men from two-parent
households—the kind of Americans whom we are supposed to admire.) But
blame for society's ills, of which there seem to be so many, needs to be
assigned somewhere. And one visible, ordinarily passive, relatively defenseless
group is still available. Thus, since the early 1980s, Americans have been told
relentlessly by prominent leaders that ours is "a nation at risk" because its
schools and teachers have failed us.

Actually, attacking the public schools has long been a popular pastime in
America. To illustrate, a 1900 article in *Gunton's Magazine* told us, "The
mental nourishment we spoon-feed our children is not only minced but
peptonized so that their brains digest it without effort and without benefit
and the result is the anaemic intelligence of the average American school-
child."[27] (Although the language is quaint, the message seems to be familiar.)
Again, in 1909 the *Atlantic Monthly* criticized the schools for: (a) not teaching
enough facts, (b) not teaching thinking skills, and (c) not preparing young
people for jobs.[28] (Does this also sound familiar?)

Our favorite early example comes, however, from the *Ladies Home Journal*
of 1912. There, Ella Francis Lynch criticized the schools because life in America had changed and the schools had not changed with it. Lynch had a wonderful way with words. She asked if the millions of middle-class women who
were her readers could

> imagine a more grossly stupid, a more genuinely asinine system tenaciously per-
> sisted in to the fearful detriment of over seventeen million children and at a cost
> to you of over four-hundred and three million dollars each year—a system that
> not only is absolutely ineffective in its results, but also actually harmful in that it
> throws every year ninety-three out of every one hundred children into the world
> of action absolutely unfitted for even the simplest tasks of life? Can you wonder
> that we have so many inefficient men and women; that in so many families there
> are so many failures; that our boys and girls can make so little money that in one
> case they are driven into the saloons from discouragement, and in the other into

brothels to save themselves from starvation? Yet that is exactly what the public-school system is today doing, and has been doing.[29]

School bashing was not confined to the first years of the century, of course. *Time* magazine charged in 1949 that the schools were failing to teach traditional subject matter because it was too concerned with life-adjustment education.[30] The year 1951 seems to have been a particularly good year for criticism. From *Readers Digest* and *Scientific Monthly* in that year one learned that

> there were complaints from frustrated university professors and angry business people that public school students were woefully unprepared for college as well as for work. The typical high school student could not write a clear English sentence, do simple mathematics, or find common geographical locations such as Boston or New York City. There were no basic standards. . . . The schools also were ignoring religion. The curriculum was inappropriate for life at mid-century, giving students worthless information and outdated training and worst of all, boring them. As one critic put it: "We are offering them a slingshot education in a hydrogen-bomb age."[31]

Nor was this all. The 1950s also witnessed savage criticisms of the schools in books by Arthur Bestor, Albert Lynd, and Admiral Hyman Rickover—and this was during a decade of unprecedented growth in and optimism about American education![32] Consider, for example, Admiral Rickover's comments:

> Everyone is aware today that our educational system has been allowed to deteriorate. It has been going downhill for some years without anything really constructive having been done to arrest the decline, still less to reverse its course. We thus have a chronic crisis; an unsolved problem as grave as any that faces our country today. Unless this problem is dealt with promptly and effectively the machinery that sustains our level of material prosperity and political power will begin to slow down.[33]

(Makes one wonder how America has managed to survive the past thirty-five years, does it not?) Nor have such wholesale attacks on American education ceased in subsequent decades—take a look, for example, at recent books by Paul Copperman and Allan Bloom.[34]

Why on earth should school bashing be so popular in our country? Perhaps playwright Jane Wagner had it right when she said "I personally think we developed language because of our deep inner need to complain." But Americans seem to attack schools in particular because they have such unrealistic expectations of those schools, and become disgruntled when the schools cannot meet those expectations. Moreover, many Americans seem to remember the boredom or repeated failures they experienced in classrooms where public competitions and competitive evaluations are practiced endlessly. And, as Richard Jaeger suggested in the quotation with which we began this section, attacks on the schools are attention-grabbing and cost very little—indeed, they often make money for the attackers.

In addition, most American schools are, after all, *public institutions* and are subject to public scrutiny and review. Public education also eats up large chunks of tax dollars; educators and their supporters are forever calling for additional support funds; and nobody likes to pay taxes. And educators are a relatively passive group, often from working- or middle-class backgrounds, who have an embattled professional status and who are also likely to be women—a traditionally unempowered group. In sharp contrast, many of the critics have been males who were educated in private schools and who presently enjoy secure and prestigious positions.

And if these weren't reasons enough, American teachers actually set themselves up for attack because of some of their most responsible, professional conduct. How does this occur? As it happens, Americans are very likely to take personal credit when they succeed in difficult tasks.[35] Not only is this tendency widespread in the United States, but it is also approved of by Americans who associate it with creating the appearance of being able to cope.[36] Moreover, the tendency is promoted in American schools by teachers, who encourage students to believe that *they* are personally responsible for their successes in schools. But if students are to take personal responsibility for their successes, what does that say about the teachers who helped them to succeed? According to data presented by Philip Tetlock, teachers are most approved of when they *downplay* their own contributions to student successes.[37] Should we then be surprised if others sooner or later take teachers' self-deprecatory styles as evidence of incompetence?

But the question remains, why were America's educators so often scapegoated in *the 1980s,* and why did *government* leaders—for the first time in American history—then lead this attack on the schools? Three reasons presumably lay behind this action by the White House. First, as we noted above, for the first time *ever* Americans had elected a government composed of individuals who subscribed to reactionary ideologies that condemned public schools, and when they scapegoated education, that government was just expressing publicly the hostile notions that right-wing ideologues had been telling one another in recent years.

Second, the administrations of Ronald Reagan and George Bush came under strong pressure from Human Capitalists in industry who wanted extensive and expensive modifications in American education. But both administrations were concerned with other matters and had no intention of spending additional dollars on education. (In fact, despite suggestions to the contrary, federal support for education *declined* in constant-value-dollar terms during most of the Reagan and Bush years.) Human Capitalists tend to be powerful business leaders, however, and neither Ronald Reagan nor George Bush wanted to annoy them. Consequently, both paid lip service to educational reform. Indeed, George Bush styled himself "The Education President." But they tried to shift the burden of that reform to the states, local communities, parents, and, above all, *educators,* who were deemed to be both incompetent and responsible for education's problems. A paradox, indeed.

Third, the Reagan and Bush administrations were faced with escalating domestic social problems that neither government wanted to tackle. (Rather, the Reagan and Bush administrations generally represented interests of the rich, and many of America's social problems got worse during their tenures—see Chapter 6.) Thus, both administrations had reasons for diverting America's attention from federal failures to deal with domestic problems, and one way to do this was to blame those problems on educators and the schools.

None of these reasons compliments the Reagan and Bush administrations, of course, and other reasons might also be unearthed for the recent explosion of educational scapegoating. Our basic concern, however, is not with assigning blame but rather with countering the evil effects that scapegoating imposes on innocent people. Educators are *not* responsible for most of the reputed shortcomings of American schools, let alone for the overwhelming problems in American society. Indeed, most of the "shortcomings" of schools suggested by critics are nonexistent; and in most cases American educators are coping well with intellectually complex, emotionally demanding, time-consuming, and often dangerous tasks.

Rather than leading us to ruin, the vast majority of teachers and administrators run a school system that works well for most American children. Educators in the schools with the least support—those who serve children who need the most help—are indeed having a hard time. These schools may indeed be failing, but as we have noted before, the causes of their failure usually lie outside the school building. Such causes are embedded in the problems and social inequities of our society, which many of our politicians seem wonderfully able to ignore.

Self-Interest Versus Public Interest

When I first heard about America 2000 and its provisions for diverting public funds to private schools, I classified it as just another attempt to reinforce the image of the Education President. . . . Further probing of the evidence, however, has convinced me that America 2000 is more than a mere quest for image.

Total expenditures for public elementary and secondary education have grown steadily over the past three decades. . . . It takes no special insight to realize that, as the original forty-niners might have said, "Thar's gold in them thar hills!"

—Richard M. Jaeger (1992b, p. 125)

It is also useful to discuss briefly some of the more invidious, self-serving reasons why critics may have attacked education during the past few years.

We examine these with reluctance. Most Americans like to think well of their fellow citizens, and some people will find it hard to believe that criticism of schools may also be motivated by hidden selfish interests; and yet, such interests often underlie campaigns of public advocacy.

To illustrate, rich and powerful people often create marvelous explanations for why they should continue to enjoy their privileges. Consider, for example, the many creative rationales offered by the tobacco industry for discounting or hiding research that links smoking with cancer, or the huge panoply of "disinterested" objections to national health care voiced by rich doctors, drug companies, and insurance executives. Such statements are obvious masks for self-interest. It seems at least possible that similar self-interest may have also motivated some recent actions of the critics of education.

For example, take the case of arguments for vouchers that could be used to support private schools. In Chapter 6 we review evidence showing how federal policies generated massive transfers of income and wealth to rich people during the Reagan and Bush years. Ronald Reagan and George Bush are both rich people, as are many of their friends. Many of their own or their friends' children have attended high-status, expensive, private high schools, and George Bush himself graduated from such an academy. Both the Reagan and Bush administrations favored vouchers, and in the spring of 1991 the latter brought forth America 2000, a proposed educational policy that would have provided, among other things, tax-supported vouchers that could be used in private schools. One does not need Albert Einstein to explain that if such a program were adopted, tuition charges at high-status, expensive, private high schools could be reduced. Do you suppose that self- or class-interests helped to motivate these enthusiasms for vouchers?

Critics in the federal administration may have had other selfish reasons for lambasting public schools. As readers may know, Chris Whittle is a business tycoon from Tennessee who operates a business that provides video equipment and news programming for schools in exchange for guarantees that those schools will show students two minutes of television commercials each day. Lamar Alexander, secretary of education in the Bush administration and a former governor of Tennessee, is a long-time friend of Chris Whittle's. His close connections with the Whittle Communications enterprise are documented in a recent article by Jonathan Kozol, which indicates that Alexander had previously served on Whittle's board, worked as a consultant for Whittle, and had profited greatly from transactions of Whittle stock.[38] Moreover, in March of 1991, the *Wall Street Journal* suggested that other leaders in the Department of Education had also benefited from relationships with Whittle.[39]

Suspicions that education policies under George Bush reflected Whittle interests escalated in 1991 when, in quick succession, the Bush administration published America 2000 (which called for school vouchers); Chris Whittle formed a new business, the Edison Project, responsible for a proposed coast-to-coast network of profit-making schools (which would have benefited greatly had America 2000 become law); and Chester Finn, former assistant secretary of education (a consistent critic of public schooling and a major architect of America 2000), signed on to work for the Edison Project. Strange.

Industrial leaders may also have selfish motives for criticizing the schools. To illustrate, during the 1980s industrialists began to complain about an anticipated "shortage" of engineers and scientists. Moreover, those complaints were endorsed by Erich Bloch, then head of the National Science Foundation, who used flawed data to support his arguments. (We detail this sad story later in the chapter.) These actions stimulated a greater supply of scientists and engineers who could be employed by industry, and, as the actions were largely successful, the salaries that industries now need to pay

---

■ EXHIBIT 4.1
Big Business Goes to School

Shortly before George Bush was defeated for reelection in 1992, John S. Friedman wrote about the suspicious alliance between corporate interests and White House education policies.

Chris Whittle, chairman and founder of Whittle Communications, represents the new intersection between business and education. Until recently, corporate America, for the most part, has avoided direct involvement in education. But it has now turned to the classroom. The Bush Administration is the point of entry and Chris Whittle is the point man. . . .

Whittle Communications is a media company [whose] centerpiece is Channel One. The Whittle formula is ingenious. His company lends the schools TVs, VCRs and satellite dishes to receive the programming and then wires the system. . . . In exchange, schools agree to show Channel One to most students on 92 percent of the days in which school is in session [which features] two minutes of ads on every Channel One program. . . .

Buoyed by its $102 million in gross annual revenues from Channel One, Whittle Communications is looking for ways to expand. About nine months ago Whittle unveiled a plan [the Edison Project] to "invent," build and open 200 private schools by 1996. His plan resembles the Education Department's original proposal to create some 535 experimental schools by the same year. Referring to his "new American schools," Whittle even echoes some of the rhetoric used by the Bush Administration in its "America 2000" education goals, announced about the same time. . . . Whittle estimates that $2.5 billion to $3 billion will be required to put his first 200 schools into operation. By the year 2010, there could be 1,000 campuses. . . .

As for Whittle's relationship with the Bush Administration, it is cozy. Although not a partner in Whittle Communications, Lamar Alexander,

for scientists and engineers have fallen dramatically. Is it possible that industrialists had this outcome in mind when they issued their complaints?

This does not mean that all advocates for policies that would harm public schools have hidden selfish motives. On the contrary, some announce their selfish motives openly. Such is often the case, for example, in arguments for vouchers made by representatives of private, sectarian schools. People making these arguments may be quite open about the benefits that vouchers would provide their constituents; indeed, they often suggest how "unfair" it is that parents whose children attend private schools should have to pay both public-school taxes and private-school tuition. Voucher programs, they argue, would merely rectify an "injustice"—an argument which suggests that rationalizations for private interests are by no means confined to the rich.

> Bush's top education official, has, in his own words, been "a good close friend for twenty years" of Chris Whittle. . . . .Conservative educational theorists and business leaders are important influences on Whittle and Alexander. For example, Chester Finn Jr. . . . who served in the Nixon White House and later was a top policy-maker at the Education Department under Reagan, is also an old friend of Alexander's [who] "worked very closely" with Alexander on America 2000, [and was subsequently hired by Whittle to work on the Edison Project]. . . .
>
> Alexander himself was on the Whittle advisory board that guided Channel One and worked for Whittle after leaving the [Tennessee] governorship in 1987. His compensation was $125,000 in consulting fees plus the opportunity to buy four shares of Whittle stock, for which he wrote a $10,000 check, according to the *Wall Street Journal*. . . . At the end of 1988, Whittle bought back the stock for $330,000, giving the Alexanders a hefty profit. . . .
>
> After his nomination as Secretary of Education, Alexander asked Whittle [and other business leaders] for their advice. In a series of meetings, three of which Whittle attended, the proposals that became America 2000 were mapped out, along with a voucher system [that would support private schools], according to one participant.
>
> [Then,] after his confirmation, Alexander sold his home in Knoxville, Tennessee, for $977,500. He had paid $570,000 for it about a year before. The buyer was Gerald Hogan, a top executive of Whittle Communications. Hogan received a mortgage of $780,000 from the First Tennessee Bank. Alexander was on the board of the bank's holding company until he became Secretary of Education. Whittle is still on the board. . . .
>
> The Whittle-Alexander connection symbolizes the new alliance between business and government to exploit the educational system. . . . Whittle sees nothing wrong in this: "Is there an inherent conflict between profits and education? No way. The biggest contribution business can make to education is to make education a business."
>
> —John S. Friedman (1992).

We don't want to suggest that all criticisms of education or proposals for reforming public schools are motivated by crass, selfish interests. Indeed, some criticism of education comes from people with genuine concern for the problems faced by our schools and are focused on the parts of education that clearly need fixing. But some school bashing certainly seems to reflect the special interests of the critics themselves; friends or business interests of the critics; or the ideological, racial, ethnic, religious, or class interests that critics represent. Such possibilities should alert us all to read criticism of the public schools with a healthy dose of skepticism.

American Individualism and the Powers of Education

The cool, disinterested judgment of thousands of investigators shows that success or failure lies within the person himself [sic] rather than with outside conditions.

—An early twentieth-century business analyst (quoted in Wyllie, 1954, pp. 32–33)

Since many people have criticized American education over the years, it seems likely that this criticism also reflects beliefs, expectations, and myths that are widely shared in American society.

One such myth concerns individual efficacy and the powers of education. Americans tend to assume that most social outcomes are generated by the characteristics of individuals—rather than, say, by unfair laws, structural forces in the society, industrial greed, accidents, or divine intervention. And we also believe that schools are given broad responsibility for molding individuals so that they are more likely to experience positive outcomes. This is all very well, but what happens when social outcomes are negative? And what happens when, as in the past twenty years, social problems escalate in America? What happens when American industries lose out to foreign competitors, when more and more people lose their jobs, when crime rates soar, when the country must deal with high rates of violence and drug addiction, when the divorce rate shoots up, or when Americans suffer in increasing numbers from sexually transmitted diseases? By extension of the above logic, the individuals experiencing those social problems are (obviously) responsible for their fates, the schools those individuals attended have (obviously) failed in their missions, and those schools should be brought to account.

Let's decompose this argument into its constituent beliefs. The first is *the myth of individual efficacy*. Almost since the country's founding, Americans have shared a tenacious belief that individuals in this country are largely responsible for their own outcomes, their own successes or failures. Thus, defying all odds, the person with enough skills and energy, and right attitude can succeed. And the person who fails does so because of factors that he or she might have controlled.[40] Robert Reich provides a good description of this myth in his "American morality tale of the Triumphant Individual":

> This is the story of the little guy who works hard, takes risks, believes in himself, and eventually earns wealth, fame, and honor. It's the parable of the self-made man (or, more recently, woman) who bucks the odds, spurns the naysayers, and shows what can be done with enough drive and guts. . . . The theme recurs in the tale of Abe Lincoln, log splitter from Illinois who goes to the White House; in the hundred or so novellas of Horatio Alger, whose heroes all rise promptly and predictably from rags to riches. . . ; and in the American morality tales of the underdog who eventually makes it, showing up the bosses and bullies who try to put him down; think of *Rocky* or *Iacocca*. Regardless of the precise form, the moral is the same: With enough guts and gumption, anyone can make it on their own in America.[41]

As Reich suggests, Americans often tell one another versions of the myth of individual efficacy and assume that such tales have the effect of encouraging individual accomplishment.

Evidence also confirms American acceptance of the individualism myth. James Kluegel and Eliot Smith reported data from a 1980 national survey of Americans' beliefs about economic inequality.[42] Respondents were asked to rate the importance of various causes of wealth and poverty, some focused on the individual, some focused on circumstances. Exhibit 4.2 gives the percentages of respondents who said that each of the listed conditions was a "very important" cause for poverty. As can be seen, only three causes were thought to be "very important" by a majority of respondents, and those three were *all* associated with the individual. (Similar results were reported for causes of wealth.) What this suggests is that in 1980, most Americans assumed that the *individual* was largely responsible if he or she became poor—despite years of media coverage indicating that American poverty is often a result of involuntary unemployment, substandard wages, medical emergencies, family crises, or other circumstances beyond individual control.

Why do Americans embrace the myth of individual efficacy? Commentators suggest that this tendency is rooted in both American political history and in the weak structure of American institutions, which provide fewer "safety nets" than are provided in other Western countries. At the same time, the numbers suggest that acceptance of the individualism myth is by no means universal. Kluegel and Smith also looked at which Americans were most and least likely to endorse the myth, and—lo—they found that beliefs about individual efficacy were weaker among people who were most likely to have experienced economic failure or discrimination—namely, those who were young, black, female, impoverished, or from poorer sections of the country. The researchers commented, "The picture of the prototypical believer in the [myth of individualism that] emerges quite clearly and, perhaps not coinci-

Exhibit 4.2   Percentage of Americans Stating That Each Condition Is a Very Important Cause of Poverty

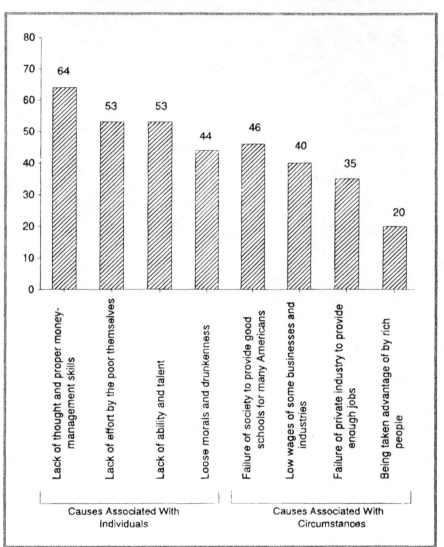

—Source: Kluegel & Smith (*Beliefs About Inequality: Americans' Views of What Is and What Ought to Be,* 1986, Table 4.2, p. 79).

dentally, resembles Ronald Reagan: an older, white, male, Westerner with a relatively high income."[43]

If the commentators are right, the myth of individual efficacy is preeminently American, and evidence is also available confirming that the myth is weaker in other countries. In an ingenious study, P. S. Fry and Ratna Ghosh asked leading academics (namely, those who had received Fulbright grants) in the United States and India to explain their professional successes and found that the Indians were *far* more likely to stress circumstantial causes such as family ties and luck.[44] Somehow, readers may not be surprised to learn that belief in individualism is lower in India than in the United States—indeed, such an effect has also been reported by other researchers[45]—but what about comparisons between the United States and other Western countries? A good answer to this question has come from research comparing Australia and the United States. An early study of American myths about poverty was reported in 1972 by Joe R. Feagin, and, two years later, Norman Feather published comparative findings suggesting that Australians were less likely to blame the poor for their poverty.[46] Moreover, in 1985 one of us collected data about the causes of poverty from matched samples from the United States and Australia and found that Australians gave much lower ratings than did Americans to individual causes, and much higher ratings to circumstantial causes.[47]

To summarize then, evidence suggests that many Americans embrace the myth of individual efficacy, that belief in this myth is somewhat less in other countries, and that belief in the myth is stronger among Americans who are rich and powerful. At best, the myth of individualism serves to motivate effort in America, but unfortunately, it also tends to discourage compassion and support programs for those who fail. Indeed, the myth is often cited by reactionary politicians in our country as an excuse for reducing public support for the poor and needy.

But what about the second part of our argument, beliefs about the responsibilities of schools for molding students? Earlier, we suggested that sharply different instructional tasks may be proposed for American schools by specific groups. (Compare, for example, demands from the Religious Right that the schools teach "creation science," requests by Neoconservatives that schools stress basic academic subjects, or proposals by Human Capital advocates that schools offer curricula for specific technologies.) Most analysts, however, also suggest that Americans tend to agree on a broad core of instructional tasks that schools should stress. A good discussion of these agreed-upon tasks recently appeared in *The Way Schools Work* by Kathleen Bennett de Marrais and Margaret LeCompte, and we reproduce the tasks they list as Exhibit 4.3.

One can argue with the specific tasks appearing in such lists, of course. (To illustrate, aesthetic interests and motor skills do not appear in it.) But the basic point is that American schools are given responsibility for a *broad range* of instructional tasks that can help students achieve success and avoid failure. Thus, if we accept the Bennett de Marrais and LeCompte list, we see

■ EXHIBIT 4.3

Instructional Tasks for Schools in America

Kathleen Bennett de Marrais and Margaret LeCompte suggest that "commonly held or conventional wisdom" has it that American schools are expected to accomplish four types of instructional tasks—intellectual, political, economic, and social.

Intellectual Tasks

1. To assist students in the acquisition of cognitive skills (reading, mathematics, etc.)
2. To assist students in the acquisition of substantive knowledge
3. To assist students in the acquisition of inquiry skills (evaluation, synthesis, etc.)

Political Tasks

1. To educate future citizens for appropriate participation in the given political order
2. To promote patriotism by teaching myths, history, and stories about the country, its leaders and government
3. To promote the assimilation of immigrants
4. To assure order, public civility, and conformity to laws

Economic Tasks

1. To prepare students for later work roles
2. To select and train the labor force

Social Tasks

1. To promote a sense of social and moral responsibility in people
2. To serve as sites for the solution or amelioration of social problems
3. To supplement the efforts of other institutions of socialization, such as the family and the church

—Adapted from Kathleen Bennett de Marrais and Margaret LeCompte (*The Way Schools Work: A Sociological Analysis of Education*, Second Edition, 1995, pp. 9–13).

that Americans believe that schools can and should assist students in intellectual tasks AND political tasks AND economic tasks AND social tasks. This does not mean that American schools can actually *accomplish* such a wide range of tasks, of course. (Indeed, evidence concerning the accomplishment of many of these tasks is, at best, skimpy.) But Americans tend to share a wide range of beliefs about the potential *ability* of their schools to do a great deal.

Let us call such beliefs *the myth of unbounded instructional responsibility*. Is there any evidence to back up the notion that Americans embrace this myth? Indeed there is. Look again at Exhibit 4.2. Of the four causes for poverty associated with circumstances, the cause involving *schools* received the highest rating for importance, which means that in 1980 Americans judged *schools* to have more of an effect on poverty than low wages, lack of jobs, or being taken advantage of by the rich. Moreover, a wide range of other studies have also reported that Americans hold broad expectations for the ability of schools to help students accomplish many goals in life.

Why should Americans hold such broad expectations for schools? Perhaps it is because they reflect a history of educational advocacy by influential Americans, ranging from Thomas Jefferson to Horace Mann, Edward A. Ross, John Dewey, and others who have argued that schools should be viewed as coming to replace the church, family, and community as the *primary* institution for socializing young people, thus solving a broad range of social problems in the country. Moreover, America's broad expectations for schools contrast with narrower expectations that have generally evolved in other Western countries.

American educators and their supporters have also generally embraced the myths of individual efficacy and unbounded instructional responsibility. Such myths flatter the public schools and may (it is hoped) promote additional financial support for education. But when educators embrace such myths they also make schools more vulnerable to criticism. Many social problems worsened during the past two decades in America, and if Americans believe (a) that the individuals who suffer from those problems are personally responsible for them, and (b) that the schools they attended had the ability, but failed, to educate those people for better conduct, the fat is indeed in the fire. How many times recently have you heard or read one or more of the following complaints?

- Because schools have provided sex education courses—or, sometimes, have *failed* to provide sex education courses(!)—young people are more promiscuous, teenage pregnancy rates have soared, and we suffer from the AIDS epidemic

- Because schools have failed, too many Americans are illiterate, lack basic mathematical skill, are ignorant of geography, or cannot write or spell correctly

- Because schools have failed, Americans do not vote, cannot name their senators, tolerate urban corruption, and know less about the history of their country than people do elsewhere

- Because American schools have failed, gangs of youth roam the streets, drug use has soared, and urban violence dominates our cities

- Because American schools have failed, American youths lack the work ethic, Christian values, concern for the environment, the habit of thrift, and respect for the flag
- Because schools have failed, the American economy is currently deteriorating—indeed, "our educational system is failing miserably to prepare young people for today's competitive world."[48]

Thus, beliefs in the myths of individual efficacy and unbounded instructional responsibility can become a major force generating criticism of public schools when, as in recent years, social problems are getting worse in America. Unfortunately, American educators have often been guilty of "selling" both of these myths. And the selling of myths can be dangerous.

The Use, Misuse, and Abuse of Evidence

Why all the fuss, then? How, if at all, did the criticisms of the 1980s differ from those that had come before? I believe that they differed in three important ways: they were more vigorous and pervasive; they were putatively buttressed by data from cross-national studies of educational achievement; and, coming at a time when Americans seemed to be feeling anxious about their place in the world, they gave every indication of being potentially more dangerous and destructive.

—Lawrence Cremin (*Popular Education and Its Discontents*, 1990, pp. 6–7)

We turn finally to a factor that sharply increased the force of recent criticisms. As never before, those criticisms were often bolstered by claims of *evidence*—by supposed findings from national surveys and cross-cultural and historical research—that seemed to point to shortcomings in American education. Whereas authors in the past could only cite anecdotes or personal opinions to back their criticisms of education, critics in the 1980s were able to draw on a host of "negative" findings from massive studies that apparently confirmed the poor performance of American schools.

Such negative findings seem to have played two roles in critical thinking about education. In some cases, particularly in the early 1980s, specific negative findings were apparently unexpected. These seem to have been accepted without question by critics, and became, in effect, a force that helped to generate sincere concern about American schools. More recently, however, ideologically driven criticism of the schools has grown more strident, and negative findings known to be questionable or wrong are now being cited in that criticism—findings that are often drawn from unidentified or secondary sources, and are used as ritualized support for lambasting education.[49]

Simplistic Analyses. As we have made clear, most of these apparently negative findings about school effects are chimerical. Or, to quote *The Sandia Report,* "much of the nonproductive rhetoric surrounding education today is based on improper use of simplistic data."[50] American education faces structural problems that are unique in the Western world, and American schools today serve the needs of students from a very broad range of ethnic, social class, and economic backgrounds. And once these factors are taken into account, it turns out that American schools today are actually doing quite well. This fact illustrates the first of several points we want to make about the misuse of evidence.

Let us assume that one is shown a simple graph, table, or statistic from survey data showing that student achievement in America is lower than student achievement in other countries. Does this mean that inadequacies in American schools "caused" this result? To jump to this conclusion is tempting but unwise, since other forces could easily have produced such a result.

To understand how this can happen, consider the effects of poverty on student achievement. Many, many studies have shown that impoverished students do badly in school. Moreover, a *much* larger proportion of students live in poverty in the United States than in other Western countries. (This dismal fact may surprise some readers; data confirming it are given in Chapter 6.) Taken together, these two facts mean that if one compares only the simple, aggregated achievement scores of students in Western nations, the United States is bound to look bad simply because it has to contend with more student poverty.

How, then, does one estimate the *true* effects of American schools on student achievement in multinational studies? To do this, in the analysis one must control for the effects of other crucial factors that are also related to achievement, such as student poverty. This can be done in various ways. Sometimes the analyst will construct a graph or table showing disaggregated levels of achievement for students who are and who are not impoverished in the countries compared. On other occasions the analyst may use complex statistical techniques (such as "regression analysis") that allow one to estimate the independent impact of several different factors—such as nationality and student poverty—that have concurrent effects on school achievement. Regardless of the technique used, when one conducts an analysis that also controls for the effects of other crucial factors, one may discover surprising things about national differences in school achievement. Sometimes the apparent national differences that appeared in simplistic analyses are increased; sometimes they are reduced sharply; sometimes they are even reversed!

This suggests a general point that we shall call the "Principle of Control," which states that to estimate the true effect of a factor using survey data one MUST control, in the analysis, for the effects of other crucial factors that can affect the relationship. Trained data analysts are very aware of this principle—indeed, it is one of the first things taught in courses on statistics. Moreover, the general public is also coming to understand the principle. Consider, for example, the many demands people have made to apply controls in studies of the effects of tobacco smoking on lung cancer.

But why then have so many critics been willing to quote simplistic "negative" findings as if they indicated the true effects of American schools? It seems possible that early critics were actually ignorant of the "Principle of Control," that a decade or two ago they may have thought that simple interpretations of aggregate survey findings were justified. That was then, but today is now, and good analyses, involving controls, are now available that examine the impact of schools on achievement—see Chapter 2. Most of these analyses suggest that the original dismal portrayal of American schools suggested by simplistic findings was *wrong*—when appropriate controls are applied, American schools look quite good in both cross-cultural and historical studies. Therefore, it is now less tenable to argue that the critics are simply ignorant. (Is it possible that they cling to simple, negative, aggregate findings because they don't like to admit error and want to continue bashing the schools?)

Liars, Damn Liars, and Statisticians. Violations of the "Principle of Control" are certainly serious, but alas, other techniques are also available for those interested in misusing evidence. Another example is provided by the work of Chubb and Moe that we discussed in Chapter 3.[51] To recapitulate the Chubb and Moe technique, their text claims that the educational programs of private schools generate higher levels of achievement than do those of public schools and implies that this claim was supported by their analyses of survey data. But in their analyses they did *not* provide findings comparing the net effects of public and private schools in a single, controlled analysis. Instead, they strung together several analyses (using different controls) which showed that, by comparison, private schools were more likely to have certain characteristics, and that those characteristics were, in turn, associated with achievement. Such procedures are statistical voodoo, and it seems likely that Chubb and Moe knew this was the case.

Other examples where textual claims are not backed up by the evidence cited are also easy to find. Consider, for example, *National Excellence: A Case for Developing America's Talent,* a document released in late 1993 by the U.S. Department of Education. This document advocates spending more for the education of talented students, "reviews" evidence concerning the issue, and makes various claims concerning the treatment of talented students in American schools. One of its claims states that

> Compared with top students in other industrialized countries, American students perform poorly on international tests, are offered a less rigorous curriculum, read fewer demanding books, do less homework, and enter the work force or postsecondary education less well prepared.[52]

This sounds as if data are available comparing the treatment and achieve ments of equivalently defined groups of "talented" students in various countries, but NO such data are reviewed in *National Excellence*. Instead, the authors of this work merely recapitulated the standard, misleading, aggregate evidence from studies comparing the total range of students in the educational systems of different countries. Thus, their claims were not matched by the evidence they cited, and we know of at least one well-meaning commentator who was bamboozled by those claims.[53]

Evidence should always be matched to results that are claimed in textual materials, and researchers or reviewers are culpable when they do not conform to this tenet, which we shall call the "Principle of Honest Claims." Unfortunately, many lay persons are either frightened or bored by statistical evidence, tables, graphs, or study details. When such people read research reports, they have few options other than to swallow whole hog the textual claims that those reports make. Needless to say, this is unwise. Most educational researchers and reviewers are also advocates for something-or-other—just as we clearly are—and sometimes the claims they make are driven more by wishful thinking or expediency than by honesty. (And for this reason, although we have tried to honor the "Principle of Honest Claims," readers should also look closely at the evidence *we* cite to back *our* assertions.) Viable plans for improving education are more likely to evolve when *honest* claims are made; and to monitor those claims, people must be prepared to grit their teeth, screw up their courage, and *look* at the evidence cited by investigators.

Confusing Science and News. A more subtle problem appears in the way in which empirical results are sometimes reported. As we noted in Chapter 3, on two different occasions James Coleman and assorted colleagues announced early conclusions to the press, based on massive survey evidence, that were damaging to public education.[54] In neither case had these conclusions been given peer review. On both occasions the conclusions had been generated by questionable techniques, and subsequent reanalyses of the data have generated findings that contradicted those of Coleman and his associates. But in each case the early, questionable conclusions set the tone for subsequent debates, and critics to this day continue to cite both sets of early conclusions as if they were gospel.

Great mischief can result when investigators trumpet premature, poorly reviewed, biased conclusions to the press in the name of research evidence. To do so violates a tenet we shall call the "Principle of Responsible Publicity." Although violations of this principle are easy to find for research on schooling and its effects, they are by no means confined to education. An egregious violation appeared recently, for example, when two investigators at the University of Utah, B. Stanley Pons and Martin Fleischmann, called a press conference in which they claimed to have found evidence for cold fusion.[55] The research conducted by the Utah group had *not* been given peer review—indeed, the researchers had not at that time submitted even a single report of their research to colleagues. But their premature claims were embraced by the gullible media, and those media reports quickly generated millions of promised dollars for research support from foundations and the Utah state legislature, as well as scores of time-consuming research projects in other laboratories trying (in vain) to replicate the Utah results.

As this example suggests, irresponsible publicity about research in the physical and biological sciences can waste dollars and the efforts of other researchers, but such irresponsibility is even more serious when it comes to education. Indeed, unwise policy decisions that affect the lives of thousands of students are *still* being made by people who cite the erroneous early findings of the 1966 Coleman Report. How can people guard against such irresponsibility? They can do so in several ways: by being skeptical, by being aware that some researchers will be tempted to violate the "Principle of Responsible Publicity," by remembering that unimpeachable results simply cannot be obtained by a single study, by checking the fit between claimed results and study evidence, by refusing to give credence to announced results unless those results have been given responsible peer review. Such strategies will not throttle all premature research publicity, of course, but they will help to blunt the damage that such publicity can otherwise cause.

Propaganda, Dissimulation, and Research. Yet another strategy for misusing evidence appeared in *What Works: Research About Teaching and Learning.*[56] This sixty-five-page publication, reportedly an unbiased review of research findings, was released amidst much fanfare by the U.S. Department of Education in January of 1986, complete with a foreword by Secretary William Bennett and a dedication by President Ronald Reagan. By midsummer of that year, over three hundred thousand copies were in circulation, according to a departmental news release. Moreover, the document was received warmly by many lay people and investigators, who were impressed that, at long last, "important personages" had something good to say about educational research.

Sounds promising, doesn't it? But let's look more closely at *What Works.* After an introduction by Assistant Secretary Chester Finn (the primary developer of the work), the bulk of the publication consisted of a set of snappy, one-page summaries of research "findings" that were expressed and interpreted so that they appeared to be extensions of "common sense." Many of these summaries were also set off by quotations from "distinguished thinkers" of bygone years, implying that the "findings" were mere confirmations of revered wisdom. In addition, the "findings" chosen were focused almost entirely on the impact of teachers or parents on pupil achievement and papered over major debates in the research literature.

All of these ploys were deliberate. In his dedication to *What Works,* President Reagan wrote of his hope that through "renewed trust in common sense, we Americans will have even greater success in our unstinting efforts to improve our schools," and in his foreword Secretary Bennett stated,

> Most readers will, I think, judge that most of the evidence in this volume confirms common sense. So be it. Given the abuse that common sense has taken in recent decades, particularly in the theory and practice of education, it is no small contribution if research can play a role in bringing more of it to American education.[57]

And in his introduction, Assistant Secretary Finn said, "In this volume . . . we draw upon the knowledge and opinions both of modern scholars and of distinguished thinkers of earlier times."[58]

Regarding the narrow focus of *What Works*, Assistant Secretary Finn acknowledged that its coverage was not "comprehensive" but suggested that materials left out reflected topics for which "not much formal research has yet been done, or that which has been done is fragmentary, inconclusive, or hotly disputed."[59] This assertion no doubt "impressed" the hundreds of authors of (totally ignored) studies on computer-assisted instruction, for which major summary articles had already appeared, or the many, many researchers who had generated well-established (but equally ignored) findings for the effects of school and community characteristics on pupil achievement. Moreover, the summaries also slighted serious debates then underway about findings concerning the effects of teachers and parents.[60]

Far from being unbiased, then, *What Works* was in fact a clever piece of propaganda—disguised as a review of research—that was designed to further the initial educational goals of the Reagan administration. What were those goals? As we noted earlier, they were generally those of the Far Right. Thus, in his 1987 review of *What Works*, Gene Glass observed,

> The political goals of *What Works* are those of the administration that produced it: to disestablish the federal bureaucracy in education, to decentralize control over education, to deregulate the practice of schooling, and to diminish financial support for schools. *What Works* seeks to further these goals by (a) arguing that the results of educational research merely confirm what has already been apprehended by common sense or revealed in the works of great thinkers, and (b) maintaining that the only needed reform in schooling is a change in the ethos of the school and classroom—a change in the way teachers and parents think about and act toward children—not a change in the level of resources invested in education. . . . [Moreover,] if, as *What Works* argues, the findings of educational research are "common sense," then the apparatus of federal support for educational research that has grown up since 1956 . . . is unnecessary.[61]

It would be disingenuous to slight *What Works* alone for biased reviewing. Virtually all works of advocacy tend to cite studies that support, and ignore those that contradict, their arguments. But honest authors explain their agenda so that readers can take the authors' biases into account when assessing their research evidence. *What Works* was culpable because it hid its intentions and pretended to be something other than a piece of propaganda. It thus violated a tenet that we shall call the "Principle of Open Advocacy." Moreover, a lot of well-meaning people were taken in by its pretenses.

Suppressing Evidence. Given that people in the Reagan and Bush administrations were willing to misuse evidence to further an agenda hostile to public education, we should not be surprised to learn that the same people were also willing to suppress evidence when that evidence contradicted their ideas. We discuss two instances where this was done systematically.

Our first example occurred during the later years of the Reagan administration and involved the National Science Foundation—of all agencies. The NSF has always portrayed itself as committed to good evidence, impeccable analysis, peer review, and honest dealing—all absolutely required in an organization dedicated to supporting scientific research in the national interest.

Despite these principles, in 1985 an employee of the NSF prepared a badly flawed study suggesting that since the number of twenty-two-year-olds in the population was declining, the nation's supply of scientists and engineers would soon suffer a serious "shortfall." This study had many defects. Among others, it provided no information at all about likely demands for scientists and engineers; thus its projection of a "shortfall" tacitly assumed that demands for their skills would remain constant. (For obvious reasons, *responsible* labor-force studies make estimates for both supply and demand.) These defects were well known in the NSF. Indeed, from the beginning the 1985 study had been roundly criticized by others in the agency.

Despite its defects, this study became the basis for a vigorous campaign and scores of speeches by the Director of the NSF, Erich Bloch, who argued that the nation faced a serious "crisis" and had to step up its production of scientists and engineers. Endless versions of the 1985 study were prepared, and these were circulated widely by NSF officials. Outside peer reviews of the study were assiduously avoided, and contradicting data were ignored or suppressed. Eventually, however, the chickens came home to roost. When the predicted "shortfall" of scientists and engineers failed to materialize, the NSF came under attack. Finally, in April of 1992, the NSF was called upon to explain its actions in a congressional inquiry. Howard Wolpe, chair of the subcommittee which conducted the inquiry, wrote a marvelous summary of the NSF story that we have abridged as Exhibit 4.4.

Not only had the NSF conducted a flawed study, but it had trumpeted the conclusions of that study widely, ignoring and suppressing contradictory evidence, in order to promote the idea that America was facing a serious "shortfall" of scientists and engineers. Why on earth did NSF officials try to sell this false notion to Americans? Howard Wolpe suggested that this action was motivated largely by desires to increase the NSF budget. Perhaps. It is also true that industrialists who embrace the Human Capital ideology were then complaining loudly about the need to train additional scientists and engineers—a need that, if met, would also mean they could hire qualified professionals for a lot less money. Is it possible that officials of the Reagan administration wanted to help those industrialists?

Unfortunately, this was not the only occasion when evidence about education was suppressed during the Reagan and Bush years. Our second example concerns *The Sandia Report*,[62] which we have described in earlier chapters. This report, initially prepared in 1990 by officials of the Sandia National Laboratories, a component of the U.S. Department of Energy, documents a careful analysis of the status of American education. Major findings in *The Sandia Report* flatly contradicted claims about education that were then being

---

■ Exhibit 4.4
How Good Are the Numbers?

The subcommittee will come to order. Good morning. . . .

In 1985 the Policy and Research Analysis Division, or PRA, of the National Science Foundation began to work on a demographically based study projecting a shortfall of 692,000 bachelor's degrees in natural science and engineering. The study was a deceptively simple one. It held that, as the participation rate of 22-year-olds in natural science and engineering degrees had been stable for a decade, and the number of 22-year-olds was dropping, there would be a shortfall of degrees.

In 1986 the then director of the Foundation took that number to Congress and started the shortfall ball rolling in his fiscal year 1987 budget testimony. In 1987 PRA furthered it by publishing and distributing to over a thousand people a "draft" of the study. It had never been peer reviewed or given any other type of serious methodological review before its release. Because of the confusing and interchangeable use of the words "shortfall," "shortage," and "scarcity," and discussions by Foundation officials of supply and demand, many members of Congress, academic institutions, the media, and the public became convinced fewer degrees meant that a real shortage of workers was looming, and government intervention in the form of increased financial support for science and engineering education was necessary.

At least 10 other drafts were produced and distributed between 1988–90 with varying numbers and years of shortfalls. They became known as NSF's "underground literature" with different people possessing different drafts. PRA settled on a constant number of 675,000, but, strangely enough, the years charted changed from report to report without any change in that number. This was relatively easy to do, as the report contained no statement of methodology, data points, lists of assumptions, or bibliography.

From the very beginning, labor economists and statisticians, including those inside the Foundation, scoffed at the methodology as seriously flawed, pointing out that new graduates were only one part of supply. . . , that it was not useful to look at supply without looking at demand, and that the market was very flexible in adjusting to demand. The Foundation's statistical unit

(continued on next page)

peddled by President Bush and others in his administration, so the report was squelched.

How this was done is largely told by Daniel Tanner,[63] and we draw much of our story from his account. By early 1990 George Bush had announced his intention to become "the education president." Since this goal involved overhauling the supposed shortcomings of schools, officials in his administration were motivated to help by gathering supportive evidence. To this end, James Watkins, then secretary of energy, made the "tragic mistake" of instructing the Sandia National Laboratories, a former wing of the Atomic

found that the "stable" participation rate wasn't stable. However, the study, through its repeated use in speeches and testimony by the Foundation's director, university administrators, and members of Congress, and countless articles and news stories, took on a life of its own that was slowed only when the engineering community publicly attacked it in late 1990. . . . Even today, the study's echoes still are heard in news stories and halls of Capitol Hill. Senator Danforth cited it in discussing the NASA authorization bill last year; *Fortune* Magazine referred to it just last month. . . .

The purpose of this hearing is to review how a study so flawed survived for so long in the Nation's premier scientific agency. The subcommittee's investigation has revealed that valid criticism was ignored and even suppressed within the Foundation. A $3000 internal, peer review report was deep-sixed in 1989. The Foundation's statistical unit, which is charged with providing information about scientific and technical personnel resources to the Administration and the Congress, never agreed with these numbers, but its objections and its work were ignored by NSF officials. . . . Although the Foundation claimed in a letter to me that the 1987 draft had been reviewed, when GAO contacted the reviewers, it found that none of them had conducted a review beyond casual conversations in the hallway.

In 1991, after the study was ridiculed publicly—and the already four-year-old projected shortfall/shortage showed no signs of materializing—the NSF quietly buried the study and removed the 675,000 number from its lexicon. The new head of the planning office admitted to us that a study of supply without demand was not "very useful." But the NSF has never publicly repudiated the study or the manner in which it was used. And as far as we can tell, it has taken no steps to prevent a recurrence. An advisory committee that recommended that publicly released policy work be peer reviewed was unceremoniously scrapped last fall during the NSF reorganization. Regrettably, there is as yet little evidence to indicate that the NSF is particularly concerned about the repercussions the study has had on the Foundation's reputation or the structural weaknesses that allowed this terribly flawed work product to be given wholly undeserved legitimacy.

—Rep. Howard Wolpe (opening statement made by its Chairman to a Hearing before the Subcommittee on Investigations and Oversight of the Committee on Science, Space, and Technology, U.S. House of Representatives, 1992).

Energy Commission, to undertake a comprehensive study of the status of American education. (Sandia had previously done some research on higher education, and it was also hoped that the study would allow Sandia to plan future activities relevant to primary and secondary schools.)

The study itself drew from existing data sources and was originally drafted in late 1990. It was then circulated among various educators and researchers for comment, and it became the subject of briefings in the Department of Education and a congressional hearing in the summer of 1991. Alarmingly (to supporters of President Bush), many of its findings flatly contradicted claims then being made by administration officials, claims that eventually undergirded Bush's education initiative, America 2000. This led officials in the Department of Education and others in the administration to demand that *The Sandia Report not* be released but instead that it be subjected to unprecedented reviews by minions of the National Center for Education Statistics and the National Science Foundation. (Ironically the task of reviewing in the NSF seems to have been assigned to the same person who had earlier prepared the flawed 1985 study, which predicted the nonexistent "shortfall" of scientists and engineers!)

These reviews were conducted, the reviewers dutifully detected trivial "flaws" in the report, and it was recommended that the report not be released but that it be rewritten and subjected to further reviews. Following these recommendations, the report *was* rewritten and was subjected to more internal review, further demands for rewriting, and even an audit by the General Accounting Office[64]—all of which effectively prevented timely release of the report.

But America is a wonderful land, where photocopying machines abound, and within a few months scores of draft copies of the report had been "leaked" and were floating around the country. A condensed version of the report was then printed by the *Albuquerque Journal* on September 24, 1991. As Daniel Tanner explains, this "prompted Secretary Watkins to issue an immediate response, . . . dated 30 September, [which] opened with this sentence: 'The Sandia National Laboratories study, "Perspectives on Education in America," reported in your September 24 issue is dead wrong.'"[65] Finally, the report itself eventually appeared in the *Journal of Educational Research*—without fanfare, without even a listing of its authors!—after George Bush had been voted out of office. To our knowledge, no former official of the Bush administration has as yet publicly acknowledged that, in view of Sandia report evidence, some claims about "the education crisis" or plans outlined in America 2000 might have to be modified.

The trouble with suppressing evidence is that it leads to policy errors that can ruin people's lives. Thus, when the National Science Foundation suppressed the truth about America's production of scientists and engineers, the federal government increased its support for training in these fields, and *hundreds* of America's scientists and engineers now cannot find jobs.[66] More-over, a host of well-known, well-intentioned Americans have been deceived by the nonsense that a shortage of scientists and engineers is impending. In 1993, for example, the American Psychological Association published a vol-ume detailing how psychologists could help to solve the "looming" shortage of scientists and engineers. As we noted in Chapter 3, this book began with a foreword by Charles Spielberger, then president of the association, which referred to "predicted catastrophic shortfalls by the turn of the century" in the supply of scientists, engineers, and technicians.[67] And many similar quotes could be cited from other academics, university administrators, and political leaders from across the nation. Seldom have so many well-intentioned people been so seriously misled by their government!

And when the Bush administration suppressed *The Sandia Report,* it al-lowed lies to be repeated that scapegoated educators and prompted actions that have harmed American schools. Moreover, lies are hard to defeat. Most Americans do not know today that much of the Bush rhetoric about education was effectively contradicted by *The Sandia Report,* which was originally drafted in 1990, and good-hearted people are still being asked to consider tragic policy proposals that follow from those uncontested lies.

These two episodes, then, involved violation of one of the most basic of all tenets concerning evidence, which we shall call the "Principle of Open and Honest Reporting." One absolute condition of democracy is that citizens have access to relevant information, and this condition is violated when gov-ernments suppress evidence. These two episodes were not the only cases of suppression of evidence by American governments, of course. (As we write, Americans are just beginning to discover how often they were lied to about "experiments" that involved dosing unwitting victims with massive amounts of radiation. Somewhere down this road one finds totalitarianism and the Nazi death camps.) But, to the best of our knowledge, prior to the Reagan and Bush administrations, *no* American government had ever suppressed evidence about primary and secondary education. And it is difficult to under-stand how the public can make effective decisions about education—or any other concern, for that matter—unless it has full access to the facts.

Press Irresponsibility. For better or worse, citizens in a modern urban society depend strongly on the mass media for much of their information. When they tune to network news programs or read the front page of their daily newspapers, they expect to find accurate accounts of newsworthy events. Unfortunately, that expectation is not always met. Sadly, news media are not generally rewarded for documenting "the truth, the whole truth, and nothing but the truth." Rather, they frequently earn their Nielsen ratings or circulation figures by pandering to public fascination with catastrophe, exaggeration, human-interest stories, and superficial reporting. Germs of truth are present in news stories, of course, but it is often difficult to separate the truth from the "chaff."

The media seem to have particular difficulty when it comes to reports of research. Some of the nation's more "responsible" newspapers—such as the *New York Times* or the *Washington Post*—will prepare stories that report not only research findings but also study details, potential problems with research claims, and the identities of investigators.[68] But this information is often stripped away in wire-service accounts or secondary reports that appear in network news programs or local newspapers. Thus, what the majority of Americans learn is only that "research shows . . . " or "a study has found . . . " something or other. This converts a tentative and questionable conclusion into "certain knowledge." Moreover, since the media feed off one another extensively, the most attractive or hysterical bits of "certain knowledge" associated with research spread like wildfire.

We could cite many examples of how this kind of media irresponsibility has hurt education, but we describe only three here. Our first example concerns press treatment of *A Nation At Risk*. As we have noted, this document made many charges about recent "declines" in the achievement of American students and about how "poorly" those students were supposedly doing in international comparisons. These charges were all said to be based on evidence, yet *not one study* was cited in the document to support those charges. By itself, this is not too surprising. Propaganda pieces often make unsupportable claims for which no citations are provided, and responsible journalists will either ignore such works or discuss their evidentiary shortcomings. But this kind of careful treatment was *not* given to *A Nation At Risk*. Instead, this document was reported in literally hundreds of newspaper and television accounts across the nation, and as far as we can tell, *none* of those reports noted its lack of citations or called for documentation of its incendiary charges. (In this case, even the "responsible" newspapers seemed to have been mesmerized by the prestigious creators of *A Nation At Risk* and did not notice its shortcomings.) As a result, the public was led to believe that the claims it made were unimpeachable.

Our second example concerns media reports of Americans' supposed ratings of "top" problems in public schools, as discussed by Barry O'Neill in his article, "The History of a Hoax." Readers may have seen one or more news reports of "surveys" from the 1940s and 1980s that compared "the public's lists of top school problems" for those decades. According to one version of this report,

> In the 40's the [top] problems were: 1. talking; 2. chewing gum; 3. making noise; 4. running in the halls; 5. getting out of turn in line; 6. wearing improper clothing; 7. not putting paper in wastebaskets. [In contrast] the top problems in the 80's had become: 1. drug abuse; 2. alcohol abuse; 3. pregnancy; 4. suicide; 5. rape; 6. robbery; 7. assault.[69]

Clearly, such evidence would indicate that our schools have become dreadful, threatening places!

Of course, this was all nonsense. No such surveys had ever been conducted. Indeed, when O'Neill was finally able to trace the story back to its roots, he found that it had first been expressed, about 1982, as a set of personal opinions by one "T. Cullen Davis of Fort Worth, a born-again Christian who devised the lists as a fundamentalist attack on public schools." Then, by a complex process of misreporting and advocacy, the lists were repeated, elaborated, and converted into "surveys" by other members of the Religious Right (Tim LeHay, Phyllis Schlafly, and Mel and Norma Gabler), officials from the state of California, and then—literally—hundreds of different newspaper, magazine, and television accounts. And given wide circulation as news stories by the press, the tale of worsening school problems has since been repeated by many columnists, leading federal politicians (such as William Bennett), education officials (such as Joseph Fernández, former chancellor of New York City schools), and academics (such as Derek Bok, former president of Harvard). Indeed, O'Neill suggests that these lists have now become "the most quoted 'results' of educational research, and possibly the most influential." Thus, once again, public schools were given a black eye because of a media "feeding frenzy."

Our third example concerns press treatment of the "political correctness" issue in higher education. A good review of this matter has recently been prepared by the National Council for Research on Women, and we draw from their account.[70] In the late 1980s and early 1990s, a set of books appeared attacking higher education in America, several of them financed by ultra-conservative foundations.[71] These works charged or implied that "liberals" had taken over American campuses and were now preventing the expression of viewpoints they deemed not to be "politically correct." In response, the press began slowly to generate stories concerning the "political correctness" issue. Then, in 1991, Dinesh D'Souza's *Illiberal Education* appeared. In this work D'Souza discussed six examples of policy conflicts at prestigious universities—conflicts that had *not* been resolved in ways approved by the Far Right—thus creating "the false impression that most of the nation's 3,500 colleges and universities were engulfed in the 'p.c.' debates and experiencing conflict over diversity in exactly the same way."[72] As a result, massive numbers of news stories about "political correctness" began to appear—3,989 in 1991 alone—the vast majority relying only on secondary accounts or drawing simply from the six incidents that had been portrayed by D'Souza.

Thus, through cupidity, bias, or desires to pander to readers, the media had created beliefs that "liberals" were on the rampage and that "political correctness" debates were rife on American campuses. These beliefs were not only false but were flatly contradicted by evidence of continuing right-wing intolerance associated with race, gender, and sexual preference on those same campuses.[73] Such beliefs have caused headaches for university administrators and have diverted attention from the real problems of American higher educa tion.

These three examples illustrate a specific form of press irresponsibility, violation of a tenet we shall call the "Principle of Source Citation." As a rule, scholars will not tolerate the citing of secondary materials but demand that their colleagues look at and cite original sources when discussing research results. It may be too much to ask that journalists actually *look* at original research documents, but it is surely not too much to demand that journalists *cite* their sources when writing about research and take responsibility for alerting readers when propagandists have failed to provide needed citations.

It is a nasty fact that many public lies are now uttered in the name of research, and those lies can cause untold mischief in education and other public-policy fields. It would help keep these lies within manageable bounds if journalists were trained to respect—and tried always to honor—the "Principle of Source Citation."

Beyond this basic point, the three examples we've given also illustrate an observation we've made in earlier chapters. For obscure reasons the press delights in stories about the failures of education but shies away from stories that report education's successes. We're not the first people to have observed this effect, of course.[74] But until and unless the press can be induced to mend its ways, Americans will continue to be given the false impression that their public schools, colleges, and universities are in deep trouble—when in fact they are doing remarkably well despite the increasing social problems of American society. This, then, is a second, pervasive form of press irresponsibility.

The Proper Use of Evidence. To summarize, recent criticisms of American schools have often been bolstered by impressive claims of evidence that appeared, on first glance, to support arguments about our "troubled" schools. On closer examination, however, many of those claims have turned out to be garbage. A decade or so ago one could be persuaded that at least some of the critics were making honest errors when they cited faulty evidence. Over time, however, the notion that misuse of evidence by the critics represents "honest errors" has worn thin. Unfortunately, recent critics of the schools have employed various tactics for misusing and abusing evidence, often aided by a biased, ignorant, or hysterical press. People who are sincerely interested in improving American education must be alert to such chicanery.

Since it is frighteningly easy to misuse and misunderstand evidence concerning education, we suggest a final tenet, which we state in the form of a three-part maxim in Exhibit 4.5. When it comes to evidence concerning education and other matters of social policy, it is very easy to misinterpret that evidence; advocates and scoundrels are only too likely to embrace or create those misinterpretations; and the press and public are far more willing to buy into those misinterpretations than to examine the evidence on which

---

■ EXHIBIT 4.5
Berliner and Biddle's Evidence Maxim

Evidence attracts misinterpretation;
Misinterpretations attract advocates and scoundrels;
Advocates and scoundrels attract the press and the multitudes
    who far prefer to be told tales than to look at the evidence.

---

they are based. Let all of the many, many friends of education take appropriate heed!

Legitimate Concerns

If there is a crisis in American schooling, it is not the crisis of putative mediocrity and decline charged by the recent reports but rather a crisis inherent in balancing [the] tremendous variety of demands Americans have made on their schools and colleges—of crafting curricula that take account of the needs of a modern society at the same time that they make provision for the extraordinary diversity of America's young people; of designing institutions where well-prepared teachers can teach under supportive conditions, and where *all* students can be motivated and assisted to develop their talents to the fullest; and of providing the necessary resources for creating and sustaining such institutions.

—Lawrence Cremin (*Popular Education and Its Discontents,* 1990, p. 43)

Finally, let us also remember that some criticism of education represents sincere attempts by thoughtful Americans to cope with serious issues in a public institution to which they are strongly committed. There is, therefore, every reason to believe that criticism of public schools will continue in America. Let us, however, learn lessons from the sorry record of the recent past and rededicate ourselves to the principle that those debates must reflect honesty, goodwill, respect for evidence, acknowledgement of the dedication and contributions of educators, and a sincere desire to improve the lives of all Americans. Agreement on these principles would seem a reasonable basis for meaningful debates about how to resolve education's many dilemmas.

Chapter Five

Poor Ideas for Reform

◆

America has long had a love affair with educational reform. Schools are held in high regard in our country, and Americans think their schools are able to accomplish a host of important tasks. Moreover, America is an optimistic nation, and most Americans believe that our institutions can and should be improved. Furthermore, most citizens have had personal experience with public schools, and they understand that financing those schools requires spending a good many tax dollars, particularly at the state and local levels. Add these factors together, and you create a climate for noisy, public debates and frequent proposals for educational reform.

But not all proposals for reform are useful. Some proposals reflect only the personal experiences or prejudices of legislators. Some are generated by special-interest groups. Some represent educational fads that will be short-lived. And some are based on misunderstandings about schools and the problems of education. For these reasons, many programs intended to "improve" our schools turn out to have little detectable effect or, worse, end up creating serious problems for educators and students.

This last result is particularly true of proposals that are based on systematic misunderstandings. And since America has just been subjected to a decade and a half of a Manufactured Crisis that involved the vigorous promotion of derogatory myths about education, it should come as little surprise to learn that literally hundreds of reform proposals have also been generated based on those myths. Since they are designed to address problems that are actually fictions, most of these proposals are poor ideas. We review here some key reform ideas that the critics most responsible for manufacturing the crisis have put forth. As we shall see, most of these ideas are not merely foolish; rather, if enacted, they would cause serious damage to American schools.

Vouchers and Private Schools

In the cities, vouchers would quickly solidify a two-tiered educational system consisting of nonpublic schools and pauper schools. That development would impoverish us all, because it would represent an abandonment of efforts to improve education for disadvantaged youngsters, who are already a majority in most U.S. cities.

—Mary Anne Raywid (Public choice, yes; Vouchers, no!, 1987, p. 763)

Not surprisingly, some of the worst ideas for reform of American education have come from representatives of the Far Right. It is tempting to judge some of these proposals as merely outlandish, but they have generated a lot of debate during the past few years—so we should at least look at them.

What would happen, for example, if, as some Far Right critics urge, the federal and state governments gave up all support for education, and control over the public schools were "returned" to parents and local communities? Among other things, this would involve abandoning all federal record keeping and support of research concerned with education, all attempts to develop national or state-wide education policies that support American economic growth, and all programs that provide support for schools in poor and needy districts from general tax revenues. Adopting these policies would thus impose chaos on American education and would create even poorer schools in impoverished communities, for only rich districts would then be able to afford adequate schools. Such outcomes would surely be recipes for disaster.

Other disasters would result if curricula were dictated by the Religious Right. American society and industry do *not* need a population that is ignorant of scientific knowledge, including knowledge about evolution, DNA, genetics, and the inheritance of traits and diseases. America does *not* need even more ignorance on the part of teens about the facts of reproduction and AIDS. And it seems doubtful that America's serious social problems would go away if only our schools refrained from talking about them. Our Constitution guarantees religious freedom, and this includes freedom to preach ideas in houses of worship that other Americans consider nonsensical and superstitious. Such freedom is not extended to the public schools, however, nor should it be. America is not served well when religious zealots confuse its public schools with its churches.

Nostrums such as these are clearly misguided and have not generated much support among thoughtful Americans. Other right-wing proposals are more seductive, however—particularly those for vouchers or tax credits that parents might use to support schools of their choice in the private sector. Such proposals have received support from a surprising variety of sources, including some Neoconservatives, misguided political liberals, urban educators, some white- and black-parent groups, the Catholic Church, and various state governors. To understand this range of support, we must look at recent history.

Recent Voucher Proposals. The notion of funding education through vouchers goes back many years, but interest seems to have been rekindled in the early 1960s by Milton Friedman[1] and by plans for a federally funded voucher program that were prepared in the late 1960s by Christopher Jencks, a Harvard sociologist then working for the U.S. Office of Economic Opportunity.[2] Congressional bills that would have funded such programs were actually introduced several times in the 1970s, but these were easily defeated. The voucher idea received a boost, however, when it was endorsed by President Reagan, and serious attempts to fund vouchers through federal legislation surfaced in 1982, 1983, and 1984. These proposals were perceived as elitist and were also defeated.

> Realizing this, conservatives decided to repackage school choice in a form that its opponents might find more palatable or at least harder to oppose. In the first installment of this new campaign, the Reagan administration introduced a bill to provide vouchers to low-income youth to purchase remedial education at whatever school, public or private, they would like.[3]

In addition, George Bush also favored vouchers, and when he became president, he initially endorsed choice among *public* schools in order to make his eventual call for vouchers more palatable. That call finally came in 1992 and garnered wider support than earlier voucher proposals. Fortunately, that attempt to fund vouchers at the federal level also failed; but lack of federal success has not daunted proponents of voucher programs, and numerous proposals for such programs are now pending in state legislatures.[4]

Proponents of vouchers argue that such programs would encourage more choice among schools, subject schools to market forces, promote school efficiency through competition, improve parental involvement, increase the numbers of private schools thus leading to higher levels of student achievement, reduce educational bureaucracy, and help to equalize educational opportunities. These arguments are seductive because they draw on the ideology of free enterprise and suggest that vouchers would enable America to solve sticky educational problems with little or no increase in tax support. Some of these arguments are at least debatable, but others are unsupportable or even ridiculous.[5]

Vouchers and Poor Families. Since poor parents lack the supplemental resources that rich people have for helping their children, it is foolish to argue that voucher programs would help to equalize educational opportunities. (For example, rich parents can afford the extra costs for transportation, clothing, and educational supplies when they send their children to a distant, private school; poor parents cannot.) And it defies reason to argue that voucher programs would *reduce* bureaucracy; if anything, those programs would require *additional* bureaucratic forces to administer.[6]

Many objections may also be raised about applying the market model to public education. For example, public schools provide not only *private* benefits to their students but also a wide range of *public* benefits to the community and society. It seems VERY unlikely that these public benefits would be protected if a market model were forced on education. And, as Alan Blinder has made abundantly clear, market forces generate great inequalities—and one wonders how long America could survive as a society if its schools became even *less* equal than they are today in their funding, staffing, and offerings.[7]

Moreover, new economic thinking has converged around a remarkable discovery, namely, that growth in a nation's economy is more likely when disparities between the earnings and education of rich and poor families are low. Today, the average income for the top twenty-five percent of America's families is $91,368, while the bottom twenty-five percent earn an appalling average income of only $11,530—which means that a huge proportion of America's population has almost no buying power.[8] This disparity is *much* worse than in other Western countries, most of which also have higher rates of economic growth. Because voucher plans would *increase* this inequality, they would generate an *additional* drag on the economy, and our entire country would suffer. As Labor Secretary Robert Reich recently put it, "A society divided between the haves and the have-nots or between the well-educated and the poorly educated . . . cannot be prosperous or stable."[9]

Voucher proposals are also sometimes embraced by less-affluent parents whose children attend underfunded, often dangerous public schools. These parents would like to receive vouchers so that they, like rich parents, could rescue their children by sending them to private schools. Such parents often believe that private schools have intrinsic advantages over public schools. Their beliefs are bolstered by stories of the marvelous achievements of students in high-status private high schools; and it takes careful analysis to reveal that weak private schools may have dreadful academic programs, that many of the achievements of high-status academies are generated not by the fact that they are private schools but rather by their superior levels of financial support and by the talented students they recruit, and that students attending well-funded, attractive public schools can also achieve wonderfully.

In addition, we must always distinguish between actions that will benefit the individual and actions that will benefit education as a whole. Given the advantages of the rich, private academy in an affluent suburb over the miserably funded public school in an urban ghetto, which parents would not choose to send their children to the former if they could afford to do so? But this does not mean that these advantages would persist if a *lot* of parents could afford private-academy tuition. Elite academies sell prestige and exclusivity—as well as academic achievement—and these comparative advantages would be taken away if too many of the poor were allowed to "mingle" with their "regular" students.

But fear not, most voucher plans would provide only token assistance to poor families—indeed, only a fraction of the amount they would need to send their children to private academies. This fact has not deterred proponents of voucher programs, of course. With great seriousness of purpose, Governor J. Fife Symington III of Arizona—compassionate to a fault—has proposed giving vouchers worth $1,500 per year to poor, mostly Hispanic families to help them send their children to "better" schools. Perhaps Governor Symington, with large holdings in real estate, has forgotten what it cost to send his own children to private academies in Phoenix; or, perhaps, given his wealth, he never felt compelled to check the bills. Armed with the governor's generous voucher, poor families might afford to send their children to about one month's worth of education at the most prestigious academies in Phoenix! But perhaps that is the governor's real plan; Arizona can send its poor to the private academies for a month so they can taste what "good" education is, and this should motivate them and their neighborhood schools to do better (with the miserly public support they will continue to receive).

The Effects of Voucher Programs. Many objections can be raised about voucher proposals, but most debates about them have focused on the First Amendment to the U.S. Constitution, which mandates separation of church and state. It is easy to understand why First Amendment concerns surface in these debates. Most private schools have sectarian affiliations, and more than half of all students who attend them are found in schools run by the Catholic Church, an institution that often supports voucher programs. But use of the First Amendment to derail voucher proposals is questionable. Recent court decisions suggest that "some" public funds can, indeed, be used to support "some" costs of private education under "some" circumstances. Moreover, focus on First Amendment issues diverts public attention from other serious defects of voucher programs. Thus,

> those who argue against private school choice programs might be better off focus-ing on equal educational opportunity issues and what a voucher plan would mean to public schools, especially those serving families least likely to have the ... resources ... that would help them compete in the educational free market.[10]

What, then, would be the likely outcomes if Americans were to embrace programs for vouchers or tax credits to fund private schools?

In the short run, such programs would divert tax dollars to the support of high-status private schools, thus providing tuition relief for wealthy parents and generating yet another way for average Americans to finance tax relief for the rich. In addition, since private schools are more often located in wealthy neighborhoods, voucher programs would also tend to transfer dollars from poor communities to rich communities. A good analysis of this second effect was provided by William Cooley, who examined the likely outcomes of a voucher scheme proposed for Pennsylvania that would provide nine hundred dollars in credits for each student in the state.[11] Because of the locations of private schools, *two-thirds* of the funds authorized by this plan would flow into the eight Pennsylvania counties with the highest per-capita incomes, while *none* of the funds would go to the state's poorest counties. Thus, under the proposed scheme, the poorest counties in Pennsylvania would, in effect, be paying additional taxes to support the richest counties!

The long-term effects of voucher systems would, if anything, be even more damaging. The reason for this is that when enough high-status private schools appear in a community, they tend to siphon parental energy, finances, and able teachers from the public schools. This sets up a two-class educational system, in which the private schools serve talented and wealthy students and the increasingly poorly financed public schools are left to cope as best they can with the poor and disadvantaged. As Cooley suggests, a dreadful example of this outcome may already be found in Philadelphia, where about 30 percent of all students attend private schools. Over time, this has generated some remarkably fine private schools in Philadelphia. However,

> there are 24 public elementary schools in all of Pennsylvania in which 80% of the fifth graders are still unable to read with minimum competence. (Can you imagine trying to teach social studies, for example, in a fifth grade classroom where 4 out of 5 students cannot understand what they read?) *All 24 of those schools are in Philadelphia.* They serve over 15,000 students, almost all of whom live in homes with income below the poverty level. From the data available it seems clear that these 24 schools represent one of the most difficult educational challenges in the state, yet their teachers tend to be the least experienced in their district, because as soon as teachers have sufficient seniority, they transfer to other schools. It is probable that parents who care about their child's education *and* who can afford to have their child escape from such schools have already done so. This illustrates what market forces leave in their wake . . . ever greater inequities.[12]

Now, what would happen across America if private schools were to be given additional support through voucher funds? High-status private schools would surely become more numerous, the position of public education would become threatened in more communities, and the "Philadelphia effect" would likely become the American educational norm.[13]

Moreover, *this scenario is not hypothetical.* As it happens, the voucher alternative is now being tried in another industrialized country, Australia, and Americans can surely learn from that country's mistake. Here is the story: As in the United States, Australia has long had high-status private academies (called *independent schools* "downunder") that serve students from families of above average wealth and status.[14] Since the early 1970s, however, the Australian governments (both federal and state), responding to political pressures unique to that country, have provided substantial per capita subsidies to non-government schools. (The amount of these subsidies has varied from about one-quarter to over four-fifths of a school's operating expenses, depending on the school's private resources.) If our argument is valid, this "voucher" program should have shifted enrollment from public to independent schools, increased the class distinctions between schools, and decreased the relative achievement of students attending school in the public sector—and lo, that is exactly what has happened!

According to data provided by Don S. Anderson of the Australian National University, between 1976 and 1986, national enrollment in public-sector schools fell from 78 percent to 73 percent in Australia, whereas enrollment in independent schools doubled, from 5 percent to 10 percent. Furthermore, the socioeconomic status of students became more polarized in communities where these two school types appear.[15] (In addition, Roman Catholic schools increased their share of enrollments.) Moreover, the effectiveness of Australian public schools has now begun to wane. Between 1985 and 1990, the proportion of high school graduates entering higher education from independent schools *rose* from 64 percent to 71 percent, whereas the proportion from public schools *fell* from 46 percent to 39 percent.[16] Anderson comments,

> there is also other evidence indicating decline in public education. For instance, public school teachers are beginning to send their own children to private schools. [By] 1984, 50 percent of public secondary teachers did; now there must be many more. . . . Soon the only representatives of the middle class in public schools will be those who stand in front of the blackboards.[17]

Australia is widely known for its equalitarian values, and one wonders how long it will continue to tolerate this failing social experiment. This does not mean, of course, that voucher programs would always have the tragic effects that Anderson documents for Australia. An interesting counterexample is provided by France, where federal support for private schools began in 1960 under the so-called Debré Act. This act and its effects have been lauded by voucher advocates in this country, but relations between public and private schools are quite different in France. As noted by Frances Fowler, school funding in France is controlled nationally, which ensures that "there are virtually no financial inequalities within the public school system," and public schools have long been "considered [slightly] academically superior to private ones."[18] (Fowler presents both interview and objective evidence supporting these points.) This means that the French school environment is vastly different from the American school environment.

> In the United States, private schools are perceived as superior to public ones, and public schools vary greatly in their resources, offerings, and academic quality. Teachers, public and private, are paid on very different salary scales. In such an environment it is all too likely that even carefully regulated choice plans will lead to increasing elitism and social stratification. . . . In contrast, French parents are offered choices between schools that are relatively equal. Therefore, increased stratification on the basis of social class has not occurred.[19]

In short, the Australian and French examples both suggest that voucher programs in *America* will lead to greater inequalities in education and thus will thwart America's traditional commitment to common schools and to equality of educational opportunity. This does not mean that voucher programs are intrinsically evil, that private education is inherently suspect, or that high-status private schools do not have substantial advantages over poorly supported public schools in today's America. But voucher programs in our country would surely transfer yet more wealth from average-income Americans to the rich, would place an additional brake on the economy, and would lead to greater degradation of our poorest public schools. (Nor are we alone in noting those likely outcomes—see Exhibit 5.1.) Citizens of good will should oppose voucher programs with all the vigor they command.

In saying this we are not suggesting that all programs that promote choice in American education are pernicious. Indeed, as a rule, students and their families have higher morale when they are offered choices among schools, and schools (whether public or private) also benefit when they have some control over the students they will enroll and retain. This means that one should look seriously at strategies for promoting choice among *public* schools.

■ EXHIBIT 5.1
Vouchers and Needy Students

Charley Reese, a columnist for *The Orlando Sentinel*, espouses politics that are avowedly conservative. Here is what he recently wrote about vouchers and school choice.

The phony conservatives—neo-conservatives if you are into political taxonomy—such as Jack Kemp, Bill Bennett, and that crowd are now touting school choice. All that shows you what a bunch of phonies they are.

What's wrong with school choice is that it asks the wrong question.

The correct question is, Do you want to offer public education to children. If the answer is no, then abolish the whole system. The more than $180 billion public education costs, if left in private pockets, would create a market for private schools. But if the answer is yes, I want to keep a system of public education, then you must reject school choice.

School choice is a pirate ship sailing under false colors. The neo-cons claim that it would inject the benefits of the free market into the public education [system]. That's false. It would not because no government program can ever respond like a free market institution. A school denied adequate resources by a political system cannot add those resources just to keep students from leaving. In other words, the principals and teachers, unlike the owners in a private business, do not control their own finances. Consequently, they cannot respond to changes in student population.

What school choicers really want is the privilege of converting part of the public school system into their own tax-paid private school system. They want parents to be able to move children to the best-equipped, best-staffed schools in the best neighborhoods while poor children are left behind in the worst-equipped, worst-staffed schools in the worst neighborhoods. This would create an utter sham of a public education system. It would amount to nothing more than resegregating schools, this time on the basis of parent income instead of on the basis of race. It would rationalize the crime many public school systems already commit. That crime is providing vastly unequal resources to the children in their system.

The true conservative position is that once we commit to a government program of public education, we undertake the moral obligation to see that the program benefits every child, regardless of race, income, or neighborhood equally.

Intensification

A . . . key assumption underlying state [reform] statutes from 1983 to 1987 [was] that education does not need to be fundamentally changed, but the existing delivery system can be intensified to meet the economic challenge. [Proposals] to drastically reorganize secondary schools or [those] favoring vouchers received scant support in state capitals. Rather, the key variable in 1983 was thought to be a more rigorous curriculum. As one legislator told me, "Let's make the little buggars work harder."

—Michael Kirst (Recent state education reform in the United States, 1988, p. 320)

Given help from Washington, some education proposals from Neoconservatives and Human Capital proponents had a lot of impact during the past decade. Many states have passed legislation encouraging or requiring school districts to de-emphasize "soft" subjects, to lay greater stress on "the basics," to lengthen the educational day or year, and to assign more homework.[20] Such programs were designed to intensify, rather than to replace, existing educational efforts and were popular with state legislators because they held out the hope of more achievement bang for fewer—or no more—educational bucks.

I hold with Andy Jackson, who said, "It is to be regretted that the rich and powerful too often bend the acts of government to their selfish purposes . . . there are no necessary evils in government. Its evils exist in its abuses. If it would confine itself to equal protection, and, as Heaven does its rain, shower its favors alike on the high and on the low, the rich and the poor, it would be an unqualified blessing."

If a public school is underfinanced, finance it properly. If it is unsafe, make it safe. That's the proper commitment every American should make to every child in the United States. The Kemp-Bennett crowd's plan is: Let the wealthy flee, but let the middle class subsidize them, and let the poor suffer because they don't vote for us high-tone Republicans anyway.

There are exceptions, but there is a correlation between parental income and parental concern about their child's welfare. Those very children suffering most from parental neglect or indifference would be the ones left behind by the exodus to the best public schools.

But in fact there should be no best public school. Not one should be any better equipped, any better staffed, or offer any better courses than any other. If they do, the children of the system are being cheated.

These neo-conservatives, these Wall Street Republicans with their phony-baloney populist rhetoric, deserve to go into the ashcan of history. . . .

—Source: Charley Reese (1993).

Curricula. Many intensification programs have focused on curricula. Some state legislatures have passed laws requiring high school students to complete a minimum number of core subjects if they are to graduate, and some have sought to limit extracurricular activities so that schools could spend more effort on instruction. Programs such as these reflected several beliefs—that educational efforts have become too diffuse; that talented students are no longer being prepared for college entrance or for useful employment; or that students are too often being coddled and, as a result, are becoming loutish or lazy.

These beliefs should be put in historical context. Until World War II, only a minority of students aspired to attend college, most of them came from WASP homes with above-average wealth, and these students usually took a demanding high-school curriculum focused on core academic subjects. Other students either took vocational courses or dropped out of high school when they could. After the war, however, greater stress was given to retaining *all* students in high school. High schools then put greater emphasis on vocational courses, on new courses that focused on students' interests, and on more remedial work for students with weak academic backgrounds. As a result, enrollment in core academic subjects declined.[21] Moreover, tough standards for grading, student conduct, and graduation were often relaxed.

But this did not mean that the high school experience had been debased for the "average" student. Indeed, since American high schools were now serving a much-expanded student population, "average" students clearly were receiving more education than they had a generation earlier. Moreover, it could be argued that even college-bound students were better off. More students were being offered courses that held their interest, and in some cases teachers were able to build a good deal of "traditional" content into courses that students elected to take. Moreover, more students were being offered remedial work to overcome early deficiencies in their backgrounds.

Be that as it may, by the mid-1970s it had become clear that increasing numbers of students were also college-bound. And since most colleges have curricula that are built on core high school subjects, the high schools came under increased pressure to expand core offerings. Response to this need was already underway by the end of the decade, but concern about the issue also surfaced in 1983 in *A Nation At Risk* and other documents crucial to the Manufactured Crisis. As a result, by the mid-1980s many high schools were increasing their core-course offerings and encouraging (or requiring) college-bound students to take those courses. The results of these efforts were dramatic. From 1982 to 1992, the number of students across the country taking the minimum core program recommended in *A Nation At Risk* rose from 13 percent to 40 percent, and the number taking the full core curriculum rose from 2 percent to 17 percent.[22] Today, more than 70 percent of college-bound seniors have taken courses in U.S. government or civics, in world history or world cultures, and in English composition. More than 80 percent have passed courses in chemistry, English grammar, and American literature. And over 90 percent have studied algebra, U.S. history, and biology. In this respect, at least, calls for intensification have had considerable effect. Today, some critics still claim that America's high schools do not stress a rigorous curriculum, but those critics have not bothered to *look* at the evidence concerning courses that are now taken by most of America's college-bound seniors.

These statistics, however, conceal a problem. Those who urge that curricula be intensified argue that such actions will lead to higher levels of student achievement. Such arguments have rarely, if ever, been confirmed by evidence. This is hardly surprising, since most curricula-intensification programs have imposed extra requirements on schools but have provided no additional resources to help meet those requirements. As a result, schools have adopted various strategies for superficial compliance but have avoided serious changes in their programs. Thus, they have responded

> by a proliferation of courses that treat academic subject matter with extreme superficiality, by the assignment of . . . teachers to academic subjects that they are unprepared to teach, and by the failure of educators to explore ways of teaching academic subjects to the many students who traditionally have not received a serious academic education.[23]

For example, in the 1980s various states passed laws requiring *all* students to take four years of mathematics in high school, but these requirements were not backed with additional funds. As a result, some schools in those states responded by expanding their curricula to include such uplifting offerings as "practical math," "discovery math," "math skills," "math concepts," or "informal geometry." Other schools reputedly decided that students could meet the new mathematics requirements by taking courses in auto-body repair, television production, or cosmetology. Still others added additional sections of traditional mathematics courses, such as trigonometry or calculus, but because of teacher shortages or administrative rules found it necessary to staff those courses with teachers who were not qualified to teach mathematics. Needless to say, coping strategies such as these did little to increase average student-achievements in mathematics. Moreover, students in the lower-status, "commercial" and "general education" tracks were more likely to be the victims of these superficial coping strategies.[24] Small wonder, then, that underfunded programs for curricular intensification have had few positive effects.

Even when it is well funded, curricular intensification is associated with other problems. One problem is deciding on what grounds one chooses the curricula to emphasize. *A Nation at Risk* recommended that high schools require a core curriculum consisting of four years of English, three years each of mathematics, history, and science, and a half year of computer science.[25] These suggestions seem attractive until one begins to think about subjects that are, potentially, left out. Once upon a time students who wanted to attend college had to take two years of a modern foreign language, but this requirement was only "recommended" in *A Nation at Risk.* Why omit this requirement when American industry is now trying to expand overseas markets? And why not require at least one year of psychology, human relations, or health science? Why omit civics or the social sciences? Why not stress at least some practical skills, such as driving? Why slight art, music, and drama? What about sports and physical education? Good cases can be made for each of these subjects. But whether they or others should be required of *all* students should be debated publically rather than decided by fiat. The authors of *A Nation at Risk* and related documents were not only responding to educational needs, they were also promoting suspect political agenda and had their facts wrong—and this should be borne in mind when assessing their recommendations.

Another problem is that proposals to intensify curricula are generally based on the assumption that all students will be subjected to a uniform standard for academic competence. But what about the many, many students who have skills or interests that are not represented in the uniform curriculum? It is easy to cite talented people, including Albert Einstein and Winston Churchill, who suffered early failures in education because they had to cope with rigid curricula for which they were not suited. A historic strength of the comprehensive American high school has been that it can offer instruction in both core *and* special-interest topics; thus it can provide students who are "late bloomers" second chances to obtain high-status education. Are students who have little initial interest in the expanded, uniform curriculum then to suffer losses in morale, be stigmatized, or be excluded from American high schools altogether—perhaps to swell the ranks of the unemployed and inflate even further America's intolerable crime statistics? Unless such issues are worked out, programs for curricular intensification run the risk of destroying the comprehensive high school and can threaten student and teacher morale.

Time Allocation.   Other intensification proposals have called for extending the length of the school day or the school year.[26] Such proposals are based on the assumption that students will learn more if only they are exposed to more classroom hours. Moreover, this assumption seems to be supported by two kinds of "evidence." First, American schools are open for only an average of about 180 days per year, while students in other industrialized countries—Japan, West Germany, South Korea, or Israel, for example—are required to attend school 200 or more days during the year. And some critics have assumed that these differences explain the putative shortcomings of American school performance. Second, studies of the effects of classroom instruction have found that students learn more when teachers spend more "time on task,"[27] and critics urging that students spend more hours in school during the year have assumed that such hours would be devoted to more "time on task."

Once upon a time, advocates of intensification programs also assumed that few, if any, additional costs would be required if the classroom day or the school year were lengthened, but teachers' professional associations and unions have now made it clear that their clients will expect to receive extra pay if such forms of intensification are adopted. This information has not daunted enthusiasts, however. For example, in 1990 Chancellor Joseph A. Fernández of the New York City public-school system proposed to spend proceeds from refinancing the city's municipal bonds—a mere billion or so dollars!—on a plan to lengthen each school day by one hour and the school year by twenty-five days, despite the fact that he had also been complaining that school facilities in the city were in terrible shape and that they needed at least a billion dollars just to catch up on deferred maintenance costs.[28]

Chancellor Fernández argued that this intensification plan would lead to improvements in reading and mathematics scores. However, we know of no strong evidence indicating that student achievement will rise if the school year is lengthened. Indeed, evidence concerning the effect of the quantity of schooling on student achievement is confusing. David Wiley and Annegret Harnischfeger reported that hours of schooling were associated positively with levels of achievement for students in the city of Detroit, but Nancy Karweit found no such effects for a host of other school districts.[29] Surely, "common sense" would suggest that students will learn more if they spend more time in school. Why should such an "obvious" effect turn out to be elusive?

One key to unlocking this puzzle is suggested by research from Sweden reported by Urban Dahllöf and Ulf Lundgren.[30] The Dahllöf-Lundgren studies began when the investigators stumbled on a strange fact. Over the school year, three types of classrooms, those composed of "talented" students, those serving a "normal" range of students, and those containing only the "less talented," all seemed to achieve roughly the same level of subject-matter competency by the end of the school year. Intrigued, the researchers decided to look at teaching activities in these three types of classrooms. They discovered that instruction in the classrooms was controlled not so much by available time as by curricular materials and by the teachers' perceptions of student learning. Teachers throughout the system had been given texts and other materials that specified levels of achievement students ought to reach during the year. The teachers dutifully carried out instruction until they thought that "most" students in their classes had reached that level, and then those teachers stopped instructing students in the subject matter. Not surprisingly, the desired level of achievement was reached earlier with "talented" students, but most teachers were able to achieve the desired level by the end of the year.

What did those teachers do for the rest of the school year? They filled classroom time with discussions of civic problems, local and national news stories, reports of summer-vacation activities—anything to keep students occupied and to avoid further engagement with subject matter. Why did those teachers stop instructing their students? They did so because the system in which those schools were embedded had lockstep curricula that specified levels of achievement for each grade level, and the teachers did not want to make trouble for other teachers who had to instruct those students the following year.

But most American school systems *also* use lockstep curricula that are designed for a fixed school year; thus, the Dahllöf-Lundgren effect surely also occurs in this country. (In fact, a decade ago Rebecca Barr and Robert Dreeben reported its presence in Chicago-area schools.[31]) And this means that if the school year is *shortened,* student achievement should fall; but if the school year is *lengthened,* student achievement may not change! (No wonder research on quantity of schooling has generated confusing results.) These predictions would have to be revised, of course, if one did away with lockstep curricula.

In addition, proposals for extending the school day or year have not generally provided guidance and resources to help teachers use the additional time wisely. To convert more time spent in school into achievement gains, that time must be used effectively on instruction. There are various ways to do this, of course: cross-age tutoring, small-group work on interesting projects, supplementary work with computers, and so forth. But most of these would require additional teacher training or supplementary resources, and all would require careful planning. Unless these are provided, extending the school day or year will have little effect on students' achievements.[32]

Other problems also dog proposals to increase the school day or year. First, surveys regularly report that the typical American teacher spends forty-five or more hours per week on professional duties—including evening hours spent on school activities, grading papers, and lesson preparation—so it is hardly surprising that those teachers resist calls for a longer school day. Second, many worthwhile extracurricular activities are scheduled during late-afternoon hours, and these might disappear if schools were required to lengthen their days. Third, many teachers work at other jobs during the summer to make up for poor academic salaries, and proposals for a longer school year may threaten those jobs. Fourth, many activities are now planned to take advantage of the long summer-school holiday, such as remedial education programs, summer camps for kids, teachers' workshops, and flexible family vacations. Finally, why on earth would American teachers and students *want* to spend more time in schools, given the devalued image of education that so often appears in the American media (see Exhibit 5.2)? Given these many problems, it's hardly surprising that, at present, teachers, students, and parents are all likely to resist calls for more school hours and days.

Homework. In brief then, most forms of intensification will cause prob
lems, some are expensive, and little evidence has yet appeared that would
confirm their putative advantages. A possible exception to this generalization,
however, concerns homework. A good deal of research has appeared on the
effects of homework on student achievement. After conducting a careful review of this research, Harris Cooper, a leading research analyst, has concluded
that secondary school students who are required to do homework probably
have a small achievement advantage over those who are not.[33] In addition,
Cooper found that homework for secondary students also conveys more advantage for simple skills that require practice and rehearsal than for skills
requiring higher-order integration of subject matter. However, research to
date does not confirm an "ideal" amount of homework for secondary students, nor has it explored adequately the conditions that maximize the effectiveness of homework. Also, despite many calls for giving more homework

---

■ Exhibit 5.2
The World of Education According to the
Media—A Test

Benjamin Barber, a professor of political science at Rutgers University,
wonders how it is possible to increase educational outputs through intensification or any other means when our young face a media culture that does
not value education. Here is a version of his test for adults to help them see
the world as our students do:

1. According to television, having fun in America means
   a) going blond
   b) drinking Pepsi
   c) playing Nintendo
   d) reading

2. A good way to gain a high income and acquire status in our society
   is to
   a) win a slam-dunk contest
   b) take over a company and sell off its assets
   c) start a successful rock band
   d) play the lotteries
   e) become a kindergarten teacher

3. Book publishers are financially rewarded today for publishing
   a) mega-cookbooks
   b) mega-catbooks
   c) mega-thrillers by Michael Crichton and John Grisham
   d) mega-romances by Danielle Steele
   e) mini-books by Voltaire

(continued on next page)

to primary school students, we know of no evidence that would confirm the usefulness of such actions.

Except for assigning homework to secondary students, then, intensification strategies alone are not likely to lead to greater student achievement. Taken alone, most proposals for intensification are based on questionable assumptions and, if adopted, will likely lead to controversy and to loss of morale among teachers, students, or parents. Indeed, most of the intensification programs of the early 1980s generated merely cosmetic changes, and many such programs have been abandoned. Intensification programs represent a set of simple nostrums for solving complex problems, and—as ever—most of such nostrums turn out to be "snake oil." Of course the curricula and the educational programs of America's schools can be improved. But just as surely, those improvements will require a good deal of thought, effort, and, often,

---

4. A major California bank that advertised "no previous credit history required" in inviting Berkeley students to apply for Visa cards turned down one group of applicants because
   a) their parents had poor credit histories
   b) they had never held jobs
   c) they had outstanding student loans
   d) they were "humanities majors"

5. Colleges and universities are financially rewarded today for
   a) supporting bowl-quality sports teams
   b) forging research relationships with large corporations
   c) sustaining professional programs in law and business
   d) stroking wealthy alumni
   e) fostering outstanding literature, history, and philosophy departments

6. To help the young learn that "history is a living thing," Scholastic, Inc., a publisher of school magazines and paperbacks, recently distributed to 40,000 junior and senior high school classrooms
   a) a complimentary video of the award-winning series "The Civil War"
   b) free copies of Plato's "Dialogues"
   c) an abridgement of Alexis de Tocqueville's "Democracy in America"
   d) replicas of the Declaration of Independence, the Constitution, and the Gettysburg address
   e) gratis copies of Billy Joel's hit single "We Didn't Start the Fire" (which recounts history via a vaguely chronological list of warbled celebrity names)

The answers are: 1—a, b, or c, but not d.   2—a, b, c, or d, but not e.
3—a, b, c, or d, but not e.   4—d.   5—a, b, c, or d, but not e.
6—e.

—Source: Benjamin Barber (A Nation of Dunces, 1993).

additional resources—and none of these is likely to appear in simple programs of intensification.

Carrots and Sticks

State monitoring and accountability systems reflect a concern that local educators will not work hard enough to support student learning unless coerced. Promotion of national achievement tests reflects a lack of trust that state and local educators will select the wisest instructional focuses unless the preferred instructional outcomes are specified. National statements of educational goals, state identification of the components of a common core of knowledge, [and] administrative efforts to articulate a clear vision of the purposes of the school all exhibit the belief that teachers and principals prefer to have their professional lives externally controlled.

[Other] reforms reflect similar beliefs about students, e.g. (1) testing will result in students working harder; (2) an agreed upon curricular core will attract the attention of students to important knowledge; [and] (3) students need to have their days structured by adults. . . . [These] also reflect the belief that improvement in student performance requires the use of "carrots and sticks."

—Terry Astuto, David Clark, Anne-Marie Read, Kathleen McGree, and deKoven Pelton Fernandez (*Challenges to Dominant Assumptions Controlling Educational Reform*, 1993, pp. 63–64)

A major belief of Neoconservatives has it that American schools are now failing because students, teachers, and other educators are confused or because they lack the ability or the will to engage in focused education. This has suggested, in turn, the need for additional state or federal controls to make sure that education is properly conducted.

As a result, a host of new state programs have recently appeared specifying standards for student conduct, effort, and achievement. Some of these programs have focused on issues of discipline—for example, on student dress, deportment, civility, and on avoiding violence. Some programs have been concerned with grades and tests—with, for example, codes for minimally acceptable grade-point-averages, frequency of testing, and standards for assigning grades. And some programs have addressed student achievement—usually assessed through statewide or national examinations.

These programs have not merely set standards but have often spelled out sanctions that are to be used to "encourage" student compliance. In some states today, students who fail to meet disciplinary standards can no longer participate in athletics or other extracurricular activities. In other states, schools are required to discharge unruly students. In many states, getting into desirable courses, certain academic programs, or high-status educational tracks—or even earning a high school diploma—now depends on students' grades or achievement-exam scores. Still other states have set up systems of public honors to reward students' academic accomplishments.

Similar reasoning lies behind other programs that attempt to control teachers. Many states have recently tightened standards for teacher certification, either by specifying additional educational qualifications or by requiring that teachers attain a given score on statewide exams of subject-matter knowledge. Other states have attempted to improve teaching by mandating regular appraisals of teachers' classroom conduct by supervisors, inspectors, or students. These appraisals are often tied to public honors or annual raises. Other states now examine teachers' ability to generate gains in the measured achievements of their students—again tying those gains to honors or raises. And still other states have set up career-ladder systems in which teachers advance through a set of ranked academic titles associated with prestige, authority, and salary. Advancement in these systems depends on teachers' assessed performances or accomplishments.

Programs such as these may have superficial appeal, but they are also associated with many problems. For one thing, programs that appraise student conduct always presuppose agreement concerning standards that will be used in those appraisals; but does such agreement exist? Surely, everyone would agree that students should pay attention in class and refrain from assaulting one another (or teachers!), but do Americans truly agree about other standards for student deportment? Is a student truant if he or she misses class in order to go on a winter ski vacation? Or are other students truant if they stay home for a few days to care for siblings when day-care services fail? Should junior high students be suspended if they violate a school's dress code or dye their hair an unusual color? Is calling another child a "motherfucker" a punishable offense or merely a regrettable use of language? Should working students who fall asleep regularly in class be suspended from high school? Is speaking one's non-English native tongue at school cause for suspension? (It *was,* believe it or not, a few years ago throughout the Southwest!) And should students in certain communities be allowed to bring guns to school (as some parents are now demanding)? Agreement about what is "proper" student behavior clearly varies depending on time, place, ethnicity, and social class, and it is not easy to get consensus on these issues.

Similarly, do Americans truly agree about the content of required courses? It is one thing to propose national standards for mathematics, but something else to suggest a single curriculum for lessons in social history or ethics. Surely the content of instruction in the social sciences should vary, in part, to meet the needs of students from diverse backgrounds—thus offering somewhat different content if one teaches students from Vietnamese, African-American, Hispanic, or Muslim homes. Moreover, Americans regularly feud over the content of courses concerned with evolution, human biology, or sexual conduct. Should teachers responsible for such topics be sanctioned if they do not offer the "proper" content?

Another problem with the carrot-and-stick approach concerns the subjective nature of evaluative judgments about student or teacher conduct. Unfortunately, such judgments often reflect personal or ethnic prejudices. Thus, conclusions that a student has violated disciplinary standards or that a teacher uses an "inappropriate" style may reflect little more than the biases of an evaluator. And for this reason, professional associations and teachers' unions have long argued against such evaluative judgments.

Still other problems concern the consequences of too many competitions. Americans are taught to value competition, and many people believe that students and teachers will achieve at higher levels when they must compete regularly with one another for coveted honors or privileges. Thus,

> [improving] competitive environments in schools is at the heart of many [recent reform proposals]. The fascination with merit pay and recognition programs for teachers is based on the belief that a direct connection between individual work and individual rewards will yield increased teacher efforts toward student achievement. [And] testing programs to monitor student achievement and compare classrooms or schools or districts on the basis of student achievement establish conditions for identifying winners—and losers.[34]

Unfortunately, those recommending such programs fail to realize that American schools already stress more competition than schools in other in-dustrialized countries and that a good deal of research indicates that, by comparison, *cooperative* learning strategies promote greater task involvement, better social integration and adjustment, more cognitive development, and improved problem-solving ability.[35]

In addition, enthusiasm for competition ignores long-term consequences for the majority who regularly lose. Students in America are taught that failure results from lack of ability or effort on their part. Thus, many students who fail regularly for reasons having to do with their home background, lack of support for their educational efforts, or bias associated with race or ethnicity will conclude that they lack the ability to do the work. Other students may decide that academic competitions are rigged, that the school is "mean," or that the "system" is unfair. Surely, none of these conclusions is in the best interest of those students or of society at large.

Similarly, competent teachers who regularly fail in competitions for scarce honors or a few large raises are likely to get discouraged and eventually be-come sullen or drop out of teaching. We cannot believe that these are desirable outcomes either.

Above all, programs that use carrots and sticks for motivating students or teachers employ *extrinsic sanctions*—the contingent application of rewards or punishments by others. A good deal of evidence now confirms the poor effects of such strategies. Consider, first, the problem for students. As psychol-ogists Edward Deci and Richard Ryan note, a generation ago thoughtful edu-cators, such as Jerome Bruner and Carl Rogers, suggested that "whereas ex-trinsic controls lead [students] to memorize well, they fail to promote the type of engagement with the task that results in conceptual learning and creative thinking."[36]

Many studies have since confirmed these insights. For example, Grolnick and Ryan conducted an experiment that compared how well fifth-graders given three different types of instruction learned a passage from a social studies text. Some of those students were told they would be tested and would receive a grade on the material; some were encouraged to learn from it; and some were asked merely to read it. Students who were to be graded and those who were encouraged to learn both scored well when tested on *facts,* but those who were encouraged to learn also *understood* more concepts from the passage.[37]

Similarly, Benware and Deci found that when college students read an article on neurophysiology, those who thought they would be asked to teach others from the article found the material more interesting, enjoyed the learning experience more, and reported being more involved in the learning experience than those who were told that they would just be tested on the material.[38] Thus, programs designed to control student academic effort through tests or other extrinsic sanctions may actually *depress* student interest and understanding of the subject (see Exhibit 5.3).

In contrast, interest in the subject, conceptual learning, and creative thinking are heightened when teachers use *intrinsic* motivators. Several years ago one of us had the pleasure of observing the classroom styles of two geometry instructors. One based his teaching on *extrinsic* sanctions, such as classroom competitions, pop quizzes, and public praise for right answers. The other used *intrinsic* motivators designed to stimulate students' choices, autonomy, belief in their own abilities, and fascination with geometry. Both of these men were known for the high scores their students earned on standardized tests, but the second teacher was also known for the number of his former students who had become mathematicians, scientists, and engineers.

Similar problems are associated with proposals to promote greater teacher effort with *extrinsic sanctions* such as honors, raises, or titles that are awarded depending on assessed performance or students' achievements. Research has shown that teachers also respond poorly to such sanctions.[39] This is hardly surprising, since teaching is a difficult, stressful, and underpaid profession; and many teachers remain at their posts largely because they are committed to their students or are sincerely interested in the subjects they teach. Extrinsic sanctions tend to destroy these commitments and interests and thus may have the unintended effect of driving the best teachers out of the profession!

A chilling example illustrates this problem. Several years ago a state with which we are familiar adopted a program that based high school mathematics teachers' annual raises on gains in their students' achievement scores. The next year some of the top teachers in the state resigned in disgust. Those who remained entered into intense competition with one another, which disrupted school programs and caused morale to drop throughout the state.

■ Exhibit 5.3
The Tricky Business of Giving Rewards

When B. F. Skinner taught pigeons to play Ping-Pong by rewarding them with food pellets, the world sat up and took notice. Clearly, his methods of producing and reinforcing behavior were impressive, and if they worked with birds, they might augur well for molding human behavior. Teachers began using more incentives . . . in the classroom, [but] . . . they found that rewards can backfire. [Other psychologists] . . . learned the same thing about college students. They also lose interest in an activity if researchers reward it to death.

Employers uncovered a nest of other problems as they restudied traditional incentive pay. In his study of piece-rate pay in industry, William F. Whyte . . . found it is tricky to know just how much more pay is necessary to get employees to work faster. And then it looked like praise, not money, might be a cheaper and more successful reinforcer. But management has had difficulty tooling up factories to give compliments. When industry began to institute piece-rate incentives, employees learned to slow down production while the rate was being set. Then they could easily earn bonuses by producing more items than necessary to earn their old salaries. Rewards, Whyte reported, motivate workers only when they fit into the social fabric of the factory or office. Humans are more complicated to manipulate than pigeons.

An old man in a folk tale, however, learned to turn confusion into order, to right the upside-down effects of rewards. He lived alone on a street where boys played noisily every afternoon. One day the din became too much, and he called the boys into his house. He told them he liked to listen to them play, but his hearing was failing and he could no longer hear their games. He asked them to come around each day and play noisily in front of his house. If they did, he would give each a quarter. The youngsters raced back the following day, and made a tremendous racket in front of the house. The old man paid them, and asked them to return the next day. Again they made a noise, and again the old man paid them for it. But this time he gave each boy only 20 cents, explaining that he was running out of money. On the following day, they got only 15 cents each. Furthermore, the old man told them, he would have to reduce the fee to five cents on the fourth day. The boys became angry, and told the old man they would not be back. It was not worth the effort, they said, to make noise for only five cents a day.

—Source: Margie Casady (insert box in an article reporting research on intrinsic motivation by David Greene and Mark Lepper, 1974).

(Among other things, some math teachers demanded that their schools restrict extracurricular activities, cancel school assemblies, and abolish out-of-school trips that might interfere with their instructional efforts.) The following year the incentive program was dropped.

To summarize then, programs that promote the use of carrots and sticks to motivate students and teachers generate a good deal of controversy, tend to lower morale, and focus attention on superficial conformity rather than on long-term interests and commitments. They are likely to lower meaningful learning among students and to drive the best teachers out of the profession. In many ways, then, they *thwart* rather than *promote* good education.

One of the tragedies of our era is that Americans have granted so much legitimacy to the tenets of conservative economic thought. It is all very well to point out that when people are doing dull and repetitive work—such as laboring in a factory—their efforts can be affected by schemes that base salaries on tasks completed and errors avoided. It is another thing entirely to try to extend this idea to the realms of professional conduct. Imagine, if you will, the absurdity of trying to control the professional conduct of pastors, psychiatrists, or Supreme Court justices with superficial, performance-based rewards! The reason why our minds rebel at such a thought is that we conceive the professional roles of such persons to involve highly complex decisions and moral commitments, and we select and train professionals with these ideals in mind. But education is also a profession that involves highly complex decisions and moral commitments. Therefore, the best ways to improve education are *not* those that are based on the factory model but rather are those that presume trust, grant autonomy, and seek ways to enlarge the lives of students and teachers. Perhaps the surest way to RUIN American education would be to expand the use of carrots and sticks with students and teachers.

Performance Indicators and Accountability

The economic/business analogy seems to have shaped and propelled the drive for accountability in education during the last decade. Since there are no profits to serve as indicators of whether or not schools are doing a good job, test scores have been assigned that function instead. The insistence on quantitative measures of school effectiveness has reduced educational outcomes to testable products and deemphasized the role of the school in other areas, such as preparing young people for civic participation, encouraging their personal development, and helping them master higher-level intellectual skills. It has also left little room for the "process" goals that are important to parents: the kinds and qualities of school experiences that they simply want their youngsters to undergo, quite apart from specific expectations regarding outcomes.

—Mary Anne Raywid (1987, pp. 764–765)

A major Neoconservative buzzword for our times is *accountability.* As funds for public education have become more threatened, many Neoconservatives have proposed programs that would tie funding for schools or salaries for educators to "objective" performance indicators such as average-gain scores on standardized tests, ratings of teaching performance, or numbers of students going on to higher education or landing suitable jobs. And this means that the efforts of local *schools* are to be controlled through state or federal mandates.

These ideas have also proven remarkably popular. Many state legislatures have proposed or enacted laws that require schools to be ranked according to average student achievement and offer honors or increased financial support to high-achieving schools. Moreover, these ideas have also surfaced at the federal level. In 1990 Linda Darling-Hammond, a policy analyst at Teachers College, Columbia University, reported that the National Assessment Board had proposed setting national "competence" levels for tests used by the National Assessment of Educational Programs (NAEP) and expanding the reach of those tests so that "they can be used to rank states, districts, and perhaps even schools. [In addition,] some policy makers have expressed the desire to use NAEP scores (along with, or in lieu of, scores from other tests currently administered to students) as means of triggering rewards and sanctions to schools or districts."[40] The following year Congress established a National Council on Education Standards and Testing (NCEST), and in its 1992 report, *Raising Standards for American Education,* NCEST recommended that nationwide curricular standards be developed for five core subject areas—English, mathematics, science, history, and geography—"with other subjects to come." The new curriculum standards would be backed up by a "national system of assessments,"[41] and a version of these recommendations was enacted into federal law in the recent Goals 2000 legislation sponsored by the Clinton administration.

As Darling-Hammond points out, accountability programs and proposals such as these presume

> that schools can be made to improve [only] if standards are set and incentives established that force schoolpeople to pay attention to them. Essentially this line of thinking assumes that problems exist either because educators don't have precise enough targets to aim for, because they aren't trying hard enough, or both. Supplying concrete goals and using both carrots and sticks to move educators to pursue them are the presumed answers to underperformance.[42]

Accountability programs apparently sound good to some untutored politicians and citizens. After all, industries demonstrate their success by making profits. Why should schools be exempt from the need to demonstrate that they are succeeding in *their* tasks? And if one grants this need, why not use standardized tests of achievement to see how each school stacks up against other schools in the state or nation? And once one has this information, isn't it also a good idea to encourage excellence in schools by rewarding "the best" schools with certificates of achievement or financial incentives?

Unfortunately, such ideas are based on badly flawed assumptions and generate a host of serious problems.[43] Let's consider only a sampling of these. For one thing, accountability programs impose *extrinsic sanctions* on educators that are largely irrelevant to the problems and goals of their professional lives. Since extrinsic sanctions tend to destroy intrinsic motivation, accountability programs can depress the morale of teachers and administrators.[44]

Teachers who work in schools subjected to such programs report that their worries about the school's status and the shallowness of accountability evaluations consume their time and energy. Over time, these programs tend to generate the three A's, Anxiety, Anger, and Alienation. Teachers feel *anxious* when their schools face accountability systems—particularly systems that are imposed by higher authorities, and that are used to make important decisions about their lives. They feel *anger* when they discover that those accountability systems are used unfairly—when they provide rewards or impose punishments on undeserving schools. And when teachers learn they have little ability to change unfair accountability systems, they become *alienated*—passive-aggressive members of a community, acting as obstructionists for other new ideas that come along. To say the least, this does not sound like a good recipe for improving American education.

Administrators also feel pressure when accountability systems are adopted. They report that they must spend additional hours defending their schools' competitive standing with parents, teachers, and the media—hours that they once spent more productively.

In response to these worries and pressures, educators also begin to adjust the focus of their efforts. Over time, their curricula and teaching efforts become more standardized and superficial.[45] Moreover, since they want their schools to look well on competitive tests, they tend to restrict instruction to the topics assessed by those tests.[46] A sad example of how this process works was recently described by sociologists Jere Gilles, Simon Geletta, and Cortney Daniels. In 1993 the State of Missouri created an accountability program designed around a new assessment instrument, the Missouri Mastery Achievement Test. This test was tied to a new curriculum that had been developed by the state's department of education, and all schools were required to administer it so that it could be used as a "report card"—letting the public know how well their own schools were doing compared with others in the state. As Gilles and his colleagues describe the outcome,

> results of this [program were most alarming]. Quality programs and textbooks were scrapped in order to replace them with materials that directly taught the test, and an unholy competition emerged between districts and communities over test scores. In some districts a week or more of instructional time each year was devoted to [preparing for] this test.[47]

Moreover, this was not an isolated incident. As testing specialist George Madaus has suggested,

> when you have high-stakes tests, the tests eventually become the curriculum. It happened with the Regents exams in New York. Items that are not emphasized in the test are not emphasized in school. That's a fundamental lesson that cuts across countries and across time. Teaching has not changed that much; it's an art form. Given basically the same set of circumstances, teachers will behave in much the same way. . . . But if you go to Europe, to the British Isles, or to Australia and look at comparable literature, [worries about] the external achievement exams . . . appear often. And they write about cramming, about how they prepared for the exams. They write about how, after taking the exams, they purged their minds of the answers that they had learned.[48]

Somehow, we doubt that most Americans are interested in promoting school learning that is narrow, test-specific, standardized, superficial, and easily forgotten—but that is exactly what accountability programs promote (see Exhibit 5.4).

It also takes a great deal of time and money to conduct accountability programs. According to a leading scholar, Arthur Wirth, citing the National Commission on Testing and Public Policy, mandatory testing in America now "consumes annually some 20 million school days and the equivalent of $700 and $900 million in direct and indirect expenditures."[49] What this

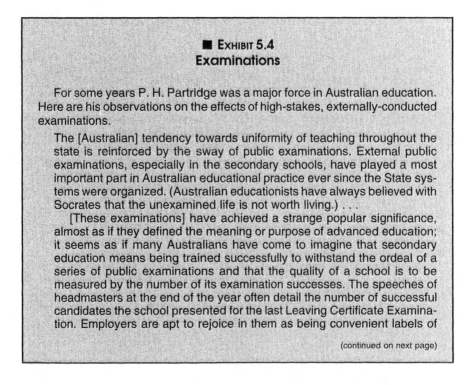

■ **EXHIBIT 5.4**
Examinations

For some years P. H. Partridge was a major force in Australian education. Here are his observations on the effects of high-stakes, externally-conducted examinations.

The [Australian] tendency towards uniformity of teaching throughout the state is reinforced by the sway of public examinations. External public examinations, especially in the secondary schools, have played a most important part in Australian educational practice ever since the State systems were organized. (Australian educationists have always believed with Socrates that the unexamined life is not worth living.) . . .

[These examinations] have achieved a strange popular significance, almost as if they defined the meaning or purpose of advanced education; it seems as if many Australians have come to imagine that secondary education means being trained successfully to withstand the ordeal of a series of public examinations and that the quality of a school is to be measured by the number of its examination successes. The speeches of headmasters at the end of the year often detail the number of successful candidates the school presented for the last Leaving Certificate Examination. Employers are apt to rejoice in them as being convenient labels of

(continued on next page)

means, of course, is that schools regularly shortchange classroom instruction to give students time to take accountability exams. Also, Americans have to pay additional taxes to support mammoth statewide and national testing programs.

In addition, the pressures of accountability programs have led some educators to cheat. School administrators may quietly distribute tests to teachers ahead of time. Teachers may teach only a restricted curriculum that is aligned with test content, teach test questions, or use tests meant for children at a lower grade. And schools may exempt low-achieving students from taking tests or report fraudulent results. As a consequence, accountability data from specific schools may be questionable, and statewide average scores for high-stakes accountability tests tend to inflate sharply over time.[50]

Also, the tests used in most accountability programs assess only a superficial range of outcomes and are systematically biased against minority students. We raised these issues in our earlier discussion of the SAT, but we were certainly not the first to have noted the problems. Regarding the superficiality of tests, Tanya Suárez and Nancy Gottovi note that since most accountability programs use tests that assess only lower-level thinking skills for specific academic subjects, such tests do *not* represent the curricular standards, broad offerings, or teaching performance of American schools.[51] Regarding test biases, Arthur Wirth has recently written,

> The poor and the nonwhite often score low on standardized testing. Women, who will make up more than half of the work force by the year 2000, score lower than

educational attainments and ability, and they are used for the award of competitive scholarships and bursaries.

The independent schools as well as the public schools prepare their pupils for the public examinations, and since they are based on the standard curricula and subject syllabuses promulgated by the State education authorities, they cause the teaching in the non-State schools to resemble closely in organization and content that of the public schools. . . . Many employers and parents also prefer the public test of the external examination, and many teachers themselves distrust the internal examination—partly from habit, partly because the "internalizing" of examinations eats further into teaching time and shifts the administrative troubles from the public examination authorities to themselves, and partly because they have insufficient faith in many schools and many of their colleagues, and believe that where examinations are conducted within schools themselves, standards tend to fall.

Thus, within the federal distribution of responsibilities, organization and practice have evolved to produce a large measure of uniformity and centralization. This is one of the cardinal features of Australian education, as every student of it has remarked, and one that differentiates it sharply from education in Britain, the United States, and many other countries.

—Source: Percy H. Partridge (*Schools, Society and Progress in Australia*, 1968, pp. 57–58).

men on certain important tests such as college entrance examinations — yet often perform better in school than men. . . . The simple idea that current standardized tests yield objective scientific facts about learning differences, and that kids who score lower are dumber than kids who score higher, is a myth.[52]

All of which means, of course, that accountability programs are seriously biased against innovative schools and against those schools that serve minority students.

Finally, accountability programs are also *unfair* because they involve competition among schools that are not playing on a level field. Earlier, we noted that America exhibits great extremes of wealth and poverty and that public schools serving impoverished children are often given a fraction of the funds given to public schools in rich suburbs. Naturally, poorly supported schools that serve our most disadvantaged children are also the schools that are most likely to "lose" in accountability competitions. Indeed, who would expect any other outcome? In fact, when considered from the perspective of America's neediest children, accountability programs are little more than ceremonies for awarding prizes, honors, and extra finances to America's best-supported schools, which serve its most privileged students!

To address these concerns, some accountability programs try to make the competition fairer by basing their judgments not on average student-achievement scores for schools but rather on average "gain scores." In such programs, schools "win" if their students *gain* more in average achievement over the course of a certain period—say an academic year—than do the students in other schools. To the uninitiated this may sound more equitable, but it turns out that the "gain score" procedure is also biased. Students (or schools) with high *initial* achievement scores are also more likely to generate high "gain scores," and this means that those schools with the highest early achievement scores are also more likely to "win" in gain-score accountability schemes.[53]

Statistical methods have even been proposed to handle this last problem. Some statisticians have suggested that schools should be clustered in such a way that they compete only with other "similar" schools, but no one has yet developed a foolproof way of judging whether or not schools are truly "similar." Other methodologists have recommended that schools' gain scores be weighted to take account of key attributes that are known to be associated with students' achievements—for example, the proportion of students who are bilingual in the school or the percentage of parents enrolled in its PTA. However, no one yet knows how to assign such weights fairly.

In short, nobody yet knows how to make a fair accountability program for American schools. Perhaps if a lot more were known about various student groups and about how school funding truly affects opportunity to learn, a fair procedure could be devised for the competitive assessment of school performance. But such procedures are *not* now available, and given the widely diverging levels of support provided to schools serving rich and poor students in America today, there is no defensible way to prevent the biases and unfair impact of accountability programs.

To summarize then, accountability programs cause *enormous* problems, and one wonders why they have proved to be so popular. One reason may be that such programs represent yet another poor strategy for applying outdated, conservative economic ideas to the complex institution of education. For untutored legislators, accountability programs also seem to hold out the hope of "improving" public schools without having to spend additional dollars. And, for those who accept the tenets of the Manufactured Crisis, and believe that America's schools are in deep trouble, accountability programs might

---

■ Exhibit 5.5
Assessment Explained

As you no doubt notice, the topic of assessment has become something of a phenomenon, comparable, for example, to a hurricane or an earthquake that just keeps on happening. Under such circumstances, it is most helpful to have a thorough understanding of matters pertaining to assessment, testing, and accountability. With that thought in mind, I offer this discourse on *homomensurmania*, which is defined as "the mad desire to engage in the measurement of human performance."

To probe the most profound levels of homomensurmania, one must explore the laws and theorems that give rise to this phenomenon. The most important law is entitled (appropriately, I think) the First Law of Homomensurmania. It reads,

> The further an educationally related dollar has to travel from source to ultimate recipient, and the more bureaucratic layers it must pass through, the greater the demands the provider will make for demonstrating that the dollar was well and properly spent.

No law can be fully elaborated in the absence of corollaries, and the First Law of Homomensurmania (abbreviated FLH) is no exception. The critical corollary, known as the Primary Corollary to the First Law, is,

> Tests are an efficient and effective way of indicating whether an educationally related dollar was well and properly spent.

Now the FLH and its sidekick, the Primary Corollary, are usually encountered in the company of another law, called the "Second Law of Homomensurmania" (SLH), which is,

> The demands made on the intelligence of those who take the tests are inversely proportional to the distance traveled by the dollar and the number of bureaucratic layers it passes through.

be conceived of as a way of achieving control over those failing schools. However, accountability programs simply do not address the real problems of America's schools. Rather, they are radically unfair and place serious and unnecessary burdens on America's best administrators and most dedicated teachers.

This does not mean, of course, that America's public school teachers and administrators should not be held responsible for their *conduct*. No society should tolerate thieving politicians, vicious policemen, incompetent firemen, careless surgeons, or clergy who prey on vulnerable youths. Similarly, no

---

The formulation of this Second Law is based on the fact that the further away the funding source is from the ultimate recipient of the dollar, the more difficult it is to convey data and information back from the recipient to the provider of funds. Thus the provider seeks information that is as brief and as descriptive as possible. Tests that are easily and accurately scored typically provide such information. Such tests also typically make very modest demands on the cognitive processing abilities and analytical skills of those who are required to take them. Ergo, the Second Law of Homomensurmania.

The First and Second Laws of Homomensurmania (along with the Primary Corollary, of course) help us to understand why we have assessment and accountability devices of the type that are so common today. What these laws do not tell us is why we take all this stuff about assessment so seriously. For an explanation, we must turn from noble laws to a mere theorem. This particular theorem is called the Assessment Policy Theorem, or APT. It reads as follows:

> Educators of good will and high intelligence are often frustrated in their attempts to make the educational system behave as they believe it should. These educators have been known to seize whatever devices for reform are most likely to yield the surest and quickest results.

The APT points out that policymakers interested in education and indeed even educators interested in education—not all of them, of course, but quite a few—look to assessment as an instrument for "bending" educational change in directions thought most desirable. This perspective on reform is sometimes called "Measurement Driven Instruction," or . . . Oh, I'll bet you've already got the acronym.

The explanation of assessment and accountability is nearly complete. There is just one more step, called the Homomensurmania Synthesis:

> Divide the APT by the FLH, subtract the Primary Corollary, and then multiply the result by the SLH. If the ambient temperature in the District of Columbia is above freezing, cube the answer; if below freezing, take the cube root.

Confused? Well . . . your feelings at the moment probably are not very different from all those students and teachers who take these tests.

—Source: Gary Fenstermacher (1991).

society should long put up with teachers who cannot instruct or administrators who cannot run schools. In fact, there is nothing wrong with accountability *in theory;* it is the *practice* of accountability that is so difficult to organize. To be fair, a person should be held responsible for what he or she *does,* for the actions that the person actually takes. (Politicians must be *caught* stealing; policemen must be *observed* to beat up innocent persons, and so forth.) And this means, if one is fair, that the competency of educators should also be judged by gathering careful information about their professional conduct. But gathering information about the behavior of individuals always costs money, and spending additional money is exactly what most proponents of accountability programs are trying to avoid. So, instead, they propose to base educational accountability on *outcomes,* as indicated by student achievement scores. The shaky reasoning and known biases of such procedures are not tolerated in America's courts when applied to other public servants or professionals, and Americans should be no more tolerant of them when it comes to education.

Immersion Programs for Language
Minority Students

> The Bilingual Education Act was most recently [re]authorized last year. [At that time] Congress had before it yet more evidence that the mandated method of instruction in the native language was no more effective than alternative methods of special instruction using English; and in some cases the mandated method was demonstrably less so. Indeed the English language skills of students in bilingual education programs seemed to be no better than the skills of those who simply remained in regular classrooms where English was spoken, without *any* special help.
>
> —From a 1985 speech by William J. Bennett, then Secretary of Education (cited by the United States General Accounting Office, 1987, p. 46)

Another persistent demand of right-wing critics is that schools in America should abolish Transitional Bilingual Education (TBE) programs for children who speak another language. Such programs conduct instruction in a child's mother tongue while gradually introducing English as the eventual language of instruction. The critics argue that TBE is divisive and that it doesn't work. They urge that immigrant students be forced into immersion programs where all instruction is in English. As we shall see, little evidence has appeared that would support the critics' arguments. Indeed, the effectiveness of TBE programs has frequently been confirmed. But this raises an interesting question. Why have these critics been so hostile to the children of recent immigrant groups?

To answer this question, we must begin with a brief history of bilingual instruction in the United States.[54] During much of the nineteenth century, instruction in their native languages was provided for most immigrant groups in this country. Students whose parents came from Italy, for example, were able to study Italian in school; those from Sweden could study Swedish, and so forth. In addition, if they had political clout, those groups were able to demand that schools conduct core-subject instruction in their native languages. German-speaking Americans even tried to get German named as the second official language of the country, and they, along with other immigrant groups, were sometimes served by monolingual public schools in which *all* courses were conducted in their native tongues.

Hysteria associated with World War I made it necessary, however, for Germans and other ethnic groups to show their loyalty to the United States, so they stopped clamoring for native-language public schools. At the end of that war, severe restrictions on immigration to the U.S. were put into effect, and this also contributed to the demise of such schools. But before World War I, bilingual and native-language public education were very common in our country and they were *not* thought to be a threat to our national identity.

Large numbers of new immigrants came to our shores again after World War II. Many were from Puerto Rico, Mexico, and various countries of Asia. English-speaking Americans again had to deal with large numbers of foreign-language speakers and their children. Then, in response to the Civil Rights Act of 1964 and the War on Poverty, the U.S. Office of Education began to support bilingual programs for children with limited proficiency in English. However, few school districts really cared about welcoming immigrant children (or, for that matter, their parents), whose native language was not English; few were worried about instructing those children in their native language; few were interested in protecting the cultures those children represented; and few wanted to spend extra money on bilingual programs. So, over the next decade, bilingual education was generally ignored by local school districts.

Then, in 1974, in Lau v. Nichols, a landmark law case, the Supreme Court affirmed the responsibility of the states and local districts to provide appropriate education for their language-minority students. As a result, districts across the country were "forced" to take seriously the needs of children from immigrant families, and opposition to bilingual education soared.

Thus the stage was set, and when President Reagan took office a few years after the Lau decision, he and his supporters were geared up to do away with bilingual programs. Moreover, they were backed in this mission by organized ethnocentric groups that refused to think of America as anything but a white Christian country (despite colorful evidence to the contrary!), as well as by other Americans who were willing to act out "language paranoia."

Such paranoia is, unfortunately, a common response to people who are speaking an unfamiliar language. It is all too easy to conclude that those people are "un-American," or that they might be up to no good. Suppose, for example, you are on a subway, in a bus, or at a public event, and two foreign-language speakers glanced in your direction. Wouldn't you wonder whether they were talking about you—or perhaps planning something you ought to be warned about? If so, you are not alone—and this common response is what we mean by "language paranoia." Most Americans, however, are willing to keep such suspicions to themselves. Only a minority act on them by expressing feelings of hostility or by seeking to limit the rights of those who speak another language.

Acting out one's "language paranoia" becomes more likely, however, when people who speak a foreign tongue enter a community in large numbers and are perceived to be a threat to native-language speakers. And that is exactly what happened in some American communities in the late 1970s and 1980s. As a result, newspapers in those communities began to report the concerns of Americans—who worried about "foreigners who use our resources and steal our jobs." And various reactionary groups began to surface that advocated restricting immigration and limiting all forms of foreign-language use, including instruction in the schools, to "English Only."

One English Only group, U.S. English, was originally co-chaired by a United States senator; claimed a large membership, including many other government officials; was endorsed by many celebrities; and was led for a time by the misguided but media-savvy Linda Chavez, a Hispanic who was once a staff-member in the Reagan White House. U.S. English and similar groups were opposed to every aspect of bilingualism and successfully promoted English Only legislation in various states.[55] In order to examine some of the concerns of those who led this movement, let's look at a memo on Hispanic immigration authored by John Tanton, co-founder of U.S. English. Tanton wrote,

> *Gobernar es poblar* translates "to govern is to populate." In this society where the majority rules, does this hold? Will the present majority peaceably hand over its political power to a group that is simply more fertile? . . . Can *homo contraceptivus* compete with *homo progenitiva* [sic] if borders aren't controlled? Or is advice to limit one's family simply advice to move over and let someone else with greater reproductive powers occupy the space? . . . Perhaps this is the first instance in which those with their pants up are going to get caught by those with their pants down! . . .
>
> How will we make the transition from a dominant non-Hispanic society with a Spanish influence to a dominant Spanish society with a non-Hispanic influence? As whites see their power and control over their lives declining, will they simply go quietly into the night? Or will there be an explosion?[56]

Why on earth should such blatantly racist sentiments have surfaced over the issue of bilingualism? Actually, this question is easy to answer. A good deal of the funds supporting John Tanton and other leaders of the English Only movement came from a member of the wealthy Mellon family, Cordelia Scaife May, who over the years had often contributed to eugenic and racist organizations.[57] Thus, in some ways, this movement represents merely the old wines of racial hatred and bigotry in new bottles. However, the targets of hatred have changed. Whereas once hate-filled people had inveighed against Irish, Polish, Italian, or Jewish immigrants from Europe, today's targets come more often from Korea, Vietnam, and various Spanish-speaking countries.

Thus, the recent bitter protests against bilingualism suggest the unhappy thought that many Americans can still be swayed by blatant racial prejudice, and that fear of the "brown" or "yellow menace" is at the root of some contemporary antibilingual sentiment. So, pandering to the fears and prejudices of ignorant Americans, by the mid-1980s Reagan and his supporters had joined the attack on bilingual education. They did so, characteristically, by making "claims" about evidence. Here are some representative quotations.

- Federal policy has discouraged the use of English and may consequently delay development of English language skills. (From an undated Department of Education "Bilingual Education Fact Sheet.")[58]
- The immersion literature is consistently positive and shows impressive levels of [second language] development. The same cannot be said for [Transitional Bilingual Education]. (From materials submitted by the Department of Education to congressional hearings during the summer of 1983.)[59]
- [E]ducational research does not justify promoting only those methods that rely on native language instruction—other methods are probably more effective in many cases. (From a Department of Education "Bilingual Education Fact Sheet" distributed to congressional offices in 1986.)[60]

These and many other quotations critical of bilingual education, made either by then Secretary of Education William Bennett, or by others in the Reagan Department of Education, were eventually assembled by the United States General Accounting Office (GAO), an agency established to audit government programs. The GAO was asked to advise Congress about whether the executive branch was accurate when it claimed that bilingual education was ineffective, that evidence favored immersion programs (which would, of course, save federal tax dollars), and that bilingual programs should be scrapped. Moreover, to promote their agenda, the Reagan Department of Education had attacked most prior research on bilingual education, and the GAO was asked to assess the claims the department was then making.[61]

What did the GAO conclude? That Secretary Bennett and the Department of Education had not been telling the truth! Indeed, in transmitting its report on bilingual education to Representative Augustus F. Hawkins, Eleanor Chelimski, the Director of the GAO, wrote that *the Secretary of Education had failed to interpret the research accurately.*[62] Bennett had been *wrong* to say that bilingual education is "the same failed path on which we have been travel-ling," that the current bilingual education law is a "bankrupt course," that as a result of the current law "too many children have failed to become fluent in English," and that Americans "throw good money after bad" by supporting this law. Evidently, either no one in the Department of Education could then read or understand research evidence, or the secretary and his minions had lied about this evidence to promote their own agenda and those of their English Only supporters.

But what does the research on bilingual education really say? To answer this question, one need only examine scholarly reviews of the literature.[63] Four main points emerge. First, many informative studies have appeared about Transitional Bilingual Education, and those studies confirm that TBE builds competency both in children's native language and in English. Second, although the implementation of TBE programs is not always good, the imple-mentation of other types of complex educational innovations—such as co-operative learning, Head Start programs, or new mathematics curricula—can also be problematic. Thus, one should not judge the overall effectiveness of TBE based on a few poor examples of implementation.

Third, various models for TBE have evolved, but the most successful are those in which competency both in English and in the child's native language are promoted throughout the school years. In addition to arguing for immer-sion programs, the Department of Education under Reagan promoted TBE programs in which native-language instruction was gradually withdrawn and immigrant students were "weaned" to speaking English only. (This led to schizophrenic recommendations by the Department of Education: on the one hand, it was trying to squelch heritage languages among young children; while on the other, it was promoting the study of those same languages among high school students!) Naturally, short-term TBE programs were less successful in developing competency in two languages than were programs that involved long-term instruction in both languages.

Fourth, studies of bilingual children, from various backgrounds—includ-ing, for example, English and Spanish; German and Turkish; or French and English—have found not only that such children have economic and social advantages, but also that they enjoy *cognitive* advantages. They are more able to accomplish challenging, higher-order cognitive tasks than are monolingual children.[64] Bilingual education, then, is simply better education! In fact, we cheat monolingual American children of a good education when we do not provide them with opportunities to learn a second language well at an early age. (Americans may think this a startling finding; Europeans would not be surprised. Most schoolchildren in Europe today are required to learn at least one second language well. Many students in Holland learn *five or more* lan-guages!)

So the research evidence provides little support for education critics who advocate scrapping bilingual education. Moreover, some of those who oppose bilingual programs seem to be xenophobic, racist, and just plain meanspirited. This does not mean that all Americans who have questioned bilingual education are so motivated. Some people may not understand how young children learn foreign languages and may assume that immersion programs "ought" to work, as they supposedly did for immigrants a century ago. Others may simply be confused about the issue, which is not surprising given the disinformation campaign conducted by William Bennett and others in the Department of Education under Reagan.

But beyond these issues, the campaign against bilingual education raises serious policy questions for Americans: How can our country best preserve the languages and cultures of our latest immigrants so that we all benefit from economic and cultural ties with the nations from which those immigrants came? And how can Americans convince their political leaders that there is an urgent need to fund good, early, second-language instruction so that *all* American students can benefit from bilingual education? As the great writer Carlos Fuentes once said, "monolingualism is a curable disease."[65]

The Elect and the Damned

The time is ripe for a reevaluation of gifted and talented education programs. . . . Gifted programs prepare future leaders, scientists, and artists. In addition, these programs help meet the individual needs of gifted children. The loss in unrealized potential of underserved gifted children is incalculable—in lost inventions, cures, discoveries, and dreams. Gifted programs help gifted students maximize their potential and increase the probability that they will make a productive contribution to society.

—David M. Fetterman (*Excellence & Equality*, 1988, p. 1)

Common sense tells many educators and parents that "gifted" or "gifted and talented" or "honors" classes offer exceptional educational opportunities to students who can profit from them. Often (though not always) that's true enough. But over the past ten years or so, the practice of tracking has been challenged in a way that the educational status quo and "common sense" rarely are. It turns out that tracking works to the *disadvantage* of most children; and it also turns out that tracking is not essential to maintain benefits for the few children who participate in the highest tracks.

—Jeannie Oakes and Martin Lipton (Foreword to *Playing Favorites* by Mara Sapon-Shevin, 1994, p. ix)

It's such a seductive idea: The typical school is obviously planned to serve the "average" child, but as we know most children are not "average." Schools now provide extra resources to help students who are disabled or who need special help. But where does this leave the student who is "talented" or "gifted"? If other students are being given extra resources, doesn't this leave our best students out in the cold? Aren't we therefore stunting their lives, and don't we risk losing their potential contributions (which the country badly needs)? Why not select those who are truly "talented" or "gifted" and give them the *enriched* educational experiences that they need and deserve?

Why not, indeed? The argument favoring special programs for gifted and talented students has formed a cornerstone of Neoconservative educational rhetoric. Some business leaders, journalists, academics, and educators have also worried about serving the needs of talented youths and don't want to lose their potential contributions to the nation. So what's wrong with the argument? Actually, there are *many* things wrong with it, each raising serious questions about proposals to provide enrichment programs for the gifted and talented. Let's look at these issues.

To begin with, *there is no foolproof way to identify at an early age those who are "talented" or "gifted."* The typical enrichment program bases decisions about which students to enroll in the program on intelligence-test scores or on a combination of scores from a battery of ability, aptitude, and achievement tests. Students are allowed into the program if their test scores exceed a certain cut-off point, let us say an IQ of 130 or an equivalent total score from the test battery. But intelligence tests and others tests used for these purposes are *not* totally reliable instruments, which means that the student whose IQ is estimated at 130 or more on a given day may very well score only 120 if retested a week or so later. And this means, of course, that one week later a child who has been selected for an enrichment program should properly be asked to leave, but that is an unlikely event, to say the least. (Schools do not like to declassify students from enrichment programs because their parents get angry.)

Moreover, tests used for making decisions about enrichment programs have only marginal validity. Actually, this shouldn't be too surprising. Intelligence, aptitude, and achievement tests are designed to predict students' abilities to do well in *school* subjects, so they assess only a small sample of students' capabilities and are normally *poor* predictors of students' adult accomplishments. This is particularly true because those accomplishments might be in a huge variety of fields—mathematics, chemistry, music, dance, history, cinematography, political leadership, ethics, electronic design, marketing, you name it—and commonly used tests are simply not designed to predict this wide range of adult accomplishments. As long as tests are the main criteria for accepting students into enrichment programs, those programs will *always* exclude some students who could benefit greatly from them.

Add these problems together, and one discovers that many mistakes are *always* made when standardized test scores are used to determine who does and who does not "deserve" to be admitted to a program having long-term consequences in the real world. A startling illustration of this principle occurred in 1976 when, due to an error in calibration for the Armed Services Vocational Aptitude Battery (ASVAB), some *three hundred thousand* recruits were admitted to the military who normally would have been rejected because of their low test scores. What happened? "Follow-up studies showed that as a group these enlistees performed only somewhat less well than those who passed the ASVAB, and many did as well or better."[66] The ASVAB, therefore, had provided only shaky evidence for making decisions about who would and who would not make good soldiers. Intelligence, aptitude, and achievement tests provide equally shaky evidence for admitting students to enrichment programs. How on earth can an enrichment program be justified for a few students when we know from the outset that many other students are excluded from the program who could also benefit from its privileges?

Another major issue concerns bias. Unfortunately, *the procedures commonly used to select students for enrichment programs are inherently biased against poor and minority students.* In Chapter 2 we reviewed evidence and discussed reasons why both intelligence and achievement tests are biased against students from poor and minority families. If candidates for enrichment programs are selected on the basis of test scores alone, those programs will inevitably enroll an unfair number of students from privileged homes. To address this problem, some program administrators also base their selection decisions, in part, on personal recommendations by teachers, counselors, or school administrators. But this leads to two problems: First, teachers are more likely to pick children for gifted programs who are neat and clean, conforming and obliging—the "nice" kids in class, who consistently cooperate with teachers—and these children may *not* be those whom experts would judge the most "gifted."[67] Second, given the many covert prejudices some Americans hold, such recommendations can easily reflect bias against students of the "wrong" race, ethnicity, or gender. Thus, unless they are forced by quota systems to behave otherwise, enrichment programs will *always* overenroll unfair numbers of students from privileged backgrounds.

In addition, the enrichment program inevitably sets up an ability-tracking system in which two groups of students—"the elect" and "the damned"—are exposed to different curricula, and *those who are not selected for the enrichment program know full well they have been found wanting.* American students are taught throughout their school years to participate in public competitions, and they think that failing in those competitions reflects their individual shortcomings. Enrichment programs, therefore, impose the burden of *failure* on the majority of students in the school. Thus, they tend to lower morale, destroy a sense of community, and decrease interest in education among the majority of students in the school.[68]

Furthermore, most curricula for the gifted, prepared by specialists in that field, *are designed to be novel and challenging* and are filled with puzzles and problem-solving tasks that deal with real-world issues. They are often planned so that the students, not the teachers, get to ask a lot of questions. And in the best classrooms for the "gifted," teachers encourage the students to learn the skills needed to answer their own questions.[69] If this is true, and if such experiences truly lead to maximal growth in the abilities of gifted students, why shouldn't *other* students be exposed to these experiences? Surely, if this is considered good education, it should be available to the *majority*.

Finally, and appallingly, *no evidence has yet appeared that confirms the touted positive effects of school enrichment programs on adult accomplishment.* Indeed, some scholars are now beginning to question whether "schoolhouse giftedness" and "adult giftedness" are not, in fact, two quite different phenomena. A good discussion of this issue may be found in a recent summary chapter by psychologists Robert Siegler and Kenneth Kotovsky.[70] As these authors point out, students who are identified as "gifted" in school tend to be very good at convergent thought, at learning what is already known, and at short-term accomplishments. In contrast, those whom we honor for their accomplishments as adults are more likely to exhibit divergent thought, discovery, and long-term, profound achievements. Since these two groups of people may not overlap much in the real world, and if we fund enrichment programs for those who are "schoolhouse gifted," we may do little or nothing to enhance the accomplishments of our most talented adult Americans.

In short, then, enrichment programs require American educators to discriminate between students who are "in" and "out" of those programs—the elect and the damned—those programs are always subject to test unreliability and bias, they have the effect of degrading educational experiences for students who are not chosen for enrichment, and they may be a complete waste of effort and money if our goal is to improve the accomplishments of "gifted" adult Americans.

Given these severe problems, why have enrichment programs proved so seductive? Their attractiveness seems to reflect three assumptions. The first is that "talents" or "gifts" are detectable qualities that usually appear in early childhood. This is, of course, a dubious assumption. True, Mozart was composing music by the age of five, but for every Mozart there are a dozen or more Tchaikovskys, whose musical talents did not bloom until they were in their twenties. And it is worth remembering that the major contributions of Charles Darwin and Sigmund Freud did not begin to appear until those titans were in their forties! Evidence now suggests that intelligence continues to evolve throughout the school years and can be promoted by exposure to high-quality education. Why then deny enriched educational opportunities to those students who, for one reason or another, do not score highly on test instruments at an early age?

The second assumption reflects the Neoconservative tenet that too much of America's limited educational resources have recently been spent on students who need special help in schools and that the country cannot survive unless it educates its truly talented students adequately.[71] And, in support of this assumption, advocates for enrichment programs often point approvingly at European education systems where "talented" students are identified through early exams and are thereafter sent to specialized, demanding, expensive secondary schools. As we have suggested, this elitist argument reflects

both disquiet over the recent growth and democratization of American high
schools and a fundamental misunderstanding of the genius of American education which encourages *all* students, provides second chances for those who
need them, and delays specialized programs until the undergraduate or postgraduate years. Why should Americans turn their backs on these unique
strengths of the American system, which already educates a larger proportion
of its citizens to higher standards than does any other country in the world?
In whose interests is it to destroy this remarkably successful enterprise?

Third, some ambitious American parents assume that their own children
are (or ought to be) "gifted" and will benefit personally if programs are set
up to service their unique needs. Some privileged parents may even assume
that "giftedness" is associated with their own race, class, or ethnicity. Thus,
proposals for programs serving the "gifted" are sometimes barely disguised
demands for special privilege.

Despite their seductive appeal, and despite their frequent promotion by
privileged Americans, enrichment programs are *not* the way to improve
American education. There is no evidence that they accomplish the goals
claimed for them, and they tend to weaken some of the most impressive
traditional strengths of America's schools.

The Clinton Administration's Agenda

Practically every school district in the country uses standardized tests to provide output
measures, and the public is encouraged to believe that schools generating the highest
(outcome) scores on statewide or district-wide tests are the "best," while those with
the lowest scores are the "worst." Such quality judgments are meaningless without
"input" data on the students when they first enroll. In fact, "outcome" scores are
probably telling us much more about the population *recruited* by the school than they
are about the effectiveness of the school's academic program. The same mindless form
of one-shot testing also characterizes the National Assessment of Educational Progress
and the testing now being proposed by the National Education Goals Panel.

—Alexander Astin (1993, p. A48)

Since January of 1993 the Reagan and Bush administrations have been
history. Americans today are faced with the educational policies of a new
administration, that of Bill Clinton and company. What have been those
policies to date, and what are their prospects for improving the American
educational scene?

So far we would have to give a mixed report card to Clintonian education
enterprises. On the positive side, Bill Clinton has appointed well-intentioned,
supportive people to leadership positions in the Department of Education
and given only low-key attention to educational issues. This doesn't sound too

impressive, but by comparison with actions of the Reaganaughts or Bushites, educational activities in the Clinton administration have been less vigorous, less dishonest, and less hostile to public schools—and these are surely improvements. Muted is the rhetoric that blames education for the growing social problems of America; absent are the lies and distorted evidence that characterized the depths of the Manufactured Crisis; abandoned are plans for mindless intensification and vouchers—and we applaud these changes.

In addition, the Clinton administration has signaled its intention to support the study of education and its outcomes, and this also is a plus. Moreover, some Clintonians have indicated enthusiasm for "outcome-based education"—programs where educational success is judged by combinations of success indicators—as a result of which, "outcome-based education" seems to be displacing "secular humanism" in the catalogue of educational evils in some broadsides from the Religious Right![72] One may quarrel with the limitations of "outcome-based education" and the idea of basing decisions about schooling on those few outcomes that can be easily measured, but at least the Clinton administration is committed to using evidence.

Also, the Clinton administration deserves praise because it views the process of educational reform as an ongoing one that should involve close collaboration among federal, state, and local authorities. Indeed, such collaboration is a major feature of Goals 2000, the recently passed bill that represents the cornerstone of Clinton's education initiatives.

Unfortunately, however, the Clinton education agenda also has some bleak features. Consider, for example, Goals 2000 itself. It is no accident that this act had a title similar to George Bush's initiative, America 2000, for a good deal of the rhetoric of Bush's initiative was resurrected in the Clinton bill. For example, America 2000 called for America to be "first in mathematics achievement by the year 2000," whereas Goals 2000 merely extended this call to "science and mathematics achievement." With the kinds of testing programs used in international studies—whose faults we discussed in Chapter 2—it is impossible for this nation, or any other nation so conceived and so dedicated, to ever achieve this goal, or to know when that goal had actually been attained! Goals such as these make sense only if one assumes: that America's comparative standing with regard to science and mathematics achievement can be detected reliably; that America is not now "first" in science and mathematics achievement; and that the nation should commit itself to becoming first in science and mathematics rather than to other commendable educational goals. Each of these is a dubious assumption.

In addition, some Clinton initiatives seem to be based on tenets of Neoconservative thought and may generate serious problems for schools. A good example of this appears in Goals 2000, which sets up a "National Education Standards and Improvement Council" that is charged with promoting national standards for accomplishment in basic academic subjects, encouraging the states to set up reform programs that will enable them to meet these standards, and certifying state procedures for assessing their efforts. Although this program is cloaked in the rhetoric of "improvement," it is also a vehicle for promoting competitive evaluations among schools within each state. And though Goals 2000 recognizes that schools presently differ in their facilities, curricula, and pedagogy and places a five-year moratorium on the use of evaluations to reward specific schools, it calls for high-stakes evaluation systems in all of the states. Thus, if it has its desired effect, Goals 2000 will generate many of the evils of evaluation systems that we discussed earlier: declining intrinsic motivations in schools, narrowed and superficial instructional efforts, added costs that are not devoted to instruction, outright cheating on evaluation exams, systematic bias against schools serving poor and minority students, and unfair awards (and support) given to schools that already enjoy advantages.

Another unfortunate example concerns the promotion by the Clintonians of enrichment programs for "talented" students. In October 1993 the Office of Educational Research and Improvement released *National Excellence: A Case for Developing America's Talent*.[73] This document was designed to promote the notion that America was now shortchanging its "talented" students, and it encourages the states to set up programs that would remedy this "problem." We have already noted that proposals to provide enrichment for "talented" students have long been urged by Neoconservatives, that they pander to the interests of privileged persons, and that, if adopted, they impose serious problems on America's schools.

Yet another problem concerns the enthusiastic way in which prominent members of the Clinton administration, such as Secretary of Labor Robert Reich, are promoting the questionable idea that more education will lead to more employment. As we have noted, the evidence suggests that the *individual* can improve his or her chances for employment through education but that educating more people does not necessarily create more jobs. Indeed, many Americans with postgraduate degrees are now unemployed or driving taxicabs, their real earnings have declined, and their anxiety about job security permeates the nation. We believe that current leaders in the Department of Education are people of goodwill who would like to improve public education in America. But compared with the substantial attention the administration has given to health care, crime, gun control, welfare reform, job creation, and other domestic issues, education has not been given high priority at the White House. Many of the increasingly serious problems now faced by America's schools stem from the wider society, so the schools may benefit, too, if the administration pays attention to some of these other problems. However, it appears that too many members of Clinton's administration have accepted myths of the Manufactured Crisis—as well as tenets of Neoconservative educational thought—and these unsupported beliefs presumably have helped to generate their enthusiasm for educational initiatives originally begun in the Bush years.

The most serious charge that can and should be laid against the Clinton education agenda, however, is that it continues to ignore or downplay soaring social problems that directly afflict American schools. For example, we can detect little concern for and less action with regard to the huge, and growing, level of poverty among America's children; the enormous differences in levels of support given to America's schools; or the low average salaries of America's teachers. Absent initiatives to improve these conditions, it is difficult to understand how the Clinton administration can hope to have a significant impact on American education.

To summarize then, so far the Clinton administration's effects on education are not likely to be as corrosive as those of the administrations of Ronald Reagan or George Bush, but that is surely faint praise. The current administration's attitudes and intentions are praiseworthy, but some of its major initiatives have been based on activities that were begun in the Bush years. These initiatives may cause damage to schools if they have an impact. But one can always hope that their impact is minimal and that leaders on the Clinton team will look a bit more closely at the evidence and begin to plan their *own* agenda of innovative actions that can help solve the many real problems of American education. And to help them and others who want to help schools today, we turn in the next two chapters to some of the real problems of American education and what might be done about them.

Chapter Six

Real Problems of American Education

◆

By now you may be convinced that American public schools have no problems, and that all concern about the present state of American education is without merit. After all, haven't we convinced you that most recent criticisms of our country's education are groundless?

Alas, such a conclusion is not warranted. Unfortunately, American schools face serious and real problems. Indeed, many of those problems are worse today than they were in earlier years, and many are more serious here than in other Western countries. It is, in fact, amazing that American educators cope as well as they do, that in the face of myriad barriers they manage to educate so many students, and to such a high standard.

But saying this is one thing, and understanding the real problems faced by American schools is something else. Unless they have this knowledge, well-intentioned Americans will be confused about what their schools can and cannot accomplish, and they may embrace ineffective or even tragic nostrums for improving education. But once they have that knowledge, well-intentioned Americans become able to design and support programs that can truly improve schools. For this reason, we turn now to the real problems that American education faces.

Societal Problems and American Schools

And even should the clouds of barbarism and despotism again obscure the science and liberties of Europe, this country remains to preserve and restore light and liberty to them.

—Thomas Jefferson (letter to John Adams, September 12, 1821)

Today, ... the challenge is clear. We see a nation whose economy is plainly failing to meet the needs and aspirations of its people. Staggering deficits choke off critical public and private investments. ... Our once-dazzling infrastructure buckles. Our nation is becoming two polarized Americas, one privileged, one poor. Our productivity grows meagerly compared to our competitors'; our savings and investment rates are a fraction of theirs. The general interest and the future are drowned out by the strident claims

215

of today's special interests. Even at a time when the electorate has made it clear it wants change, many elected officials dare not speak the truth. . . . The American Dream—the promise of steady improvement in private and public life and parents' conviction that their children's lives would be better than their own—is now at risk of extinction for many citizens and may survive for future generations as but a wisp of historical memory.

> —Senators Warren B. Rudman and Paul E. Tsongas (foreword to *Facing Up* by Peter G. Peterson, 1993, p. 13)

As in all countries, Americans tell one another myths, and if you are like us, you may have grown up believing that the United States is not only a land of freedom, wealth, and democracy, but that it also offers more opportunity, more equality—in short, a better deal—to its citizens than does any other country. Indeed, so pervasive are these myths that people who question them are sometimes accused of being unpatriotic. Thus, you may be surprised to learn that *major* social problems afflict our country, that many of these problems are longstanding and are often worse here than elsewhere, and that some of these problems have escalated during the last few years.

These problems also afflict education, and sometimes their effects are devastating. We consider several of these problems here and the difficulties they generate for America's schools.

Income and Wealth Inequity. Americans have always known, of course, that some people are rich and some are poor, but they have not generally known that *income and wealth are much less evenly distributed here than in other Western nations.* By comparison, in *our* country, rich people are a lot wealthier and poor people are a lot more numerous—and this condition has recently been getting worse. You may think that we are exaggerating this problem, but we're not. Let's look at the evidence.

Few topics have generated more heat among economists than debates about how to assess income and wealth inequality, although such debates often concern "Gini coefficients," "Theil coefficients," "Lorenz curves," and other wonderfully obscure concepts. Rather than get into these matters, let's take a simple measure of economic inequality among nations, the percentage of people who are *truly poor.* To compare different countries, however, we need a definition of poverty that can be applied everywhere. Recent comparative studies have defined *the poor* as those who live in families whose net income is less than half the median net income for all families in the population. Thus, should median net income for a family of four be, say, thirty thousand dollars per year in a given country, a family of four trying to make do with less than fifteen thousand dollars per year would be considered poor. In addition, we should understand that "net income" includes not only the salaries earned by family members, minus taxes, but also the value of social services that are transferred to those families from public funds.

Information for comparing net-income statistics among Western countries has recently become available in a database called the Luxembourg Income Study (LIS) which summarizes surveys that were conducted in several countries around the year 1980. Various publications have now appeared from the LIS, and we've prepared Exhibit 6.1 from one of these sources, an article by John Coder, Lee Rainwater, and Timothy Smeeding, that estimated percentages for those who were poor in ten Western nations in 1980.[1]

Coder and his colleagues calculate that 16.6 percent of Americans were living in poor families around 1980; that is roughly *three times* the percentage of people who were then living in poor families in Norway, Sweden, or West Germany. This figure seems bad enough, but look also at the data for children—the major clients of schools. The authors estimated that *more than a fifth* (21.4 percent) of American children were living in poor families fourteen years ago! In other words, compared with Germany, Norway, or Sweden, a child in the U.S. was more than *four* times as likely to be living in poverty in 1980. And the problem has been getting worse. According to the National Commission on Children, the number of children living in poverty *increased* by roughly *two million* in our country between 1980 and 1990.[2]

("But wait a minute," some skeptics may mutter. "Aren't the two of you assuming that average incomes are roughly the same in Western nations? Isn't it also true that America is the richest nation, so poor people in this country live better than they do elsewhere?" The answer to these questions is no. America was indeed the richest nation in the world for a brief period, after World War II. But our country has fallen behind in recent years, and today poor people are worse off here than in most of Western Europe.)

Why are there so many more poor people in the United States? Maldistribution of income in this country results from many forces, among them the fact that for the past two generations Americans have spent *much* more of their tax dollars on the military than on the social services that taxes support elsewhere. (Did you know that Americans spend from *two to four times as much*, per capita, on armaments as do citizens in other Western countries, that ours is the *only* Western country that does not have a national health care system, that most other Western countries provide a basic wage for *all* unemployed people as a matter of right, and that most Western countries support *free* day-care services for infants and *mandate* paid maternity leave?) Indeed, given the paucity of citizen services supported in this country, it is surprising that America's income maldistribution is not worse than it is.

Income maldistribution creates problems for public schools for several reasons. To begin with, poor families lack resources and cannot afford to pay much for school taxes, which means that sooner or later others in the population may come to resent paying to educate their children. In addition, when rich people have a lot of extra money, that money becomes optional, disposable income that they can spend on luxuries. One of the luxuries rich people

218

Exhibit 6.1 Percentage of People Who Were Poor in 1980

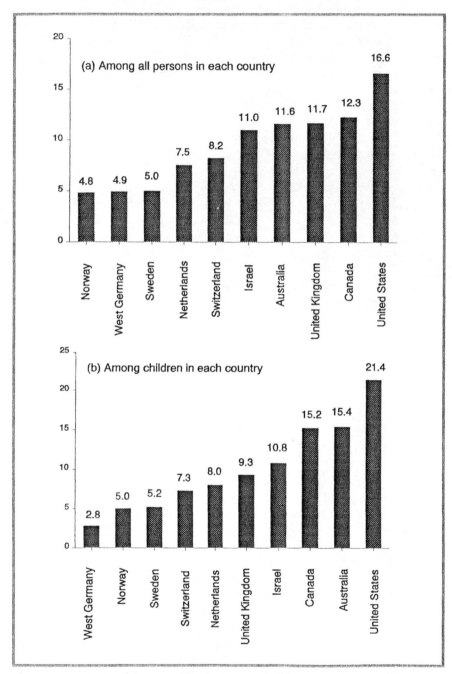

—Source: John Coder, Lee Rainwater, and Timothy Smeeding (Inequality among children and elderly in ten modern nations: The United States in an international context, 1989, Table 2, p. 322).

sometimes buy is private schooling for their children, which, in turn, reduces the financial and moral support they would otherwise give to public schools.

Above all, income maldistribution creates problems because it is *very* difficult to provide good schooling for impoverished students who may come to school hungry or in cast-off and torn clothing, who suffer from untreated medical problems, who live in neighborhoods that are rife with crime and violence, or who come from homes that lack even basic amenities—let alone books and other supports for education. A frightening portrait of the many ways poverty affects American children appears in Jonathan Kozol's *Savage Inequalities*.[3] Kozol begins his book by discussing East St. Louis, Illinois (see Exhibit 6.2). As he points out, parents in this community are desperately poor and have but scant resources to give their sons and daughters. As a

---

■ Exhibit 6.2
Poverty and Children in East St. Louis

East St. Louis—which the local press refers to as "an inner city without an outer city"—has some of the sickest children in America. Of 66 cities in Illinois, East St. Louis ranks first in fetal death, first in premature birth, and third in infant death. Among the negative factors listed by the city's health director are the sewage running in the streets, air that has been fouled by the local plants, the high lead levels noted in the soil, poverty, lack of education, crime, dilapidated housing, insufficient health care, unemployment. . . .

As in New York City's poorest neighborhoods, dental problems also plague the children here. Although dental problems don't command the instant fears associated with low birth weight, fetal death or cholera, they do have the consequence of wearing down the stamina of children and defeating their ambitions. Bleeding gums, impacted teeth and rotting teeth are routine. . . . Children get used to feeling constant pain. They go to sleep with it. Sometimes their teachers are alarmed and try to get them to a clinic. But it's all so slow and heavily encumbered with red tape and waiting lists and missing, lost or cancelled welfare cards, that dental care is often long delayed. . . .

Compounding these problems is the poor nutrition of the children here—average daily food expenditure in East St. Louis is $2.40 for one child—and the underimmunization of young children. Of every 100 children recently surveyed in East St. Louis, 55 were incompletely immunized for polio, diphtheria, measles and whooping cough. . . .

On top of all else is the very high risk of death by homicide in East St. Louis. In a recent year in which three cities in the state of roughly the same size as East St. Louis had an average of four homicides apiece, there were 54 homicides in East St. Louis.

—Source: Jonathan Kozol (*Savage Inequalities*, 1991, pp. 20–21).

result, those children not only lack home support for education but are surrounded by filth, foul air, and sewage. Moreover, they are often undernourished and in pain from untreated health problems, and they are victimized by the violence that is endemic in their community. Nor are these problems confined to East St. Louis. Kozol has equally alarming tales to tell about children and poverty in Chicago, New York City, Washington, D.C., and other American cities.

Given these problems, we should not be surprised to learn that "children from families with incomes below the poverty level are nearly twice as likely to be held back a grade as their more advantaged classmates, [and that] the proficiency level of an average 17-year-old in a poor urban setting is equivalent to that of a typical 13-year-old in an affluent urban area."[4]

Thus, an important reality: *the larger the proportion of citizens who live in poverty, the greater the challenge for public schools.* And since truly impoverished students have a *much* harder time with education than students from wealthy, middle-class, or working-class homes, when the poor are more numerous, the aggregate performance of public schools will suffer. All things being equal, then, even if average income and support for education are equivalent in two countries, the country that has more extremes of wealth and poverty will generate *lower* aggregate educational achievement scores than will the country where incomes are distributed more equitably—and this is a major reason why the United States sometimes looks bad when its aggregate achievement scores are compared with those of other countries.

Several forces have worsened the problems of poverty for schools in recent years. For one, the 1980s generated a *massive* redistribution of income and wealth in the United States, so that the rich became a lot richer and the poor tragically poorer. Data illustrating this point appeared in a book by Kevin Phillips, and we have reproduced a table from his book here (see Exhibit 6.3).[5]

As can be seen, if we compute income in constant 1987 dollars, we find that the poorest 10 percent of the population (the first income decile) *lost* about 15 percent of their average family income in the eleven years between 1977 and 1988. In contrast, the richest 10 percent of the population (the tenth income decile) *gained* more than 16 percent in average income, and America's richest 1 percent gained an outrageous 50 percent in real income during this same period!

Given these sharp differences in gained and lost income, it is not surprising that rich Americans have also taken possession of more of the nation's assets. Using data furnished by the Federal Reserve Board, Phillips estimated that the share of wealth held by the richest 0.5 percent of American households *rose* from 14.4 percent in the mid-1970s to 26.9 percent in the mid-1980s. Using slightly different figures, provided by the Census Bureau, Michael Hinds, writing in the *New York Times,* recently estimated that the share of the nation's wealth held by the top 1 percent of Americans had *increased*

Exhibit 6.3   Income Gains and Losses, 1977–88

Changes in Average Family Income (1987 Dollars)

Income Decile	Average Family Income		Percentage Change 1977–88	Change in Average Family Income 1977–88
	1977	1988		
First	$ 4,113	$ 3,504	−14.8%	$ −609
Second	8,334	7,669	−8.0	−665
Third	13,140	12,327	−6.2	−813
Fourth	18,436	17,220	−6.6	−1,216
Fifth	23,896	22,389	−6.3	−1,507
Sixth	29,824	28,205	−5.4	−1,619
Seventh	36,405	34,828	−4.3	−1,577
Eighth	44,305	43,507	−1.8	−798
Ninth	55,487	56,064	1.0	577
Tenth	102,722	119,635	16.5	16,913
Top 5%	134,543	166,016	23.4	31,473
Top 1%	270,053	404,566	49.8	134,513

—Source: Kevin Phillips (*The Politics of Rich and Poor*, 1990, Table 1).
—Statistical Sources: *Challenge to Leadership* (Urban Institute) and Congressional Budget Office.

from 27 percent in 1981 to 36 percent in 1988.[6] Thus, both estimates suggest that roughly *one-tenth* of the entire wealth of the nation was transferred into the coffers of the superrich during the 1980s.

What caused this massive, upward redistribution of income and wealth in the 1980s? Two factors seem to have been largely responsible. First, the labor market has been changing, with the gradual disappearance of nonskilled and well-paid, blue-collar jobs and a weakening of union power. These trends have meant reduced income for many working-class and lower-middle-class families. Second, and more important, between 1980 and 1992, the White House was occupied by two presidents who represented the economic interests of the rich. Aided and abetted by lobbyists and the Congress, the administrations of these two presidents sharply reduced social services and promoted tax reforms that transferred ever more income upward.

Let us look at the latter process. Before the Reagan years, Americans were still paying federal taxes that were moderately progressive—i.e., that levied higher tax rates on those with higher incomes—but progressive taxes were largely obliterated during the 1980s. As a result, those with low or even moderate incomes now paid a *larger* tax share than the superrich.

We are not exaggerating this effect. Respected journalists Donald Barlett and James Steele have recently contrasted federal taxes paid in 1991 by the

American family with a median income with those paid by George and Barbara Bush. According to Barlett and Steele, the median American family earned $35,035 in 1991 and paid $6,116 in federal taxes—which works out to be a tax rate of 17.6 percent. That year the Bushes reported an adjusted gross income of $1,324,456 and paid federal taxes of $209,964—thus their tax rate was only 15.9 percent![7] Moreover, the Bushes were living in the White House at that time, so although their expenses for food and clothing may have been comparable to those for the median American family, that year their housing and transportation costs were paid largely by American taxpayers. But, do not think the Bushes were getting an extraordinary deal; in fact they may have been tax pikers. According to Barlett and Steele, IRS records from 1989 show that more than one thousand individuals and families with incomes greater than two hundred thousand dollars legally paid *not one dollar* of federal income tax that year![8] (And you wondered why the rich have recently been getting richer?)

Poverty also poses a growing problem for education because of changes in the composition of those poorest in the nation. Once upon a time America's poorest citizens were likely to be elderly, but this is no longer true.

> Today, children are the poorest Americans. One in five lives in a family with an income below the federal poverty level. One in four infants and toddlers under the age of three is poor. Nearly 13 million children live in poverty, more than 2 million more than a decade ago. Many of these children are desperately poor; nearly 5 million live in families with incomes less than half the federal poverty level.[9]

We don't have to look far to see why this shift is occurring. Not only does America fail to offer many of the social services that are provided by law to impoverished and single-parent families in other Western countries, but federal tax laws actually work against families with young children. For example, leading industrialist Peter G. Peterson calculates that in 1992 the "typical" working-age couple who had one child and who earned $30,000 would have paid a federal tax bill of $7,155. On the other hand, the "typical" retired couple, with no children and the same income, would have paid a mere $900![10]

Thus, not only must American schools contend with the effects of massive and growing poverty in the general population, but they must also cope with increasing numbers of poor *children,* their immediate clients. America's schools must, therefore, deal with a vast and growing challenge—the need to educate sharply rising numbers of "at risk" students. (Later in the chapter we examine the extent of that challenge.)

All of which illustrates a point that underlies much of what we will say in this chapter. Some Americans of modest means wonder why they should be concerned about the poor. Many believe that America is "the land of opportunity," that a good deal of poverty is transitory, or that the poor are themselves at least partly to blame for their plight. Thus, when Americans think about poverty, they may believe that the plight of the poor has little relevance for the lives of ordinary citizens. We argue that this is shortsighted, indeed that the widespread poverty in our country affects *all* Americans in many ways.

Apart from the appalling immorality of tolerating poverty in the midst of affluence, our country simply cannot compete with other nations if 20 percent or more of our children come from destitute homes and cannot complete the education they need. America's schools are severely stressed when they have to cope with large numbers of impoverished students, and America cannot afford the massive amounts of crime and violence—and the huge social-service and punishment systems needed to contend with them—if poverty and ignorance remain widespread. (Recently, the citizens of California voted for a tough law requiring an enormous expansion of their prisons. Diverting tax dollars for this expansion will impoverish the state's once-esteemed social services and educational systems, thereby degrading the lives of many working-class, middle-class, and upper-class Californians. What a tragic outcome of failure to distribute income and wealth more equitably.) Indeed, EVERYONE is harmed by poverty. Truly, no person is an island.

Growth and Stagnation of the Economy. Many Americans also seem not to be aware that the economy of their nation has been largely stagnant for two decades and that other nations have been passing us by in per-capita income and standard of living. Although, come to think of it, why should they be aware of these events? If there is one thing that motivates our federal governments, be those governments Democrat or Republican, it is the desire to paint a rosy picture of the economy. So instead of talking about the standard of living in per-capita terms, they trumpet the growth of the total economy—which may or may not keep up with the growth of the population and with inflation. To counter such propaganda, let's look at the evidence.

We begin with data showing the growth of real income during the last forty years. It is easy to express median per-capita family income in terms of constant 1988 dollars, and we do this in Exhibit 6.4. This figure reveals a remarkable pattern. As can be seen, per-capita family income in America increased substantially and at a predictable, even pace throughout the decades of the 1950s and 1960s, but around 1970 it suddenly stopped growing, and it hasn't grown much since. (Moreover, two additional problems have multiplied the effects of this stagnation. Over the past twenty-five years, average wages in America *fell behind* the rate of inflation, and the only reason American families have been able to keep even is that more and more of those families have been supported by two wage earners. Also, costs of crucial basic needs—particularly those for housing and health care—have increased

Exhibit 6.4   Median Family Income (in constant 1988 dollars)

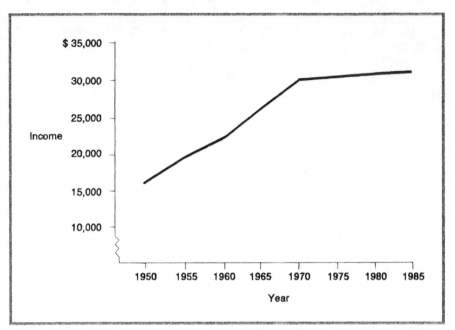

—Source: *Statistical Abstracts of the United States, 1979, 1990* (Bureau of the Census, 1979, Table #734; 1990, Table #726).

sharply in recent years. This means that the typical American family now has *less* disposable income than it had a generation ago.)

Why has per-capita income leveled off? One camp of analysts attributes the problem to the corrosive effects of the Vietnam War and its aftermath, which caused the government to divert national resources from domestic needs to huge military demands and to servicing an enormous national debt. If this explanation is correct, it should also follow that economic growth would *not* have faltered in other Western countries where less money is spent on the military and where the national debt is smaller. Indeed, that is *exactly* what has been happening, and those countries have been catching up with us or even surpassing us in standard of living.

Analysts differ regarding methods for comparing standard of living, but according to figures for Gross Domestic Product per capita (based on exchange rates) that have recently become available, the United States is now in eighth place among Western nations (see Exhibit 6.5). Similarly, according to leading economist Lester Thurow, "in terms of international purchasing power, the United States is now only the ninth wealthiest country in the world in terms of per capita GNP. We have been surpassed by Austria, Switzerland, the Netherlands, West Germany, Denmark, Sweden, Norway and Japan."[11]

Exhibit 6.5   Gross Domestic Product Per Capita for 1989 (based on currency exchange rates)

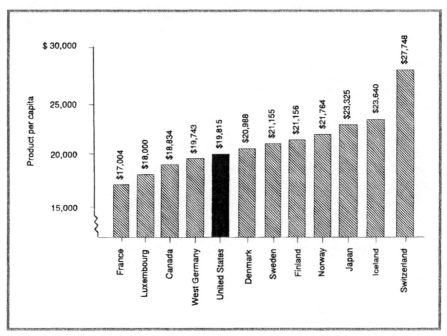

—Source: Miles Smith-Morris (*Book of World Statistics*, 1990).

Thus, although the American economy grew substantially and predictably during the 1950s and 1960s, it largely stalled during the past two decades, and this pattern of growth followed by stagnation has created difficulties for public schools. Americans become generous during periods of economic growth, and a generation ago that generosity was extended to the schools. As a result, schools were then encouraged to expand and to build new facilities, teachers' salaries went up, and educators experimented with new school equipment and curricular innovations. But generosity declines when the economy is not growing, people become less willing to pay taxes for purposes whose benefits are delayed, and support for the public schools becomes threatened. These days, school buildings and facilities are aging, class sizes are increasing, teachers' salaries are stagnating, curricular experimentation is withering, and calls for "accountability" are heard in the land. Truly, it is difficult to operate public schools—indeed to make the case for public education at all—when the economy is stagnant.

Racial, Ethnic, Religious, and Linguistic Diversity. America is a multi-ethnic society. Americans take pride in the many different groups of people who live in their country, but this diversity also poses problems for American schools.

Although most Americans are identified as white, about 12 percent are black, another 2 percent are of Asian ancestry, and about 0.6 percent are Native Americans. These four racial groups have had diverse histories and have evolved somewhat different cultures and needs. Many Americans also cling to ethnic identities associated with immigration. During the nineteenth century, immigrants to this country came largely from Northern Europe, especially from Germany and the British Isles. Immigrants at the turn of the century were more likely to represent Eastern Europe, Italy, and Russia. By the decade of the 1980s, however, the greatest number of immigrants came from Mexico, Central America, the Philippines, Korea, and Vietnam. People representing these and other national backgrounds have each brought their own beliefs, customs, values, and divergent needs to the United States. Americans also represent a wondrous array of religious affiliations. In addition, although most Americans speak English, recent immigrants are likely to speak other tongues; so that other languages, particularly Spanish, are spoken today by large minorities in some states and may predominate in certain communities.

Since these population groups have different needs, this diversity also generates problems for schools. Racial and ethnic minorities would like the schools attended by their children to offer curricula that honor their cultural heritages and urge those schools to hire teachers who can serve as role models for their children. Methods for teaching or evaluating students that work well for some groups may be less valid when applied to other groups in the population. Some religious groups may demand or object to the teaching of specific topics (such as sex education or the theory of evolution), while others may advocate or oppose prayers in public schools. Parents whose native language is not English may insist that instruction be provided in their native languages or that additional course work be offered to teach their children to speak English "properly." Meeting these diverse needs is not easy for the American schools; indeed, serious conflicts sometimes erupt in school districts over whether to spend scant resources to meet the needs of specific groups or to devote those resources to "traditional" purposes.

Moreover, these diverse groups are not distributed equally around the nation. Very few African Americans live in some states (Iowa is an example), whereas in others (mostly in the South), blacks make up more than a quarter of the population. Asians are more likely to be found in urban centers, especially in the West, and Native Americans are more numerous in states such as Arizona, New Mexico, Oklahoma, Minnesota, and Wisconsin. People of Irish ancestry are more likely to be found in the Northeast; Jews more often live in older East Coast cities; Christian fundamentalists appear in the South and the Midwestern Bible Belt; Hispanics cluster in New York, Chicago, Florida, and the states that border Mexico; and so forth. And this means that public schools in one region or community may face problems that are far different from those encountered elsewhere in the country.

In addition, population groups vary sharply in their responses to public education. Some have traditionally excelled in school, but other groups have done less well; and these differences have generated problems. Consider the recent wave of refugees from South Vietnam. On average, children from Vietnamese homes have done very well in American schools. Reasons for their successes are explored by Nathan Caplan, Marcella Choy, and John Whitmore.[12] According to these writers, Vietnamese children have done well because their families value education highly, they spend a lot of time on homework, and they are strongly coached in their studies by family members. So striking is the effect of family support that students from larger Vietnamese families actually outperform those from smaller families—which reverses the negative relationship between family size and academic achievement typically found for other groups.

One can learn a lot from the Vietnamese example, but problems are surely created when schools in a state or district are asked to meet the needs of two or more groups who differ sharply in their educational values, in their ability to provide home support for schooling, or in their understandings of public education. The United States is not the only Western country whose population contains unmelded groups—Belgium, Canada, and Northern Ireland, for example, each struggle with this problem. But no other Western country has ever tried to cope with so *many* partially-assimilated groups, and this fact poses significant problems for public schools in America.

Prejudice, Discrimination, and Black Americans. Some forms of prejudice occur around the world, and whenever they surface, social problems arise. The United States has been particularly harmed because of the malignant discrimination it has practiced for years against its most visible minority, black Americans. The history of African immigration differs significantly from that of other groups in our country. Blacks were first brought to this country as slaves, of course, and as such were often subjected to brutality, humiliation, and deculturation. After the Civil War, blacks continued to suffer violence, overt mistreatment, and the denial of basic rights and opportunities for education and economic advancement. Even today, after the Civil Rights movement of the 1960s, African Americans are still subject to prejudice, ethnic stereotyping, and discrimination. And they are disproportionately poor and are often ghettoized in rural hamlets in the South or in urban slums in the North.

The condition of black Americans today is a national disgrace that attracts worldwide attention. Consider the following from a British source:

> Nearly half of black teenagers in the city of Chicago fail to graduate from high school. In Washington, D.C., in 1989 nearly four times as many black men were jailed in the district's prison as graduated from its public schools; the leading cause of death among black men is murder. In the country as a whole a staggering

two-thirds of black babies are born to unmarried mothers; 43% of black children are, by government criteria, born poor; many do not live to see their first birthday. Last year's unemployment rate among blacks was 10.5%, more than twice that for whites.[13]

Americans are not unaware of all this, of course. Indeed, data reporting the poverty, lack of education, and criminal behavior of black, underclass Americans are regularly reported in the American press, and television coverage of riots—as in Detroit or South Los Angeles—often focuses on black violence. Thus, the stereotypical person from an American slum tends to have a black face.

But what do white Americans make of the fact that blacks are disproportionately unemployed, undereducated, and serving time in prison? Once upon a time, many white Americans believed that the causes were inherent—blacks were thought to be innately lazy, promiscuous, and stupid. Today enlightened Americans believe that those explanations are false and only indicate bigotry. Many Americans now understand that black problem behavior often results from poverty and discriminatory treatment. Too many whites, however, still offer explanations that blame African Americans themselves for their plight. Thus, they argue that blacks are handicapped "because" they lack human capital (e.g., skills, education, or appropriate work habits), because they come from single-parent, female-headed homes, or because they prefer welfare checks to employment. Such arguments have the effect of allowing white people to avoid feeling guilty about racism in this country.

But are these arguments valid? Evidence bearing on this question appeared in a recent article by Steven Shulman.[14] Using data from the Department of Commerce, Shulman matched black and white families in terms of human capital, family structure, and welfare status. Having done this, he found that black families were *still* substantially poorer than white families. Why? Because black wage earners are often denied access to well-paying jobs because of discrimination. But do white, affluent Americans want to hear this message? They do *not!* Instead, they cling to myths that allow them to blame black Americans themselves for the poverty that has been imposed on them (see Exhibit 6.6).

White prejudice against blacks also generates problems for schools. One of these problems concerns "white flight"—the tendency of affluent white Americans to move from districts where their children must attend racially integrated schools to other districts, where there are few black students. White flight tends to defeat the goal of assimilation. In addition, because of local funding of schools in suburban districts, it often allows affluent white parents to avoid responsibility for supporting schools that serve poorer, mostly black students.

Another problem concerns the intrusion of racism into debates over support for public education. During the 1992 election campaign, for example, a candidate for governor in a state where one of us lives authorized TV

■ **EXHIBIT 6.6**
Prejudice, American Style

Unlike class, a person's race is visible. The black poor are not simply poor. They visibly represent a set of stereotypes that support the values and sense of worth of the non-poor. In the era when racism was openly expressed, blacks were identified with laziness, promiscuity, and stupidity. Today these stereotypes are expressed in a more roundabout fashion: black poverty is blamed on welfare disincentives (that is, laziness), out-of-wedlock births (that is, promiscuity) and lack of human capital (that is, stupidity). Despite the lack of evidence supporting any of these explanations for black poverty, they persist in the academic literature as well as the popular imagination. They are values not in the instrumental sense of reinforcing positive life processes, but in the ceremonial sense of reinforcing status distinctions. It is far more comfortable to perceive black poverty as resulting from the deficiencies of the black population than to see it as the outcome of a racial hierarchy that skews the distribution of income toward whites. The former has the pleasant corollary of explaining the success of whites as resulting from their alleged characteristics, such as hard work, self-discipline, and skills. The latter has the unpleasant connotation of discrimination that deserves to be ended but that inevitably entails equalizing the competition for a limited set of rewards. Furthermore, the former reflects and reproduces the individualistic ethos of the marketplace, while the latter calls into question capitalism's self-images of opportunity and democracy. It is no wonder that racial myths have proved so enduring. They are part and parcel of the myth of America itself.

—Source: Steven Shulman (The causes of black poverty: Evidence and interpretation, 1990, p. 1014).

---

advertisements that promised to "correct" court decisions which had generated extra funds for urban schools. None of these advertisements said that those schools served black students (although viewers knew they did), and none reminded viewers that those schools had had miserable funding for many years (although this was also true), but each was designed to appeal to the prejudices of whites who were thought to be angry because they were being forced to spend tax dollars to upgrade schools for blacks. Fortunately, this candidate did not win the election, but racial politics have often been used to thwart support for public schools in the nation.

Unfortunately, discrimination also appears within schools themselves. To understand this problem we must go back in time. Before 1954, many school districts in this country provided only inferior, racially segregated schools for black children. Such practices were outlawed, however, in the Supreme Court's famous Brown v. Board of Education decision, and today many black students are enrolled in public school systems that are nominally integrated. Moreover, many white Americans believe that legal school integration has "solved" the problem of discrimination in American education. Alas, this is not true. Covert discrimination is now practiced in many American schools.

Covert discrimination was recently studied by Kenneth Meier, Joseph Stewart, and Robert England in a survey of urban school districts in the United States using data that were gathered by the Office of Civil Rights.[15] These investigators found that schools in some of these districts used racially loaded procedures for sorting and disciplining students.

> [In these districts] a black student is nearly three times more likely to be placed in a class for the educable mentally retarded than is a white student. A black student is 30 percent more likely to be assigned to a trainable mentally retarded class than a white student. At the other end of the sorting spectrum, a white student is 3.2 times more likely to be assigned to a gifted class than is a black student.
>
> In terms of discipline, a black student is more than twice as likely as a white student to be corporally punished or suspended. A black student is 3.5 times more likely than a white student to be expelled. [And, at the end of the road,] a black student is 18 percent more likely to drop out of school and 27 percent less likely to graduate from high school.[16]

Why have these policies evolved? According to the authors, it is because they enable bigoted members of white school boards and prejudiced educators to limit interracial contact and to maximize opportunities for white students within schools that are legally integrated. How do we know that these practices reflect discrimination rather than simply the inadequacies of black students? We know because they were not found in other districts that had powerful black communities, large populations of lower-class white students, or large percentages of black teachers.[17]

Does such educational discrimination matter? Of course it matters. Repeated studies have shown that educational attainment is a major predictor of subsequent career entry-level and earnings, and this is particularly true for the children of poor parents, for whom education may be the major, if not the sole, avenue for escaping poverty.[18] Thus, today's covert discrimination in public schools promotes poverty and problem behavior among black Americans and is yet another reason why the aggregate achievement of public school students in this country may look bad when compared with achievements from elsewhere.

To summarize then, the American tragedy of racism poses serious problems for our public schools, problems that are less evident in other Western countries that have lower levels of prejudice. These problems have threatened support for public schools and have sometimes meant that those schools did not serve equally the needs of the white and black students who were their clients. Not only are prejudice and discrimination inherently evil, but racism in this country has historically meant that Americans were willing to tolerate for worse conditions for the poor (who are thought to have black skins) than are tolerated in other Western countries. This tolerance of inadequacy for the poor has generated appallingly bad schools, where the educational accomplishments of the students are dismal.

Suburbs, Ghettos, and City Centers. Americans who travel abroad often come to an "original" insight after visiting cities in other Western countries. Somehow those cities don't quite look like their American counterparts. They are far more likely to have viable city centers and center-city residential neighborhoods, fewer slums and suburbs where poverty and wealth are concentrated, modern public transportation systems, safer streets, and well-scattered public institutions that serve the needs of the public. In short, non-American Western cities—from Oslo to Oostende, Paris to Prague, Montreal to Melbourne—all tend to be less ghettoized and more livable than are New York, Cleveland, Detroit, Milwaukee, St. Louis, or Los Angeles. Why should this be so? Why are American cities so neglected and ghettoized?

As a rule, American cities looked a lot like European cities before World War II. Like their European counterparts, most had viable city centers, good public transportation systems, and local neighborhoods with populations that tended to be stable. Most also had areas of relative affluence and poverty, of course, but these areas were either within walking distance of one another or were laced together by rail or bus services. And though cities in both the U.S. and Europe suffered during the Great Depression, public programs were also then available in most countries for city maintenance.

Several factors prompted postwar changes in American cities, however. Americans had always been geographically mobile; but after World War II, they stepped up their mobility and moved in increasing numbers from farms and small towns to urban centers. The result was that many cities were flooded with "newcomers" who had no commitment to traditional neighborhoods. And although American cities had always housed immigrants, after the war large numbers of a more visible minority, blacks, flooded into those cities. Americans also developed an early love affair with the automobile and began to dismantle their public transportation systems in favor of superhighways. And many American cities were surrounded by cheap acreage that could easily be converted from farms into suburbs or industrial parks. Suburban growth was also encouraged by real-estate speculation, economic boosterism, and freedom from the traditions and legal restrictions that often constrained municipal growth in Europe. Finally, many American women had entered the work force during World War II, and afterwards the federal government generated propaganda advocating suburban living and stay-at-home wives as a way of persuading those women to release their jobs to the servicemen who were then returning to the country.

These factors combined, then, to create a postwar climate in which affluent Americans deserted the city centers for the suburbs, leaving the cores of cities to the poor, who often represented stigmatized minority groups. The suburbanites who worked in the city usually commuted by automobile and drove on express highways. In addition, many suburbanites could avoid paying taxes to the core city, so facilities in the suburbs blossomed while those in the central cities decayed. As a result, the centers of our metropolitan areas became overwhelmed by crime, poverty, and violence. All of which means that America's cities are now more difficult to live in—and more ghettoized—than cities in other Western countries.

Needless to say, the decline of American cities has also created problems for the schools. Since American city centers often lack recreational facilities, city-center schools are frequently asked to provide those facilities. Since those schools are often located in neighborhoods that are impoverished and beset by crime, they have great difficulty meeting educational goals. And since American public schools are supported primarily through *local* taxes, suburbanization often allows affluent parents to avoid paying for schools in the urban core, thus generating sharp differences in levels of support for schools. Each of these problems is less prevalent in other countries where cities are less ghettoized and easier to live in.

Violence and Drugs. America has also had a long history of violence. In our culture individuals have been encouraged to take up arms to defend themselves or to attack others if they found them offensive. During frontier days violent acts were committed against native peoples or were frequent in communities where law enforcement was weak. During the Era of Reconstruction violence was practiced against blacks, who were frequently lynched, and Prohibition promoted the institutionalization of violence by criminal gangs in our major cities. Today, violence in America is encouraged by gun laws (unknown in other countries) that allow citizens to carry weapons freely, and is justified in "morality plays," to which Americans are repeatedly exposed on television and in the movies. These forces generate rates of personal violence in America that are appallingly high.

How violent are Americans? Until 1984 *Statistical Abstracts of the United States* regularly reported homicide rates for various countries. If we compare rates for homicide among individuals reported that year, for example, we find that Americans killed one another about *eight* times as often as did citizens from other industrialized countries (see Exhibit 6.7). These figures indicate that America was then the clear, sole, and exclusive "winner" among industrialized nations in the individual homicide derby. (On the other hand, American rates of violence against *property* are not much different from those elsewhere, and *communal* violence, generated by religious or ethnic bigotry, is greater in locales such as Northern Ireland or Bosnia-Herzegovina.)

Violence imposes many problems on the United States. It can degrade horribly the quality of life for children, and it forces some schools to devote many of their resources to security measures. Moreover, these problems fall

Exhibit 6.7   Individual Homicide Rates per 100,000 People in 1978

United States   9.4

Australia	1.8	Ireland	.7
Austria	1.4	Japan	1.1
Canada	2.5	Netherlands	.8
Denmark	.5	Norway	.7
Finland	3.0	Sweden	1.0
France	1.0	Switzerland	.7
Germany (West)	1.2	England (& Wales)	1.2
Greece	.7	Scotland	1.5
		Average (except USA)	1.2

—Source: *Statistical Abstracts of the United States, 1984* (Bureau of the Census, 1984, Table #295).

particularly on urban ghetto schools, where rates of violence are the highest. Thus city-center schools that often receive only a fraction of the funding given to suburban schools are further stressed because they must support terrified and grieving students and spend sizable portions of their meager funds on barbed-wire fences, metal detectors, and armed guards to protect students and teachers from assault (see Exhibit 6.8.)

Mind you, the effects of extreme violence do not appear in most American schools. According to a recent Louis Harris poll conducted nationally, 90 percent of students said they felt "very safe" or "somewhat safe" in their schools, and 74 percent said they lived in neighborhoods that had "hardly any" crime or "none at all."[19] Such news is nice to receive, but overall rates do not reveal what is happening in some of America's worst neighborhoods. Sadly, some of our public schools are now found in "war zones" and have great difficulty conducting education. However, violence is largely ghettoized in our country—which often allows middle- and upper-class Americans to turn their backs on its evil consequences.

In recent years American schools have also had to contend with problems caused by illegal drugs. Since the 1960s large amounts of marijuana, heroin, cocaine, and hallucinogens have been sold to America's youth, and a good deal of that drug trade has been conducted in America's schools. In response, American schools have developed various measures designed to curtail drug use—including special curricula dealing with the effects of drugs, people who are employed to monitor student behavior in the hallways and lavatories, and searches of students and their lockers. Such measures also divert attention and funds away from instruction. In addition, since young people are heavily involved in the drug culture, rates of violent and non-violent crimes have recently soared among American youth. This has sharply increased our prison populations and made many adult Americans wary of, or hostile to, young people and the institutions that serve them.

In other countries, where rates of violence and drug abuse are lower, schools can spend more of their resources on the education of their students. That greater investment in education helps, in turn, to keep the rates of violence and drug abuse in check. And where young people are less obviously involved in violence and the drug scene, adult citizens tend to be more sympathetic to their educational needs.

■ Exhibit 6.8
Listen to the Children

The teen-ager called to ask if he could be excused from classes. Something bad had happened. He had attended a christening and a shootout had erupted. "I have to go with my mother to visit my brother in jail," the boy told school officials. "He's up for attempted murder. Then I'm going with her to bring my other brother's body home. He was killed in the shootout and I still have to go to the doctor because I got shot in the pelvis." Officials of the Bushwick Outreach Center, an alternative high school in Brooklyn, were understanding. They said yes, the boy could be excused.

Another time a student asked if he could "delay" coming to school for a week. "We found my brother dead in the hallway this morning," he said. Yes, school officials replied. Of course. A week's absence would be O.K.

Once there was a time when kids stayed home because of the flu, or a cold, or a stomachache. Serious illness was unusual and the death of a student was rare. That is no longer the case in inner-city schools. Like a poisonous wind, misfortune and tragedy are sweeping relentlessly across the children of the big cities.

Teachers and guidance counselors recalled some of the other reasons given by students for missing classes at Bushwick Outreach: "The guy upstairs got shot and the blood dripped on my mother's head, so we're moving." "My uncle was killed in front of our house." "My girlfriend gave birth to twins and they're both dead." Ellie Weiss, a teacher, remembered a girl who told her she couldn't come to school because one of her grandmother's foster children had been raped, beaten, and murdered in a city park. Ms. Weiss knew the student was telling the truth because the story was already in the newspapers. . . .

The excuses at Bushwick Outreach provide a chilling glimpse into the real lives of big-city youngsters across America: "I'm moving. The marshal is putting us out." "I have to be tested for TB. My mother tested positive." "I can't come to school until my bruises heal." Times have changed. Lunch boxes and thermoses are out. Guns and knives are in. Before the roll call you have to walk through a weapons detector. These kids don't go to pep rallies. But they do go to funerals. Death is so prevalent that some schools are equipped with mourning rooms. . . .

"It's like we're living in some kind of weird place," Ms. Weiss said. "It's shocking. It's very upsetting. Students come to school who are cut up or shot up, or we hear from kids who can't come to school because people are after them."

We have not even begun to confront the enormity of this problem. We have children across America living in neighborhoods as lawless as Mogadishu. We have children who believe that the death of other children is normal. . . . A three-year study of "Adolescents in High-Risk Settings" was released last week by the National Academy of Sciences. It says, "We believe that the problems of America's young people are getting significantly worse, not better". . . . [Meanwhile] the big story in Washington is the struggle over the federal budget, but that means nothing to the children of the cities. They're nobody's constituents. We hear about them mostly when they are killing somebody, and sometimes when they are dying. Given a choice, most of the country would like not to hear from them at all.

—Source: Bob Herbert (1993).

The Aging of the Population. Americans are getting older. In 1965 more than 35 percent of Americans were under eighteen, but now that age group constitutes only 25 percent of the population. And this proportion is expected to decline to about 20 percent by the year 2010. In contrast, people who are age sixty-five and older constituted less than 10 percent of the population in 1965 but now represent more than 13 percent, and that percentage will continue to increase in the near future (see Exhibit 6.9).

The aging of the population stresses America's educational system in several ways. For one thing, if the size of the population were static, it would reduce the need for primary and secondary classrooms in the country. The American population is *not* static, however, but continues to grow through immigration. Therefore, the aggregate, national need for classroom space continues to expand, albeit at a slower pace than in the past, but the need for that space is unequally distributed around the country. More classrooms are needed in communities that are growing, but shrinking or static communities may find that they have a surplus of primary and secondary classrooms.

More seriously, America's older population has become a potent voting bloc that promotes its own interests—which often do not include the needs of young people. Self-interest can be seen, for example, in recent changes in federal tax policy that have protected the elderly at the expense of children. In addition, older Americans may actively oppose spending tax dollars on schools. This problem has become serious in certain states that cater to retirees (such as Arizona or Florida) where elderly citizens sometimes refuse to vote

Exhibit 6.9   Children and the Elderly As a Proportion of the U.S. Population

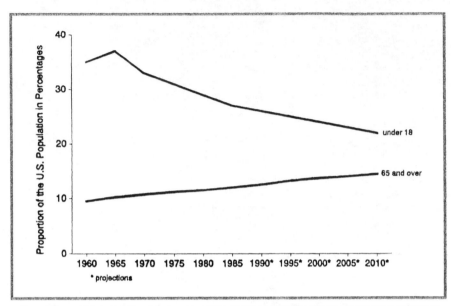

—Source: *Beyond Rhetoric: A New American Agenda for Children and Families* (National Commission on Children, 1991, Figure 2-1).
—Statistical Source: *Projections of the Population of the United States by Age, Sex, and Race: 1988–2080* (Bureau of the Census, 1989, p. 8, Table G).

for bonds or taxes to support local schools. In some cases this problem has been "solved" by setting up retirement communities that have their own public school districts—which of course do not support any schools at all. But this "solution" allows a segment of the population to duck responsibility for the next generation and reduces overall support for public education. Increased political effort will be needed to maintain enthusiasm for public schools among older Americans.

Competing Demands for Funds.   Once upon a time only a few institutions in this country were supported with tax dollars. Most of those dollars were spent for schools, roads, water and sewage services, public parks and buildings, and law enforcement. Other needs for tax dollars have evolved in this century, however, and now schools must compete with new and powerful forces for their share of strained public budgets.

Since World War II, Americans have spent huge sums on the military and health care. As can be seen in Exhibit 6.10, military expenditures peaked in 1955 and again in 1970 (corresponding, respectively, to the Korean and Vietnam Wars), and health-care costs have soared since 1980; but public expenditures on education have managed only a modest growth during the period. (Moreover, the figures for education are misleading because they include

Exhibit 6.10   Expenditures for Public Education, Health, and Defense (as percentages of Gross Domestic Product)

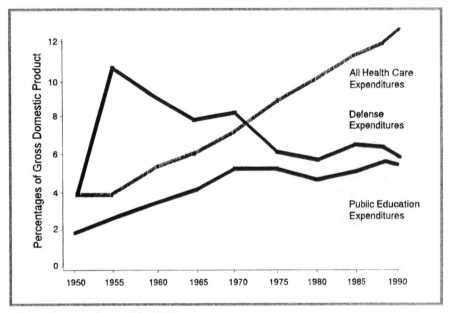

—Source: *Consumer Reports* (July, 1992).
—Statistical Sources: National Center for Education Statistics, Health Care Financing Administration, U.S. Office of Management and Budget.

public expenditures not only for schools, but also for colleges and universities; and most of the postwar growth in educational spending has reflected expansion in post-secondary institutions.) Before 1940, public schools did not have to compete with huge military and health-care demands when they made their case for tax support. Naturally, such competition is less intense in other countries, where military needs are fewer and health-care costs are more effectively restrained.

But this is only part of the problem. In recent years, nine-tenths or more of funds for public schools have come from state and local sources. Those resources have become stressed because of increasing needs to pay for health insurance and public-aid programs—costs often transferred to the states and local communities during the Reagan years.[20] As a result, although state and local taxes have risen, support for public schools as a proportion of total state and local budgets actually *declined* by about a third between 1960 and 1984. Moreover (as we noted earlier), during this same period major American industries have found ways to wiggle out of paying state and local taxes, which means that public-school funding has fallen more heavily on the individual taxpayer. Furthermore, *federal* aid for education also declined during the Reagan and Bush years.

All of which means that it is becoming a lot more difficult to make the case for education when other, insistent, competing needs for tax dollars are being pressed.

The Restructuring of Work. Finally, problems are also generated for education because work is being restructured in America. This restructuring has involved several different processes, two of which pose specific problems for schools.

To understand the first of these processes, we need to distinguish among several types of work.[21] Some occupations fall into an *extractive* sector, which concerns agriculture, fishing, mining, quarrying, oil wells, and the production of basic materials. Others involve *manufacturing*, through which materials are converted into finished products. Occupations associated with making automobiles, television sets, carpets, refrigerators, food stuffs, clothing, houses, bridges, and roads fall into the manufacturing sector. Other occupations constitute *services*. These include occupations associated with transportation, warehousing, water and energy, waste disposal, cleaning, beauty care, food and drink, sports and recreation, and the many activities performed by the armed forces, police, doctors, and dentists. Finally, still others concern *information processing* through teaching, research, public service, the media, banking, the creative arts, religion, and politics.

Needs for these several types of work have varied over time. Before the Industrial Revolution, extractive work was most in demand; need for manufacturing became greater during and shortly after the Industrial Revolution; and now, in our Post-Industrial Society, needs are greater for jobs in information processing and service, with the latter gaining more quickly today. Thus, immediately after the Civil War, perhaps half of those employed in this country were engaged in extractive occupations such as farming and mining; manufacturing reached its apogee around 1950, and today, jobs in information processing and particularly service involve perhaps 80 percent of the work force.

These shifts in occupations have posed obvious problems for education. Curricula appropriate for extractive and manufacturing jobs are now less needed than are those preparing students for positions in service and information processing. This change has meant that some schools have had to retool their course offerings, personnel rosters, and physical plants. Moreover, many extractive and manufacturing jobs required only minimal literacy and numeracy, so that in earlier times youngsters could expect to find work if they dropped out of school when it was legal to do so. In contrast, jobs in the service and information processing sectors tend to require higher levels of education.

A second form of work restructuring has concerned the long-term effects of labor-saving machinery and of medical technology. In the past, society was powered by human beings and domestic animals, with occasional help from wind and water, and life expectancy was little more than thirty years.

Today, society is powered by fossil and atomic fuels, and much of the technol ogy that allows us to use such fuels is automated. Moreover, medical advances mean that citizens of advanced countries often live into their eighties—or longer. Thus, Americans today not only live longer than their parents or grandparents did, but they enjoy, on average, more leisure and a higher standard of living.

But if people are to have more leisure time, how is that leisure to be distributed among different segments of the society? In earlier times Americans would have thought it easy to answer this question—those who were poor obviously had to work, and those who were rich enjoyed leisure—but answers are more complex today. Americans are now taught that success comes to those who work hard, and our country has, in fact, organized its affairs so that full-time employment is associated with many benefits—among them status, wealth, power, medical insurance, and retirement benefits—so of course Americans often prefer work to leisure. (It is no fiction that Americans tend to be "workaholics.")

In fact, employed Americans work more hours during the year than do citizens of other industrialized countries (except for Japan) and often protect their jobs by requiring that others meet strict "qualification" standards before they can be considered for employment. Moreover, since employers often must provide fringe benefits for each extra, full-time worker they hire, they prefer to encourage those already on the payroll to work overtime. And this has meant problems for education. As fewer and fewer young people are welcomed into the full-time work force, higher and higher qualifications are set for attractive jobs, and schools (and colleges) are now called upon to provide meaningful experiences for young people who often will not enter full-time employment until they are in their mid-twenties or older.

In addition, since the real wages of Americans have been dropping over the last two decades, many wage earners are now working more hours in the week or more days in the year, and many families find that they now need two incomes just to stay even.[22] This sharply curtails the amount of time parents can spend with their children and places additional demands on schools, which may be asked to provide noncompensated day-care or recreation facilities—or, at least, to keep their doors open for longer hours. (Contrast these practices with the typical Western European country, where tax-supported day-care services are provided to all families in the land and long summer holidays are mandated by law.)

In the long run, however, even Americans are having to cope with the need to fill leisure hours with activities that are attractive, creative, and socially useful. This, in turn, generates additional problems for education. Some schools are filling this need directly, by providing leisure activities for citizens in their communities—activities such as sports spectacles, adult education courses, public lectures, and recreational programs. Other schools have responded to the need by providing courses that teach students about recreation, music, and the arts. But given America's present love affair with "the work ethic," both of these uses of resources tend to provoke criticism.[23]

Processes leading to changes in the work force have also posed problems for America's schools. But note that our analysis of these problems bears little resemblance to claims about work-force problems that are made by some major critics of education. As we indicated in Chapter 4, some critics have expressed concerns about "de-industrialization" in America and have assumed an escalating need for high-tech occupations. We have made our reasons clear for rejecting these analyses. The work force certainly evolves, but the need for jobs in the service sector now seems to be exceeding that for jobs in information-processing. And the critics have quite ignored problems created by the increasing availability of leisure. American ideology has yet to come to grips with leisure, but it seems to us that the schools have a major role to play in providing and educating people for meaningful leisure activities.

Summary. We have reviewed *nine* problems in American society that create distress for American schools. These are certainly *not* the only features of our society that threaten schools today; indeed we could have discussed others. Each poses serious difficulties, however, and each must be taken seriously by those who would make effective plans for improving America's schools. Unfortunately, many people who propose reforms for education seem to be unaware of these problems, and as a result their proposals are unrealistic. Effective reforms must begin by taking these problems seriously.

Everyday Features of Education and Their Effects

Until the first few decades of the 1900s, there was really nothing that could meaningfully be called a public "system" of education in the United States. Schooling was a local affair. . . . And as [people] proceeded—all across America, without plan or coordination—to fashion the kinds of schools they wanted for themselves and their children, the great heterogeneity of the nation came to be reflected in the diversity and autonomy of its local schools.

—John Chubb and Terry Moe (*Politics, Markets, and America's Schools,* 1990, p. 3)

Obviously, schools and public school systems existed in the United States before the 1830s. What was different about the common school movement was the establishment and standardization of state systems of education designed to achieve specific public policies. . . . [Thus, according to Horace Mann, writing in the 1840s,] children in the common school were to receive a common moral education . . . [and] a common political creed. . . . The result would be the creation of a society with a consensus of political and moral values. . . . [Moreover] common schooling was to create a common

... class consciousness among all members of society. By mixing rich and poor within the same schoolhouse, social-class conflict would give way to a feeling of membership in a common social class.

—Joel Spring (*The American School 1642–1985*, 1986, pp. 70–89)

These contradictory quotes come, first, from a pair of authors interested in attacking public education, and, second, from a reputable historian. We contrast these assertions to make a point. In their zeal, the critics have sometimes painted a distorted picture of the history and current organization of American schooling. This is too bad. Real problems for schools are also generated by some of the everyday features of American education, but when distorted pictures of those features are painted, the public is likely to misunderstand these problems.

It may be difficult to think about everyday features of education as a source of problems simply because they *are* familiar and are not normally examined closely. And yet, if we compare education in different countries, we discover that American education often has features that don't appear elsewhere. Moreover, it requires a historical perspective to understand some of the common, everyday features now found in American education and their consequences.

The Age-Graded Classroom. Consider, for example, America's standard form of primary schooling that places students of roughly the same age in day-long classes, where they are exposed to standardized curricula thought to be "appropriate" for their grade level. This form of schooling became popular in earlier decades when students needed to be trained for repetitive industrial jobs. It has remained popular because it is easy to understand and manage, but it also generates a host of problems.

Age-graded curricula are designed for the "average" student, but only a few students are actually "average." As a result, many students are bored, while others are anxiously confused by a good deal of primary instruction. And this means that the standard, age-graded classroom is not an efficient educative setting. This problem is well known; indeed, it is often cited by those who advocate computer-assisted instruction, which can respond to individual students' levels of knowledge. But high-quality, computer-assisted instruction is expensive and is so far available only in a small number of schools. Therefore, America's dependence on day-long, age-graded classrooms persists and continues to generate needlessly low aggregate levels of student achievement.

Age-graded classrooms are also associated with lockstep curricula, and as we noted earlier, such curricula tend to focus and restrict teachers' efforts in the classroom. As a result, when a school has lockstep and weak curricula, students in its age-graded classrooms may actually be *prevented* from learning. Now, suppose also that weak curricula are more often assigned to schools

that serve minority students. What outcome would you predict from such blatant discrimination?

Unfortunately, this is not a hypothetical question. About a decade ago reading specialist Rebecca Barr and sociologist Robert Dreeben studied first-grade curricula, teaching practices, and student achievement in nine Chicago-area schools.[24] They found striking differences in the demands of the basal readers assigned in those schools, with the toughest readers appearing in schools that served white students and easier readers assigned to schools whose students were black or racially integrated. And this meant, of course, that students in the black and racially integrated schools were subjected to fewer demands and learned less. As Dreeben described the situation,

> since primary grade teachers usually try to complete the curriculum in their high- and middle-level reading groups no matter how demanding the materials, but will rarely go beyond it, the selected basal [reader] normally sets a ceiling on how much material will be covered during the school year. . . . This means that the district administration, through its book selection practices, greatly influences the level of learning opportunity and . . . of learning itself. . . . [And] *this means that learning deficits found in black as compared to white children can be attributed in part to the actions of district and school administrators before classroom instruction ever takes place.*[25]

Discriminatory practices such as these are more likely when age-graded classrooms and lockstep curricula are the rule.

In addition, what happens when bored and confused youngsters are forced to sit in day-long, age-graded classrooms? They learn to conform, of course—to control their impulses, to conceal their thoughts, to raise their hands, to take turns, and to defer to the teacher. Thus, the day-long classroom is, among other things, a device for teaching conformity to authority—an effect that is surely problematic if one wants to promote creativity and self-expression among students, as most of us do.

The day-long, age-graded classroom also exposes the individual student to only a few other students, who become a small reference group against which that individual can judge his or her achievements. This may lead children to form beliefs about their abilities that have negative long-term effects. Consider, for example, how many Americans suffer from math phobia. Mathematics is one of the few subject-matter fields in which answers are either "right" or "wrong," and in the age-graded classroom it is all too easy to focus on which students have the correct answers rather than on the logic used to get those answers. Thus, aversion to mathematics often begins in primary classrooms and results, in part, from loss of confidence when students see others who (for seemingly magical reasons) always seem to know the "correct" answers.[26]

Moreover, the day-long, age-graded classroom encourages the development of odd roles for students that may have long-term effects. A thoughtful

discussion of this process appeared in a study by Louis Smith, a psychologist, and William Geoffrey, a seventh-grade teacher.[27] These authors observed and analyzed an urban classroom for some months and were able to trace how one student developed a role as "classroom clown." Their report noted that this role evolved not only from the characteristics of the student but also from the responses of others in the classroom, as well as from the managerial strategies employed by the teacher. Once the role was in place, however, it became a prominent feature of the classroom's culture. Other students may come to play different roles in day-long classrooms, of course—"dunce," "flirt," "bully," "helpless victim," "teacher's pet," "vacant dreamer," or the like—with results that can warp students' long-term concepts of themselves or others.

Many educators now understand the shortcomings of the day-long, age-graded classroom. And various programs have been proposed to break such classrooms into transient instructional groups that bring pupils of different ages but common skill levels together to study specific subjects. In addition, it is useful to remember that at one time much of primary education in this country was conducted in one-room schools, where children of many ages and abilities were taught together and where older students often mentored the work of those who were younger. Surely it is time that this common, everyday feature of education today—the day-long, age-graded class-room—disappear from the American scene.

Public Competitions, Success, and Failure. American schools are also remarkable for the stress they place on public competition among students. Students are forever being given tasks that call for competition and public evaluation—homework assignments that are graded openly, demands for recitation, spot quizzes, examinations, and so forth. Thus from an early age those students are taught to compete with their friends, that such competitions are "natural" and fair, and that the results of such competitions will often be made public.

Public competition within the classroom is less prevalent in most other countries. In socialist countries it is often discouraged for ideological reasons; and elsewhere it is unlikely to occur because tests are delayed until the end of the instructional unit, the term, or the school year. In contrast, educators in the United States have long believed in giving students frequent feedback and in the motivational advantages of public competition. In fact, some American teachers even use competition to organize classroom maintenance tasks, or they make up competitive games to fill empty class time.

This pattern of public competition has effects on students and their parents. To begin with, it reinforces Americans' beliefs about individualism and suggests that rewards will, indeed, come to those who are talented and hard working. American students are taught from an early age, in their schools, that academic success can be attained by "anyone" and that success reflects only their qualities as *individuals* (rather than, let us say, help provided by others or teacher prejudices). Americans learn this lesson well, for the rhetoric they use to justify competition in the schools is frequently repeated on the sports field, in the business world, and in the political arena—where it is assumed that success also reflects individual skill and effort.

Of course, American school competitions do teach a few students how to succeed—what to believe and how to feel and behave when their work is judged "the best." And sometimes a few other students, whose work was "nearly the best," will learn that they should work harder and prepare more diligently before the next competition. But *most* students' work will not be judged "the best," or "nearly the best." So repeated competitions also teach a lot of students how to fail—what to believe and how to react when their work is frequently judged to be substandard or merely mediocre. Predictable patterns of failure lead students to believe that they have little talent for the subject matter—or, worse, that they are generally inept or stupid. Unfortunately, far too many students are victimized by public competitions today and decide that they are "failures." The consequence of such beliefs are discussed in Exhibit 6.11.

Beliefs that students are personally responsible for "failing" are often undeserved. Those who succeed in academic competitions may do so because they have people to help them study, because they come from homes that support education, or because important people in their lives *expect* them to do well. Those who fail may do so because they are distracted by hunger or family crises, because their native language is not standard American English, because others will be upset if they succeed, because they do not understand competitions or do not believe it appropriate to compete in them, or because the teacher is unprepared to deal with their race, gender, or ethnicity. Minority and female students, in particular, are not always well served by public competition in school; indeed, their lives may be warped by negative beliefs they develop about themselves as a result of too much competition.

At a more profound level, public competitions create problems because they set students against one another and thus interfere with social integration. Consider what happens when a minority student is called on to compete with others who represent a majority group. Regardless of whether the minority student succeeds or fails, public competition is likely to highlight that student's minority status, thus making it more difficult for the student to be accepted into the larger group. On the other hand, when students are engaged in cooperative learning, they can pay attention to how each contributes to the common task; thus, students can base their opinions of each other on their contributions to the group rather than on their race, accent, or gender, and social integration becomes more likely. Forms of cooperative learning are being studied and implemented today,[28] but classroom competition is still much more common than cooperation.

■ Exhibit 6.11
Cooling Out the Failures

Although our schools can be a golden avenue of opportunity for those who succeed in them, they are also the arena in which many confront failure that condemns them to the more subservient positions in our society. How are those who "fail" handled so they do not become bitter revolutionaries intent on overthrowing the system that so brutally used them?

"Cooling out" is the process of adjusting victims to their loss. When someone has lost something that is valuable to him [or her], it leads to intense frustration. This frustration and its accompanying anger are dangerous to society because they can be directed against the social system if the social system is identified as being responsible for the loss. But our educational system is insidiously effective, and many who fail within it (perhaps most) never even need to be cooled out. They learn early in grade school that they are stupid and that higher education is meant for others. They suffer miserably in school as they continue to be confronted year after year with more evidence of their failure, and they can hardly wait until they turn sixteen so they can leave for greener pastures. Such persons are relieved to end their educational miseries and need no cooling out.

For those who do need to be cooled out, however, a variety of techniques is used. The primary one makes use of . . . the ideologies of individualism and equal opportunity. [Students] are taught that people make their own way to the top in a land of equal opportunity. Those who make it do so because of their own abilities, while those who do not make it do so because of a lack of ability or drive on their own part. They consequently learn to blame themselves for failure, rather than the system. It was not the educational system that was at fault, for it was freely offered. But it was the fault of the individual who failed to make proper use of that which society offered him. Individualism provides amazing stabilization for the maintenance of our social system, for it results in the system going unquestioned as the blame is put squarely on the individual who was himself [or herself] conned by the system.

If this technique of cooling out fails to work, as it does only in a minority of cases, other techniques are put into effect. Counselors and teachers may point out to the person that he [or she] is really "better suited" for other tasks in life. He may be told that he will "be happier" doing something else. He might be "gradually disengaged" from the educational system, perhaps be directed to alternate sources of education, such as vocational training.

The individual may also be encouraged to blame his lack of success on tough luck, fate, and bad breaks. In one way or another, as he [or she] is cooled out, he is directed away from questioning the educational system itself, much less its relationship to maintaining the present class system and his subservient position within it.

—Source: James Henslin, Linda Henslin, and Steven Keiser (Schooling for social stability: Education in the corporate society, 1976, pp. 311–312).

Finally, public competition in American schools also creates problems because it generates habits that are inappropriate in many life contexts. Since the days of Adam Smith, conservative economists have thought that competition has generally beneficial effects, and many Americans support competition in the schools because they believe it will give students subsequent advantages. But is this true? Consider life at home, activities of the church choir, the problem-solving meeting in industry, a group of climbers scaling a mountain peak. Success in each of these contexts depends on *avoiding* competition, and competition in school provides few clues for success in such enterprises.

In fact, thoughtful Americans are now beginning to question whether the model of individual competition is even appropriate for American industry. They point out that successful industries overseas are often built around *groups* of workers, who cooperate in solving problems or in constructing units of production, and competition among individuals would ruin such groups. Thus, American schools may actually be contributing to a *decline* of American industry by stressing competition rather than cooperation. Clearly, public competition is not required in American schools, and it is also time to limit this feature of American education.

Comprehensive Schools and Tracking Systems. American public education also lays great stress on the operation of *comprehensive* schools, a stress that is not often found in other countries. Consider this quotation from James Coleman:

> Perhaps the ideal most central to American education is the ideal of the common school, a school attended by all children. The assumption that all social classes should attend the same school contrasted with the two-tiered educational systems in Europe, which reflected their feudal origins. Both in the beginning and at crucial moments of choice (such as the massive expansion of secondary education in the early part of this century), American education followed the pattern of common, or comprehensive, schools, including all students from the community and all courses of study. Only in the largest Eastern cities were there differentiated, selective high schools, and even that practice declined over time, with new high schools generally following the pattern of the comprehensive school.[29]

Although we certainly support Coleman's major thesis, today we would add a minor caveat. With the development of the magnet-school movement, some school districts have moved back toward "differentiated, selective high schools." Nevertheless, Americans have certainly rejected the two-tier model that provides different high schools: one for elite students, and another for the non-elite students. Thus, it is difficult to find a public high school in our country today that offers only a college-preparatory curriculum—or, in contrast, only trade, technical, or vocational courses—whereas England has traditionally had both "grammar" and "secondary modern" high schools, Germany funds both *Gymnasien* and *Berufsfachschulen,* France supports both the *lycée* and the *technique,* and so it goes.

What this means is that in other Western countries students are often sorted out in mid-adolescence by means of state-administered examinations and may thereafter enroll in an "academic" high school only if they pass those exams. Such exams are a source of great anxiety, of course, and are supposed to reflect only students' knowledge of academic subjects. In fact, such exams also reflect students' social backgrounds and thus serve, in part, as screening devices that tend to send students from working-class homes to technical and trade schools while children who come from families that are affluent and well-educated tend to be allowed into "academic" high schools and eventually into college or university.

In contrast, Americans have long embraced the common-school ideal and have supported comprehensive high schools because they presumably offer more opportunities and bring students from all walks of life together. But does this mean that "student sorting" is avoided in American education? Not at all. American schools also sort students, but the sorting procedures are different because they are based on academic *tracks* associated with different curricula that are offered in a common school building.

Tracking in American schools actually involves two types of sorting. Comprehensive high schools offer a wide range of subject-matter courses associated with different occupations in the adult world. No student could possibly take all of these offerings, and it is assumed that the school is responsible for steering students toward courses that are matched to their abilities and needs. To accomplish this, students in most high schools are sorted into *curricular tracks,* each track involving a specific sequence of courses. Unfortunately, curricular tracking has been associated with status labeling over the years. The traditional high school offered curricular tracks for "college preparation," "vocational careers," and "general education," or some such, and all students within the traditional high school understood that the first of these tracks had higher status than the other two.

In addition, it is thought that students learn best when they are grouped with other students with similar abilities. Thus, many high schools (and even some primary schools) also sort students into *ability tracks*—also associated with status labeling—and differing "levels" of instruction are offered to students in the various ability tracks. It should be understood, however, that the exact forms of curricular and ability tracking differ around the nation. For example, schools may recognize many tracks or just a few; schools may link curricular and ability tracking closely or loosely; and schools may or may not tie tracks to specific subjects or to blocks of subjects.

Tracking is also associated with serious problems. To begin with, *it doesn't work.* Tracking is supposed to benefit *all* students and to "increase [all] students' learning [and] enhance students' attitudes about themselves and schooling," but evidence strongly suggests that it does not accomplish these goals.[30] Instead, repeated studies have shown that even when tracking systems have positive effects, those effects benefit only students who are assigned to high-status tracks. In contrast, when students are assigned to low-status tracks, they experience decline in self-esteem, aspirations, and academic achievement. Their attitudes toward school are also adversely affected, and they are likely to have poorer job prospects than students in high-status tracks.

These contrasting effects are generated, of course, because tracking decisions are also forms of public competition, and they too are thought to reflect students' capacities. Thus, students assume that a major judgment has been rendered about them when they are assigned to a high- or low-status track. Such awareness affects their beliefs about their abilities and prospects, and those beliefs tend to become self-fulfilling prophecies (see Exhibit 6.12).

Exhibit 6.12   The Long-Term Effects of Academic Tracking

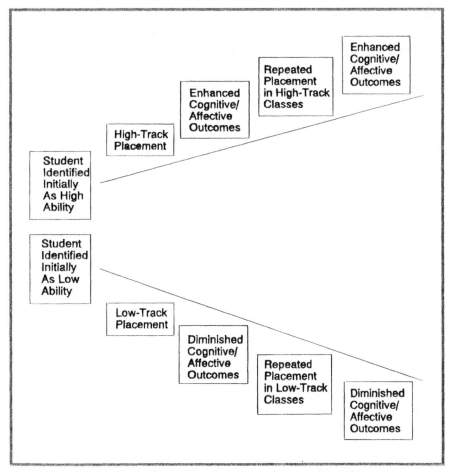

—Source: Jeannie Oakes (Tracking in secondary schools: A contextual perspective, 1989).

In addition, schools presumably assign students to tracks through a combination of "standardized test scores, teacher and counselor recommendations, prior placements and grades, and (for some senior high schools . . .) student choice."[31] This system is supposed to generate fair and informed decisions, but it doesn't. Instead, various studies have shown that students from minority groups and from working- or lower-class homes are more likely to end up in lower-status tracks, and this effect persists even when controls are entered for test scores and prior grades.[32] This relationship is widely understood, or at least suspected, by privileged parents. In fact, ability tracking systems are sometimes but barely disguised means for maintaining racial, ethnic, or social-class segregation within the comprehensive school setting.

What do we conclude from all this? The common-school ideals of community and equal opportunity have produced comprehensive high schools in this country, but those ideals are threatened by the tracking systems that also appear in those schools. Evidence suggests that even when tracking systems provide benefits, only those students who are assigned to high-status tracks receive them, and that students from minority and impoverished backgrounds are likely to be harmed. Thus, like sorting systems in other countries, American tracking procedures also operate as screening devices that assign students from advantaged and disadvantaged homes to different curricula and divergent life courses.

Ability tracking persists in America because it benefits the sons and daughters of advantaged and powerful parents, but it is difficult to justify on moral or evidential grounds. In contrast, some form of curricular tracking is probably necessary—indeed, the need for curricular tracking will increase if magnet schools become more popular—but there is no inherent reason curricular tracking should be associated with status. One can imagine a school system of the future in which various curricular tracks associated with differing career paths are offered as options to all students on an equal basis, and entrance into different curricular tracks is based only on students' interests and their completion of appropriate entry requirements.

The Feminine Profession. For more than a century, the majority of schoolteachers in America have been women. This is particularly true of primary teachers, where men constitute less than 15 percent of the teaching force.[33] It is less true at the secondary level, where the number of men and women is roughly balanced. Until recently, however, most teaching was done at the primary level, public school teaching has traditionally been one of the few occupations open to women, and Americans have long assumed that schoolteaching was a "feminine" occupation. In addition, there are more female teachers in the United States than in most comparable countries. In the latter half of the 1980s the percentage of women in primary teaching was

Exhibit 6.13 Percentages of Women in Primary Teaching in
Some OECD Countries in 1986 or 1987–88

Italy	89.8	Canada	68.9
United States	86.2	Sweden	68.1
Austria	80.6	France	67.0
West Germany	79.6	Netherlands	63.3
United Kingdom	78.1	Norway	61.3
Ireland	76.3	Japan	56.6
Belgium	74.7	Greece	49.3
Spain	73.1	Turkey	41.6
Yugoslavia	71.5		

—Sources: *Education in OECD Countries: 1987–88* (OECD, 1990) and *Status of the American Public School Teacher: 1990–1991* (National Education Association, Research Division, 1992).

higher in the United States than in all other OECD countries except Italy (see Exhibit 6.13).

Why did the teaching profession become dominated by women in the United States? Teaching was perhaps the first profession open to women on a regular basis,[34] and people held stereotypic beliefs in the nineteenth century that associated women with "natural" child-rearing talents and moral purity.[35] However, school systems had to expand rapidly during the middle of the last century, and Joel Spring suggests that economic forces had something to do with early decisions to hire women as teachers (see Exhibit 6.14).[36]

What happens when women come to dominate the teaching profession? Some have argued that this dominance is responsible for differences in the

Exhibit 6.14 Average Weekly Salaries of Teachers, 1841 to 1864

	Rural		City	
Year	Men	Women	Men	Women
1841	$4.15	$2.51	$11.93	$4.44
1845	3.87	2.48	12.21	4.09
1850	4.25	2.89	13.37	4.71
1855	5.77	3.65	16.80	5.79
1860	6.28	4.12	18.56	6.99
1864	7.86	4.92	20.78	7.67

—Source: Joel Spring (*The American School: 1642–1985*, 1986, p. 121).
—Statistical Source: Willard Elsbree (*The American Teacher: Evolution of a Profession in a Democracy*, 1939, p. 274).

average academic achievement of boys and girls in specific subjects, but evidence supporting this thesis has been weak.[37] One problem is clearly associated with the feminine dominance of teaching, however; for years, teachers have been paid low salaries. As in many other countries, Americans hold sexist prejudices and tend to assign lower status to other professions—such as nursing or social work—that are staffed largely by women. In addition, women in America are still paid less than men for equivalent, and sometimes even identical, work. Thus, the fact that most teachers are women becomes an excuse to pay lower average salaries for teaching than for other comparable occupations. To illustrate, in its 1986 report, *A Nation Prepared: Teachers for the 21st Century*, the Carnegie Forum on Education and the Economy compared the 1985 salaries of teachers and accountants (the latter being another occupation requiring an undergraduate degree). As can be seen in Exhibit 6.15, not only was the average teacher paid less than the average accountant in 1985, but by comparison teachers' salaries exhibited less variation. Thus, "teachers' starting salaries are at the low end of the spectrum for college

Exhibit 6.15 Annual Salaries of Teachers and Accountants for 1985

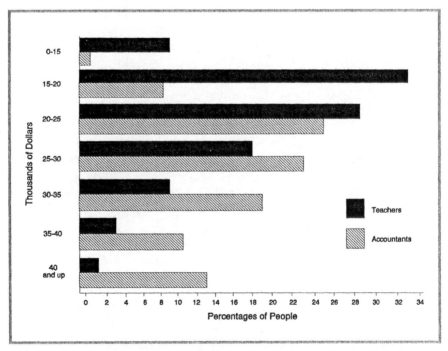

—Source: *A Nation Prepared: Teachers for the 21st Century* (Carnegie Forum on Education and the Economy, 1986, p. 97).
—Statistical Sources: *National Survey of Professional, Administrative, Technical, and Clerical Pay, March, 1985* (Bureau of Labor Statistics, 1985) and *The Metropolitan Life Survey of the American Teacher 1985: Strengthening the Profession* (Louis Harris and Associates, Inc., 1985).

graduates, and [teachers'] prospects of salary growth do not compare with [those of] other occupations."[38]

Domination of the teaching profession by women and sexist prejudices are surely not the only reasons teachers are paid poorly, but it is surprising how rarely these reasons are noted by those concerned with teachers' salaries. (On the other hand, why should one be surprised? Most of those who write about the salaries of teachers are, after all, men.) Higher salaries for teachers would raise morale in the profession and bring more talented people into the field. And these effects would surely generate greater student motivation and achievement.

Bureaucratization. Recent critics of American education are right about one thing, at least. Schools in large school districts are often controlled by large bureaucracies, and this causes many problems. A bit of history will help us understand this issue.

Before the Industrial Revolution most artifacts were made by artisans such as carpenters, seamstresses, and blacksmiths who worked independently and had all the skills necessary to produce a given product. Then, as the Industrial Revolution got underway, people with similar skills were often brought under a single roof—a factory—so that they would presumably learn from and enhance one another's work. This was not sufficient to produce really complex products, however, so new forms of industrial enterprise were invented. These involved the specialization of work and, eventually, the assembly line. But the latter industrial forms generated problems; they separated those who planned and supervised from those who did the work, and they reduced work to a set of simplified, specialized, boring tasks—a far cry from artisanship.

In our country's early days, most schools were located in small communities and operated independently of one another. As small communities grew into cities, however, public school districts began to model themselves after the industrial forms that were then becoming common in the private sector. Thus, by the end of the nineteenth century, the typical school district had these features:

> 1) A hierarchy with a superintendent at the top and [with] orders flowing from the top to the bottom of the organization; 2) Clearly defined differences in [the] roles of superintendent, principals, assistant principals, and teachers; 3) Graded schools in which students progressively moved from one grade to another; 4) A graded course of study for the entire school system to assure uniformity in teaching in all grades in the system; [and] 5) An emphasis on rational planning, order, regularity, and punctuality.[39]

But this was not the end of the process. As school districts grew larger, they tended to evolve more complex bureaucracies to control ever-larger realms of the educational enterprise. Thus, by 1972, in the seventh edition of their text, *American Education*, Chris DeYoung and Richard Wynn would

Exhibit 6.16   Administrative Organization of a Large School System

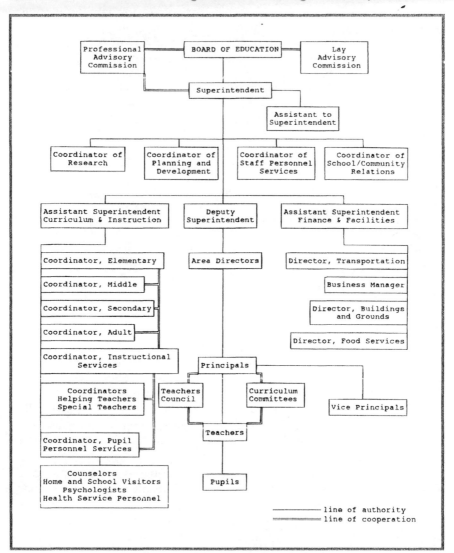

—Source: Chris DeYoung and Richard Wynn (*American Education,* 7th ed., 1972, p. 136).

portray, approvingly, the bureaucracy of a "typical" large school system in the form we display as Exhibit 6.16.[40] (One can only assume that those who would plan and work in such bureaucracies believe that teachers and school principals should not be trusted with making *any* decisions on their own.)

Large educational bureaucracies create many problems, of course. First, they tend to evolve criteria for judging performance that have little to do with the task of instruction. In his classic 1962 study, *Education and the Cult of Efficiency,* historian Raymond Callahan observed that in some large public-school systems, not only was having a centralized authority considered the best means for making educational decisions, but that such decisions were largely based on cost effectiveness rather than on sound educational benefits. As a result, some administrators of large systems "saw schools not as centers of learning but as enterprises which were functioning efficiently if the students went through without failing and received their diplomas on schedule and if the operation were handled economically."[41]

Second, educational bureaucracies tend to strip teachers of all opportunities to exercise professional autonomy. In other words, in large bureaucratic systems,

> schools [are] viewed as factories, the students as the raw material, and the teachers as workers. . . . Teachers are thus divorced from the process of actually constructing materials that could embody specific, personal meanings and values. The routinization and depersonalization of teaching has effectively "deskilled" it, not unlike the segmented work of blue-collar factory workers.[42]

Third, like other large bureaucracies, those in education create a host of rules, procedures, and paperwork that can interfere with the tasks of instruction and cause untold annoyance for teachers, principals, students, and parents. To defend themselves against such bureaucracies, teachers often join unions, and parents, out of frustration, may form angry action groups.

Finally, large bureaucracies also inflate the cost of public education. Look again at Exhibit 6.16 and note that most of the titles displayed represent salaried people *who do not teach.* Some may argue, of course, that the lives of students are ultimately enriched by "coordinators," "directors," "managers," and their assistants and secretaries, but the argument seems a bit thin. Somehow, some really excellent schools manage to appear in small public-school districts and in the private sector without the benefit of such supernumeraries. Strange.

Why then have educational bureaucracies become so popular in large cities? Part of the answer seems to be that school bureaucracies have responded to sexist stereotypes suggesting that women were "naturally" emotional (rather than logical) and therefore should be subordinate to men. Thus, since the majority of teachers were women, it seemed reasonable to set up a bureaucracy of men to control them.[43]

In addition, in 1911 Frederick W. Taylor's influential book, *The Principles of Scientific Management,* was published. This book stressed the need for planning, efficiency, and centralized control. It advised basing decisions on "scientific" evidence and on economies of scale.[44] This work had enormous impact not only in private industry but, ironically, in public institutions such as school systems. Thereafter, the pursuit of efficiency and "scientific management" made school bureaucracies grow, and the profession of "school administrator" became established as a distinct entity.

It can be argued, however, that the growth of bureaucracies in education is actually self-generated. Bureaucracies are rather like the proverbial Arabian camel whose nose must never be allowed under the tent, because once in place they tend to expand "naturally" and to evolve weird definitions of reality that generate endless mischief for others. Regarding the former, surely the best (and funniest) explanation for bureaucratic growth ever to appear was *Parkinson's Law* (see Exhibit 6.17). Moreover, lest you think that Parkin-

■ EXHIBIT 6.17
Parkinson's Law

In brief, Parkinson's Law posits that the size of a bureaucracy has nothing whatever to do with its responsibilities; instead, *all* bureaucracies tend to grow because of their own internal dynamics. Why?

Omitting technicalities (which are numerous) we may distinguish at the outset two motive forces. They can be represented for the present purpose by two almost axiomatic statements, thus: (1) 'An official wants to multiply subordinates, not rivals' and (2) 'Officials make work for each other.'

To comprehend Factor 1, we must picture a civil servant, called A, who finds himself overworked. Whether this overwork is real or imaginary is immaterial, but we should observe, in passing, that A's sensation (or illusion) might easily result from his own decreasing energy: a normal symptom of middle age. For this real or imagined overwork there are, broadly speaking, three possible remedies. He may resign; he may ask to halve the work with a colleague, called B; he may demand the assistance of two subordinates, to be called C and D. There is probably no instance, however, in history of A choosing any but the third alternative. By resignation he would lose his pension rights. By having B appointed, on his own level in the hierarchy, he would merely bring in a rival for promotion to W's vacancy when W (at long last) retires. So A would rather have C and D, junior men, below him. They will add to his consequence and, by dividing the work into two categories, as between C and D, he will have the merit of being the only man who comprehends them both. It is essential to realize at this point that C and D are, as it were, inseparable. To appoint C alone would have been impossible. Why? Because C, if by himself, would divide the work with A and so assume almost the equal status that has been refused in the first instance to B: a status the more emphasized if C is A's only possible successor. Subordinates must thus number two or more, each being thus kept in order by fear of the other's promotion. When C complains in turn of being overworked (as he certainly will) A will, with the concurrence of C, advise the appointment of two assistants to help C. But he can then avert internal friction only by advising the appointment of two more assistants to help D, whose position is much the same. With this recruitment of E, F, G, and H, the promotion of A is now practically certain.

(continued on next page)

Seven officials are now doing what one did before. This is where Factor 2 comes into operation. For these seven make so much work for each other that all are fully occupied and *A* is actually working harder than ever. An incoming document may well come before each of them in turn. Official *E* decides that it falls within the province of *F,* who places a draft reply before *C,* who amends it drastically before consulting *D,* who asks *G* to deal with it. But *G* goes on leave at this point, handing the file over to *H,* who drafts a minute that is signed by *D* and returned to *C,* who revises his draft accordingly and lays the new version before *A.*

What does *A* do? He would have every excuse for signing the thing unread, for he has many other matters on his mind. Knowing now that he is to succeed *W* next year, he has to decide whether *C* or *D* should succeed to his own office. He had to agree to *G*'s going on leave even if not yet strictly entitled to it. He is worried whether *H* should not have gone instead, for reasons of health. He has looked pale recently—partly but not solely because of his domestic troubles. Then there is the business of *F*'s special increment of salary for the period of the conference and *E*'s application for transfer to the Ministry of Pensions. *A* has heard that *D* is in love with a married typist and that *G* and *F* are no longer on speaking terms—no one seems to know why. So *A* might be tempted to sign *C*'s draft and have done with it. But *A* is a conscientious man. Beset as he is with problems created by his colleagues for themselves and for him—created by the mere fact of these officials' existence—he is not the man to shirk his duty. He reads through the draft with care, deletes the fussy paragraphs added by *C* and *H,* and restores the thing to the form preferred in the first instance by the able (if quarrelsome) *F.* He corrects the English—none of these young men can write grammatically—and finally produces the same reply he would have written if officials *C* to *H* had never been born. Far more people have taken far longer to produce the same result. No one has been idle. All have done their best. And it is late in the evening before *A* finally quits his office and begins the return journey to Ealing. The last of the office lights are being turned off in the gathering dust that marks the end of another day's administrative toil. Among the last to leave, *A* reflects with bowed shoulders and a wry smile that late hours, like grey hairs, are among the penalties for success.

—Source: C. Northcote Parkinson (*Parkinson's Law,* 1957 [1986], pp. 12–15).

son was exaggerating, his text also provides data from the British Admiralty and Colonial Office showing that in the years after World War II these two bureaucracies grew and grew—predictably, steadily, substantially—while their assigned responsibilities shrank! Regarding the latter, who among us has not received off-the-wall demands in the mail from bureaucrats in government agencies, insurance companies, banks, or school systems that would never have been sent had even a moment of objective reflection intervened?

This does not mean that educational bureaucrats are evil people, that large school systems do not sometimes benefit from bureaucracies, or even that education is, in general, overly bureaucratic. (In fact, since most school districts in the country are small, educational bureaucratization tends to be held in check in most American communities.) Nor does it mean that educational bureaucracies are unique to America. In fact, public schools are run by *state* or *national* authorities in most other countries, and this can, indeed, lead to massive bureaucracies. But, even at their best, bureaucracies tend to force *their* definitions of "reality" on people, in and out of the system; and this is pernicious in large districts where the philistine values of central administrators are allowed to defeat the educational commitments of teachers and principals. At their worst, educational bureaucracies become endlessly expanding financial sinkholes that eat up resources and create only mischief and red tape.

Public, Parochial, and Elite Schools. Americans are aware that the educational system in their country includes both public and private schools, but they may not understand why this creates problems. In fact, during Colonial times, children were educated only in private schools, mostly representing the Protestant churches of the Europeans who had settled each region. When the Industrial Revolution began in the early nineteenth century, however, it brought floods of poor immigrants to this country, and in response, the states organized public schools that were to ensure literacy for all and promote a common set of values.

Two problems threatened these goals from the beginning. First, the pre-existing private schools were left in place and thereafter continued to serve the needs of affluent families; thus, a two-tiered system of education was actually created. Second, the values promoted by public schools became a source of controversy, and later in the century various religious groups, particularly Catholics, began to set up parochial schools to promote their own value systems.

Today roughly 88 percent of America's students attend public schools; about 7 percent are educated in Catholic schools; and the remainder attend both high-status elite academies (which may or may not be affiliated with religious authorities) and an assortment of schools representing other religions, educational programs that are not offered in the public sector, and ethnic commitments and prejudices.[45] Private schools are by no means confined to the United States, however. As can be seen in Exhibit 6.18, among OECD countries for whom the public-private comparison is available and meaningful, a larger proportion of students attend private schools in Spain, Australia, France, and Denmark than in America. On the other hand, the private sector is smaller in *most* OECD countries and is effectively nonexistent in Norway, Turkey, and Sweden.

Various problems are associated with private education. First, each state in the country requires that young people be educated appropriately, and yet

Exhibit 6.18   Percentage of Students in Private Schools in Some
OECD Countries in 1986

	Primary	Secondary
Spain	35	35
Australia	24	29
France	15	22
Denmark	9	14
United States	11	8
Japan	1	13
United Kingdom	5	8
Austria	4	7
Canada	3	7
Greece	6	4
West Germany	2	7
New Zealand	2	5
Switzerland	2	5
Norway	1	3
Turkey	1	2
Sweden	1	1

—Source: Don S. Anderson (Is the privatisation of Australian schooling inevitable?, 1991b, p. 147).
—Statistical Sources: *Education in OECD Countries 1986–87* (Organisation for Economic Co-operation and Development, 1989), and *Development of Private Enrollment First and Second Level Education 1975–1985* (UNESCO, 1989).

some private schools may decide not to offer curricula that are required in public schools. How then can states guarantee that students are receiving a "satisfactory" education in the private sector? This problem can generate angry debates, but in most states minimal educational standards are enforced by requiring that private schools offer certain basic courses or by testing all students in the state on a regular basis for skill mastery.

Second, parents who send their children to private schools may come to resent the fact that they are paying *twice* for education: once, through taxes, to support the public schools; and a second time, through tuition payments, to support the private school of their choice. And this resentment has helped fuel debates about whether public funds should be used to support private schools. Advocates for Catholic schools have often led these debates, but so far their urgings have been blocked by court decisions stressing that to spend public money for private, sectarian schools would violate the constitutionally mandated separation of church and state. Full-scale *political* debate has not yet taken place on this question in the United States, however, and it is certainly true that public funds are sometimes used to support both public and sectarian schools in other Western countries. In fact, this outcome is quite likely where, as in the Province of Quebec, two strong school systems are operated, one secular, the other representing a dominant religion.

Third, and most damaging, when elite and public schools exist side by side in a community, the former tend to debilitate the latter. The reason for this is that elite schools tend to attract wealthy and concerned parents, as well as talented and ambitious students, and this creates a dual educational system in which private schools cater to "the richest, the best, and the brightest" youngsters, while public schools are stuck with educating "the leftovers." And once this process starts, ambitious (and thoughtful) parents become less interested in supporting the public schools or in sending their children to them. So the elite schools spiral upward, the public schools spiral downward, and this creates "the Philadelphia effect" discussed in Chapter 5.

To summarize, various problems are created because America tolerates both public and private schools. This doesn't mean that all private schools should be prohibited. To the contrary, private schools provide a useful safety valve for dissident groups in the society, and some private schools have pioneered important innovations in education. But it is useful to bear in mind the problems that private schools can create. In particular, we should be alert to the damaging effect that elite private schools can have on the public sector.

Local School Districts. As a rule, public education is operated by local school districts in America, and in this respect the United States is unique among Western countries. The idea that public schools should be run by locally elected boards of education seems to have appeared first in a Massachusetts law dating from 1789, but the idea spread quickly to the other New England states and eventually across the nation. Today the idea of local control over schools forms the basis for public-school organization in all the states except Hawaii.[46] Early in this century, there were roughly 150,000 public-school districts in America, and although many of these have vanished because of consolidation and the abandonment of one-room schools, even today the country has some fifteen thousand local school districts.[47]

The influence of these districts "is extraordinary in world perspective. Despite the recent growth of state and national power, these districts make a great range of decisions, including those that bear on levels of funding, the nature of educational programs, and the teachers to be hired."[48] These features are simply not found in other Western countries. Elsewhere, public schools are largely operated by state or national governments, and many nations have no tradition favoring even minimal local control over education. Thus, in other countries decisions concerning features of the education system such as funding, curriculum, teacher assignment, testing procedures, and resource allocation are typically made by central authorities. They make these decisions through a combination of parliamentary debates that set educational policies and actions by state bureaucracies that presumably implement (but often "reinterpret") those policies.[49]

The American system arose out of suspicion of central government and has some obvious advantages. Among them, it encourages citizen participation in school governance at the local level, it helps schools to respond to local problems, and it tends to facilitate educational innovation. However, it also generates problems.

First, it is simply not cost-effective. Although most school-board members serve without pay, expenses are associated with their regular meetings. In addition, it is more expensive for a metropolitan area or state to control its schools through scores of local bureaucracies than through a single organization. And, of course, all of these expenses inflate the costs of public education. (One of America's largest cities, Phoenix, Arizona, has roughly thirty separate school districts in its metropolitan area and over forty in its county. Each district has a board, a superintendent, separate purchasing and payroll departments, and so forth. Savings could be effected by amalgamating some of these services.) Thus, even if the United States spends as much per capita on public education as other Western countries—a dubious thesis—less of that money is available to pay teachers and to equip classrooms.

Second, the American system tends to generate great variability in school programs. This occurs because schools in different districts may offer divergent curricula, use "strange" textbooks, adopt differing systems for grading and promoting students, or promote values in their schools that people in other districts detest. Some of this variability is welcome, of course, and American schools are known throughout the world for their willingness to try out new ideas. But some of it is counterproductive. Public education should promote common standards of literacy, numeracy, scientific knowledge, social understanding, aesthetic appreciation, and respect for cultural traditions across the nation; and some commonality in school programs is necessary to accomplish these goals. In addition, American parents move around a lot, and their children are at a disadvantage when they must enter schools in new districts if the schools have markedly different programs. So some coordination of school programs is necessary, and this requires additional mechanisms that either are not needed or are less prevalent elsewhere. And for this reason, Americans have developed numerous agencies that review and accredit schools; state, regional, and national professional associations; city, state, and national testing services; and so forth. These coordinating agencies also add to the cost of education in our country.

Third, school districts in America are given the power to tax their citizens and to issue bonds to support education, and the bulk of funding for schools has traditionally come from local rather than state or federal sources. This means that wealthy American school districts are able to build and staff *much* better schools than are poor districts. These inequities pose serious problems for our country, and we return to them shortly.

We certainly do not recommend that local control of education be done away with in America. (As observers from other countries often comment, it is absurd to assume that a central parliament can make intelligent decisions for all public schools in a country, and state educational bureaucracies are often isolated from the concerns of citizens.) But one must also be aware of the problems generated by local school districts and take these problems into account when planning programs for improving education.

Multiple and Competing Tasks. In early years, public schools in America were conceived of as institutions that served local communities. However, over time those communities grew into cities with serious problems that resulted from the Industrial Revolution, immigration, and inadequate social services; and powerful voices began to argue that schools should expand their missions, should take on additional tasks, should provide additional services for those cities. To illustrate, William Torrey Harris opened the first public school kindergarten, in St. Louis in 1873, claiming that kindergartens were necessary because traditional socializing agencies such as the family, the church, and the community had collapsed.[50] And early in this century, John Dewey urged that schools be used as social centers in order to reduce the growing problem of alienation in industrial society, Edward A. Ross argued that schools were agencies that could provide needed social control, Edward J. Ward promoted the use of schools as centers for political activity, and Henry Curtis wrote that schools should provide playgrounds and other recreational facilities as antidotes to crime and idleness.[51] As Lawrence Cremin has suggested, such arguments created a broad, "Progressive" vision for American education that may be contrasted with the narrower conceptions of education prevalent in other Western countries where social services are often provided by other institutions.[52]

Today, American schools are asked to take on a large number of tasks. All schools are supposed to provide *instruction* for students, of course—teaching courses in subjects that society deems necessary or that are of interest to groups of students. In addition, American schools regularly *test* students for their knowledge of subject matter they have been taught. These two tasks are so basic to American notions of how to run schools that it may come as a surprise to learn that "testing" is not always performed in schools in other countries. Instead, in other Western countries educators often argue that schools should be responsible only for instruction, so testing is done by outside agencies, which administer statewide or nationwide examinations in designated subjects. Such customs allow schools to devote more of their energies to instructional activities but also tend to restrict the range of curricular offerings in schools to just those subjects examined.

In addition, "every society must make some provision for deciding which of its members shall occupy the various positions in the society and perform the roles necessary for its continuation and development."[53] In the United States this task—*pupil allocation*—is assigned to the schools. As we noted a few pages ago, this task tends to produce curricular tracking. It also provides employment for counselors and school psychologists—professional roles that do not appear in many Western countries—and this increases the costs of education.

In response to the progressive agenda, American schools are also likely to provide services for the wider community—to assume responsibility for some forms of *public entertainment, community enlightenment,* and the *creation of community spirit.* High schools may provide various forms of entertainment, ranging from football games and other sports events to lectures, music, and theatre. They may also offer adult-education courses and recreational facilities that are used by adults in the community. Moreover, the local high school's football team, facilities, and social events may become a source of community identification and pride. This becomes strikingly evident, for example, when one studies the consolidation of rural schools in Midwestern America. Smaller towns that lose their high schools tend to die; those lucky enough to acquire the consolidated high school tend to prosper.

American schools have also taken on an increasing range of tasks involving the *socialization and supervision* of youth. Some of these tasks have reflected the evolving needs of society; for example, most high schools offer courses in driver's education and on the creative use of leisure time. Schools have also taken over some of the tasks that were once performed by churches and families; thus many high schools offer social events, such as dances and parties, that have little relevance to the task of instruction. And yet busy parents would far prefer to have their children supervised by educators than to have them on the streets, in bars, or "hanging out" on street corners.

As well, American schools are increasingly being asked to provide *baby-sitting* and *leisure-time* services for society. As more and more mothers choose to work, primary schools are being asked to provide pre-school programs and day-care centers. And as fewer and fewer jobs are available for young people, high schools and colleges are being asked to provide curricula sufficiently attractive to hold older youths in education until high school graduation or later.

Some schools are also called on for programs that will *maintain subgroup traditions* for specific immigrant or ethnic groups. And in some communities, public schools are now viewed as agents of *social reform* and are thus called on to "solve" the problems of racial segregation through student busing, to conduct "outreach" programs that will help specific groups, or to seek greater contacts with industries or other institutions in their communities.

This wide range of tasks reflects not only the general shortage of social services in America but also the high regard Americans have for their schools. Unfortunately, they also create problems. First, it is not clear that the school is the best place for accomplishing some of these tasks. It is questionable, for example, whether most schools are equipped to meet adults' recreational needs well, and true social reform simply cannot be accomplished within the school alone. Second, some of these tasks may be incompatible with others; fielding a winning football team may seriously interfere with academic instruction in the high school.

But crucially, whenever the school takes on yet another task, it must devote resources to that task; and unless the community is willing to provide additional support, those resources must come from the base budget of the school. Thus, the school that has wonderful sports teams, that offers music and drama programs for the public, that has first-rate vocational counselors, that provides adult education courses, may in fact be diverting resources away from instruction for ordinary students. And the school that tries to keep disaffected youngsters off the street by offering "attractive" curricula—courses concerned with souping up hot rods, rock music, or craft and hobby interests—may have fewer resources to support traditional instruction in basic academic subjects.

We do not propose to judge whether American schools should or should not take on such a wide range of tasks. Although some critics of education in the U.S. pretend that Americans agree broadly that the resources of public education should be focused on instruction in "the basics," we detect no such agreement. Like the progressive educators of the past, we believe that American schools *should* take on various tasks, indeed that some of the more recent tasks given the schools are more important today than they were at the beginning of the century. But Americans should understand that schools are able to take on only a finite number of tasks, and citizens must be prepared to debate the need for those tasks and then must fund schools appropriately when additional tasks are assigned to them. American schools *can* accomplish various goals, but only if those goals are clearly articulated, are judged to be appropriate by the community, and are reasonably funded.

Summary. American education has indeed had a unique history, and has today a number of recognizable, everyday features that sets it apart from education elsewhere. Some of these features are true strengths, but others cause serious problems. The latter must be understood if we are to make effective plans for improving America's schools.

A case can be made that America has, in the words of historian David Tyack, "The One Best System" of education in the world.[54] Indeed, much of what we wrote in earlier chapters was devoted to persuading you of the many virtues of American schools. But this does not mean that our schools cannot be improved. Rather, American education today faces some truly severe problems that require broad understanding and serious effort if we are to avoid tragic consequences—and we turn now to three of these. We have written briefly about each of these problems in earlier chapters, but here we describe them and their consequences in greater detail.

Unequal Support of Schools

What are the messages of schools with "insufficient heat," "perennially clogged toilets," and "inadequate lighting"? What are schools such as one in the South Bronx, "a 66-year-old dull, brick building down in a landscape of vacant lots, dead cars, stray dogs and troubled men," telling the students about society's commitment to their future? . . . If some schools are preparing students for power, can we not postulate that other schools, those in our poorest neighborhoods, are all too often training many of their young people for a life of failure and despair? Many of our young people do not come out of school with the skills or the credentials to work in the regular economy. Why, then, are we surprised at the rate of teen pregnancy, crack addiction, gang membership, or at the flourishing of the underground economy?

—Ruth Sidel (*On Her Own: Growing Up in the Shadow of the American Dream,* 1990, p. 80)

Some Americans like to pretend that public education in this country is of one piece and that it provides equal opportunities for all. Moreover, among the hundreds of works published recently that criticize schools in the United States, compare American schools with those in other countries, or suggest ways to improve American education, it is difficult to find more than a half dozen that even raise questions about unequal support for schools. And yet, *huge* differences persist in the levels of support given to public schools in this country—differences that are far greater than those found in other advanced countries. Funding levels are also closely tied to community affluence, which means that America's wealthy suburbs have some of the world's best schools, while appallingly bad schools appear in our urban ghettos. Thus, instead of funding an educational system that provides equal opportunity, America operates a system of public education that discriminates against poor students because the schools they attend are badly underfunded.

Let's examine the evidence for these claims. When we speak of inequality, what are we talking about? How large *are* the differences in support between the richest and poorest public schools in America? Actually, the answer to this question changes as one goes from state to state. In some states (Hawaii, for example) per-student support of schools varies very little as one goes from rich to poor communities. In contrast, within the worst states (Texas, for example) schools in a rich community may receive more than *five* times as much per-student funding as schools in a poor community. In a recent article, Ronald Ferguson reports that the 1986 per-student support for Texas public school districts ranged from an abysmal low of $2,042 to a munificent high of $11,082.[55] Or, if you prefer data for a single metropolitan area, Jonathan Kozol indicates that the 1986 per-student support in the New York City area ranged from $5,585 in New York City itself to more than $11,000 each in the suburban school districts of Manhasset, Jericho, and Great Neck.[56] Moreover, Kozol also reports sharp disparities in financial support *within* large school districts, with schools serving the more affluent children receiving a lot more support than those serving the less affluent.

In 1991 the Educational Testing Service published a report entitled *The State of Inequality,* which provided state-by-state data for annual per-student support of public education.[57] ETS calculated the average 1986 per-student expenditure in the ten wealthiest and ten poorest school districts for each state and then divided the former by the latter. The resulting ratios are displayed in Exhibit 6.19. By this calculation, in some states (notably Texas and Ohio), the typical wealthy school district spent roughly 2.8 times as much, on average, as did the typical poor school district. Ratios varied elsewhere, but in roughly half of the states, wealthy school districts spent, on average, 1.7 times as much, or more, on education than did poor school districts.

The fifty states also vary sharply in their general willingness to support public education. ETS also calculated each state's average per-student expenditures, based on 1989 information, and then adjusted those averages for the cost of living in each state. As a result of these adjustments, the state averages can be compared directly, without concern for differences in living costs. The adjusted averages ranged from a miserly $2,928 for the state of Utah to a healthier $6,994 for the state of New York. Thus, in 1989 New York State effectively provided more than *two-and-one-third* times as much per-student support for public education as did Utah, with the rest of the states scattered in between.

In short, students can lose out in the "public education funding race" in America either because they live in poor communities in states that allow unequal funding or because they live in states that generally fund education poorly. And if students lose out in this race, they can attend a public school that is given *one-fifth or less the level of support* that is provided to public schools in wealthier districts in the country. Are these differences large? Yes, they are enormous.

But why are public schools unequally supported in America, and why doesn't that inequality occur in other Western countries? As we explained earlier, the basic reason for unequal support in our country is that a good deal of funding for our public schools comes from local taxes. Affluent communities in America are able to tax themselves to support wonderful public schools, but impoverished communities have few resources for schools beyond what is provided by the state and federal governments. According to the National Center for Education Statistics, support from local sources has declined somewhat since the 1930s but in the 1980s provided, on average, about 45 percent of all funding for U.S. public school districts.[58] Another 45 percent came from the states, and the remainder came from the federal purse. Since local school districts *simply don't exist* in most other countries, public education abroad is largely supported by general tax revenues; and those funds are normally assigned to schools on a per-student basis. (Indeed, educators from other countries are usually shocked when they learn that we fund

Exhibit 6.19 Ratio of Education Spending Differences Between High and Low Spending Groups of Districts, 1986–87

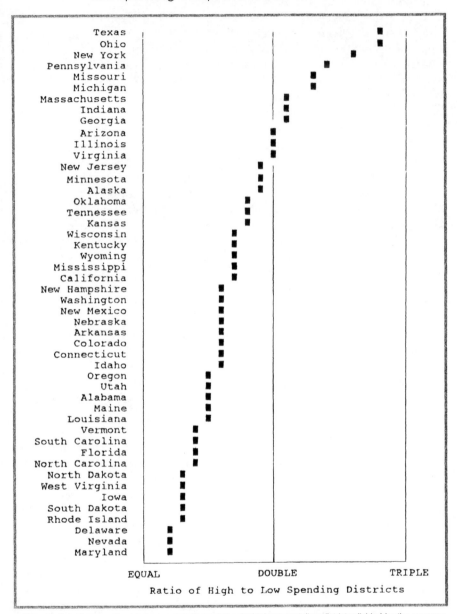

Ratio of High to Low Spending Districts

—Note: Ratios given are the average expenditure of the 10 highest-spending districts divided by the average expenditure of the 10 lowest-spending districts in each state. Data are presented for unified districts only and exclude districts with enrollments below 500 and special purpose districts. Hawaii and Montana were omitted because they have no unified districts. Because of small numbers of districts, only the highest and lowest spending districts were used in Nevada, Rhode Island, and Wyoming.
—Source: *The State of Inequality* (Educational Testing Service, 1991, Figure 4).
—Statistical Source: Riddle (1990).

schools in this country largely through local taxes, which allows rich Americans to avoid responsibility for supporting schools in poorer districts.)

To be fair, we should also point out that the legitimacy of unequal funding is sometimes questioned in the United States, and lawsuits against funding formulas for public schools have been filed in about half of the states.[59] These lawsuits have led to some reforms and to a gradual expansion of statewide per-student funding; but they haven't always been successful, and state-funding formulas are often defended vigorously by representatives of affluent school districts.

However, the issue of unequal funding is even more serious than the raw statistics indicate. Even if the millennium should arrive and public schools throughout America were given equal per-student support, inequality would still exist because of the far greater needs of schools in decaying urban centers. Many of America's urban schools now spend a good deal of their meager funds defending themselves against crime and violence. Many are located in areas that are crowded, unattractive, and depressing. Many are housed in ramshackle and unsafe buildings that reflect years of neglect. And many are burdened by efforts to provide extra health, recreational, and social services for students and other citizens. Thus, if we truly wanted to fund schools based on need, we would not provide support on a per-student basis. Instead, *extra* funding would be provided for schools in impoverished communities where needs are greater. Programs providing extra support sometimes appear in other Western countries, but we know of no such programs in America.

But does it really matter when schools are unequally supported? Of course it matters, and in the most obvious and cruel ways. Well-supported public schools have handsome buildings, small classes, well-paid and highly motivated teachers, excellent facilities that support education, and (for good measure) are usually blessed with affluent students who are growing up in supportive physical and social environments. Impoverished public schools must make do with decaying and crowded quarters, have huge and overcrowded classrooms, have difficulty recruiting and holding teachers, lack basic facilities, and often must contend with impoverished and "at risk" students who are growing up in the dangerous environments of America's inner cities (see Exhibit 6.20).

We began this chapter by noting that poverty is much more widespread in America than in other Western countries, and that the plight of the poor is worsening here. Students from poor families lack resources and are handicapped for education by comparison with students from wealthy or even middle-class homes. If America's public-school system were truly to offer *equal* opportunity, it would have to provide *extra* resources for schools serving the poor. Instead, America turns its back on the educational needs of its poorest children and offers them the *worst* public schools in the nation. Moreover, many Americans don't seem to know that this is happening. Instead, influenced by diversionary rhetoric, they often seem to be unaware of or unconcerned about unequal support of public schools, to give more attention to other problems of education, and to take for granted that the system is "fair."

What are the effects of such obliviousness and the persistence of educational inequality? For affluent and middle-class Americans: good educational opportunities, complacency about the system, and reinforcement of beliefs that the poor are largely responsible for their own plight. For Americans who are trapped by poverty and must attend America's worst schools: few opportunities, a sense of being trapped, degradation, self-blame, resentment, and lives that are more likely to involve crime and violence. Thus, for want of equitable funding for education, America pays a terrible price in correctable

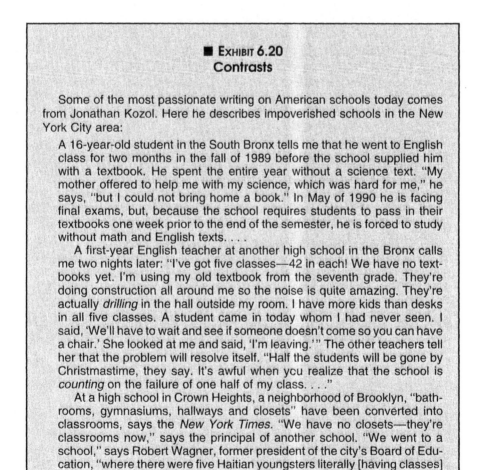

■ EXHIBIT 6.20
Contrasts

Some of the most passionate writing on American schools today comes from Jonathan Kozol. Here he describes impoverished schools in the New York City area:

A 16-year-old student in the South Bronx tells me that he went to English class for two months in the fall of 1989 before the school supplied him with a textbook. He spent the entire year without a science text. "My mother offered to help me with my science, which was hard for me," he says, "but I could not bring home a book." In May of 1990 he is facing final exams, but, because the school requires students to pass in their textbooks one week prior to the end of the semester, he is forced to study without math and English texts. . . .

A first-year English teacher at another high school in the Bronx calls me two nights later: "I've got five classes—42 in each! We have no textbooks yet. I'm using my old textbook from the seventh grade. They're doing construction all around me so the noise is quite amazing. They're actually *drilling* in the hall outside my room. I have more kids than desks in all five classes. A student came in today whom I had never seen. I said, 'We'll have to wait and see if someone doesn't come so you can have a chair.' She looked at me and said, 'I'm leaving.'" The other teachers tell her that the problem will resolve itself. "Half the students will be gone by Christmastime, they say. It's awful when you realize that the school is *counting* on the failure of one half of my class. . . ."

At a high school in Crown Heights, a neighborhood of Brooklyn, "bathrooms, gymnasiums, hallways and closets" have been converted into classrooms, says the *New York Times.* "We have no closets—they're classrooms now," says the principal of another school. "We went to a school," says Robert Wagner, former president of the city's Board of Education, "where there were five Haitian youngsters literally [having classes] in a urinal. . . ."

disadvantage for perhaps a quarter of its citizens. And we all suffer the consequences of this disadvantage in massive rates of murder, pillage, drug addiction, and imprisonment in our nation. A school principal from the Bronx
asks,

> Will these children ever get what white kids in the suburbs take for granted? I
> don't think so. If you ask me why, I'd have to speak of race and social class. I don't
> think the powers that be in New York City understand, or want to understand, that
> if they do not give these children a sufficient education to lead healthy and produc-
> tive lives, we will be their victims later on. We'll pay the price someday—in
> violence, in economic costs. I despair of making this appeal in any terms but
> these. You cannot issue an appeal to conscience in New York today. The fair play
> argument won't be accepted. So you speak of violence and hope that it will scare
> the city into action.[60]

> At P.S. 94 in District 10, where 1,300 children study in a building suita-
> ble for 700, the gym has been transformed into four noisy, makeshift
> classrooms. The gym teacher improvises with no gym. A reading teacher,
> in whose room "huge pieces of a ceiling" have collapsed, according to
> the *Times*, "covering the floor, the desks and the books," describes the
> rain that spills in through the roof. . . .
>
> And here Kozol describes a suburban public high school, just outside New
> York City:
>
> The high school . . . built of handsome gray stone and set in a landscaped
> campus, . . . resembles a New England prep school. . . . The principal . . .
> takes me to see the auditorium, which, he says, was recently restored
> with private charitable funds ($400,000) raised by parents. The crenelated
> ceiling, which is white and spotless, and the polished dark-wood paneling
> contrast with the collapsing structure of the auditorium at [a high school
> in the city]. . . . In a student lounge, a dozen seniors are relaxing on a
> carpeted floor that is constructed with a number of tiers so that, as the
> principal explains, "they can stretch out and be comfortable while
> reading. . . ."
>
> The library is wood-paneled, like the auditorium. Students, all of whom
> are white, are seated at private carrels, of which there are approximately
> 40. Some are doing homework; others are looking through the *New York
> Times*. . . .
>
> According to the principal, the school has 96 computers for 546 chil-
> dren. The typical student, he says, studies a foreign language for four or
> five years, beginning in junior high school, and a second foreign language
> (Latin is available) for two years. Of 140 seniors, 92 are now enrolled in
> [Advanced Placement] classes. Maximum teacher salary will soon reach
> $70,000. Per-pupil funding is above $12,000 at the time I visit.
>
> —Jonathan Kozol (*Savage Inequalities*, 1991, pp. 110–4, 124–5).

The Dilemmas of Radical Expansion

Whereas in previous economic crises the secondary schools served only a minority of those eligible and higher education remained an elite preserve, the schools in the post-War period have become the central institution for socializing and selecting virtually all the young people of advanced capitalist societies into their adult pursuits. To reorient such a pervasive institution in response to economic crisis has become an extraordinarily difficult and delicate matter.

—David Livingstone (*Class Ideologies and Educational Futures*, 1983, p. 9)

American education expanded radically after World War II. It now serves a *much* larger portion of the student population than it did in 1945. That expansion reflected economic forces, high expectations for education, the growth of the economy, and democratic values; but it also created many problems for American education—problems that are often more serious in this country than elsewhere.

What do we mean by "radical expansion"? Of all students entering fifth grade just before the U.S. entered World War II, only half completed high school, and only a fifth entered college. In contrast, by 1960 three-fourths of fifth graders were graduating from high school and 45 percent were entering college. Thus, in the two decades following the war, American high schools had to find places for something like 50 percent more students, and American colleges had to expand their facilities by more than 100 percent, on a per-capita basis.

These trends would continue. As Exhibit 6.21 shows, the proportion of adults in America completing less than four years of high school has continued to decline, while the proportions completing at least a twelfth-grade education and four or more years of college have continued to grow. This means that per-capita enrollment in secondary and post-secondary education programs has continued to expand. (Moreover, throughout these years the number of students in the system also grew in response to immigration and a high postwar birthrate, and this required additional expansion of secondary and post-secondary facilities.)

Growth in secondary and higher education during this period was not confined to the United States. Comparative figures published by UNESCO and OECD suggest that although America led the way in expanding its schools and colleges, most other Western countries did so also.[61] Today, enrollment rates for secondary education are fairly similar among many Western countries, although some countries—the United Kingdom, for example—lag behind.[62] But, the United States continues to enroll a larger proportion of its population in post-secondary education than do other countries. Using data from UNESCO, Edith Rasell and Lawrence Mishel estimated that "in 1985, 5.1 percent of the entire U.S. population was enrolled in some form of higher

Exhibit 6.21   Years of School Completed by People 25 Years Old and Older, 1940 to 1991

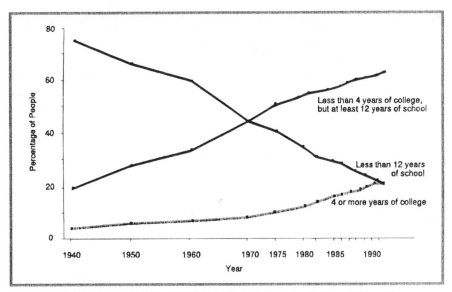

—Source: *Digest of Education Statistics 1993* (National Center for Education Statistics, 1993, p. 11).
—Statistical Sources: U.S. Department of Commerce, Bureau of the Census, *1960 Census of Population,* Vol. 1, part 1, and *Current Population Reports,* Series P–20; and U.S. Department of Labor, Bureau of Labor Statistics, Office of Employment and Unemployment Statistics, "Education Attainment of Workers, March 1991"; and unpublished data.

education, a figure two to three times larger than the percentage of enrollments of any other country, except Canada."[63]

Why did this educational expansion take place? In part, it reflected America's long-held beliefs about the efficacy of education, coupled with real growth in the American economy during the 1950s and 1960s. In part, also, it was financed directly by the federal government, as an alternative to massive unemployment, through direct grants to students under the G.I. Bill program. Further, educational expansion reflected the long-standing American commitment to extending educational advantages to more groups in the population. And education expanded because the labor market was changing, unskilled jobs were becoming scarce, and many occupations were requiring additional qualifications for entry-level positions.

What problems were created for schools by this radical expansion? First, the expansion took place during a period of unprecedented economic growth and was associated with unrealistic expectations about education. As we noted above, early in this century, progressives advocated an expanded role for education. They wanted the schools to solve many social problems in their communities. During the 1950s and 1960s, however, new schools were needed, and their supporters portrayed those schools in almost mystical terms. Not only would such schools lead to better career opportunities for their students and greater economic growth for society, but they would also provide moral education, cultural uplift, facilities for hobbies and recreation, social integration, and a host of medical, psychological, and social services for their communities. Thus, people had unrealistically high expectations for their schools; and when the economy soured in the 1970s and 1980s, those expectations became standards against which schools were judged and found wanting. Nor was this first type of problem confined to the United States. Other nations experienced a similar malaise when their expanded educational systems did not live up to high expectations (see Exhibit 6.22).

Second, problems also arose because American schools were not funded sufficiently to finance their expanded programs. In general, school expansion in the 1960s and 1970s was matched by increased funding. Some of this increase came from local and state resources and was provided in order to build new school facilities, but some also came from expansion of federal support for various entitlement programs.[64] However, expansion in education since the early 1970s has not, in general, been matched by increased

---

■ Exhibit 6.22
Reactions to the Era of Growth

At the risk of caricaturing history by oversimplifying the contrasts between one period and the next, there can be no doubt that today the period of the 1960s and 1970s exercises a profound influence on perceptions of and the shape of education systems. That was a period of unparalleled growth in expenditures and enrollments. Far-reaching structural reforms of schools were initiated in many countries. There was a strong conviction that education was a positive good—for an individual, the route to social mobility; for society, the motor of prosperity. If perceiving the roots of one era in the one that went before has any validity, then that of the 1960s was itself a reaction to the 1940s and 1950s—years of reconstruction from the miseries of pre-war depression and war-time stress. The optimism of the immediate post-war years intensified as more wanted to enjoy the fruits of increasing affluence. Education appeared to be the most obvious means of acquiring it. Predictions were common place that industrialised societies were already becoming "post-industrialized," dependent not so much on the production of goods as on the production of knowledge.

Coincidentally, the birth-rate was rising sharply and schools were filled to overflowing. The overriding problems for many education authorities was simply how to build enough new schools and find enough teachers to staff them. Expansion was both demographically and socially impelled, underpinned by the economic rationale that educational growth was a key determinant of the generation of wealth.

(continued on next page)

local or state funding—and federal support for public schools has *declined* since 1980 in real dollar terms. These constraints have resulted in two decades of scrimping and in the reduction of educational programs. In sharp contrast, most educational expansion in other Western countries has been funded more adequately. So the United States has recently been falling behind in the "education-funding derby."

Third, the radical expansion of education has left us with problems associated with curricula and educational standards that have yet to be resolved. Contrast the typical American public high school of the early 1940s with the school of today. Before World War II, about 50 percent of the students in each high school class dropped out before graduation, and only 20 percent actually went on to post-secondary education. This meant that in the 1940s, public high schools would track about a quarter of their students into a demanding "college-preparation" curriculum, offer "vocational" curricula to another 25 percent, and impose "general education" on the remainder (who would shortly leave school anyway). Contrast this with today's high school, where any student who withdraws from education before graduation is stigmatized as a "dropout," all students are encouraged to consider at least some

The seeds of later discontent, and ultimately of the present concern about quality, were thus sown. [Western] economies faltered in the 1970s in the wake of the first oil-price shock. Unemployment levels rose sharply, initially hitting hardest the young and only later giving rise to the widespread phenomenon of long-term unemployment among all age groups. Not only had the simple formula "more education, more prosperity" been found wanting, but the severe difficulties young people experienced in entering the labor market at all caused some people to blame schools for failing to prepare them adequately for working life. The link between education and social mobility no longer appeared self-evident.

As public expenditures on education ceased to increase or even diminished, and as other sectors of government became fiercely competitive for scarce resources, the sheer size and expense of education systems fell under scrutiny—how efficient were they? Did they give value for money? Just as demographic and expenditure growth had gone hand-in-hand in the 1950s and 1960s, so the economic downturn coincided with a declining birthrate and falling school rolls. With the hunt for new teachers to staff schools no longer a priority, the spotlight could begin to focus on the performance of the teachers already employed and those few being newly recruited. Had rapid expansion brought in its train too many teachers, ill-suited or ill-prepared for the onerous task of educating the next generation, who would nevertheless remain in service for many years to come? Many critics so pronounced.

—*Education in OECD Countries 1986–87* (Organisation for Economic Co-operation and Development, 1989, pp. 15–16).

form of post-secondary education, and over 50 percent of all entering students will actually enroll in colleges or universities.

By comparison then, the high school of the 1940s could impose tough standards on those few students selected for higher education, whereas today's high school has difficulty doing so because *all* students are encouraged to consider higher education—and *none* are to be forced out of the system. And the high school of the 1940s offered a narrower range of courses that were focused on careers, whereas today's high school offers a wide range of courses, some of which are focused on leisure-time interests of students whom the schools are trying to retain. Thus, radical expansion has enlarged and democratized the curriculum, but it has also introduced confusion over the setting and enforcing of standards. Moreover, note that this last type of problem is generated, in part, because America remains committed to the *comprehensive* high school. Countries that operate two or more tiers of public high schools are less bothered by the issue.

Good and compelling reasons lay behind the radical expansion of education in our country, but that expansion has certainly created problems. Most discussions of expectations for schools, educational funding, and confusion about curricula and standards have failed to come to grips with these problems. Indeed, some critics who argue for going "back to basics" would apparently have American schools return to a fictive "golden age," when higher education was reserved for the well-trained, deserving few, and the *hoi polloi* were left to fend for themselves. We find such ideas repugnant and inappropriate.

The Changing Student Population

The question before us is whether we have time to reverse the present course and make substantial improvements in the education of disadvantaged youth. Our nation has faced and overcome more severe crises in the past, and there is reason to believe that, if we became committed to educating the disadvantaged, we could overcome the current bleak picture. However, in recent years we have become a society unwilling to make sacrifices and particularly unwilling to place the interests of others above our own interests. . . . Whether we as a society act to improve the education of the disadvantaged may hinge upon leadership that understands and communicates [the message] that failing to make sacrifices now condemns us to a declining national standard of living in the future, and that the interests of the disadvantaged are increasingly intertwined with the self-interests of all of us. It is a message we may not want to hear, but it is one that we dismiss at our peril.

   —Gary Natriello, Edward McDill, and Aaron Pallas (*Schooling Disadvantaged Children: Racing Against Catastrophe,* 1990, p. 201)

For various reasons, students from several population groups have long been disadvantaged in American schools. These groups are also becoming more numerous in the population, and this will put great pressure on America's schools. Good programs for assisting these disadvantaged groups are available, but such programs require supplemental funding. Thus, unless we in America are willing to provide additional funds for education, more and more of the students in our schools will be struggling, and the *aggregate* achievement of American students is likely to fall.

Several different student groups are thought to be "at risk" in American education, beginning with those who are *impoverished*. As we documented earlier in the chapter, a great many students come from poor families in America today, and the number of impoverished students has risen sharply in the last decade. Poor students lack resources and would have a hard time in school even if they were given an equal chance, but (as we have also noted) they are *not* given an equal chance in our current education system, and the evidence is overwhelming that they do not do as well as affluent or middle-class students in our schools.[65] Thus, poor students are *badly* disadvantaged in American education today.

Children who come from *broken homes* are also thought to be "at risk." At present about 27 percent of American children live in families that are headed by one parent or no parents at all. Of these, the vast majority are headed by single mothers.[66] Evidence also indicates that students from broken homes have poorer educational outcomes.[67] Three reasons have been suggested for these findings: First, families with missing parents are also very likely to be impoverished (see Exhibit 6.23), and poverty certainly reduces students' ability to take advantage of school. Second, America provides appallingly few social services to help single parents, and this means that the children of single parents must face additional problems that may interfere with their schooling. Third, some argue that single parents are simply unable to provide adequate educational support for students. (Evidence certainly backs up the first two of these arguments, but is the last tenable? Studies to date of the impact of family structure have not generally controlled for the effects of poverty or examined the effects of supportive social services, so it is difficult to answer this question. We suspect that some of those who have argued that single parents cannot provide the support needed for education were reflecting sexist biases against single mothers.[68])

Black and Hispanic students are also thought to be "at risk" in American education, and this conclusion seems to be supported by analyses of educational statistics that provide separate data for students who are said to be white, black, and Hispanic. These analyses are actually quite confusing, since the first two of these categories are racial whereas the third is ethnic; and tabular footnotes are always needed to indicate that " 'Hispanic' persons might represent any race." Moreover, students identified as "Hispanic" in our country may have come from families originating in Mexico, Central or South America, Puerto Rico, Cuba, or even Spain, and these groups have had very different histories. However, if we accept this (awkward) distinction,

Exhibit 6.23   Poverty Rates Among Children by Family Type, Race, and
Ethnicity, 1990

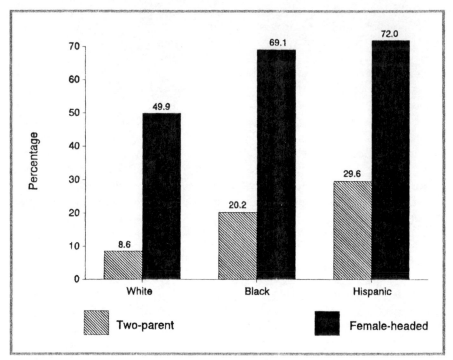

—Source: *Beyond Rhetoric: A New American Agenda for Children and Families* (National Commission on Children, 1991, p. 25).
—Statistical Source: *Statistical Abstracts of the United States* (Bureau of the Census, 1992, Table #719).

we learn that at present about 15 percent of American students are black and about 11 percent are Hispanic.[69]

For some years black and Hispanic students have suffered by comparison with white students in educational achievement; and although these differences have narrowed in recent years, they are still substantial today.[70] Several reasons have been suggested for these differences—among them discriminatory treatment and unique elements in the black and Hispanic cultures. However, black and Hispanic students are also very likely to come from impoverished homes (look again at Exhibit 6.23), so some of the apparent disadvantage of these groups is surely a result of poverty. Unfortunately, research has so far been insufficient to disentangle the causes of black or Hispanic educational disadvantage, but we suspect that most of it is indeed caused by poverty and discrimination.

As it happens, all of these disadvantaged groups are growing in size. The proportion of black and Hispanic students is actually increasing rapidly. Both groups have high birthrates, and the rate of Hispanic immigration is also

Exhibit 6.24   Projected Racial/Ethnic Composition of the U.S. Population
Under Age 18, 1988–2020

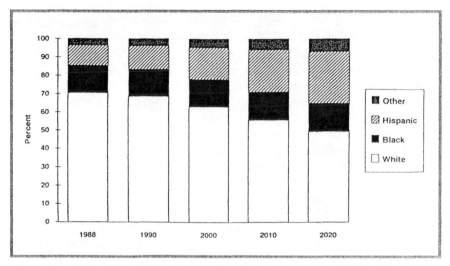

—Source: Gary Natriello, Edward McDill, and Aaron Pallas (*Schooling Disadvantaged Children: Racing Against Catastrophe,* 1990, p. 36).

high. In fact, if present growth rates continue, by the year 2020, whites will constitute less than 50 percent of the student population in America (see Exhibit 6.24).

The proportion of impoverished students and those from single-parent homes is also likely to increase, in part because of increasing numbers of black and Hispanic students. (The growth rates for these two population groups alone suggest that by the year 2020 the proportion of impoverished children in the country should increase by roughly 33 percent and the proportion from broken homes should rise by about 18 percent.[71]) In addition, it seems unlikely that the forces leading to ever increasing numbers of impoverished and broken homes in the country will abate in the near future.

All of which indicates that American schools must be prepared to help a *lot* more educationally disadvantaged students over the next few years. Is it possible to help these disadvantaged students? Indeed, it is quite possible to do so, and a good summary of programs that have been found effective for this purpose appears in *Schooling Disadvantaged Children: Racing Against Catastrophe* by Gary Natriello, Edward McDill, and Aaron Pallas.[72] Some of these programs have concentrated on maternal health or on compensatory preschool experiences. Others have been designed for primary schools—for example, that provide cooperative learning, individualized teaching, tutoring, and computer-assisted instruction. And some programs have focused on high schools. These include, for example, Upward Bound, the Job Corps, alternative schools, and programs in which curricula are adjusted to students' needs or are designed to help students find employment opportunities.

All of these programs would require additional funding if incorporated systematically into American schools. However, the research supporting these various programs has been carried out within the context of an education system that provides miserable support for schools that serve poor neighborhoods. So some of these programs *might not be needed* if per-student funding were equalized across America. But even if funding were equalized, some compensatory programs would surely still be useful, because extra effort will always be needed to provide fair chances for students who are disadvantaged because of poverty or other problems.

To summarize then, students from impoverished homes are *badly* disadvantaged in American education. In addition, evidence also suggests that students who are from single-parent homes, who are black, and who are Hispanic are also disadvantaged—but whether the latter effects are generated by poverty alone or by other factors associated with these groups is not yet clear. Regardless, *all* of these groups are large and should increase in the population over the next few years. Unless Americans are willing to provide additional resources for public schools, larger and larger numbers of American children will be given a raw deal in their educations, and the aggregate achievements of American students will presumably fall.

A Perspective on Problems

There are plenty of problems in education that we ought to be working on. But we should be dealing with them because, like Everest, they are there. Americans have a natural inclination to seek improvement [in education]. Good! Let's work to make things better. But let's not do it while telling people in the schools what a crummy job they're doing.

—Gerald Bracey (Why can't they be like we were?, 1991, p. 117)

Clearly, then, American schools face a series of daunting challenges. Some reflect serious problems in the society at large, and some result from the everyday features of American education. Some problems in American education are endemic, but others have recently escalated; and many are either unique in our country or are worse here because America so often lags behind other Western countries in matters of social justice. Given the scope of these challenges, it is actually amazing that American schools do as well as they do and that despite enormous problems they still manage to educate the majority of American students to a relatively high standard. It is even more amazing that our schools have managed to withstand the torrent of undeserved criticism they have received in the past few years.

It is surely time for Americans of good will to turn away from the myths of the Manufactured Crisis and focus once again on the *real* problems of American education. The problems we have reviewed in this chapter pose pressing and serious challenges for American schools, and our nation ignores them at its peril. Real problems such as these must be taken into account when realistic plans are made to improve our schools. And let it be clear. Those plans *must* be made. The future of millions of American students depends on whether we can spread the best features of our schools more equitably. Our society simply cannot afford the enormous economic and social costs that will follow if we fail to assist more of our citizens through education. Truly, civilization *is* a race between education and catastrophe.

Chapter Seven

Toward the
Improvement of
Education

◆

As Chapter 6 detailed, education currently faces various dilemmas and problems—some unique to our country, and many posing growing challenges for our schools. What can be done to resolve these dilemmas and solve these problems? What steps can concerned Americans take to improve the conduct of their schools?

We are not alone in asking these questions, of course. Over the past decade educators and others have made hundreds of recommendations for improving the organization, staffing, curricula, aims, and procedures of our public school systems. Many of these ideas have stimulated pilot projects or legislative action across the nation, and other ideas are waiting in the wings. Indeed, interest in improving our public education system has recently been intense.

Some of this activity has been generated by critics associated with the Manufactured Crisis, and we gave our reasons for rejecting their poor ideas for "reform" in Chapter 5. In fact, we think that the very notion of "reforming" education is pejorative. If American education is not now in crisis, then surely its schools don't need to be reformed. This does not mean that our schools can't be improved, of course. On the contrary, not only can we improve our system of education, but many useful ideas for improvement have been suggested by educators and others who wish our schools well. We turn now to some of these ideas.

In writing this chapter, we decided to focus on basic principles rather than to list specific school-improvement programs that are now being tried out across the country. We made this decision for several reasons. First, given the many programs one might review, such a list would be unwieldy.[1] Second, the results of many of these programs are as yet poorly documented; and although they may be promising, we hesitate to recommend them without seeing evidence of their successes. And third, good programs seem not yet to have appeared concerned with some of the worst problems that now face America's schools—and we wanted to write about these issues too.

In addition, it is often hard to replicate the effects of a successful educational program at a different site, but this does not mean that one cannot learn from those programs. On the contrary, successful programs often illustrate broad principles for improving educational efforts. So, in this chapter we have chosen to review those broad principles. For convenience, then, each section of the chapter begins by stating a broad principle for improving education.

On Dignity and Hope

[**Principle:** *Schooling in America can be improved by according parents more dignity and their children more hope.*]

Where there is no vision, the people perish.
   —Proverbs 29:18

In his book *Savage Inequalities* Jonathan Kozol wrote about a New York City school in terrible distress.[2] One of us had a very personal response to the conditions he described. Tears came to that reader's eyes because it was the school he had attended from kindergarten through ninth grade. It was always an ugly school, serving the poor, and that certainly has not changed. But now, because of worse poverty and more unemployment, lawlessness in the neighborhood, and reduced funding for social services and education, the school that had served so many, so well, for so many years, is now barely functioning at all. Two features of this sad situation stand out: the tragic loss of dignity among families in the area; and the decline of hope among the students who now attend this school.

People in the neighborhood around this school have always been poor. Indeed, few adults who grew up in this working-class area would say they had a glorious past, although their memories of childhood are often quite positive. This is possible because through the decades of the forties and fifties the average working-class family near this school functioned in ways that provided most parents with a modicum of dignity. Jobs were available for the men (the primary wage earners in those days), and those jobs paid enough for families to afford a basic apartment. Also, women were able to stretch their husbands' dollar incomes by doing a good deal of unpaid labor. Thus, in spite of their limited finances, these families were able to provide food, shelter, clothing, and medical care for their families. Furthermore, the growth of the economy gave them some optimism about their lives and their families' futures.

Streets were also a lot safer for children in those days, and children in those families were led to believe that they would do better in life than their parents had. Almost everyone in the neighborhood thought that better days were ahead. Affordable higher education, better jobs and higher incomes, improved housing, and a secure if not luxurious retirement—all of this seemed to be within the reach of people who strived and persevered. In those days, then, parents had dignity and their children had hope, and this meant that children in the neighborhood had good reason to attend school and to work hard there. Educating those children was actually an easy task (although teachers in the school may not have thought so at the time). But what is it like in the neighborhood today?

Today, there are very few job opportunities in the area; the few jobs now available are likely to be part-time, to pay low wages, to provide few fringe benefits, and to offer no opportunities for advancement. Single mothers struggle to provide for their children and, in the absence of affordable child-care facilities, are sometimes forced to leave their children unattended in order to go to work. Even two employed parents find it difficult to make ends meet and often have to make do without health or retirement benefits. Well-maintained apartments near the school are difficult to find, and even the most neglected apartments are very expensive. Recreational, health, and other support facilities are rare in the neighborhood, and few people can afford the cost of transportation to find them elsewhere. But these people are *Americans,* and like everyone else in the country, they have been exposed repeatedly to media images of successful living. Thus, because their community lacks the social services, the job opportunities, and the standard of living that are found elsewhere, the parents of schoolchildren in this neighborhood have very little dignity.

Young people in the neighborhood also have little hope. Some have no legal source of income and, as a result, get involved in theft, prostitution, violence, and drug pushing. Since their parents have little dignity, family ties are weak, and these young people often turn to gangs for social support. And since sport and recreational facilities are rarely available, they lead boring lives and are attracted to illegal activities. Also, their school is miserably funded, most of their academic records are mediocre, and few care about finishing high school—never mind going on to college. Most youths in the neighborhood also believe, correctly, that the cost of a college education is beyond their means and that scholarships for needy students are very rare. Thus, the everyday activities of their lives provide no vision of a better life for these young people, and they find it difficult to think of paths by which they might "make it" in the mainstream of American society. So they become angry, embittered, alienated—and too often they end up in prison or the morgue. And since parents who now live in the neighborhood have little dignity and their children lack hope, motivating those children in school is a much, much harder task.

For decades social scientists have studied what happens to families when they lose dignity and hope. Unexpected loss of jobs in the family can generate lowered self-esteem, disruption of respect and commitment, alcoholism, spouse and child abuse, divorce, crime, vandalism, lower achievement in schools, and other symptoms of dysfunction.[3] Researchers have also found that when previously stable families from Eastern Europe or Puerto Rico came as impoverished immigrants to our country they had a very hard time.[4] In fact, it has often taken a generation or more for such immigrant groups to regain a sense of personal dignity and family stability, although these processes have also been affected by the ethnic stereotypes, discriminatory practices, educational opportunities, and socio-economic conditions prevailing when they arrived.[5]

As our example from New York City suggests, these serious problems afflict not only individuals and families today but neighborhoods and whole communities in our country. Unfortunately, this fact is ignored by many critics and politicians, who like to pretend that problems in our schools and communities result solely from a "lack of family values." They contend that families no longer seem to be working. This is, in fact, a favorite theme of former Vice President Dan Quayle, who has often decried a "loss of family values" throughout the nation. Critics like Quayle are partly right—families are *not* working in America, that is, literally, *not working.* In too many American families, *no* member of the family has been able to find meaningful, legal, remunerative work—or, if someone is employed, that person works only on a part-time basis or at a job that pays less than the minimum wage, provides no health-care or retirement benefits, and offers only a bleak future. In addition, in too many cases the children of those families have few reasons to expect their lives to improve. These harsh realities are *real* causes of educational failure in our nation.

The achievement levels of our poorest and most alienated students will not be raised by lectures about responsibility from the critics, setting higher standards, or developing better tests (as recommended by our federal government and by many state legislatures). And school vouchers, another vacuous "solution" now being touted by Speaker of the House of Representatives Newt Gingrich, will not rescue impoverished families from despair. Rather, a decent standard of living, social services, jobs, and reasons to hope for the future are needed to improve the lives of those families and their students' educational achievements.

Hope and School Achievement. The importance of dignity and hope for educational achievement has recently been demonstrated in findings from a massive research project, the National Education Longitudinal Study (NELS). NELS researchers examined changes in achievement and a host of other factors for about 25,000 nationally representative students who were in the eighth grade in 1988. The students were followed through twelfth grade (in 1992), but to the best of our knowledge only the data for eighth and tenth grades have been reported so far.

One recent analysis of NELS data explored factors in families and among students that might predict student achievement.[6] When a host of such factors were examined, the *largest* effect found was for a characteristic called "student ambition and plans for the future." Students who had hopeful but realistic visions for themselves as successful in the future achieved well; those who had weaker visions did not. (Some associated factors also predicted student achievement: parental expectations for achievement, time spent doing homework, parental monitoring of friends and activities, and school-attendance rate; but these were weaker effects. Whether the student did or did not attend a private school or came from a single-parent family did *not* predict achievement.) Essentially, then, when children have strong visions for their futures, they achieve more. A strong vision for the future—hope—is a major predictor of learning!

Doing Something About It. As we know, poverty is now a *lot* worse in America than in other Western countries, and the problem of poverty has become much worse in the past decade. Thus, in all too many American neighborhoods parents have indeed lost dignity and children have little hope. From the small towns of Appalachia to inner-city ghettos and barrios—from depressed rural communities to defunct industrial towns and many native-American reservations—indeed, in perhaps a quarter of the neighborhoods of our land—dignity and hope are threatened because of widespread unemployment, poorly paying jobs, lack of social services, and despair. What can we Americans do about such devastating problems?

Actually, we can do a lot of useful things. For one thing, we can take steps that are common in other Western countries to generate greater equity in incomes. Raising and extending the minimum wage is a good place to begin. The federal minimum wage is presently set at a very low figure and has never been applied to more than a portion of the jobs in the country, in part because investors are greedy for immediate profit, and in part because few voices are willing to speak up for poorly paid workers. But shouldn't responsible people be worrying about how long a consumer economy can last *without consumers?* It is the height of folly for our nation to be *reducing* the purchasing power of its less prosperous citizens, but that is exactly what we have been doing since the early 1980s. Not only does this mean that many of our citizens now cannot meet their basic needs, but it is a terribly shortsighted policy in an economy that demands consumer spending for its maintenance.

Other actions can also be taken that will help to improve job prospects for more Americans. As a rule, American industries choose to pay overtime wages instead of hiring more employees (who would require additional fringe benefits), but such policies are prohibited by law in many countries. Other industrialized countries require that full fringe benefits also be paid for part-time workers. Many other advanced countries require business and industries to pay for four weeks or more of vacation each year, to provide "refresher leave" programs, to fund the costs of retraining programs for workers whose jobs have been terminated, and to allow workers to retire with full benefits after a specific term of employment. Some countries have cut the work week to thirty-six or thirty-two hours, and others provide tax-funded employment

programs for youth, workers in communities where industries have disappeared, and other population groups known to be "at risk" for unemployment. If we were to take steps such as these, *many* more Americans would
be able to find full-time, secure jobs.

In addition, most advanced countries use various mechanisms to redistribute income from well-off to less well-off people. Many governments mandate that employers pay equal wages for jobs of comparable worth, regardless
of who may be doing those jobs. Most industrialized countries employ a
progressive income tax system that truly takes a larger tax bite from the best-
paid workers in the land. Most advanced countries use their taxation systems
to provide more social services to alleviate problems for poor citizens. For
example, *all* other Western countries have national health-care systems that
are at least partly financed through taxes; and, as a result, those countries
pay a *lot* less for health care, have *lower* rates for many diseases, and, on
average, live *longer* lives than do Americans. Most advanced countries also
use taxes to finance fully paid maternity leave, free day-care centers for infants,
community health and recreation facilities, and a guaranteed minimum income for all people who are unemployed. Most also provide better support
for their colleges and universities through taxes; and many offer extensive,
tax-supported, scholarship programs that pay the bulk of higher-education
costs for talented but less well-off students. Clearly, services such as these
could be provided in our country and would help to redistribute income and
improve the lives of America's neediest citizens.

Here is one illustration of this effect. Several years ago one of us participated in research that compared the activities of inner-city youth in Australia
and the United States who had dropped out of school. The values and interests
of the two groups of young people were nearly identical, but the activities
they reported doing were sharply different. Australia uses taxes to fund many
recreational facilities in inner-city areas, and the Australian youngsters reported using those facilities regularly. America provides few such resources, of
course, and the American kids (who said they *wanted* access to such facilities)
reported much higher rates of boredom and illegal conduct.[7] (All of which
makes us wonder about the sanity of those in Congress who so vigorously
opposed funding for "midnight basketball" and other recreation programs
for inner-city youths in the recently passed national crime bill.)

It is not healthy for our nation to be so divided between haves and have-
nots! The supposedly egalitarian United States of America is beginning to
look more and more like the oligarchies of Central America and South America that we once derided. If concentrating the wealth among the few is allowed
to continue, this nation will see the same kind of social unrest that has marked
other nations for decades. Our country now has more private security guards
than public safety officers, and this is just one of the inevitable outcomes of
this kind of unequal distribution of wealth. In contrast, by redistributing
income, increasing the number of job opportunities, and providing more

social services, we could assure that more people in our country would experience or aspire to middle-class life styles; and this would accord more families the dignity and hope they need. Surely this would also mean greater student achievement, because children in the nation's poorer neighborhoods would then come to their schools with a sense of hope and a desire to learn. Schooling is, after all, about the future. To paraphrase the biblical quotation with which we opened this section, "When students have no vision, school achievements perish."

Prejudice, Dignity, and Hope. Although poverty, poor job prospects, and inadequate social services are prime reasons why families lose dignity and hope, other reasons can also be cited—particularly the destructive influences of prejudice and discrimination. To illustrate, highly educated African Americans and Hispanic Americans regularly face outrageous indignities. An African American professor of religion at Princeton, Cornel West, recently described an experience he had in New York City:

> [I] stood on the corner of 60th Street and Park Avenue to catch a taxi. I felt quite relaxed since I had an hour until my next engagement. . . . I waited and waited and waited. After the ninth taxi refused me my blood began to boil. The tenth taxi refused me and stopped for a kind, well-dressed smiling female fellow citizen of European descent. As she stepped in the cab, she said, "This is really ridiculous, is it not?"
> Ugly racial memories of the past flashed through my mind. Years ago, while driving from New York to teach at Williams College, I was stopped on fake charges of trafficking cocaine. When I told the police officer I was a professor of religion, he replied "Yeh, and I'm the Flying Nun. Let's go nigger!" I was stopped three times in my first ten days in Princeton for driving too slowly on a residential street with a speed limit of twenty-five miles per hour. . . . The memories cut like a merciless knife at my soul as I waited on that godforsaken corner. Finally I decided to take the subway.[8]

Prejudice, stereotyping, racist jokes and the like rob even the most affluent minority family of dignity, and they keep less affluent minority families in castelike servitude and perpetual anger. The pervasive prejudice in our society against people of color engenders a kind of nihilism among them—feelings of hopelessness and that life is without meaning. Indeed, Cornel West continues,

> The major enemy of black survival in America has been and is neither oppression nor exploitation but rather the nihilistic threat—that is, loss of hope and absence of meaning. For as long as hope remains and meaning is preserved, the possibility of overcoming oppression stays alive. The self-fulfilling prophecy of the nihilistic threat is that without hope there can be no future, that without meaning there can be no struggle.[9]

Ultimately, prejudice corrodes all Americans. It harms African Americans, Asian Americans, Hispanics, Native Americans, and other minority victims *directly* by robbing them of dignity and hope. In addition, it harms other Americans in *indirect* but serious ways. For example, it prevents many citizens from recognizing that the children of poverty—often of a different color and ethnicity—are *their* children too. Thus, prejudice prevents otherwise decent people from embracing a broader community, which hurts us all. Too often the children we ignore today—the "throwaway" children—become tomorrow's flotsam and jetsam, who can only command our attention when we have to spend precious resources imprisoning them or coping with the real threats they represent to our safety and economic welfare. But even if we are lucky, those same children will eventually become tomorrow's workers, part of the community on whom we must depend to help support us in our old age. Eventually, as Malcolm X once warned, "The chickens will come home to roost."[10]

Summary. It is clear, then, that the difficulties faced by many of our schools are closely tied to problems in their local communities—problems that are, in turn, a reflection of unwise social policies in the nation. Widespread poverty, inadequate job prospects, and lack of social services all contribute to loss of dignity in many families in the country and, therefore, to loss of hope among children. This is especially so for the most vulnerable of our citizens, those who must endure the additional burdens of prejudice. Given these facts, "school improvement" often really requires improvement in the overall quality of life of the members of the community. Unfortunately, many federal and state politicians seem disinterested in this message. They ignore it at our collective peril.

On Money and Equality in School Funding

[
Principle: *Schooling in America can be improved by making certain that all schools have funds needed to provide a decent education for their students. This will require more fairness in school funding.*
]

If the New York City schools were funded . . . at the level of the highest spending suburbs of Long Island, a fourth grade class of 36 children . . . would have had $200,000 *more* invested in their education during 1987. [This extra money] would have been enough to hire two extraordinary teachers at enticing salaries of $50,000 each, divide the class into *two classes* of some 18 children each, provide them with computers, carpets, air conditioning, new texts and reference books, and learning games—indeed with everything available today in the most affluent school districts—and also pay the costs of extra counseling to help those children cope with the dilemmas that they face at home. Even the most skeptical detractor of the "worth of spending further money in the public schools" would hesitate, I think, to face a grade-school teacher in the South Bronx and try to tell her that "this wouldn't make much difference."

— Jonathan Kozol (*Savage Inequalities*, 1991, pp. 123–124)

What the best and wisest parent wants for his own child, that must be what the community wants for all of its children. Any other ideal for our schools is narrow and unlovely; acted upon, it destroys our democracy.

— John Dewey (*The School and Society*, 1900, p. 3)

In addition to the serious problems that poor neighborhoods pose for their schools, those schools also face a huge additional burden. All too often in America they are funded at sub-standard levels. As we made clear earlier, our country now tolerates HUGE differences in levels of support for its public schools. In some states, schools in rich suburban districts may receive *five times* as much, or more, per-student funding than is provided to schools in poor, inner-city or rural, districts. Thus, our nation operates a viciously discriminatory system of public education that allows the sons and daughters of wealth to attend far better schools than those available for the children of poverty. This system reflects our custom of tying a good deal of school funding to local school taxes, and, as a result, school quality and student achievement are shortchanged for the poor. Such inequitable school funding normally does *not* exist in other advanced countries.

The Effects of Better School Funding. Is it actually true that student achievement would rise if funding for schools in poor neighborhoods could be increased and those funds were used in appropriate ways? Good but indirect evidence supports this idea.

As we know from Chapter 3, recent studies now show that school funding affects student achievement in ways that are independent of the effects of parental and community affluence; but this does not mean that we yet know what would happen if a sample of impoverished schools were given reasonable financial support. If Jonathan Kozol is to be believed, that extra support would enable those schools to repair their dangerous buildings, buy long-needed equipment for instruction and recreation, build classrooms to relieve overcrowding, and hire enough teachers to cover core subjects. This would surely improve the morale and achievement of students in those schools. But alas, to the best of our knowledge, nobody seems yet to have funded the experiment that would confirm these ideas.

Mind you, the students in those hypothetical, experimental schools would still, on average, come from impoverished families, so most of them would not have the higher levels of home support for education that middle- and upper-class families can provide. Thus, one would predict only a modest rise in their achievement. This suggests that nontraditional, supplementary programs may be needed if schools that serve impoverished students are truly to help their youngsters "make it" into the mainstream of American life. Various efforts *have* appeared that explore this idea.

For example, in 1981 Eugene Lang, a self-made millionaire, came back to the New York City elementary school he had attended half a century earlier. He was there to give the sixth-grade commencement address. But now this East Harlem school was filled with extremely poor African American children. In an off-hand remark at the end of his talk, Lang promised the children that if they finished high school and got into college he would pay their tuition. One might think he was making an idle offer, but Lang became intrigued by the challenge his promise represented and decided to help the children take advantage of it. He also believed that these impoverished children needed tutoring, counseling, guidance, and friendship; so he set up an "I Have a Dream" Foundation, which provided these forms of supplementary help.

So what happened? The program has had effects that can only be described as amazing. As of March, 1993,

> Six students have bachelor's degrees, and 30 others are attending college. In all, at least 45 students graduated from high school or obtained equivalency diplomas. . . . For P.S. 121, one of the worst schools in a bad system, the record is stunning. School authorities [had] told Lang in 1981 that he would be lucky if two of his students graduated from high school.[11]

Why has the program had its amazing success? Eugene Lang has suggested that the college scholarship he offered was only part of the picture. Indeed, it may not have been as important as the personal involvement of mentors, himself included, who cared for the children over the next six years of their lives. Those six dangerous years on the streets of East Harlem were successfully negotiated by this group of young people because someone gave them and their families the hope and resources to help them realize their dreams. Moreover, Lang's efforts did not stop with this first demonstration project. He has also fostered and helped a number of other programs in which affluent Americans and their institutions have "adopted" groups of children from impoverished schools, pledging them future support, and providing them assistance, friendship, and help along the way.[12]

The Eugene Lang story suggests a moral. The scholarships he offered were a tangible and visible signal of opportunity, true; but hope for children arises out of everyday interactions with caring adults who provide them with reasons for believing in themselves and with tangible help. If children are lucky, they get this support from their families, but they might also receive this kind of emotional nourishment from teachers or other caring adults associated with their school.

This moral is very exciting, of course, and one test of it is being conducted by the Josiah Macy Foundation, which also developed an innovative program in the 1980s, now called Ventures for Education. This program provides supplementary support for high schools that have a history of poor student achievement.[13] The first group of schools in the program had large numbers of poor and minority children, many of whom spoke English as a second language. They were located in New York City; in New Haven, Connecticut; in Alabama; and near the Navajo Nation in Arizona. The program encourages more rigorous high school course work; provides college preparation experiences throughout high school; helps students prepare for SAT and ACT examinations; funds visits to universities, summer academic programs, and camps; and supports field trips involving hands-on research. But, perhaps most important, it provides counseling and guidance for students from caring adults as well as continuous support for teacher involvement with students and further development of the program.

So what has happened in the schools that were initially helped by the program? Evidence suggests that teacher expectations for both their own performance and for student achievement have risen, and the program has brought handsome dividends to students. In 1987 the high school graduation rate for the impoverished students in Ventures was 30 percentage points higher than the national average for all students. About 90 percent of the black, Hispanic, and white students in the program went on to college—a number far in excess of rates for these groups in the general population. (Many Native American students also went on to college, but the level of "success" for this group could not be assessed since comparable national data were missing.) Moreover, many students from the program chose to enter some of the most difficult and prestigious colleges in the nation—including Brown, Columbia, Cornell, Johns Hopkins, Vassar, and Yale.

In addition, the initial Ventures students have done well in college. Most report that they were well prepared for college classes and that they tended to earn high grade-point averages. When compared with other students, they also obtained scholarships and loans at a higher rate, despite working more hours while in college than did the general population. In sum, the first cohort through the program appears to have achieved marvelously. Caring, attention, and exposure to rigorous course work have helped these poor and minority students start productive lives that should eventually place them in the mainstream of American society.

Another way to provide supplementary services for the children of poor families is suggested by the work of Edward Zigler at Yale. Zigler has argued for years that local schools need to be active places for community renewal. They should be providing parent education, health care, job training, and high quality day care if they are to serve well the children and adults of the communities in which they are located.[14]

Yale is also the home of James Comer, whose model of school improvement is tied to family involvement. Comer's own family experience suggested that children from poor and minority families are more likely to achieve when their families have dignity and hope, and this means that involving those families in their neighborhood schools may be as important as providing a rigorous and well-taught curriculum.[15]

Schools hoping to fulfill the broad visions of Zigler and Comer are now being tried in four cities in Texas, with support from the Hogg Foundation.[16] It is still too early to know whether changing schools into providers of more comprehensive service will produce desired effects, but we are hopeful. In addition, other programs are being explored that could provide models for school districts truly interested in spending money to help impoverished students improve their lives through education.[17]

Is Equity Sufficient? Although many recent critics of American schools may find this a surprising idea, it can be argued that the cheapest and most efficient way to raise the *average* achievement levels of American students is to provide additional dollars for our worst-funded schools! Thus, at a minimum, our country badly needs at least the same kind of equity in public school funding that is common in other Western countries. But is equity sufficient? Since children in poor neighborhoods usually do not come from families that can provide extensive support for education, their schools will need *extra* funds if America is to realize its long-cherished goal of providing equal opportunity for all students through public education.

Schools in poor neighborhoods need extra funds for several reasons. First, unlike suburban schools, they often have to erect barbed-wire fences, buy weapon-detectors, and hire armed guards in order to be secure. Second, they may need to hire additional school counselors merely to cope with the problems that impoverished and distressed students bring to the school. Third, these schools are often asked to provide outreach services to supplement social or recreational facilities missing in their neighborhoods. But, above all, supplemental programs that can generate dignity and hope, such as those we described above, require additional funds. Thus, instead of merely demanding strict equality in funding, Americans should spend *more* money on schools located in communities where the needs are greatest.

Perhaps you think this is a utopian ideal, unlikely ever to be realized. Think again. In some European countries, particularly in Scandinavia, whenever a school is having difficulty, that school can get extra money. For example, when a school must serve students who have language problems associated with immigration, or when parents become poor because a nearby factory has closed, that school can petition for and receive extra funding. This procedure sounds so fair and sane, and it so obviously would seem to reflect deeply felt American notions about equality of opportunity. Why didn't *we* think of it in *our* country?

In addition, some schools must serve children who have no place to go after school. It would be cheaper by far to fund recreational programs in those schools, to keep children off the streets, than to cope with the crime those children might commit—or at least the mischief they will create—if they are left unsupervised. Some impoverished communities would also benefit from school-based investments in parental education, outreach programs, or family health education. In other areas, such as in the cities of Los Angeles, Miami, and New York, schools serving new immigrants may want to fund bilingual classes for children, English-as-a-second-language classes for adults, and health care for everyone.

Yes, programs such as these will require extra funding for schools in impoverished neighborhoods. But what is the alternative? The problems of those neighborhoods will not go away, and the challenge they pose raises not only moral but very practical questions. Do Americans want to spend money now or later? Do they want to spend money now on education which offers constructive solutions to the needs of young people, or later on punitive actions to cope with problems they might have prevented?

Our own preference is, of course, to spend money now, to provide funds when local educators and their communities have devised plans that respond appropriately to clear needs. Critics suggest that "throwing money at problems" doesn't work, but that is *not* what we are recommending here. Instead, investing in school-based programs designed by local people in response to local needs makes both moral and economic sense—and such investments are clearly preferable to doing nothing.

Doing Something About It. How much funding should we then plan to provide for schools in poor neighborhoods? Our richest communities believe they know what constitutes good public education and are willing to spend ten to fifteen thousand dollars per child per year for it. Since some of the best schooled and most successful citizens in each state live in wealthy communities, we can reasonably assume that those communities provide guidelines for what good education should look like and cost elsewhere in their state. We should, then, use the per-pupil expenditures of those communities as guidelines that indicate the level of funding needed to support high quality education. Through the use of such guidelines, every district in each state would know what a high-quality educational program looked like and how much it cost. And if some communities have exceptional problems, they should be given *more* funds than those provided in wealthy communities.

Where will the money come from to provide equity and these extra resources? During the 1960s and 1970s, Americans turned largely to the federal government for funds that would help impoverished students, and by 1980 federal entitlement programs were generating nearly 10 percent of funds given to schools. However, federal support has proved to be weak. During the Reagan and Bush years, federal funds for education were slashed, and today only about 6 percent of the costs in primary and secondary education are covered by federal dollars.[18] Nor does it seem likely that this figure will rise in the near future. Demands for debt reduction and for funding medical and defense costs remain high at the federal level, and education (which Americans have traditionally conceived of as a local and state responsibility) will probably continue to receive short shrift.

Moreover, it does not seem likely that local school districts, which lacked resources for adequate school funding in the past, will magically acquire these resources in the near future.

This leaves the states as the most likely sources of additional revenue, and here one finds rays of hope. In fact, efforts to reform education funding have already appeared in about half the states, and some of these efforts have actually resulted in some equity. To date, most of these efforts have not involved legislative action. Rather, some citizens from poorer school districts have filed lawsuits demanding that state tax dollars be used to supplement local support. These lawsuits have not always succeeded, however, and even when they were successful, they have only partially solved the problem. Nevertheless, in some states it is now illegal to allow markedly unequal funding among school districts in the state, and one can hope that this principle will presently be applied to even more states across the nation.

But legal action alone will not correct these inequalities totally. Instead, well-meaning Americans must face up to a task they have long shunned, that of persuading their *state* legislators that it is in the public interest to fund schools equitably and to provide extra funding for schools that face special challenges. This will, of course, be a daunting task since most state legislators are successful, affluent people who do not normally think about the long-term advantages of investing tax dollars in ways that will benefit only poorer citizens now—but *all* citizens of their states down the road. In addition, we should remember that sharp differences also appear among the *states* in their present willingness to fund public education. It will eventually require *federal* legislative action to solve this problem.

Summary. Let it be clear—money matters in education; or, to be more precise, money spent *wisely* matters. Money can buy improvements in school buildings, more facilities, more textbooks and computers, smaller class sizes, and a better-paid, better-qualified, more numerous teaching staff—and these improvements will pay off in higher morale and higher achievement levels if applied to schools that are now badly underfunded. In addition, some schools will require extra funding if they are to establish programs needed to meet the needs of America's huge and growing numbers of students from impoverished families.

Plans for raising levels of funding for America's poorest schools *must* be devised. Well-functioning societies have always invested in resources for the common good—among them highway systems, the police, the armed forces, parks and libraries, medical research, public health, and the like. Public education is one of these common goods, and the fundamental goal of public education is defeated when its benefits are unfairly lavished on those who had the happy fate of being born to rich parents. High-quality public education and the opportunity to learn are *rights,* not privileges, in this democracy of ours. And if we do not uphold those rights for *all* our citizens, we can ultimately kiss our affluent democracy good-bye.

On School Size

[
Principle: *Schooling in America can be improved by reducing the size of our largest schools.*
]

The large school has authority: its grand exterior dimensions, its long halls and myriad rooms, and its tides of students all carry an implication of power and rightness. The small school lacks such certainty: its modest building, its short halls and few rooms, and its students, who move more in trickles than in tides, give an impression of a casual or not quite decisive educational environment.

These are outside views. They are illusions. Inside views reveal forces at work stimulating and compelling students to more active and responsible contributions to the enterprises of small than of large schools.

—Roger G. Barker and Paul V. Gump (*Big School, Small School*, 1964, p. 195)

Some primary schools in Finland are built to house only a few classrooms and are placed in local neighborhoods, right in the midst of residential areas. Why? Because the designers of those schools want children to be in small, close-to-home settings; to be in environments they know and in which they feel comfortable; to be close to their parents; and to feel that school and home are interwoven. That sounded good to us, so one of us suggested to a local school board that it buy a large house in each of the new housing tracts that were then under development in the community and use these houses for kindergarten and first-grade classrooms. That person was treated as if he was from Mars! It was unheard of! It couldn't be done! A big, anonymous elementary school was built instead. And the young students in these neighborhoods must now be bused to their school, away from their home neighborhoods, away from their nearest care givers and the environments in which they feel most comfortable. No money was saved, and the interests of the children were certainly not served.

Somehow Americans have come to believe that big schools are good and small schools are bad. This notion comes partly from the cult of efficiency that influenced industry early in the century.[19] In response to the efficiency ethic, schools are often designed to mimic production lines, where the economy of size takes precedence over human relationships. Also, Americans seem to be overly influenced by a form of civic boosterism that automatically equates bigger with better. Thus, we are all supposed to rejoice when our communities grow, when more highways are paved, when our industrial plants get bigger, when our population expands, and—by extension—when our schools increase in size.

Americans believe in the virtues of large schools also because of the writings of James Conant, a former president of Harvard and an influential educational theorist, who extolled the virtues of the large comprehensive high school a generation or more ago.[20] In the 1950s, in an era of cheap fuel for buses, the comprehensive high school was lauded for providing the variety of curricular offerings and extracurricular activities that a small rural school could never afford—advanced-placement courses, higher levels of mathematics and science, more foreign languages, sports and cultural clubs, and so forth. Thus, across the country the large regional school was promoted, and small, local high schools were abandoned.

Yet, a good deal of evidence has appeared indicating that large schools have many disadvantages. In pioneering research, completed decades ago, ecological psychologists Roger Barker and Paul Gump studied the activities of students in high schools of different sizes.[21] The authors indeed confirmed that the *very* small high school cannot provide the range of courses and extracurricular activities we have come to expect from the well-run high school in America. But when they compared a middle-sized high school with a large one, they discovered that students' lives were *very* different in these two settings. The two schools offered quite similar types of activities, but because the middle-sized high school had far fewer students, its typical activity tended to have too few participants. As a result, each activity constantly competed for more participants, and the average student participated in *many* more activities. In contrast, too many students in the large school were allowed to remain anonymous. More than enough students were available to fill each of the specialty classes (e.g., Conversational French), the varsity teams, the school clubs, the year-book staff, the cheer-leading squad, and the like. This meant that in the large school many students did *not* take specialty classes and did *not* participate in extracurricular activities; worse, they were not missed. Those without marked skills or high status in favored cliques were simply left out of prestigious events. Moreover, they often felt excluded, because, in fact, they *were* excluded.

Schools of modest size tend to have additional advantages. They promote community feeling and the ideal that students should be sharing ideas and experiences with each other. Affiliation, self-concept as a learner, and motivation to achieve all seem to be higher when a student is in a smaller, more intimate environment. This suggests that student achievement levels should be lower in truly large schools, and this effect has been confirmed by research evidence. Earlier, we mentioned the National Education Longitudinal Study (NELS), a major, ongoing research project that involves about 25,000 students across the nation. Another recent study of NELS data has examined the effects of school characteristics on student achievement. After controlling for other factors known to affect achievement, the authors found that achievement levels were substantially *lower* in large high schools.[22]

In addition, smaller elementary schools and high schools can be run both *by* and *for* the teachers and the students. In contrast, the truly large schools too often are run by and for administrators and bureaucracies distant from the site. Control typically becomes more impersonal in large settings, and for this reason, some researchers have recommended that high schools serve no more than 250 students. In larger schools, these researchers claim, administrators become preoccupied with the problems of control and order; thus, teaching, learning, and *caring* are subordinated to those administrative concerns.[23]

Researchers have also put forth a persuasive theory about why students drop out of high school.[24] The theory suggests that dropping out is less likely when a student bonds with the school. Though not a profound insight, this idea summarizes various findings from the research literature and suggests that student attendance and graduation rates can be improved when schools find ways for students to bond with, identify with, and participate in the life of the school. Clearly, students are *far* more likely to bond with smaller schools than with very large ones. (Of course, keeping schools small is not the only way to foster bonding with the school. Later in the chapter we discuss cooperative learning and other strategies that can also help to promote students' bonding.)

All of this suggests that Americans should bend their efforts to prevent the construction of very large schools. But what should be done with very large school buildings that are already in place? Two solutions have been explored for this problem: a large school may be broken up into separate "schools-within-a-school"; or, distinct, specialized programs may be conducted on the site. Today, these specialized programs are commonly called magnet schools.

Schools-within-a-school recreate *some* of the advantages of the small school, albeit within the larger campus. For example, smaller school units might be formed to respond to themes of community service and might be "homes" for cohorts of junior and senior high school students. Each unit might develop a flexible class schedule so that students could work in the community on certain days, and parts of its curriculum could reflect the nature of the work students were doing. Or, a large, comprehensive high school of perhaps two thousand students could be divided into schools of, let's say, four hundred or so students each, in grades nine through twelve. In this model, the smaller school units share some services in common while also maintaining close relationships with students in their own unit. Each of the smaller units is administered by its own cohort of teachers so that every student is known personally to his or her team of teachers. This model fosters cooperative endeavors and high rates of participation within the smaller units and allows for rivalries between units for academic and athletic honors.

The magnet school concept offers another configuration that is useful at the high-school level. Magnet schools are smaller, special-purpose units that offer focused curricula (often leading to early career entry) in specific fields—for example, the performing arts, computer skills, foreign languages, or aerospace technology. Typically, these units are located physically within large, urban high schools or sit on their peripheries, sharing their campuses. They enroll a select group of students, who may take core courses from the larger school setting but who are also offered specialized courses in the magnet school proper. The magnet school keeps students focused and together as it promotes their special interests.

Magnet schools are also considered beneficial for promoting racial and ethnic integration and are sometimes used to bring talented and ambitious students to large, urban school buildings that had previously served only impoverished or minority students. For example, one of us recently helped to study an urban high school that enrolls large numbers of minority students. Five different magnet schools had been established in it to attract students from all over the district. Last year the graduation rate remained low among the school's two thousand regular students; but for the roughly two hundred students enrolled in each of the five magnet schools, the graduation rate was well above 90 percent.

The general moral of our argument should now be clear. Whether students are poor or rich, white or black, average or brilliant, it is easier to teach—and students have richer lives—in medium-sized schools. Large schools discourage high rates of student participation in school activities; students and teachers have difficulty identifying with the culture of the school; and students' bonding with classmates and with the school itself is reduced. As a result, student achievement suffers. Those who design schools for tomorrow need to consider this moral seriously and be prepared to resist arguments for larger and larger schools. And districts that are presently stuck with large school buildings should seriously consider plans for creating smaller units within those schools.

On the Aims of the School Curriculum

Principle: *Schooling in America can be improved by enlarging the goals of curricula. This will require developing thoughtful learning environments where the emphasis is on skills needed for membership in a democratic society.*

Most students, parents, teachers, civic leaders and other citizens have consistently made the cultivation of thoughtfulness a low priority among educational aims, in spite of paying lip service to the ideal for years. Why? [Because] higher-order thinking often calls for the resolution of conflicting views, tolerance for uncertainty and ambiguity, self-criticism, independence of judgment, and serious consideration of ideas that may challenge or undermine conventional wisdom.

Critical thinking also increases the probability of youth challenging adult authority and of citizens challenging economic and political centers of power. Thus, thinking can be considered subversive and socially dangerous by dominant interests whose legitimacy is questioned. Some would argue that the survival of certain social institutions (e.g., advertising, hierarchies of labor within corporations) depends on limiting the opportunity to think to a small segment of the population.

—Joseph Onosko and Fred Newmann (Creating more thoughtful learning environments, 1994, pp. 45–46)

We turn now to an issue that affects nearly all aspects of American education. Unfortunately, a great many Americans have traditionally held concrete and quite limited notions about the aims of school curricula. Worse, narrow and traditional ideas about curricula have been pushed strongly by critics of education during the past few years. We argue that these views are badly out of step with today's world. We need a broader, revised view of curricular aims if efforts to improve America's schools are to succeed.

Traditional Views. Let us assume that Americans were asked to explain what constitutes a good high school education. Many people might answer this question by citing a list of core courses that should be completed—English, mathematics, foreign languages, American history, and so forth. Others might stress knowledge units from those courses. They would argue that well-educated Americans should be able to appreciate literary works, write grammatically, solve compound-interest problems, read graphs, interpret menus in an Italian or a French restaurant, recognize quotations from Shakespeare, know about Franklin Delano Roosevelt, and so forth.

Such answers stress concrete accomplishments on the part of students. The first type of answer stresses specific, core courses that students should take while the second lists facts or skills that students should learn. Both approaches are backward looking and assign a passive role to the student. The aim of education, they assert, is to pump specific types of knowledge from the past into students, and if those students have passed core courses or are able to regurgitate information from those courses, they are—ipso facto—educated people.

One might assume that these traditional views about the aims of education are widely shared, and yet Americans have never actually agreed about them. Before World War II, high schools applied this traditional type of curriculum only to the small, select group of students who were planning to enter college. After the war, as high schools were asked to serve more and more students from different backgrounds, many high schools came to stress a broad range of curricula that focused more on specialized student interests and specific vocational needs. But more and more students were also becoming interested in college. As a result, the traditional curriculum was sometimes no longer required for young people who would eventually enroll in colleges, and traditionalists became worried about a putative "decline" in standards and to argue for a "return to the basics" in curricula.

Arguments for traditional curricula formed one important theme of the Manufactured Crisis, and these arguments have now become quite strident. A good illustration of them can be found in the recent writings of E. D. Hirsch, particularly in his book *Cultural Literacy*,[25] and in a series of works setting forth what children at particular grades need to know to be culturally literate.[26] Hirsch urges, for example, that children should know about James Monroe, DNA, tectonics, the Treaty of Versailles, Ichabod Crane, and so forth. These concrete bits of knowledge are to be learned by taking core courses in history, biology, earth science, literature, and the like; and high schools should encourage or require all students to take the courses that disseminate these "factoids."

This limited, traditional view of curricular aims was also pushed by leading educationists in the Bush administration and has since been endorsed by the Clinton White House. As we noted earlier, in 1992 the National Council for Education Standards and Testing recommended that concrete, nationwide standards be developed for five core subject areas—English, mathematics, science, history, and geography—"with other subjects to come."[27] These standards were to be backed up by a national system of assessments. Unfortunately, this approach to curricular reform has since been embraced by President Clinton and his supporters.

The New Curriculum: Skills for the Twenty-first Century. The traditional view suggests that schools are mechanisms for pumping bits of knowledge from the past into passive students. Such a view has always been questionable, but today it is truly archaic. Many thoughtful people have discussed problems in our society and the likely needs of the twenty-first century. Not only have vast changes taken place in our country in recent years, but the rate of those changes is clearly accelerating. Most Americans will now have to shift occupations at least once, perhaps many more times, during their lifetimes. Our work force now requires more and more people who can assume professional responsibilities, and this trend will surely continue. The problems of governing our nation become more complex each year, which means that if we are to understand and evaluate the performance of our government, Americans must develop more sophisticated understandings of those problems. And as our mechanical servants make more and more leisure time available, Americans must develop the ability to use their leisure time in independent and socially responsible ways.

All of these changes mean that America needs citizens who are flexible, who embrace new ideas, who can reason well when faced with complex ideas, and who are capable of self-directed learning. It is difficult to understand how citizens with these skills and interests are likely to develop if our high schools merely pump concrete bits of knowledge from the past into passive students. Americans need a broader, revised vision of curricular aims. Now is the time to reconceive the aims of high schools in ways that are more appropriate to the twenty-first century.

Not only is this possible, but various scholars have begun to take up the challenge. To illustrate, let's take economist and educational reformer Henry Levin's advice and list some of the goals of a good high school education in terms of attributes that will be needed in the work place of the next century.[28] According to Levin, the well-educated high school graduate should fit the following description:

- Has initiative: possesses the drive and creative ability to think and work independently
- Demonstrates cooperation: participates in constructive group activities that accomplish group goals
- Can evaluate both self and others: has the ability to assess people or products; can determine their worth and merit
- Can train others: has the ability to provide formal and informal instruction and advice to others; can mentor, coach, advise, tutor and train
- Can obtain and use information: knows how to find things out and decide what is relevant for the particular purpose for which the information is needed
- Can communicate effectively: can speak and write intelligibly and can listen and comprehend what others say or write
- Can reason sensibly: can make and evaluate deductive and inductive logical arguments
- Can plan: can order priorities so that reasonable schedules for accomplishing things are set and goals are met
- Can solve problems: can identify problems, offer potential solutions from among alternatives, and implement actions that might reasonably be expected to solve the problems
- Can engage in metacognition: can monitor his or her own activities while doing them
- Can earn respect in multicultural settings: can work productively with people from other cultures who are likely to possess different communication styles and values as well as speak different languages

This list of skills is not definitive, of course, but it differs enormously from the concrete bits of knowledge listed by E. D. Hirsch and others who promote traditional curricular ideas. Moreover, the two approaches differ strikingly in their implications for classroom activities. To implement fully a traditional curriculum requires drill and practice, rote learning of facts and definitions, and tests of memory. In contrast, the skills we listed above suggest a curriculum that is more thoughtful, has less focus on rote memory, and allows more student involvement and problem solving. To implement it would require greater stress on teaching methods that feature student-initiated projects, cooperative-learning activities, self-evaluation, peer and cross-age tutoring, having students solve complex and ambiguous problems, self-aware thinking, and multicultural education.

These are radical ideas, far different from the stand-and-deliver classroom model that still dominates American high schools today. As a society, we need to decide which type of student would have an easier time of it and make a better citizen in the twenty-first century—one who knows hundreds of unintegrated facts, or one who can think independently, plan, cooperate with others, and solve complex problems.

Let there be no mistake. We are *not* arguing here that students should be ignorant of the knowledge base that constitutes our cultural heritage. On the contrary, our country badly needs a citizenry that shares such a heritage, but those who cannot think beyond the traditional image of a fact-oriented high school curriculum confuse the necessary with the sufficient. It is *necessary* that students have an appropriate knowledge base, but such a base is far from *sufficient* if students are to be well educated. To have well-educated students, we must greatly expand our view of curricular aims and recast learning activities.

Our argument applies to most, if not all, academic subjects that are now taught. Moreover, it is backed by arguments from experts in various subject fields. For example, leading science educators recommend that science lessons should open with questions about phenomena rather than answers to be committed to memory.[29] They argue that science should begin with discourse that builds on what students already know. Young people must be given opportunities to form hypotheses, collect data, analyze their findings, and talk about what they have learned. They must be allowed to design and carry out scientific projects that are intellectually challenging and require creativity. Alone, or more typically in small collaborative groups, with teacher guidance, young people should be asked to *do* science—not just to study it.[30]

The National Council for the Social Studies recommends that through a "process of active construction of knowledge" teachers and students should think reflectively and make informed decisions about real issues.[31] Teachers should reduce their direct instruction and find ways to help students become independent, self-regulated learners who can work collaboratively to solve authentic civic and community problems.[32]

Teachers of mathematics are also urged to encourage children to explore, develop, test, discuss, and apply mathematical ideas so that they can construct their own mathematical understandings.[33] Mathematics must not be about the teaching of algorithms for the solution of artificial problems. Rather, it should be an active and collaborative activity in which young people learn to uncover the underlying mathematical features of a topic, issue, or situation. "In contrast to current classroom practice in which much of the activity involves students practicing procedures that have been explained or modeled by the teacher, classrooms should provide ample opportunities for students to verbalize their thinking and to converse about mathematical ideas and procedures."[34] Thus, if leading mathematics educators have their way, the new mathematics curriculum will resemble social studies and literature curricula more than the old mathematics curriculum. Truly a revolution in pedagogy is being proposed.

Curriculum Aims and the Psychology of Learning. The types of curricular changes we are recommending also fit well with new understandings about the psychology of learning that have evolved over the past two decades.[35] Ideas psychologists held in the past were more compatible with the notion of a fragmented and decontextualized curriculum, which students were supposed to learn partly through drill and practice. Many psychologists once thought that it was sufficient to encourage individual students to learn through rewards and punishments and then to test them on their ability to reproduce what they had memorized, and this certainly fits with traditional ideas about curricula.

In contrast, psychologists now describe learning as more complex. This reflects greater understanding about the situational specificity of knowledge and how difficult it is for people to transfer knowledge from one realm to another. What students often learn by studying *Julius Caesar*, for example, are bits of knowledge about Rome, and perhaps something about the writing style that Shakespeare employed. It is often very difficult for students to take those knowledge bits and apply them to their own lives and to contemporary issues in city, state, and national politics—for example, to issues of power, political popularity, crowd manipulation, law, and the possibility of justifying political murder. If these kinds of transfer are to be promoted, teachers must lead students to explore how the themes of *Julius Caesar* relate to issues in their own lives or perhaps to create their own meanings from related reading or acting out bits of the play in contemporary settings.

In addition, psychologists are now more likely to view knowledge as something that is actively constructed by the individual.[36] Thus, meaningful knowledge is never really transmitted from an authority to a passive learner; instead, knowledge is created anew by learners as they struggle to integrate what they are learning with everything else they know. So teachers need to help students construct their own interpretations of ideas. But to do all this requires a good deal of time devoted to teacher-student interchange and discussion, and this may mean giving up extensive but superficial coverage of other matters. If we truly wanted students to have *broad* exposure to Shakespeare's tragedies, teachers could whip through *Julius Caesar* in ten days, give multiple-choice or short-answer tests, and then move on to *King Lear*. But the price of such a process is that the students' knowledge remains inert, tied only to the contexts in which it was learned, of little use or interest in the students' subsequent lives. Somehow, we doubt that most Americans would think that such an approach is appropriate for education in the twenty-first century.

Psychologists are also now more aware of the social forces that encourage learning.[37] They now understand that learning and thinking often are collective as well as individual enterprises, that in the real world they often take place during group interactions. The distinguished Stanford psychologist James Greeno has recently provided a good example of this insight.[38] We all know Rodin's great sculpture, *The Thinker*. This art work has become a widely accepted cultural icon for "Rational Man," for "Reflective Man," for a representation of thinking as a solitary task and the hard work entailed in thinking deep and long.

Now let us envision three girls and two boys, perhaps in the fifth grade, sitting around a computer and talking fast and with great animation to each other, trying to convince each other how they can estimate the world population in the year 2050 from data now available. Greeno rightly asks, why is *this* vision not our cultural representation of people thinking? Why did we choose a solitary, dour figure, possibly in some distress, to represent what can clearly be a joyful, social encounter? The students in the classroom are also thinking hard and for a lengthy period. They, too, are thinking deeply. Why should Rodin's model remain the icon?

If we assume that the small group of students around the computer are indeed learners and thinkers, then some of our old notions about learning and thinking must be expanded. Psychology offers new ideas that emphasize that knowledge is often constructed in group settings, among communities of learners; and in the classroom those communities will include both the teacher and the students. The goal in such settings, then, should be to construct jointly knowledge that is personally meaningful, and this calls for new and innovative types of pedagogy. (It also calls for new and different types of assessment, a matter to which we return later in the chapter.)

Summary. Traditional views of curricula have conceived the school as a means for pouring discrete and relatively unintegrated ideas into passive students. These views have always been suspect, but they are now truly obsolete, given the type of citizens America needs for its evolving, postindustrial society. The new curricula we envision should be more concerned with developing thoughtfulness—and we make this recommendation regardless of subject-matter field and regardless of the students' socioeconomic backgrounds. The new curricula should also reflect current understanding of how learning takes place—about knowledge transfer and the social nature of knowledge acquisition. And such curricula will imply many changes in the ways in which Americans conceive of and conduct education in their schools.

On Innovative Teaching Methods

[**Principle:** *Schooling in America can be improved by adopting innovative teaching methods that serve enlarged curricular aims.*]

Social research has gathered impressive evidence to show that when people work together for group goals, there are a number of desirable effects on people's feelings for one another. When groups engage in cooperative tasks, they are more likely to form friendly ties, to trust each other, and to influence each other than when the task stimulates competition among members. . . . Studies of cooperative learning in classrooms show similar results. When students [are] taken out of class and given a group task, those who [come] from classes using cooperative learning [show] far more helpful and cooperative behavior—and much reduced negative or competitive behavior—than those coming from classrooms where only whole-class instruction [is] in use.

—Elizabeth Cohen (*Designing Groupwork*, 1994a, p. 17)

The traditional model for instruction featured, of course, a single room full of students who listen, in common, to lectures or engage in group discussions that are led by the teacher. But if Americans are to take seriously the enlarged curricular aims we have discussed, they must also be prepared to adopt new and different methods of teaching. Here we examine some methods now being proposed for this purpose.

Encouraging Thoughtfulness. Promoting thoughtfulness should be a central goal of the new curricula in any field, in mathematics or art, science or dance. But to promote thoughtfulness requires ways of teaching that are not now common. Educational researchers Joseph Onosko and Fred Newmann suggest new methods that teachers can use to encourage thoughtfulness.[39] Higher-order thinking occurs when people use their minds to meet new challenges—when individuals must interpret, analyze, and manipulate information to solve problems that cannot be solved by lower-order, routine thinking. Thus, classrooms where higher-order thinking is promoted would demonstrate many of the following features:

- Sustained involvement with a small number of topics, rather than superficial coverage of many topics
- Classroom lessons that exhibit coherence, continuity, and a logical progression of ideas
- Pacing that gives students time to think about topics of interest
- Questions or activities that are genuinely challenging
- The modeling of thoughtful behavior for students
- Treating students' ideas and contributions with respect
- Encouraging students to justify their contributions

Other strategies promoting thoughtfulness might include: encouraging students to express novel ideas; allowing students to play the roles of teacher, questioner, or critic; and rewarding responses that are focused on the topic.[40]

Unfortunately, many barriers stand in the way of implementing these methods. Many Americans, including some educators, still believe that teaching is simply the transmission of knowledge. Classroom activities that promote thoughtfulness often don't look like traditional lectures or whole-class discussions, which may make some people nervous. Furthermore, some people think that responsible teaching involves covering "everything" that is known about a given topic. As Onosko and Newmann note, "what is there to probe or explore in a curriculum that is a mile wide and an inch deep?"[41]

Although not often used with any students today, thought-provoking methods are used even more rarely with poor and minority children—and this reflects blatant prejudice. Because some educators think that such children lack ability, they confront those children with teaching styles that stress drill, practice, and other mind-numbing strategies. Henry Levin has been active in designing new curricula for disadvantaged students. Levin suggests that what such students need most is *an accelerated and enriched teaching style,* not one that bores them to tears, implies that they are stupid, and increases their deficits when compared with students from more-advantaged homes.[42] Levin and the teachers who have adopted his programs have shown conclusively that the capacity for thoughtfulness is not confined to the suburbs.

In addition, teachers may hesitate to adopt methods that promote thoughtfulness because they know that the achievement level of their students will be assessed by standardized tests that stress the acquisition of facts. To illustrate this principle, each year about five hundred thousand students take Advanced Placement classes in some of our nation's leading high schools. By taking these classes and passing rigorous tests, students can get college credits in specific subjects—calculus, biology, physics, chemistry, and so forth. Unfortunately, those tests consist largely of multiple-choice questions that focus on facts. But since teachers know this to be the case, they often conduct Advanced Placement classes as semester-long test-preparation exercises and leave little time for class discussion or other experiences that would promote student interest or thought. Thus, although Advanced Placement courses are conceived of as experiences that will help bright students, their conduct may actually discourage student interest and stifle student thoughtfulness.

Despite these problems, it is clear that we need to encourage greater student thoughtfulness. So those who are sincerely interested in improving America's schools should support educators who are willing to experiment with teaching methods that promote higher-order thinking.

Cooperative Learning. Another set of methods associated with new ideas for curricula come from the cooperative learning movement. This movement began in the late 1970s and early 1980s, when a number of major contributors, working independently, began to develop models that encouraged cooperation and collaborative learning within small groups in classrooms.[43] The basic idea here is that a classroom can be subdivided into smaller groups and that these can work cooperatively toward group goals, sometimes independently and sometimes in competition with other groups in the class. Depending on the cooperative-learning model, these groups may work holistically, or individuals in them may be assigned specific tasks. Usually grades (or other rewards) are assigned to whole groups for their achievements, thus assuring that the more able students will help the less able students and not compete against them. A lot of research has been reported on some of these models, and good summaries of this research have now appeared.[44] Texts and handbooks are also available explaining the advantages and pitfalls of various strategies for cooperative learning.[45]

Some cooperative learning models seem to be better than others for certain purposes, but most forms of cooperative learning tend to improve student achievement when compared with independent student effort. Moreover, this effect seems to hold for both *talented* and *less-talented* students. The effect is not hard to understand. Classroom subgroups can provide more excitement and greater opportunity for students to both tutor and learn from other students. In addition, cooperative learning is known to encourage a host of other desirable outcomes, including the reduction of ethnic, racial, and gender stereotypes and barriers; increased student self-confidence and positive evaluations of others; higher leadership and task-analysis skills; and better integration of students with disabilities.

Given these many advantages, why is cooperative learning rarely found in American schools? Several factors may help explain this. One is that many educators and others interested in improving education know little as yet about cooperative learning and its effects. Another is unwillingness on the part of teachers to accept changes in the traditional power and authority relations of the classroom. Some parents and educators may also find it difficult to believe that students are, indeed, competent to accept more authority for their own learning. Still others may resist cooperative learning because they assume, in error, that talented students will be "held back" if they have to cope with less-talented students in cooperative groups.[46] But above all, many Americans have long embraced an ethic that justifies untrammelled competition and rewards for individual achievement, and they find it very hard to believe that good things happen when students work together in groups.

Regardless of these problems, it is clear that cooperative learning is consistent with the enlarged view of curricular aims we outlined earlier and that it provides a major means for improving education in our country. Cooperative learning should also be strongly encouraged.

Cross-age and Peer Tutoring. Cross-age and peer tutoring are also compatible with new curricular aims, and effective tutoring programs are known to generate high levels of student achievement. In fact, some scholars have argued that of all the methods recommended in the last decade for improving education, cross-age tutoring generates the *largest* gains in learning for the *least* financial cost.[47] When it comes to cost-benefit analysis and seeking the biggest bang for the educational buck, peer and cross-age tutoring programs may be the clear winners. Moreover, the model for education that was once offered in America's many thousands of one-room schoolhouses used peer and cross-age tutoring extensively, and we are all losers because these methods have largely disappeared today.

Unfortunately, everyday features in today's schools often stand in the way of peer and cross-age tutoring, particularly America's standard form of primary schooling, which features day-long, age-graded classrooms and standardized curricula. How can a sixth-grader, for example, provide tutoring for a fourth-grader if the two of them are penned up in separate classrooms and must study different materials? We need to think again about the ways in which schools are organized if these methods are to be embraced seriously. This is hardly an insurmountable problem, of course, and *many* good things would ensue if primary-school organization were revamped in our country. But one of the biggest gains would be generated by increased opportunities for one-on-one student tutoring, where the payoff is often high indeed.

Evidence suggests that tutors and tutees can both learn from the tutoring experience. Tutors learn because they are given the opportunity to teach another student, since one of the most valuable techniques for learning something well is to try to teach it to someone else. Tutees learn more, of course, when the teacher's efforts are supplemented by those of an interested, "prestigious" older student. Furthermore, in tutoring programs more personal bonding can take place as older students take on the "big sister" or "big brother" role.

Like all teaching methods, peer and cross-age tutoring can be mishandled or abused, but evidence indicates that these methods serve broad curricular aims and often generate a great deal of success. Clearly, greater attention should also be given to these methods if we really want to improve America's schools.

The Project Method. Finally, we also recommend that teachers use the Project Method, yet another technique that is clearly compatible with enlarged notions of curricula.[48] Involving students in individual projects is actually an old idea and was once quite common in America's schools. But this method tended to be pushed aside as leadership in education passed to people who embraced standardized curricula and who worried about curriculum coverage because they wanted their students, schools, and districts to get the highest possible test scores.

Nothing is inherently wrong with encouraging children in a class to learn different things; after all, those children do have various interests. Furthermore, since students in a given class vary sharply—in the length of their attention span, in their ability to comprehend, and in their sociability—even if we try to teach them a common curriculum, they will learn different things. It is also no great loss if some children do not cover every topic that is recommended in the curriculum guide. Most of us manage to operate competently in the world even though we do not remember all the rules about how to parse sentences, how to divide by negative numbers, or the names of all fifty state capitals. We walk around with these little gaps of knowledge, and it is no great problem. We thrive in our lives if we are able to understand and solve problems, and promoting this ability should be a major task of our schools. Our schools should be promoting experiences that help their students become flexible, self-aware problem solvers, and the project method is remarkably good for this purpose.

When students and their teacher pick a project that has *depth, duration,* and *complexity,* wonderful things can happen. In a fifth-grade class the project might be for a small group of children to collaborate in building a simple robot. In an eighth-grade class a single student might choose a project requiring collecting and analyzing water samples from different parts of a large, nearby bay or lake. In a high school class a project might entail organizing a community effort or rehabilitating a local park.

Projects that have sufficient depth, duration, and complexity challenge students to develop many of the skills they will need to function well into the next century: initiative, planning, collaboration, ability to find information and to communicate it, ability to solve problems, and so forth. Such projects require thoughtfulness over extended periods. Also, they allow students to explore and to capitalize on their different skills, knowledge bases, and learning styles, and this leads to greater student motivation. Teaching becomes collaborative when teachers offer well-conducted, challenging projects rather than didactic lectures. When teachers and students collaborate on a project, the teachers tutor and advise, comment and supervise, ask questions and listen to explanations—but rarely do they "tell," and never do they attempt to "cover the curriculum." Thus, when used well, the project method allows us to take seriously former HEW secretary John Gardner's reminder:

> The ultimate goal of education is to shift to the individual the burden of pursuing his [*sic*] own education. . . . All too often we are giving our young people flowers when we should be teaching them to grow their own plants. We are stuffing their heads with the products of earlier innovation rather than teaching them to innovate. We think of the mind as a storehouse to be filled when we should be thinking of it as an instrument to be used.[49]

Summary. At a minimum, then, we recommend that people who are genuinely interested in improving education in America give greater stress to methods that promote thoughtfulness among students—among them, cooperative learning, peer and cross-age tutoring, and the project method. These recommendations do not, of course, exhaust the topic of useful teaching methods that might also serve enlarged curricular aims; indeed, they barely scratch the surface of this rich subject. But they allow us to make a general point. For years, American education has proved to be a hotbed of ideas about how to improve teaching and the conduct of schooling. Once we have enlarged curricular goals in mind, we can fairly easily locate innovative ideas for methods that may help to realize those goals. But will these ideas work? That is another question, to which we return in the next chapter.

On the Content of Curricula

Principle: *Schooling in America can be improved by adjusting the content of curricula. This will require deemphasizing the tie between schooling and employment and expanding curricula tied to the productive use of leisure.*

I must study politics and war that my sons may have liberty to study mathematics and philosophy. My sons ought to study mathematics and philosophy, geography, natural history, naval architecture, navigation, commerce, and agriculture, in order to give their children a right to study painting, poetry, music, architecture, statuary, and porcelain.

—John Adams (1780)

John Dewey liked to define the aim of education as growth, and when he was asked growth toward what, he liked to reply, growth leading to more growth. That was his way of saying that education is subordinate to no end beyond itself, that the aim of education is not merely to make parents, or citizens, or workers, or indeed to surpass the Russians or the Japanese, but ultimately to make human beings who will live life to the fullest, who will continually add to the quality and meaning of their experience and to their ability to direct that experience, and who will participate actively with their fellow human beings in the building of a good society. To create such an education will be no small task in the years ahead, but there is no more important political contribution to be made to the health and vitality of the American democracy and of the world community of which the United States is a part.

—Lawrence A. Cremin (*Popular Education and Its Discontents,* 1990, p. 125)

So much for the aims of school curricula, but what topics should students be studying? Which subjects should be offered in America's schools, and which should be required of America's students? What courses should education be stressing in this postindustrial age?

These questions are important because of ongoing changes in our economy, our work force, and the way we live. Consider the past fifty years: many jobs requiring manual labor have disappeared; middle-class occupations that earlier flowered have now become threatened; jobs in primary and secondary industries have been replaced by jobs in human services and information processing; and our economy now requires intense interaction with other nations. Moreover, robots, computers, and advances in transportation and telecommunications are creating greater amounts of leisure time and new ways for citizens to fill that time. And changes in our institutions have weakened some institutions—the community, the church, the family—while strengthening others, such as social- and personal-support services. These changes pose many problems for our society and suggest the need for adjusting the content of school curricula.

Unfortunately, American debates about curricular content are often mired in the past. One still hears some people arguing for curricula that reflect nineteenth-century, small-town America. Other advocates seem oblivious of the fact that Americans now must interact regularly with people from other countries who don't speak English. Many peoples' ideas about curricular content seem to reflect merely the high school offerings of past generations or traditional views of what is needed for university entrance. And many debates about curricula are dominated by outdated ideas about job opportunities and what contributes to the growth of the American economy.

Above all, current debates about curricular content give too much stress to presumed ties between schooling and employment. For years, assumptions about this tie have been made in American education. Schools in our country were first assembled to promote literacy, citizenship, and the study of the Bible, but by the end of the nineteenth century public schooling was being supported—albeit grudgingly—by industry as a means of giving young people and immigrants basic skills to make them employable. And though leaders of the progressive-education movement argued later for other functions of education—its liberating and transformative powers, and the need for schools to take on social-service responsibilities—many Americans continued to link education with jobs.

The association between schooling and employment was strengthened by events following World War II. Immediately after the war, government officials were worried that returning GIs would create an unemployment problem and urged those men to get higher education credentials in order to land "better jobs." Human Capital theory reappeared in the late 1950s, arguing that education should be thought of as "investing" in human resources that could benefit industry and the national economy. Economists also got into the act and began to publish research showing how much income one could expect to gain from each additional year of education completed. And then, a decade ago, *A Nation at Risk* and other documents crucial to the Manufactured Crisis gave great stress to links between education, employment, and the health of the economy. It is, therefore, not surprising that today many Americans assume that curricular content should focus largely on preparation for employment and should reflect the supposed needs of industry.

This assumption is played out in several ways. At the primary level, students face a common curriculum focused on basic literacy and numeracy.

In secondary schools, several curricula are offered. Some secondary students are offered vocational and special-interest courses that presumably prepare them for nonprofessional jobs. Other students—those interested in higher education—may be required to take a standard, core curriculum of courses in English, history, mathematics, and the sciences, designed to prepare them for college entrance and professional careers. In addition, some exposure to the arts, recreational interests, physical education, mental health and social relationships, and specific skills (such as drivers' education) appear at both the primary and secondary levels—although these offerings are thought to be "less important" than those leading to jobs and careers.

Such a view of curricular content is remarkably narrow. Among other things, it assumes that the worth of peoples' lives are to be measured largely by their contributions to activities for which they earn a salary. Such an assumption is both sexist and classist. It devalues both voluntary service and much of the traditional work of women that has never been salaried, and it implies that occupations that are better paid inevitably make more valuable contributions to the society. In addition, in a world where the tie between education and employment is becoming less predictable, it sets people up for disaster. In earlier chapters we noted that the annual supply of people with bachelor's, master's, and doctoral degrees in America is now exceeding the demand. As a result, more and more people who have earned these degrees now find they must take what others consider to be "menial" jobs. What shall we say to the young man or woman who has studied hard, incurred large debts, and sacrificed in many ways to complete a degree in higher education only to discover that the job for which he or she trained cannot be found?

Moreover, the problem is not confined to entry-level positions. In her terribly sad book, *Falling from Grace,* anthropologist Katherine S. Newman writes about the huge problem of downward mobility in America.[50] Much of downward mobility occurs because people lose jobs they thought were secure and face large losses in income or status. Newman estimates that between one-fifth and one-third of our population has suffered downward mobility during the past fifteen years. Although some of those who face this experience eventually find other attractive positions, many eventually must take poorly paid or part-time jobs; or they may face permanent unemployment. And this means, of course, that the average wages of American workers have recently been falling and that more and more Americans are now worrying about job security.

How do individuals interpret the experience of downward mobility? Since many Americans depend on employment for their sense of self-worth, they take it very badly. Here is how Newman describes the plight of the many thousands of middle-level managers who have recently lost their jobs in America:

What underlies the experience of managerial downward mobility is the damage it does to the victim's sense of identity and feelings of social embeddedness. Downwardly mobile managers are skewered by three beliefs that they hold dear: that occupation is the measure of a person's moral worth; that rewards flow to those who are really deserving; and that people are the masters of their own destinies. They are victims of their belief in meritocratic individualism as much as they are victims of economic adversity.[51]

But what leads to meritocratic individualism? Among other things, it is fueled by assumptions about the tie between education and employment—hence, the belief that the basic reason for seeking education is that it will lead to a better job and therefore to more money, higher status, and greater contributions to industry and to society. Such assumptions motivate many Americans to seek ever higher levels of educational qualification. But when jobs become scarce—when the economy no longer needs as many middle-level managers, when a host of other occupations are replaced by robots and computers—this association also puts those same Americans in danger of experiencing an ugly slide, which leads to occupational failure and a degraded sense of self-worth.

To be fair, some of the reasons why Americans focus too much on employment do not come from our schools but rather from problems in the larger society. Consider, for example, the problems resulting from the huge inequities in income that Americans tolerate between our best-paid and worst-paid workers. We've seen figures indicating that the CEOs in some industries are given salary and bonus packages that add up to *hundreds* of times the annual wages earned by the best-paid workers in their plants. And some surgeons we know of take home annual salaries of a *million* dollars or more, earned in part by providing services to clients who, though employed full-time, earn *less than ten thousand dollars* per year. Why do Americans allow income disparities of this enormous magnitude when they are not tolerated in most industrialized countries? Instead, in much of the Western world, those who are paid the top salaries earn only ten times, or less, as much as those who earn the least—and this means not only that CEOs and surgeons are paid less outrageously in other nations, but also that custodians, beauticians, store clerks, and hospital orderlies are paid a living wage. If such conditions prevailed in the United States, then downward mobility would carry less social stigma, and people would more often choose an occupation because it interested them, not just because it paid well. So if Americans were to find ways to dramatically reduce income disparities in our country—and we should do so—such a step would help to reduce obsessions with certain types of employment.

Another step would be to provide greater job security for American workers. Again, this is now done routinely in most other industrialized countries, which seem to be much more aware of the enormous personal and social costs that result when workers are fired. According to Katherine Newman,

When we look to our chief rivals in the international arena—Japan and West Germany, among others—we find countries that understand the dangers [of widespread downward mobility] and implement policies to prevent them. They adhere to industrial philosophies and employment practices that . . . are suffused with an ethos of loyalty and reciprocal commitment: of employee to firm and firm to employee, of commitment to product, to quality, to the customer. Their labor turnover statistics are a fraction of the levels routinely seen in America.[52]

In contrast, most American industries have reserved the right to fire workers whenever they please and to assume little or no responsibility for employees when they change to a new product line or close their plants. Indeed, the CEOs of American corporations are often given enormous bonuses when they devise new techniques that allow them to "downsize" their work forces without provoking legal sanctions or union actions. Such cavalier behavior is thought to be idiotic or is forbidden by law in many other countries, where it is understood that employee morale, industrial productivity, and social welfare are all ultimately tied to job security. So Americans would worry less about employment if our country passed laws, common in other Western nations and Japan, to make jobs more secure here.

Another problem is associated with the many benefits that we load onto employment in America. In most Western countries, for example, day care for children is provided as a public benefit; but in our country parents must pay for it out of their salaries. Many other countries provide an automatic "dole" for those who cannot find work; in America this benefit is available only to those who have already been employed and lasts for only a limited period. Much of the industrialized world provides a host of tax-supported services for those who are impaired or elderly, but such services often must be paid for by the salaries of individuals in our country. Above all, national health-care systems are provided in other advanced countries, but health care in the United States is the individual's responsibility and is tied to employment. What this all means is that when a person suffers downward mobility in America, that person also loses many benefits that are associated with employment. In other countries, those benefits are also available to unemployed people, so that downward mobility is less punishing and less frightening. Americans would worry less about employment if more benefits were provided through taxes rather than through salaries.

It is also time that Americans faced up to the fact that technological advances are now creating more leisure time—thus, the economy needs fewer and fewer work hours to maintain high levels of productivity—and this means that new mechanisms must be created for legitimating leisure and distributing leisure time more equitably. Unfortunately, America has largely accommodated increased productivity by reducing the size of its work force—by making it harder and harder to find decent employment, by firing "superfluous" workers, and by increasing the number of part-time, poorly paid jobs.[53] These are rotten solutions for the problem.

So far, the major useful solutions in our country to "the leisure problem" are those associated with age. We prevent young people from entering the labor force by holding them in schools for longer and longer periods of time, and we encourage older people to leave the labor force through earlier retirement. Both policies are viewed as legitimate; thus, it is quite acceptable for youths to spend their summers in indolence and for the elderly to tool around the country in RVs. However, America has just about pushed these policies to their limits. It's becoming a lot more expensive to hold young people in higher education, and many older people simply don't want to retire.

How else, then, might America distribute its increasing leisure time equitably? Other countries solve this problem in various ways. Many European countries now require their industries to provide at least a month of summer vacation time for their employees. Other countries have already reduced their standard work week to less than forty hours. Others make it possible for people to choose early retirement by providing pension plans that encourage this alternative. (And then there is Australia's marvelous long-service leave program. Many Australian industries provide regular, full-pay, "sabbatical" leaves whenever their employees have completed a given term of service. Moreover, in many cases those employees receive extra pay, which they can use for travel or for other recreational expenses, when they take their long-service leaves.) These methods help people in other countries to accept and enjoy the greater leisure that is now being created by their mechanical and electronic "servants." But so far Americans have shown little willingness to debate or even think about ways to structure and encourage leisure. People in our country would obsess less about employment if more mechanisms were provided that encouraged people to enjoy the additional leisure hours that are now being generated.

The problems resulting from changes in America's economy and work force can also be eased by shifts in the content of school curricula. We suggest two principles that can help guide those shifts: adjusting curricula to meet changes in work-force needs; and expanding curricula to focus on worthwhile activities that are *not* associated with employment.

To illustrate curricular adjustment, America is now increasing its rate of contacts with other countries where people do not speak English. This means that more and more jobs will exist for people who are fluent in foreign languages, which suggests, in turn, that our schools should be offering a lot more foreign-language instruction. Since job opportunities are expanding in the hospitality industry, more attention should also be paid to sensitivity training and to the intricacies of travel and resort services. Since more jobs are being created in human services, American schools should be enlarging their offerings in psychology and in the social sciences. And since the need for information-processing skills will increase, more attention should be given to academic courses that service these needs. Moreover, the latter means a lot more than just word-processing skills. Ours is an information age, and students must be able to understand and use information of unsurpassed quantities. Schools, therefore, have a special obligation to train intelligent and ethical users of information (see Exhibit 7.1).

Also, job opportunities are declining in some sectors of the economy, and this means we should give less stress to curricula that serve those sectors. For example, if the economy continues to need fewer scientists, mathematicians, and engineers, then fewer students should be urged to take specialized course work associated with these fields.

This recommendation may provoke controversy. For years advocates have urged that more students be required to take *calculus,* a specialized course needed for careers in the sciences. When we were students, both of us took calculus. We enjoyed the experience, and we have used the skills the course provided in our professional lives. But we cannot understand why a person who dislikes mathematics and does not want to work in a science field should be forced to take calculus. We grant that calculus can generate insights about the physical world, but we still say that most Americans do not need its specialized knowledge and should not be told that taking it is necessary if they are to get "good" employment in the new postindustrial economy. If we had to nominate a topic in mathematics that is needed today by all informed citizens, it would be *statistics.*

Others may differ with this recommendation, of course, and this suggests a general point. Decisions about whether to require calculus, statistics, or indeed any other specific course in the core curricula should not be left to individuals (including us). No single person or advocacy group is wise enough to design a curriculum for the evolving needs of America's work force, but perhaps some consensus about the matter could be fostered by funding study groups concerned with the issue. Above all, our country needs continuing, thoughtful, national debate on curricula appropriate for our evolving needs.

In addition, curricular content should be expanded so that it gives greater stress to matters that are *not* associated with employment—to avocational interests, to recreation, and to the creative use of leisure time. Students should be given opportunities to explore socially acceptable activities that can provide nonvocational meaning and pleasure in their adult lives. These activities might include, for example: various kinds of community service; hobbies; sports; music; enjoying and performing the arts; reading philosophy or history; travel; studying comparative religions; and so forth. Thus, Americans need to confront the fact that they will be spending more and more of their lives in leisure pursuits, and that the schools bear a responsibility for educating students so they can fill those leisure hours with rewarding and socially useful activities.

In making these recommendations, our concern is that Americans must now take more explicit control over the planning of school curricula. One of the many unfortunate aspects of the Manufactured Crisis was that powerful

■ Exhibit 7.1
On Schooling and Technology

[T]he great problems of education are of a social and moral nature and have nothing to do with dazzling new technologies. In fact, the new technologies . . . are themselves not a solution to anything, but a problem to be solved. The fact is that our children, like the rest of us, are now suffering from information glut, not information scarcity. In America there are 260,000 billboards, 17,000 newspapers, 12,000 periodicals, 27,000 video outlets for renting tapes, 400 million television sets, and well over 400 million radios, not including those in automobiles. There are 40,000 new book titles published every year, and every day in America 41 million photographs are taken. And, just for the record (thanks to the computer), over 60 billion pieces of advertising junk mail come into our mailboxes every year. Everything from telegraphy and photography in the 19th century to the silicon chip in the 20th has amplified the din of information. From millions of sources all over the globe, through every possible channel and medium—light waves, air waves, ticker tapes, computer banks, telephone wires, television cables, satellites, and printing presses—information pours in. Behind it in every imaginable form of storage—on paper, on video and audio tapes, on disks, film and silicon chips—is an even greater volume of information waiting to be retrieved. Information has become a form of garbage. It comes indiscriminately, directed at no one in particular, disconnected from usefulness. We are swamped by information, have no control over it, and don't know what to do with it.

And in the face of all of this there are some who believe it is time to abandon schools.

Well, if anyone is wondering whether or not the schools of the future have any use, here is something for them to contemplate. The role of the school is to help students learn how to ignore and discard information so they can achieve a sense of coherence in their lives; to help students cultivate a sense of social responsibility; to help students think critically, historically, and humanely; to help students understand the ways technology shapes their consciousness; to help students learn that their own needs are sometimes subordinate to the needs of the group. I could go on for another three pages in this vein without any reference to how machinery can give students access to information. Instead, let me summarize. . . . If a nuclear holocaust should occur some place in the world, it would not happen because of insufficient information; if children are starving in Somalia, it's not because of insufficient information; if crime terrorizes our cities, marriages are breaking up, mental disorders are increasing, and children are being abused, none of this happens because of a lack of information. These things happen because we lack something else. It is the "something else" that is now the business of the schools.

—Source: Neil Postman (Of Luddites, learning, and life, 1993, p. 26).

(and ignorant) forces in our federal government and industry took it upon themselves to tell Americans what should be taught in their schools. It is time now for citizens to reassert their right to control the curricula of their schools and to demand open and informed debates about what courses their schools should and should not be offering to students. If this were done, we believe that the content of what is taught in American schools would change significantly and would become more relevant to the true, evolving needs of our changing, postindustrial society.

On the Evaluation of Achievement

[
Principle: *Schooling in America can be improved by rethinking and redesigning the system for evaluating student achievement.*
]

Widely used standardized tests may be hampering efforts to improve math and science education, and they hurt minority students the most.

—Susan Chira (1992)

Let us take this statement from Susan Chira seriously. How can it be that traditional standardized tests might hurt students? One answer to this question was suggested earlier in the chapter. The typical standardized test is constructed of multiple-choice questions that assess students' recall of facts, definitions, and other bits of knowledge; and these tests encourage teachers to use teaching methods that stress little more than acquiring this concrete level of information. And, because teachers who instruct minorities are under the most pressure to produce gains on these tests, minority children often receive the most drill and practice. And in this way they often get the most boring curricula and are hurt the most.

In addition, standardized multiple-choice tests force teachers to focus on broad, superficial coverage. Teachers must maximize curriculum coverage because they do not know the exact test questions students will be asked each time the tests are given. This means that they must cover course content at a gallop, foreswearing the time that might be "wasted" on encouraging reasoning, student thoughtfulness, or applications of course content—which are, of course, the goals of education that most scholars now advocate. The lesson to be learned, then, is that *it is difficult to have both a new curriculum and traditional, multiple-choice tests.* The new curricula and traditional tests make poor bedfellows.

As we stressed in earlier chapters, standardized multiple-choice tests tend to drive the curriculum. If such tests feature no expository writing, expository writing drops out of our schools; and if those tests do not or cannot assess scientific reasoning, then such reasoning will not be taught in science classes.[54] In the end, fewer and fewer changes will appear in our curricula if current, standardized, multiple-choice tests continue to be the sole way we assess student achievement. Unfortunately, though the educational community knows full well how to build better tests, textbook and test publishers are making a lot of money from traditional testing methods. Thus, the testing industry is not keen on ideas that challenge traditional tests, since some of the newer forms of assessment may limit their profits.

What might more useful tests look like? The tests we have in mind should be more *authentic, performance oriented,* and *locally evaluated.* An authentic test confronts students with contextualized, complex, intellectually challenging tasks that represent knowledge in a given discipline. It often requires some form of performance assessment; therefore, authentic tests resemble more the dance recital or art show than they do the annual "herd 'em up, sit 'em down, get 'em going" ritual that accompanies standardized achievement tests.

It is odd that Americans readily accept performance tests as appropriate measures of achievement in the arts and athletics, or for school clubs, while we reject them for core academic subjects. The sports contest, the recital, the debate, the play, and the juried show have long been acknowledged as appropriate means for displaying skill and ability; but we rarely think about performance measures for English, mathematics, history, or physics. However, Grant Wiggins, a critic of traditional testing, has promoted a movement to do just that. He asks, do we truly want to find out whether our students are "deficient in writing, speaking, listening, artistic creation, finding and citing evidence, and problem solving? Then let the tests ask them to write, speak, listen, create, do original research, and solve problems."[55]

An authentic test, then, might ask students to demonstrate a law in physics to parents and other students. Or it might entail a group report for a biology class on the amount of *e. coli* and other bacteria in a stream that runs through the students' town. Or it could be the presentation of a year-long project in social studies on the oral histories of local female senior citizens as they reflect on the role of woman over the course of their lives.

The criteria for success on such authentic tests are designed to be transparent—to be known and understood by both the judges and those who are to be judged. Assessments for an art course or in ice skating provide good models. Generally, over a few months, students prepare their art work or their skating routine for a public exhibition. They prepare with help from parents, teachers, or coaches; and ultimately they are judged by competent individuals from the local community who have expert knowledge of the arts or of ice-skating techniques. The trick with performance assessments is, of course, to have tests worth preparing for and judges with appropriate vision of what constitutes good and bad performance on the tests. But these are not insurmountable problems. Moreover, many people will agree that when students actually demonstrate their literacy, numeracy, scientific thinking, or research skills to panels of judges (classmates, other teachers, parents, community members), their performances provide better indicators of knowledge than do 30-item, multiple-choice, end-of-the-semester examinations. And this seems to be true even with all the subjectivity and lack of standardization that may accompany performance assessments.

As in much of real life, authentic assessments allow people to get help preparing for the test over an extended period of time. Thus, preparing for an authentic performance test also becomes a major part of the new, integrated curriculum, which students often see as more intrinsically motivating than traditional curricula. Rather than cramming all night before the standardized test, students acquire knowledge of the subject over an extended period. Moreover, if parents and others from the community act as judges, community understanding of what the schools are trying to accomplish will increase.

Results from performance tests and other records from the student's school work can also be stored in a portfolio, making it easier for teachers to understand a student's growth. Portfolio assessment can also help teachers explain to parents what the class has been doing and how their own child has been growing. (Compare this with the teacher's report of a standardized test result, which might be phrased, "Your child's raw score was 78, which means a grade equivalent of 6.3"; or ". . . a normal curve equivalent of 57." What can a typical parent make of such information?)

Given commitment, leadership, and support, many teachers are quite capable of designing creative, authentic assessment programs; and when such programs are explained to parents, many parents will choose them over standardized multiple-choice tests.[56] Traditional, standardized tests are clearly hampering efforts to improve the schools. If we are to hasten change we must develop and experiment with more performance tests. Performance and portfolio assessments are not yet in widespread use, largely because they are so different from past visions of what assessment ought to be. But they are surely an important part of the school-improvement effort. As our vision of curricular aims is expanded to promote greater thoughtfulness, self-awareness, and competence in students, we will also need a lot more testing procedures that are authentic, performance oriented, and locally evaluated.[57]

This does not mean that standardized multiple-choice tests should be done away with completely. On the contrary, such tests provide an effective means for assessing concrete information, and they will presumably be retained for their ability to evaluate students' command of basic skills, such as the elements of "reading, 'riting, and 'rithmetic." In addition, it is argued that scrupulously prepared, multiple-choice tests are able to tap into some aspects of higher-order skills—although performance assessments provide a more obvious, more integrated way to measure these complex outcomes. Standardized tests are useful tools, then, which have their own strengths and limitations. But we should give greater stress to other procedures, such as performance tests and portfolio assessments, for evaluating advanced levels of students' skills and knowledge.

On Managing Heterogeneity

> **Principle:** *Schooling in America can be improved by changing the ways in which schools manage heterogeneity. This change will mean abandoning the age-graded classroom and finding alternatives for ability groups and tracks.*

Tracking [as a way of dealing with heterogeneity] is partly, but not only, about race. Whereas African American and Latino children disproportionately wind up in the lower-track classes, most of the children who are disadvantaged by tracking are poor and working-class Whites. The segregative mechanism of tracking, at least ostensibly, is ability. However, like racial segregation, tracking builds inequalities into school that both devalue and materially disadvantage those groups that are least able to defend themselves. Ability, like race, is a social construction that leads schools to define and treat children from powerless groups—Black, Brown, and White—as expendable. Thus, like racial segregation, tracking carries with it class-based damage that can neither be avoided nor compensated for.

—Jeannie Oakes (1994)

Americans worry a good deal about heterogeneity in their schools and classrooms. From time to time they have allowed or encouraged practices that segregated children by gender, race, ethnicity, or religion. Moreover, these practices have generated a lot of heat. Those favoring and opposing educational segregation have often felt these were important issues and that the ultimate effectiveness of our public schools was tied to whether such patterns of segregation were tolerated or not.

Today, American public schools commonly segregate students by age and presumed ability. Students having roughly the same chronological age are assembled into classroom groups representing specific "grades," and often those students are also sorted into ability groups or "tracks" that are to be given different curricular experiences. In fact, so common are these practices today that many Americans assume they are "natural" and cannot conceive of other procedures for conducting education.

Such beliefs are contradicted by history, of course. Until quite recently, a good deal of public education in our country was conducted in small schools where students of various ages and ability levels were clustered together into common classrooms. Thus, segregating students by age and ability is actually quite recent. These practices reflect an assumption that education is more effective when students having similar levels of knowledge are clustered together and exposed to an appropriate curriculum. Whereas this assumption is almost certainly correct, Americans made serious mistakes when they tried to implement it by setting up schools that featured segregation by age and presumed ability.

Age and Ability Segregation. As we pointed out earlier, age-segregated classrooms create many problems. Students who share a given chronological age are far from equal in their interests and levels of knowledge, and this means that many students are bored while others are confused when they are exposed to a common curriculum that was designed for the "average" student in the room. Also, age segregation leads to lockstep curricula for the various grades in the school system, and these curricula often restrict teachers' efforts and inhibit students' learning. Further, age-segregated classes are mechanisms that promote docile conformity and odd roles for students that may have long-term, destructive effects.

Age segregation is bad enough, but in our country it is also associated with ability grouping or tracking. Tracking systems are supposed to benefit *all* students, but repeated studies have shown that even when they have positive effects (and they don't always), they benefit only students who are assigned to high-status (high-ability) tracks. Such findings reflect two sorts of forces. On the one hand, students believe that tracking decisions reflect judgments about their personal abilities and prospects; thus, those decisions set up expectations in students that tend to become self-fulfilling prophecies. And since most students are *not* placed in high-status tracks, this means that ability and tracking systems repeatedly give most students the cruel and unfair message that they just don't measure up.

Tracking decisions also create prejudices and may be associated with discriminatory treatments that favor students in high-ability groups and tracks.[58] To illustrate, studies have shown that

- Less able teachers are more often required to teach students in low-ability tracks.
- Teachers prepare less for low-ability track classes.
- Teachers often form the same number of ability groups within their classrooms regardless of whether their students are relatively homogeneous or heterogeneous in ability.
- Students in lower-status groups frequently pick higher-status students to socialize with, but higher-status students don't reciprocate.
- Students judged to be more capable tend to be given tasks with more complexity and more meaning, and they have more chance to perform publicly. Students judged less capable are assigned more drill and practice and have less chance to assess their own capabilities.
- Students judged to be more capable are given more new content to learn, are afforded more choices about tasks to do, are assigned tasks that require more challenge, and get to work more often with other students who are high in motivation and achievement.

In addition, students are normally assigned to ability groups and tracks through a combination of test scores and teacher judgments. Such criteria are supposed to reflect students' native talents and abilities, to be reliable and valid, and to generate fair and impartial judgments—but none of these suppositions can be supported. Intelligence tests and other standardized instruments used for classifying students reflect background experience as well as "native" talent, are not perfectly reliable, and have little ability to predict adult achievement levels. And this means, of course, that tracking systems serve to "choke off the supply of highly trained students" preparing for entry into crucial fields.[59] Moreover, both test scores and teacher judgments are known to be biased against impoverished and minority students, so those groups of students are *always* underrepresented in higher-status groups and tracks. No means for correcting these problems is available, nor will any appear since standardized tests have inherent biases, and prejudice against minorities is all too frequent in America. Indeed, enthusiasm for ability grouping has always been greatest among parents from majority groups who assume that "talent" and "ability" are inherited traits and have long thought that ability grouping was an appropriate way to segregate their (talented, high-ability) children from "less deserving" others so that they can be provided the enriched educational privileges they "need and deserve."

Given such beliefs, representatives of privileged groups can become quite strident when called on to defend ability tracking. In 1990, for example, the Association for Supervision and Curriculum Development asked several "experts" whether gifted students should (or should not) be taught in special programs.[60] Linda Silverman, director of the Gifted Child Development Center in Denver, Colorado, replied in part,

> Absolutely. There is no research indicating that the gifted are best served in heterogeneous groups. . . . It would be ridiculous to expect a regular classroom teacher to plan a program for self-feeding one child and beginning calculus for another.

John Feldhusen, director of the Gifted Education Resource Center at Purdue University, wrote,

> Yes. The movement to do away with ability grouping is based on the faulty conclusion of [some] researchers . . . that heterogeneous groups are good for low-achieving students and, hence, for all students. . . . Heterogeneous grouping will create chaos and severely lower achievement for all students at all levels of ability.

And James Gallagher, Kenan Professor of Education at the University of North Carolina at Chapel Hill, cited a problem of

> excruciating boredom suffered by many gifted students who feel trapped in programs whose pace and depth, geared to the average student, are insufficient to challenge them. . . . It is envy and a twisted concept of democracy, not research, that ungroups gifted students.

Opinions such as these signal that many high-status people are now strongly committed to ability grouping and tracking—and the notion of inherited talent on which such practices are based—as the means by which their personal and social class interests can be served within the American public school system. Such people are unlikely to welcome efforts by scholarly advocates such as Jeannie Oakes, Anne Wheelock, or Mara Sapon-Shevin, who have urged strongly that ability groups and tracks be done away with.[61]

In this sense, schooling in America seems to be at an impasse. On the one hand, the practices of segregating students by age and supposed ability are flawed, badly biased against poor and minority students, and known to create many problems. On the other hand, these same practices are defended strongly by the rich and powerful, who view them as a means for providing special but "deserved" privileges within the public system for "talented" students—who just happen to be their own children or children of "the best" people. Is there no way out of this impasse?

An Insight. Indeed there is, but in order to understand it we must entertain an insight. It may come as a surprise to some readers, but many studies confirm that, given enough time and professional support, all but a very small number of students can master the curricula we set for our primary and secondary schools. The determining factor in achievement, then, is *time*, not ability. Students simply move through the curriculum at different rates. We tend to label fast-moving students as "talented," and we assume that the speed of their learning reflects native ability; but there might actually be many reasons why a student learns specific subjects quickly or slowly: idiosyncratic interests, help at home, energy level, native-language facility, cultural traditions, study habits, state of health, and so on.

There is, however, no inherent reason why we should organize education in ways that provide kudos for those students who happen to move quickly and brickbats for those who move more slowly. Indeed, since all but a few students will make it through the curriculum eventually, the key to maximizing the effectiveness of schools lies in creating subject-matter lessons that bring together *all* students whose levels of knowledge about the subject are about equal—regardless of whether they acquired the knowledge they now possess quickly or slowly.

In making this suggestion, we draw heavily on the ideas of John B. Carroll.[62] It was Carroll who developed the insight that what we perceive as ability is little more than rate of subject-matter learning. Moreover, his research indicates that time spent in learning school subjects turns out to be a better predictor of student achievement in those subjects than measured intelligence, social class, or other background characteristics. Thus, if students merely have the time they need as individuals for learning to take place—a characteristic we can surely adjust in our schools—then learning can be maximized for nearly all students. *All* can complete the curricula we desire, although they will do so at different rates; but their achievement levels will be maximized (and they will enjoy education best) if we organize lessons so that students with roughly the same levels of competency in the subject area are assembled together and given appropriate challenges in a common lesson.

This insight has all sorts of implications. For example, the notion that children can start kindergarten if they reach five years of age by, say, November 30 of the school year may be a reasonable administrative rule, but it is nonsensical education. Such a rule means that the child born on December 1 must wait an extra *year* to enter the public school while the child who is only one day older is considered "ready" for school. What nonsense! And yet, some such cutoff date for entering school is in force in almost every school district in the nation.

What is the alternative? Let us propose that schools take in children on the day of their fifth birthday or some other agreed-on marker age. It would not matter when during the school year the child reaches that age. At that point in the year, whenever it occurs, the child would enter a public school and be placed in a supportive homeroom, under the direction of a small team of teachers and aides. Each child would then be assessed for his or her knowledge in various subjects, and the professional staff would move the child into appropriate-level reading and other academic lessons depending on those assessments. And as soon as the child was able to master basic skills for each subject, the child would be moved on to more advanced lessons.

In such a model for schooling, *the child is moved upward through the curricula as fast as the child's achievements warrant.* This model for schooling does not run on the age-grade organizational pattern. Such a model takes "rate of learning" seriously, using this as the major characteristic for dealing with heterogeneity in the schools. Under such a model, all lessons taught, from kindergarten to high school graduation, would be designed to help students move through the curriculum at their own rates. And this means that *all* students would be challenged in the most benefical ways throughout their schooling.

It would also mean, of course, that classes would be composed of students who varied greatly in age. A specific ten-year-old, for example, might be a whiz in mathematics and would be found in a calculus lesson early in the day. But the same child might also have less interest in or willingness to study other topics, so he or she would appear in a sixth-year reading lesson later in the morning and a fourth-year lesson in writing in the afternoon. Thus, any given lesson might involve students of many different ages. In fact, the lessons we envision would look more like courses offered in America's universities—which also involve students of differing ages—than the traditional, age-graded classroom of today's primary or secondary schools. And, like our university system, the school we envision would help both those who are "speedy" and those who are "slow" in various subjects to get the most out of their educations—and achievement levels for all students would shoot up.

In such a school, the entire curriculum would be designed as an integrated and continuous set of learning experiences in each of the subjects taught. Students would be monitored regularly and placed in learning experiences that are appropriate for them as individuals. Flexible, *nonpermanent* groups of students would replace age-graded classrooms and ability tracks, and this would have all sorts of good effects.

The way in which we presently organize schooling encourages Americans to assume that ability is innate and immutable. On the other hand, if students were regularly reassembled into differing groups that reflected levels of accomplishment, Americans would begin to think of ability as *rate of learning;* hence, to be malleable. They would then be more likely to pay more attention to the child's motivation, opportunity to learn, conditions facilitating creativity, perseverance, and other qualities that educators, students, and parents can do something about.

In addition, teachers, students, and parents would learn quickly that children may excel in one subject but move quite slowly in another, and this would reduce their tendency to make holistic judgments about students who are thought to be either "superbright" or "hopeless." Thus, such a school system would help to eliminate the stigmas presently acquired by large numbers of students who are thought to be "poor learners" or merely "ordinary." At present a large number of children are subjected to such judgments, and for this reason alone they learn to dislike school and academic subjects. They are also subjected to discriminatory treatment; they go through school assigned to low-ability groups and tracks, are given only easy assignments to do, are graded on the basis of "effort" rather than accomplishment, are treated by school personnel as less than capable, and are eventually told by their parents and counsellors that some kinds of jobs are out of their reach.

Thus, the ways in which Americans presently conduct schooling conspire to make "losers" of many children. In contrast, the type of school organization we envision would sharply reduce this type of stigmatizing. Students who are slow in one subject would know that they are fast movers in others. And those who were truly interested in moving more rapidly could explore ways to do so. Thus, the new system of organization would not only promote more learning and higher morale, it would also be more humane.

Special Education and Retention in Grade. If schools were reorganized as we have suggested, they could also avoid many of the problems associated with programs for special education. This is because many of those whom we presently think of as "learning disabled" are merely slow learners in one or more crucial subjects. By providing relatively open time limits, the majority of special-education students can be served in multi-age classrooms by teams of well-trained teachers and aides; and the heavy expenditures now made for special education can be reinvested in other educational programs.

Notice too that the need for programs serving "the gifted" would be eliminated. Children whom we think of as "gifted" are merely those who learn certain subjects at a fast pace, and their needs can also be served in multi-age classrooms. Moreover, let us remember that it is the rare person indeed who is a fast or slow learner in *all* fields. Since most of the ten-year-olds who can cope with calculus have the social, emotional, and athletic skills of typical ten-year-olds, they belong with their agemates when it comes to friendship, sports, and other academic subjects.

In the kind of schooling we envision, a student would graduate from high school only when he or she mastered agreed-on levels of accomplishment in the basic curriculum. Since students would achieve this level of mastery at different rates, those receiving their diplomas each year might range from, let us say, fourteen to twenty years old. But when students *did* receive their diplomas, it would be because they had fulfilled all requirements satisfactorily, and this would reduce ambiguity and disputes about the meaning of high school graduation.

The flexible, continuous-learning school would also eliminate the need for requiring students who are thought to be immature or far behind in their work to repeat a grade. School districts throughout the nation regularly retain students as a way of dealing with diversity in ability. Well over a million American students are retained in grade each year, and the overwhelming majority of them are poorly served by that practice. Making students repeat a grade stigmatizes those students and suggests to the world that they are incompetent. Retention in grade is also a very good predictor of drop-out rates. And students who are retained learn less than if they had remained with their agemates. All considered, there is remarkably little to recommend retention in grade as a strategy for handling diversity.[63] Since the design for school organization we recommend largely does away with grades and provides appropriate experiences for both fast- and slow-learning students, it eliminates the need for grade retention.

Summary. The practices of segregating students by age and presumed ability were set up to bring students with equal levels of knowledge into common classrooms. But they don't work very well, and they generate a host of serious problems. It would be far better to reorganize schools so that their lessons truly serve students who possess equivalent levels of knowledge, achievement, understanding, or skill in a subject, regardless of those students' ages.

Other ways have been proposed for reorganizing schooling to do away with tracking and within-class ability grouping, of course. Alternative approaches to tracking include: (1) the provision of a rich core curriculum that is complex for all, (2) taking informal knowledge seriously, (3) allowing for multiple right answers to many types of problems, (4) promoting the social construction of some types of knowledge, (5) promoting long-term projects for students to work on, and (6) developing authentic assessment devices that do not pit one student against another.[64] Cooperative learning activities can also do away with the need for in-class ability grouping. Other options that can help reduce ability segregation include peer and cross-age tutoring, after-school and home visitation programs to help students keep up to speed, and the use of aides and specialists to help with the unique problems of a diverse classroom. Unfortunately, however, many of these useful ideas are already being resisted by powerful advocates who (correctly) believe that they are designed, in part, to do away with the unfair advantages that grouping and tracking systems generate for affluent children. Our guess is that such advocates will be less likely to resist proposals for nongraded schools once they understand that such schools provide marvelous educational experiences for *all* students, fast and slow, rich and poor.

Segregation by age and presumed ability are *not* good solutions for the problem of heterogeneity. The proper solution is to treat heterogeneity as an asset, as a part of life, and to design school experiences to accommodate it and take advantage of it. To do this properly would maximize student achievement and create a better climate in schools. And it would mean that we are conducting education in ways that are far closer to our democratic ideals. Multi-age classes and ungraded schools are designed to accommodate differences in children's rates of learning and may even save money when compared with traditional forms of instruction that require extra expenses for special education. It is surely in the interests of the nation to experiment more with such flexible structures for schools.

On Parent, Teacher, and Community Involvement

Principle: *Schooling in America can be improved by strengthening ties between communities and their schools. Such ties can be promoted through programs that encourage more active roles for parents, more contacts between parents and teachers, and expanded visions for the responsibilities of schools.*

Although parent involvement is positively linked to school success, many parents are not as involved in schooling as teachers would like. This lack of involvement is not random: social class has a powerful influence on parent involvement patterns. For example, between forty to sixty percent of working-class and lower-class parents fail to attend parent-teacher conferences. For middle-class parents these figures are nearly halved, i.e., about twenty to thirty percent. . . . In the areas of promoting verbal development, reading to children, taking children to the library, attending school events, enrolling children in summer school, and making complaints to the principal, middleclass parents consistently take a more active role in schooling than do their workingclass and lower-class counterparts.

—Annette Lareau (*Home Advantage*, 1989, p. 3)

Americans have long assumed that public schools are more responsive to local needs, and are more effective institutions when they are closely tied to their local communities. That is why we in the United States manage our public schools through local school boards. Indeed, this assumption seems so "natural" that Americans may be startled to learn that public schools are usually operated by state authorities in other countries. Citizens of these countries often think that educators have unique, "expert" knowledge of school matters, and teachers in these countries may be encouraged to keep their distance from parents.

But what does research say about the issue? Studies of school-community integration have been conducted largely in our country, but the evidence of those studies certainly suggests that parental involvement in education *is* associated with high levels of morale and achievement in schools.[65] These are not mysterious effects. When schools are more involved with their communities and when teachers and parents see and talk more often with one another, they are more likely to know about one another's needs and are better able to work in tandem to promote the learning and welfare of students. And this implies that the conduct and achievements of education can often be improved if schools become more involved in the lives of their local communities.

Barriers to Involvement. Unfortunately, several barriers may stand in the way of strong ties between schools and their communities. One such barrier is the large number of American parents who now must work. In the past, most mothers in our country were not employed outside the home and had free hours during the week that might be spent visiting their children's schools or supplementing those schools' educational efforts. But now, most women in our country hold full-time jobs, as do most men. And this means that parents often have little time for contact with the schools their children attend.

This problem falls most heavily on working-class and single parents, of course. Wives in more affluent families can still be full-time homemakers if they choose; and parents who hold middle-class, professional jobs may have flexible work schedules that allow them to have some contact with their children's schools during the work week. These privileges are not available, however, to working-class mothers or fathers, who must punch time clocks or keep regular office hours. Such parents often have *no* opportunities for contact with their children's schools during the day and only a few free hours available in the evenings or on weekends. And the problem is *much* worse for single parents who must deal with far too many responsibilities and often feel they have no free time at all.

Schools in our country were designed, in part, to serve the needs of two-parent families in which mothers remained at home, helped to rear children, and supplemented the efforts of the school. Unfortunately, some schools are still operated by educators who think this type of family is (or perhaps should be) the norm. Obviously, schools are more effective when teachers and school administrators make sincere efforts to arrange their schedules to accommodate the real needs of parents in their communities.

Moreover, schools should be especially sensitive to the employment problems faced by working-class or single parents. We know of one study that described a teacher who complained about a family's presumed disinterest in their child's education. The teacher had reached this conclusion because the child's parents didn't come to the school's open houses and didn't respond to school communications.[66] What that teacher did not know—because she had never bothered to investigate the situation—was that the mother of this child was a poor, single, working woman who lived across town from the school. Through discussions with friends and family, the mother had chosen the school for her child because she thought it the best in the city. She drove the child across town every morning, though barely able to afford the gas and the time. Each afternoon after school, the child stayed with an aunt who lived nearby until the mother could pick the child up after work. As a result of this arrangement, some of the messages the school sent never got to the mother. And because of the needs of her other children, the mother could not attend the school's open houses that were held during the evening. Surely this teacher and her school should have made more effort to reach out to such a motivated parent.

Another barrier concerns disjunctures between the culture shared by educators in the school and that of the parents in the community. Even under the best of circumstances, some tension always appears in relationships between teachers and parents.[67] Teachers are, after all, trained professionals who are responsible for evaluating as well as instructing their students. Parents, in contrast, often feel they lack expert knowledge but must sometimes challenge teachers when they think their children are not being treated well.

The problem escalates, however, when teachers and parents represent different ethnic or social-class backgrounds. Most teachers today come from middle-class backgrounds or have been trained to exemplify middle-class, mainstream values. Communication problems are likely to crop up when they teach in impoverished communities—especially where the race or ethnicity of the community differs from their own. For one thing, parents in those communities may not initiate communications as often as some middle-class parents do. Thus, one study found that low-income, non-English-speaking and African American parents didn't know how to contact their schools and didn't believe they had a right to ask anything special of those schools.[68]

Teachers sometimes portray or embody styles of conduct or values that are not shared in the community. This can create a barrier between the school and the community. Consider, for example, the dilemmas faced by the teacher who is asked to teach the rules of mainstream, middle-class English in a community that normally speaks black urban English. In the worst cases, teachers may reject optional customs or styles of behavior common in the local community simply because of racial or ethnic prejudices. Moreover, because they were often forced to attend underfunded schools or were subjected to discrimination, failure, or humiliation at school when they were young, less-affluent parents may bear grudges that make contact with their children's schools problematic.

Also, many parents in poor communities may be embarrassed or fearful, or they may speak another language; and as a result, minimal efforts to reach out to them may fail. Though they often care deeply about their children's education, some parents do not know how to respond to requests from the school, and, as a result, they do not come to the school on open-house nights. On other occasions, they cannot get to phones; they may feel they are not dressed properly; they lack transportation; they must work at second jobs in the evening; or they have extended family responsibilities that prevent them from having contact with the school. Life is very hard for most poor families, and as we know, the number of poor families in our country has recently been soaring.

Two studies illustrate the problems of reaching out in poorer communities—one concerned with African American parents, the other focused on Hispanics.[69] In both of these communities, the parents tried hard to do what the schools asked them to do. If the schools sent home requests that their child watch a *National Geographic* television special on Christopher Columbus, or if they were asked to take their child to a museum for a special exhibit, or if they were asked to engage in some special tasks in preparation for an upcoming test, parents tried hard to honor the requests. In fact, rates of compliance with these requests were about the same as in middle-class communities. Nevertheless, parents in both of these communities had difficulty communicating with the schools. Middle-class parents generally know not only how to respond but also how to make their needs known to the school. Lower-income parents have more difficulty initiating contact, and this may suggest to (middle-class) teachers that lower-income parents don't care about their children. And this, in turn, may lead those teachers to turn away from low-income parents, isolating those parents even more from the schools.

Bureaucratic pressures constitute yet another barrier that can stand in the way of school involvement with the community. This barrier is more likely to create a problem in large school systems, of course, where school autonomy may be buried under rules and regulations that prohibit or discourage creative responses to local needs. Many schools in large districts have scant control over their personnel, their curricula, their extracurricular offerings, or their working hours; and this means that those schools have little ability to adjust any of these program features to suit local needs. Some educators are eventually defeated by bureaucratic pressures. We know of several principals in large systems who seemingly cannot make the simplest decision without authorization, and some teachers in large systems seem to be mere time servers who have little interest in the communities they serve.

Thus, various barriers can make close contact between a school and its community difficult. What can be done to break down these barriers and facilitate school-community integration?

Encouraging Parental Involvement.

The school that wants to increase its involvement with the local community might begin by promoting more parental participation.[70] Some schools we know of have asked parents to become more involved in local school politics. Others have welcomed parents to volunteer in the school as classroom aides, as test graders, or as hall monitors or lunch-room helpers. Others have sought to involve parents as "partners in learning," thus making parents responsible for education programs at home that complement those of the school. In some of these programs, parents monitor homework and television viewing, promote reading, and prepare children for specific school tasks.

Another approach asks parents to share their unique knowledge with teachers and students in the school. One school we know about has sought to ferret out the unique pockets of knowledge that exist in its community and to bring parents with that knowledge into the school.[71] (Indeed, such knowledge appears in all communities, no matter how impoverished—knowledge about cooking and baking, repairing automobiles, glassmaking, weaving, plumbing, ethnic history, farming, constructing musical instruments, and so on.) This school not only empowers parents but enlarges teachers' perspectives and gives children in the school substantive information they can use later in their lives.

Local Autonomy and Parental Choice.

The best strategies for promoting parental involvement will certainly vary from community to community, and this means that neighborhood schools in large urban districts should be granted autonomy to plan their own involvement programs. Such ideas suggest a broad principle governing school-community integration. As a rule, parents are more likely to involve themselves in the school if *they* feel that they have some degree of control over what goes on in the school and that they can influence their children's education. Thus, schools should not only encourage parental involvement, but they should also set up mechanisms that allow parents to have a say in school policies and procedures. At a minimum, this argues for the creation of school councils and parent-teacher associations; but it may also suggest other mechanisms to promote morale, commitment, and feelings of control among parents.

One possible mechanism is to promote opportunities for parents to choose among public schools for their children. Earlier, we reviewed the many reasons why Americans should *not* support vouchers and other mechanisms that promote private education and debilitate the public schools. But this does not mean that choice among *public* schools is necessarily a bad thing. Indeed, there are many good reasons why a parent might want to send his or her child to a distant public school. The distant school may provide an academic program that is unavailable in the local school; or personal friends or close relatives of the child may already attend the distant school; or the distant school may allow the child to get away from unpleasant associates or social problems in the local school.

This suggests that parent and student morale should be higher when parents and their children are allowed to choose their own public school.[72] These notions have been examined recently in research by Mary Driscoll, who studied a number of different contexts in which parents did or did not have the ability to choose the schools their children were to attend.[73] She reports that parental choice *does,* indeed, lead to higher levels of parent and student morale.

A good discussion of this effect may be found in Peter Cookson's book, *School Choice.*[74] Cookson (citing Driscoll) points out that when parents are able to choose among schools, they perceive the school they have chosen to be "special," and this leads to higher morale and more involvement. Thus, if larger school districts really want to promote higher morale and greater involvement among parents, one simple thing they might consider is to allow parents to choose among schools in the district. Some urban districts fear that this would cause chaos, unwanted competition among local schools, and increased ethnic or racial segregation, but the evidence so far available does not support such fears. Choice among public schools seems to work well as long as those schools receive approximately equal per-capita funding.

Mentoring and Youth Organizations. Other models for involvement may cause us to expand our traditional notions of schooling. For example, a good deal of effort is now underway to provide mentoring experiences for urban youth. Throughout the country, adult mentors are now providing role models, support, counseling, and real-world assistance to impoverished young people on a one-on-one basis; and a good review of the efforts and successes of these programs may be found in Marc Freedman's *The Kindness of Strangers.*[75] As Freedman points out, most current mentoring programs involve voluntary efforts by affluent people, and we provided a good example of such a program when we discussed the work of Eugene Lang earlier in the chapter.

There is no inherent reason why mentoring could not become part of public schools' efforts—but to make this happen would require that schools reach out to motivated adults in the community; set up programs in which those adults are commissioned as mentors; and facilitate, support, and supervise their services to young people. Something like mentoring programs may in fact be a necessity if we are to rescue significant numbers of ghetto youth from the horrors of poverty, discrimination, violence, and drugs. But education will have to be given additional funds and accept an expanded mission if such programs are to be vested in our public schools.

Another model for involvement is offered by the recent blossoming of youth organizations outside of schools.[76] These include youth choirs, community theater programs, and art and dance groups—as well as the traditional Girl Scout and Boy Scout programs, Little League, Pop Warner League, church clubs, midnight basketball leagues, and so forth. For inner-city youth these clubs provide meaningful activities, supervision, and instruction during after-school hours. They may be every bit as important in the lives of some young people as are school and family. They provide an alternative to street gangs by offering an equivalent sense of belonging and cross-age bonding, and these groups honor traditions and provide security while promoting activities that are legal and socially acceptable.

Leaders of youth organizations are usually of the same race or ethnicity as are their members, and often those leaders were once members of street gangs. So youngsters learn from the leaders' example that it is possible to lead an alternative, useful life, outside of street gangs. Such organizations often provide inner-city youth with opportunities to learn skills that may bring success in real-life projects. For example, they may hold car washes and candy drives to raise money; they may put on art fairs and dance performances that take months of preparation; they may have tournaments and games that require regular practice, teamwork, and analysis; or they may have picnics, outings, and field trips that must be planned and funded.

Successful youth organizations seem to have common characteristics. They begin by assuming that their members are not problems but assets and that every person is needed if the group is to function. They ensure that learning occurs regularly, not just at certain times of the week, month, or year. They plan work designed to build to a peak, such as a culminating competition, performance, hike, or cleanup of the neighborhood—something the group plans for over an extended period. They offer safety off the streets, out of view of more troubled youth. They make it possible for youngsters to travel out of their home communities to see how others live their lives. They insist that members of the group evaluate each other honestly, whether that evaluation is of a performance, an athletic event, or a contribution to a discussion. They enforce a few simple, but meaningful, rules. And they provide the members with nicknames and rituals—symbols of belonging.

In the otherwise chaotic world of the inner city, these organizations provide safety and learning. They teach responsibility and discipline, and they help to develop identity and character. They teach problem solving by solving problems in the real world. In fact, the type of learning that takes place in these organizations is strikingly similar to the authentic learning that we recommend earlier for our public schools.

Since these youth organizations are, in effect, extensions of efforts that should be encouraged in public schools, it makes sense that school districts might also assume responsibility for them. Most are presently running on a shoestring and barely survive. America's obligation to provide youngsters a safe educational environment does not end at three o'clock at the schoolhouse door. The more supervision that responsible adults can provide for inner-city children and others who need it, the better served we all are. But if schools are to sponsor youth organizations, our country must be prepared to provide extra funding and an enlarged sense of mission for its schools.

Community Schools. These last two ideas suggest that the time may finally be at hand for Americans to rethink and enlarge their assumptions about public schools. This is not a new idea. As we pointed out earlier, progressive educators argued the need for multipurpose community schools in America's cities early in the century. Americans have managed to ignore this suggestion for at least seventy-five years, but with the escalation of poverty, crime, violence, and unemployment in our inner cities, the need is becoming more urgent. Let us take this argument seriously and ask, What would a true community school look like?

Clearly, a community school would have to take on tasks that go far beyond instruction. Poverty and the factors associated with it are so overwhelming in some inner-city neighborhoods that school curricula have to be secondary to the social and economic survival of families. Concern for basic family functioning will always take precedence over school activities in the lives of very poor students, so schools should be prepared to step in and help to meet basic needs when other social services fail. For this reason, the community, or full-service, school should be prepared to offer health care, voter information, job training, parent education, supplementary nutrition, community leadership training, community recreation facilities, and a host of other key services if they are not otherwise provided in the community. Many advocates have written about how schools might take on such responsibilities, and a good illustration of reasoning along these lines may be found in psychologist Wayne Holtzman's *School of the Future*.[77]

An example of how a community school might operate was provided by the principal of a New York City school who was late for an appointment with one of us. When she was asked what had delayed her, she replied that she was helping an immigrant Salvadoran family get their electricity turned back on. When it was pointed out that most principals did not have such duties listed in their job descriptions, she laughed and said, "Yes, but how can we teach their two kids if the kids are worried that they won't be able to see at home, and their family is going to be cold tonight?" This principal ran one of the most successful schools in New York despite the fact that it was located in one of Manhattan's poorest neighborhoods. All the educators in the school took seriously their responsibilities to help with community service when needed, and the children in the school benefited.

This does not mean that, by itself, this underfunded school could make up for even a fraction of the poverty and missing social services in the community. Thus, it provides only a partial model for the true community school that would combine sensitivity and vision with sufficient funding to provide a wide range of needed social services. Even now the concept of the true community school may seem to be visionary, but some versions of such schools are badly needed in many of our urban ghettos, and it can be argued that their costs would be far less than those we are now paying to cope with the catastrophes that are now generated in our neglected inner cities.

Summary. We have suggested various strategies that might be adopted for promoting ties between schools and their communities. Strategies such as these have been found useful in some schools, and people who seek to improve the effectiveness of their own schools should consider these strategies seriously. This does not mean that all approaches will work in all contexts. Each school and community are unique, and the best strategy for promoting greater involvement will vary from setting to setting. But all schools should be challenged to promote greater involvement with parents and their wider communities; when these schools decide to accept this challenge, they will find many ideas in programs that have been pioneered elsewhere in the nation.

On Professionalism in Education

[**Principle:** *Schooling in America can be improved by strengthening the professional status of teachers and other educators.*]

Something must be done to change the perceptions that educators lack any special expertise. Such perceptions negatively affect how students, administrators, and the public at large interact with educators. These negative perceptions also influence how educators feel about themselves, about one another, and about their profession.

If we are going to attract and retain truly competent teachers, these perceptions must change. We must take steps to demonstrate that effective teachers possess (and apply) a unique body of specialized knowledge. The way to accomplish this goal is to help display teachers as the experts that they are.

—Robert T. Tauber (Those who can't, teach: Dispelling the myth, 1992, p. 98)

The crucial players needed to transform, reform, or improve schools are teachers and other educators. Literally nothing good will happen in our schools unless the professionals who run those schools make it happen. Of course, resources must be provided. Of course, the school board is important. Of course, the students in the school must be energized and their parents must be involved. And of course, workable ideas for improving education must be entertained. But no matter how important all these other factors are, it is in the schools and classrooms that the rubber meets the road, and no improvement will occur unless the educators who run our schools are able to perform *their* decisive parts.

How can we help educators take a more active role in educational innovation? We suggest that this is more likely to occur when the teachers and administrators who run our schools are treated with respect. These hard-working people are at least as intelligent and as capable as the critics who regularly attack them. Most have completed many years of higher education; most have a good deal of technical knowledge they can use and express; and most have sincere moral commitments to the welfare of the students and communities they serve. They have typically earned the right to be treated as knowledgeable professionals, and the quality of their efforts—and the academic achievements of our students—depend ultimately on whether they receive this treatment.

Does this mean that every teacher and school principal deserves our respect? Of course not. But then, one can also find incompetents and charlatans among doctors, lawyers, clergymen, psychologists, and other professionals. Does it mean that our schools should not be criticized? Again, of course not. But legitimate criticism can also be leveled against our hospitals, law firms, churches, clinics, and other types of professional organizations. Nevertheless, even when these organizations are criticized, the professionals who staff them are generally treated with respect and are thought to be doing their best under perhaps adverse circumstances. When our schools are criticized, the educators who staff them deserve this same level of professional respect. And if respect for educators is not included in passionate public debates about education, improvements in our schools are surely *not* likely.

Respect is not shown, for example, when top-down forms of innovation are imposed on teachers by school boards, superintendents, state departments of education, or federal mandates. Top-down attempts to change schools have a notorious record of failure.[78] Sometimes top-down reforms are "merely" confused or unworkable, but sometimes they are all too clear in their implications for educators; and then the trouble begins. Teachers and school principals are as human as other citizens. When they are told they now *must* teach reading by a new method, *must* cover certain topics by the end of the year, *must* learn to use the computer, *must* compete for resources with other schools, those educators may comply—barely—but no one should be surprised if they become resentful and look for ways to return to old and tired procedures with which they are familiar. If top-down change does not work well in other professional fields, it is surely inappropriate in education, where we are trying to teach and model the values of independence and responsibility for our students. Management by fiat is "demeaning to teachers and students alike. If we are to take the issue of schooling seriously, schools should be the one site where democratic social relations become a part of one's lived experiences."[79]

By way of contrast, bottom-up strategies for improving schools involve educators in meaningful discussions of the problems they face. Such strategies allow teachers and principals to look at how those problems might be solved, to examine evidence about proposed changes, and to send representatives to sites where proposed innovations are supposedly working. Such strategies grant professional status to educators, and are surely more likely to succeed.[80]

Not surprisingly, bottom-up strategies for change have a better record than do top-down strategies. This means that school improvement is more likely to occur when educators at a school are themselves organized into communities of learners. This takes time to establish, but once in place, such communities allow for meaningful discussion of proposed changes, provide appropriate environments to initiate and support change, and generate procedures to study the effects of change.[81] Thus, to promote bottom-up change, we need to establish norms of collegiality and experimentation among the teachers and administrators of schools.[82] When this occurs, school improvement becomes a continuing process, not a one-time attempt to boost test scores or attack another superficial goal. In such collegial environments, teachers feel empowered, and responsible, high-quality leadership can develop.[83]

Respect for teachers and administrators in schools may also be shown in other ways: by paying educators well and publicly recognizing their efforts; by creating mechanisms to protect teachers from irrational individuals who try to promote idiosyncratic agenda for education (for example, religious bigots, pushy academics, neurotic parents, or entrepreneurial business persons—each of whom may want access to the teacher's attention); by supporting teachers' attendance at in-service development programs so that educators do not have to pay for these out of their own pockets (today about one-fifth of all staff-development costs in education are paid for by the teachers themselves); by providing some budgets and authority to teachers so they can buy things they need for their classrooms without filling out forms or paying for them personally; by providing teachers with offices to work in, personnel to cover their classes so that they can go to the bathroom occasionally, and time for individual and group planning.

We show teachers respect when we give them enough time to do their jobs properly. Educators must have the time they need to make innovations work. They need extra time to implement a new curriculum, extra time to discuss problems and progress, and extra time to attend workshops and meetings related to school improvement. Teachers who are trying out new innovations cite *lack of time* as a major complaint.

Other steps have been proposed at the national level that are aimed at raising the status of the teaching profession. Influential leaders have suggested that the traditional professions, for example law and medicine, have enhanced their status by exerting control over standards for entering and practicing their jobs. Teachers have not traditionally done this, and various steps have been proposed to rectify this perceived problem.[84] These have included suggestions for a national examination for new teachers,[85] proposals by an activist group of education deans to upgrade standards of teacher education,[86] and various career-ladder programs that would provide extra pay for teachers judged to be "outstanding" in their work.

While many of these efforts have been well-intentioned, they have not generally had much success. The reasons for this are not hard to understand.

> Teaching [is] a mass profession, largely employed by public authorities or non-profit organizations, and could never organize itself along the lines of the small, elite, and often self-employed professions. Nor, in many views, should it want to. Teaching can never be or try to be arcane, unexplained, or closed.... Teaching must be a *public profession*.[87]

Such reasoning suggests that efforts to enhance the professional status of teachers and other educators are likely to be more effective if they focus on conditions within individual schools.

Another strategy, site-based management, is also sometimes urged as a means of increasing the autonomy and professional status of educators in schools.[88] We suggest that such arguments should be viewed with caution, however. On the one hand, site-based management presumably vests power to make decisions in the hands of teachers and principals and thus can grant educators more control over matters that are salient at the local site. This would tend to enhance their professional status. On the other hand, site-based management can also do harm. For example, the need to make site-based decisions about trivial matters may interfere with education. Moreover, site-based decision making without real budget authority is vacuous. Money is the basis of administrative power, and many site-based plans we know about continue to vest budgetary authority in a central administrative office. So teachers and principals get to decide how to spend a pittance, while decisions about the big dollars and big issues are made by others.

Moreover, in many site-based plans, teachers and administrators at the school site cannot choose their personnel, their tests, their methods of evaluation, and so forth. The site-based educators are still seen as untrustworthy to make such decisions. Self-government without authority is a sham, and site-based management programs can be a hoax when it comes to enhancing professionalism.

On the other hand, there is every reason to believe that school improvement is more likely when schools are run on the premise that most teachers want the freedom to make their own decisions, are able to improve, innovate, and take risks, and are willing to assume responsibility for the decisions they make. When premises like these are actually the basis of site-based decision-making programs, those programs can, indeed, lead to greater teacher professionalism.

We thus echo the words of policy analysts Terry Astuto and David Clark, who note that *people* are the keys to increased efficiency, productivity, and growth in organizations and that administrators who forget this principle do so at their peril.[89] It is the *people* in organizations who have the ambition and the capacity—the intelligence and the creativity—to solve organizational problems. Such talents are *not* narrowly distributed, held only by the top administrators and missing among employees at lower levels. Rather, such talents are widely distributed and are demonstrated when the environments in which people work encourage their display. The creation of this kind of supportive working environment is far too often overlooked by those who would reform or improve our schools.

For obvious reasons, much of the reform movement in education has focused on the students. But in so doing the reformers have often failed to think about the teachers, perhaps because citizens have so often been told that teachers' inadequacies were the root cause of America's putative school failure. We should remember, however, that schools must be pleasant places to work. If schools are boring, threatening, dangerous, or undemanding environments for teachers, they will shortly become poor learning environments for students. Educator and social scientist Seymour Sarason makes this point when he suggests,

> Teaching is [often] regarded as something you can do (and do well!) day in and day out, month in and month out, year in and year out, without any decrease in motivation or change in style, satisfaction, patience, sensitivity, and sense of challenge. . . . It should make no difference if the teacher does not experience any collegiality, has no role in decision making, . . . and regards him or herself as a member of the educational proletariat.[90]

Of course such views are unacceptable. School improvement must begin with the recognition that anything which "diminishes [teachers'] flexibility and autonomy, and ignores their need for self-development and recognition has no chance of succeeding with students."[91] Schools will have to provide better, more professional working environments for teachers if those schools are to become better environments for students to learn in. Thus, school improvement must also be concerned with creating environments in which teachers can succeed too.

Summary: A Bounty of Ideas

> Ours is a time of remarkable ferment in U.S. education. The recent school reform movement initially focused on the "basics," but then took off in a dramatically new direction in the late 1980s. Reformers started to demand more thoughtful and intellectually ambitious instruction. Leaders in politics and business argued that students must become independent thinkers and enterprising problem solvers. Educators began to say that schools must offer intellectually challenging instruction that is deeply rooted in the academic disciplines.
>
> —David Cohen and James Spillane (Policy and practice: The relations between governance and instruction, 1992)

Interest in educational change is probably higher now than at any time in American history, and in this chapter we have covered only a fraction of the literature on school improvement and reform. We have instead focused on what seem to us sensible principles or guidelines to follow for those who are sincerely interested in improving the conduct and effectiveness of American education.

As we were writing, however, we came across another list of principles. These are by sociologists Margaret LeCompte and Anthony Dworkin, and they seemed to parallel our own thinking.[92] They have written that

- A child's education should not be stigmatized by derogatory labels or disparity of esteem.
- Curricula should not be stratified into advanced, college prep, "ordinary," and remedial streams, because this contributes to labelling and disparity of esteem.
- Education for every child should be individualized and case managed.
- School schedules and facilities should be organized to make it possible for today's children to attend, regardless of their need to work, to fulfill their own parenting responsibilities, or to be provided special services.
- Teachers and students should have adequate materials and working conditions.
- A child's success in school should not require two residential parents and a nonworking mother.
- Similarly, a child's success in school should not be predicated upon the help of able parents.
- The assumption that better education can be had for less money should be rejected.
- Pedagogy should not be decontextualized, fragmented, and narrowly skills-based. Just as the whole child is taught, so also should the whole subject, the whole curriculum, be taught.

These ideas certainly sound good to us, but on the basis of what we have written in this chapter, we would want to add the following:

- Schools should be a size that allows every child to have an adult at the school site who would miss them if they were absent.
- Greater stress should be given to nongraded schools and cooperative classroom learning.
- The content of school curricula should be changed to give less focus to job opportunities and employment, but changes in curricula should be subject to public debate.

• New ways of thinking about the aims of curricula and the methods of teaching lead to a need for new methods of assessment.

Above all, we should bear in mind that the best ways to improve our schools are those that enhance the dignity of parents and the autonomy and professional status of educators. When they are able, the adults of our country who care most about our youngsters—our parents and the teachers—generally take care of their charges well. When they fail in their missions, they fail because they no longer have meaningful and fulfilling employment, because they cannot earn wages that provide a decent standard of living, because they are not given respect, and because, as a result, the youngsters they serve no longer have hope.

When Americans are confronted with evidence about poverty, drugs, unemployment, school dropouts, teen pregnancy, domestic violence, crime, and the like, they should realize that these are symptoms of a society that has lost its way and no longer cares for its citizens. Most of these problems exist because too many people have too little access to the American dream. Our parents and our teachers, indeed our whole nation, would have fewer problems if the goals we set for the nation included creating jobs with decent wages, restoring fair tax rates on corporations and wealthy individuals, providing universal coverage for high-quality health and day care, providing equitable funding for schools, and developing organizations to build more caring relationships among all members of our communities. School improvement doesn't begin in the classrooms, though that is where most school improvement plans must have their impact. School improvement begins with concerns about the dignity and respect accorded to the adults in the community who care for our young.

school boards, or local educators are based neither on evidence nor on careful reviews of relevant theory—and it would be difficult indeed to find cases where a decision-making body refused to consider a proposal for improving education because the relevant research had not yet appeared. For example, various states passed laws in the 1980s that attempted to reform education by intensifying school curricula or standards. As we noted earlier, these laws were *not* based on research evidence or on the analytic scholarship of the research community, and most did not work. Similarly, current federal efforts to promote programs for gifted students fly in the face of both theory and evidence. "In short, the 'radical' notion of supporting calls for educational reform with research knowledge seems not yet [to be] popular among many reformers."[2] And Americans pay the price by instituting a host of reforms that cannot, and do not, work.

Why do so many reformers behave this way when it comes to education? This question has elicited a lot of interest, and scores of scholars have written about it.[3] In part, most research on education is conducted by social scientists, and social research is not thought to have the "definitive" character, the importance, that is accorded research in the physical and biological sciences.[4] In part, also, our society has not yet evolved efficient mechanisms for getting the knowledge generated by research on education to those who must make decisions about our schools. In part, research on education also came under direct attack as part of the Manufactured Crisis, so that many concerned Americans have been given the false impression that educational research is less valid or useful than research in other fields.[5] And in part, since most Americans have had personal experience with public schools, they seem to think of themselves as "experts" on educational topics; hence, they feel little need for guidance from research when making decisions about schools.

Above all, however, research on education is not used because there is so little of it! Some readers may find this statement surprising, given our extensive citations of research evidence in the first six chapters of this book. However, we were lucky. The educational topics we reviewed for this effort are among the few for which research truly *has* been accumulated. Indeed, when constructing the Manufactured Crisis, those hostile to public education chose topics for which research had been conducted; and to counter their myths, all we had to do was to look at the evidence they had misrepresented. Research has simply not yet appeared for many important educational issues. For example, we cited relatively little research evidence on ways to improve education in Chapter 7. The reason is that little research has yet appeared that bears *directly* on most of the topics we reviewed in that chapter. Good ideas and relevant scholarship have appeared, true, but empirical studies on most of these topics have not yet been reported. Thus, those who look for research that will help them plan a specific program for improving education may find their search to be fruitless.

Chapter Eight

Fundamentals of School Improvement: Research and Compassion

◆

At this point it's useful to pause and reflect on what we have written and what it implies for American education today. By now it should be clear that American education has recently been subjected to an unwarranted, vigorous, and damaging attack—a Manufactured Crisis. Early in the 1980s, prominent figures in our federal government unleashed an unprecedented onslaught on America's schools, claiming that those schools had recently deteriorated, that they now compared badly with schools from other advanced countries, and that as a result our economy and the future of our nation were seriously threatened. These claims were said to be supported by evidence, although somehow that evidence was rarely cited or appeared only as simple, misleading analyses of limited data.

Nevertheless, this attack was waged with great vigor, was eagerly supported by prominent figures in industry, and was widely reported and endlessly elaborated by a compliant press. And as a result, many of the claims of this attack came to be accepted by good-hearted Americans, including a lot of powerful people and leaders in the educational community; and great mischief resulted because of the misunderstandings and poor policies this attack created.

In Chapters 2 and 3 we examined the actual evidence bearing on major claims of this attack and found that most were unsupported. Instead, the evidence suggests that, on average, American schools are not only holding their own but are also improving in modest ways. Thus, the major claims of the attack turned out to have been myths; the Manufactured Crisis was revealed as a Big Lie.

But these conclusions raised related questions. Why did this attack appear in the early 1980s, and what did research suggest about the educational agenda being pushed by those responsible for the crisis? As Chapter 4 suggested, the crisis was indirectly generated by escalating problems, both in the larger society and in education itself; but it was also promoted by specific groups of ideologues who were hostile to public schools and who wanted to divert attention from America's growing social problems. And in Chapter 5 we examined evidence indicating that key educational policies urged by promoters of the crisis would, if adopted, seriously damage America's schools and debase the educational experiences of its students.

Our analysis did not stop at this point, however. One of the worst effects of the Manufactured Crisis was that it distracted Americans from the real problems of American education and from thinking about useful steps that we might take to resolve those problems and improve America's schools. So, in Chapter 6 we examined a number of dilemmas faced by America's schools, some created by serious and escalating problems in the society at large, some resulting from questionable traditions for conducting education in our country. And given these pressing dilemmas, in Chapter 7 we set forth a set of principles that seem promising for improving American education.

As we've seen then, the average American school is a *lot* more successful than those responsible for the Manufactured Crisis would have us believe. This does not mean that our schools are perfect; indeed, they face serious problems, and their programs and achievements vary enormously. But this variation is due, in part, to huge differences in income, wealth, and support for schools in our nation. Thus, whether or not one accepts the principles for improving education that we outlined in Chapter 7, the task of improving our schools remains a serious and ongoing challenge for Americans.

Since this challenge is unlikely to go away, it is useful to suggest conditions that will govern how well that challenge is to be met.

The Need for More Research

Knowledge will forever govern ignorance, and a people who mean to be their own governors must arm themselves with the power knowledge gives.

—James Madison (1822)

Americans share many concerns about education, and because of our energy, optimism, and willingness to tinker with social institutions, we often set out to "reform" the public schools. And yet, most programs for improving education fail. Many turn out to have few good effects, others are unworkable, others cost a lot more than anticipated, and still others are found to create serious problems for educators or students. As a result, most programs for improvement are eventually abandoned.

And yet, some attempts to improve education succeed, and America's schools clearly do change over time. What makes for a successful improvement proposal? How can we tell ahead of time whether a reform effort is likely to succeed or fail? These questions have been addressed by various scholars, and we offer here a brief summary of only some of their ideas.[1]

In general, reform proposals are more likely to succeed if

- they reflect genuine (rather than fictitious) problems faced by schools;
- they are based on attainable goals that are shared by the people concerned;
- they are planned with an understanding of structural forces in the society and the education system that will affect the proposed changes;
- they encourage and respond to debates about alternatives among educators, students, parents, and others affected by those proposals;
- they involve plans for both starting *and* maintaining the program;
- they enlarge (rather than restrict) the lives of affected people; and
- they are adequately funded.

This list sounds impressive, but it actually skirts a truly crucial criterion. Attempts to improve education are more likely to succeed *if they are associated with research suggesting that they actually work.*

Thus, plans for improving education should solve the problems they were supposed to solve or generate other lasting benefits that educators, students, parents, or others concerned with education can detect. Unfortunately, only a few improvement efforts actually generate benefits—positive and detectable outcomes; and this is surely a major reason why most reform efforts are abandoned. Despite good intentions, a lot of effort, and no little expense, a great many programs designed to improve our schools fail simply because they don't work.

Is there no way to detect ahead of time which proposals for improving education are likely to work and which are not? To answer this question we need only look at other arenas of endeavor in which policy decisions are contemplated. Suppose our community, state, or nation were thinking about building a bridge, sending astronauts to the moon, or authorizing an expensive program to control a disease. In each case, we would want to base our decision about the issue on *research*—on relevant theories and evidence that investigators had assembled concerning our decision. Moreover, in many cases we would *demand* to see the results of that research before we made our decision, and if the research had not yet been conducted, we would commission that research as a necessary step *before* we took action. Thus, for such crucial matters, we would turn to research to reduce the chances that errors would be made. But education can surely be studied and is no less crucial in its effects on us and on the future lives of our children. Thus, it is reasonable to believe that Americans would also turn to research to avoid making errors when planning ways to improve education.

Unfortunately, they don't. Only a few efforts to change education seem to be based on knowledge generated by research. In all too many cases, reform programs that are set in motion by our federal government, state legislatures,

The reason why so little educational research exists is that funding for it is almost nonexistent. Most support for research in many fields comes from the federal government, of course, and Americans annually spend billions of their tax dollars to support research in the physical and biological sciences. Annual federal support for research in medicine alone is now running at more than five billion dollars, and billions more are spent each year on research relevant to defense. And yet, the *entire* federal outlay for research on education—including that on the costs of keeping records of the nation's schools, all research on school issues funded by all federal agencies, and the salaries of all those who administer education-research budgets—currently amounts to only a few hundred million dollars each year. And in recent years the annual amount set aside by the Office of Educational Research and Improvement for new studies by competent and motivated scholars has been a piddling five hundred thousand dollars—or about what it would cost to fund fully the research efforts and staff of three scholars in the fields of biology or medicine.

Or perhaps percentage figures would make more sense. Our federal government currently funds nearly *all* of the costs of defense but only about 6 percent of the total cost of primary and secondary education (down from about 10 percent in 1980).[6] Nevertheless, "while 15 percent of the federal dollars that go for defense are used to support research, only 0.1 percent of the federal dollars spent on educational programs are used to support research."[7] This is indeed peanuts.

For the government to provide such picayune support makes no sense. Each year scores of decisions are made throughout the country about new programs for improving or reforming American schools. Many of those programs will fail and thus will waste a great deal of money and possibly disrupt the lives of educators, students, and parents. Much of this waste of tax dollars and needless disruption could be prevented if Americans would only demand that reforms in schools not be initiated without benefit of relevant research and that a good deal more funding be set aside for research on pressing issues in education.

Education is not fundamentally different from other fields of human endeavor. It is perfectly possible to conduct research that bears on major decisions we need to make concerning the organization, staffing, curricula, and teaching methods appropriate for America's schools. When that research is conducted, it can produce knowledge that helps us avoid serious and costly errors. But good research does not come cheap. It requires competent and highly-trained workers. It also requires forethought and planning, and it always takes more time than decision makers would like. But if America is to avoid the wasted dollars and disrupted lives that poor policy decisions in education generate, we must step up our regular investment in educational research. Certainly, failure to fund educational research is a case of "penny wise, pound foolish."

The Need for Compassion

No poor, rural, weak, or black person should ever again have to bear the additional burden of being deprived of the opportunity for an education, a job, or simple justice.
　　—Jimmy Carter (1971)

Research will certainly help, but it alone is not sufficient if America really wants to reform public education. Thus, we turn to a second, crucial criterion for successful reform. Public schools can *never* be judged successful until they provide equal opportunities for all, and true improvements in public education will not come about unless they are based on compassion.

Of all the ugly assumptions of the Manufactured Crisis, two of the worst are the ideas that useful improvements in American education can be initiated by scapegoating those who labor in America's schools and that education for poor and minority students doesn't matter. Time and again, those responsible for the crisis told us how rotten our schools were—how the performance of those schools had declined, how they had lost direction, how their standards and discipline had been debased—and that this was all the fault of the untalented, poorly trained, unmotivated teachers and administrators responsible for those schools. And when the critics grew tired of bashing educators, they tried to blame America's students as well (and, indirectly, their parents) for the supposed shortcomings of our public schools.[8] In addition, the same critics consistently asserted that too much attention has been given to America's poor and minority students (many of whom must attend the country's most poorly funded schools), and they have tried to cut funds for programs that support those students—by fair means or foul.[9] And the critics have studiously ignored evidence indicating that, although those students are now making better progress, they still need additional help.

We simply cannot believe that effective reforms in education can follow from premises that scapegoat educators, blame students, or heap indignities on minorities and those who are impoverished. Rather, we believe that *all* Americans respond best when they are treated with dignity and respect; and this clearly should be the case in public schools, which are, above all, institutions that should teach and exemplify intellectual values and moral conduct. Most of the poor reform ideas we reviewed in Chapter 5 would treat educators as if they were unskilled hacks, punish students for unsatisfactory conduct, or redistribute tax support so that schools for the poor are further debased and those for the rich are given even more support. Such proposals are almost guaranteed to harm both the intellectual and moral efforts of America's public schools.

Let us return to basic principles. Public schools were instituted in our country to ensure that *all* children would have access to a common store of ideas, skills, and moral instruction so they could learn how to live in harmony with each other and how to build useful adult lives and institutions. And those schools were to be staffed by professional educators who could both impart the common store of knowledge and respond to the needs of individuals, thus helping all students to develop a love of learning. Great harm can result if we forget these ideals.

If we pay teachers substandard wages and treat them like recalcitrant incompetents, won't they eventually come to think of themselves in this light? And if we foolishly structure schools so that many students are regularly bored, threatened, or punished in them, who would be so naive as to assume those students would thereafter love learning?

Above all, if we structure our public school system so that large groups of students are not provided equitable education, we create a host of problems. Students who are not exposed to common moral standards learn to lie, cheat, steal, and assault other people. Students who are forced to attend badly underfunded schools become angry and alienated; indeed, they may eventually form dissident movements and seek to destabilize our government. Students who are not provided good schooling wind up ignorant, and ignorance is expensive. Those who know nothing contribute nothing; rather, they blunder and make messes with their lives that others must clean up. But, as we now know, America's current system of public education is massively inequitable and imposes badly underfunded schools on some of America's neediest students. And the result is that many young people in the country today are violent, angry, and alienated, and lead ignorant, messed-up lives.

Of course, these social problems are not solely the result of inequities in our public-school system. Violence, anger, alienation, and ignorance are also the results of poverty, drugs, gang warfare, police brutality, poor job prospects, discriminatory treatment, mindless television, and other features of contemporary American civilization. But surely what goes on in our public schools also has an effect. Who, then, would be surprised to learn that rates of violence, anger, alienation, and ignorance are lower in other industrialized countries where public education is more equitable?

If we are truly to improve American education, and through those improvements help to solve serious problems in our country, we must change our public schools so that all those who labor in them are treated with compassion. We will stimulate the best efforts from educators if we treat them as responsible professionals. Our students will grow most effectively if we encourage their achievement and project images of adult responsibility for them. And our poor and minority students are more likely to realize their dreams and join the mainstream of American society if we provide them with genuinely equal opportunities through our public school system. To paraphrase Goethe: If you treat people as they are, they will stay as they are. But if you treat them as if they were what they ought to be, they will become what they ought to be and could be.

To summarize then, Americans hold high expectations for their public schools. Moreover, they assume that those schools are responsive and that their programs can be improved. Thus, efforts to improve those schools will surely continue in our country. For the past decade many of those efforts have been misdirected by the myths and false premises of the Manufactured Crisis. As Americans turn away from these damaging ideas, we will want to address the *real* issues that the public schools of our country face—issues that are tied to serious and growing social problems in the nation. And as we debate ways to address these issues and plan programs that we hope will improve our schools, we should remember that reforms in education are far more effective when they are based on knowledge derived from research. Research is not a frill; rather, it is badly needed if our efforts to improve public schools are to be effective.

In addition, *compassion* is needed if Americans truly want to realize the goals of public education. Compassionate reforms are not only moral, but they are required if we are to improve education and enable our schools to help solve some of America's worst social problems. In Lincoln's words, it has always been clear that effective reform of education must begin "with charity for all." We now suggest that compassion in education is an utter necessity if we in America are to realize our long-held aspirations for equality, justice, true democracy, and a decent standard of living for us all.

Endnotes

◆

Chapter 1 Thinking About Education in a Different Way

1. *Japan Times* (1987, August 23).
2. Schooland (1990, p. 121).
3. Schooland (1990, p. 122).
4. *Japan Times* (1986, January 30).
5. Schooland (1990, p. 121).
6. *Japan Times* (1985, November 20).
7. Stanglin (1985).
8. Schooland (1990, p. 179).
9. Yates (1985); *Arizona Republic* (1993); Schooland (1990).
10. *Japan Times* (1986, April 24).
11. National Commission on Excellence in Education (1983).
12. Richburg (1985).
13. Richburg (1985).
14. Educational Testing Service (1993).
15. Celis (1993); Jordan (1993).
16. See Kaufman & Rosenbaum (1992).

Chapter 2 Myths About Achievement and Aptitude

1. The College Entrance Examination Board (1993, Table 3).
2. O'Reilly (1994).
3. Crouse & Trusheim (1988).
4. The College Entrance Examination Board (1993).
5. Smith (1994); Zionek (1994).
6. Bracey (1991, p. 109).
7. See Educational Testing Service (1990, p. 31); Grissmer et al. (1994).
8. DeWitt (1990).
9. Carson, Huelskamp, & Woodall (1991) and Sandia National Laboratories (1993). Also see Grissmer et al. (1994).
10. Again see DeWitt (1990).
11. Educational Testing Service (1990, p. 9).
12. National Center for Education Statistics (1991a, pp. 7–8).
13. Educational Testing Service (1990, p. 20).
14. From a letter to the Hon. William D. Ford and the Hon. Dale E. Kildee by Eleanor Chelimsky, Head of the GAO, March 11, 1992, quoted in Jaeger (1992a). See also United States General Accounting Office (1993).
15. Saxe (1988).
16. See Dossey et al. (1988).
17. National Center for Education Statistics (1991a, p. 1).
18. Wirth (1992, p. 21).
19. Linn, Graue, & Sanders (1990).
20. Hieronymus & Hoover (1986).
21. Actually, we suspect that Kilpatrick (1983, p. 5) was merely repeating cant from *A Nation At Risk*.
22. Ravitch & Finn (1987).

23. Hirsch (1987), Bloom (1987), and Bennett (1984).
24. Whittington (1991).
25. Whittington (1991, p. 778).
26. Educational Testing Service (1991a, p. 33).
27. Solomon (1983), Graduate Management Admission Council (1993), and Hillhouse (1994).
28. Solomon (1983), Carr (1994).
29. Association of American Medical Colleges (1993), and Hackett (1994).
30. Flynn (1987).
31. Hunter (1986).
32. See Gould (1981) and Kamin (1981).
33. Binet (1913) as cited in Kamin (1981, p. 91).
34. Again, see Gould (1981) and Kamin (1981).
35. Cited in Kamin (1981, p. 94).
36. Herrnstein & Murray (1994).
37. Bloom (1964, p. 88).
38. Bloom (1964, p. 88).
39. Cahen & Cohen (1989).
40. Husén & Tuijnman (1991).
41. Husén & Tuijnman (1991, p. 22).
42. Ceci (1991).

43. National Commission on Children (1991).
44. Husén (1967).
45. See Jaeger (1992).
46. See Rotberg (1990).
47. Lapointe (1992) quoted in Bracey (1992, p. 108).
48. Bracey (1992, p. 8).
49. Crosswhite et al. (1986), Robitaille & Garden (1989), and Travers & Westbury (1989).
50. Westbury (1992).
51. National Commission on Children (1991).
52. See Coder et al. (1989, Table 2).
53. National Center for Education Statistics (1993a).
54. Cogan et al. (1988).
55. Elley (1992) cited in Bracey (1993, p. 108).
56. Bracey (1993, pp. 107–108).
57. Mayer, Tajika, & Stanley (1991).
58. National Center for Education Statistics (1993a).
59. See Kaplan (1992) cited in Bracey (1993, p. 108).

Chapter 3   **Other Myths About American Schools**

1. Rasell & Mishel (1990) provide details on statements from various officials in the U.S. government about alleged overspending on education.
2. Rasell & Mishel (1990).
3. Rasell & Mishel (1990).
4. Kozol (1991).
5. National Center for Education Statistics (1992).
6. Organisation for Economic Cooperation and Development (1992).
7. Verstegan (1992) reviews and summarizes various methods for estimating educational spending in different nations. Her conclusions

agree closely with those of the OECD report.
8. Bush (1989).
9. This remark was apparently greeted with considerable applause (see Rippa, 1988). Prior to World War II the NAM had long inveighed against spending for public education, regarding it as wasteful, unnecessary, and perhaps reducing the supply of cheap labor.
10. Coleman et al. (1966).
11. Coleman et al. (1966, p. 325).
12. Coleman (1990, p. 247).
13. Coleman (1972, pp. 146–167).
14. See, for example, Averch et al. (1972); Jencks et al. (1972); Meyer (1970, 1977); and Hanushek (1989).

15. Block (1983, p. 17).
16. See Bridge et al. (1979).
17. Hedges et al. (1994).
18. Hanushek (1989, p. 47).
19. A second recent study by Howard Wainer (1993) took on the old calumny that expenditures for education within each state are unrelated to levels of student achievement. This charge had been made (and refuted) on several previous occasions but was recently repeated in a *Wall Street Journal* article (Manno, 1993), citing the Heritage Foundation, which based its arguments on aggregate SAT scores. But, for reasons we discussed in Chapter 2, aggregate SAT scores are not meaningful, so Wainer decided to study the issue using NAEP test scores. He found, of course, a strong, positive relation between state expenditures for education and average NAEP scores.
20. Chubb & Moe (1990).
21. Chubb & Moe's findings about academic climate have recently been confirmed and extended by two new studies that involved large samples, longitudinal data, and extensive controls. Roger Shouse (1994) studied the effects of "academic press" and "school communality" and found both substantially related to student achievement, particularly among schools that served working- and lower-class students. Valerie Lee and Julia Smith (1994) examined the effects of "traditional" and "restructured" schools and found both student academic engagement and achievement gains greater in the latter.
22. Ferguson (1991).
23. Ferguson (1991, pp. 465–466).
24. See, for example, Manski (1987).
25. Card & Krueger (1992).
26. Card & Krueger (1992, pp. 36–37).
27. National Center for Education Statistics (1993c).
28. National Center for Education Statistics (1992).
29. Robinson & Brandon (1992, p. 14).
30. Robinson & Brandon (1992, p. 14).
31. Bureau of Labor Statistics (1991).
32. Robinson & Brandon (1992, p. 16).
33. Robinson & Brandon (1992, p. 17).
34. Robinson & Brandon (1992, p. 10).
35. Rothstein (1993).
36. Again see Rothstein (1993).
37. Robinson & Brandon (1992, p. 12).
38. Our title is not original, see the Louisiana Coalition for Tax Justice (1993).
39. Again see the Louisiana Coalition for Tax Justice (1993). This resource guide provides a model for other states which might like to document corporate giveaways that have reduced the tax base for school funding. The additional data we cite for Louisiana come from this source.
40. Reich (1991a, p. B1).
41. Jonathan Kozol (1991) provides a truly moving account of the predicament of East St. Louis.
42. In this booklet, apparently given to all Motorola employees and associates, Mr. Tooker failed to mention that many of the 4,000 American daily "drop-outs" eventually return to school for their GEDs, and that our high school completion rate is now higher than that of all other countries except Sweden and Japan. His booklet also went on to repeat many other myths and fictions of the Manufactured Crisis.
43. Kotkin (1991).
44. Commission on the Skills of the American Workforce (1990).
45. Reported in Rothstein (1993).
46. Readers are reminded that *The Sandia Report* was a major review of evidence concerning American school performance that was originally prepared in 1990 by officials of the Sandia National

Laboratories, a branch of the Department of Energy (see Carson, Huelskamp, & Woodall, 1991; and Sandia National Laboratories, 1993). This important document produced findings that contradicted many of the claims about education that were then being made by the Bush administration, so the report was suppressed until George Bush was no longer in office. Chapter 4 tells this sad story in greater detail.

47. Kearns & Doyle (1988).
48. Ray & Mickelson (1993).
49. Ray & Mickelson (1993, p. 7).
50. Kilborn (1993).
51. Berry (1993).
52. McKinsey Global Institute (1992).
53. *Newsweek* (1992, pp. 40–43).
54. *Newsweek* (1992, p. 42).
55. Berry (1993).
56. National Commission on Excellence in Education (1983, p. 9).
57. Gordon (1990). See also Levitan & Gallo (1991).
58. Carson, Huelskamp, & Woodall (1991) and Sandia National Laboratories (1993).
59. Carson, Huelskamp, & Woodall (1991) and Sandia National Laboratories (1993).
60. National Center for Education Statistics (1993c, Tables 255, 258, & 261; pp. 275, 278, & 281).
61. National Center for Education Statistics (1993c, Table 253, p. 273).
62. See *The Sandia Report* (Carson, Huelskamp, & Woodall, 1991; Sandia National Laboratories, 1993).
63. Again, see *The Sandia Report* (Carson, Huelskamp, & Woodall, 1991; Sandia National Laboratories, 1993).
64. Zachary (1993).
65. Carson, Huelskamp, & Woodall (1991) and Sandia National Laboratories (1993).
66. Broad (1992).
67. Mishel & Teixeira (1991).
68. Reich (1991b).

69. Reported by Rothstein (1993).
70. This fact was brought to our attention by Dennis W. Redovich (no date) who has written numerous newspaper articles showing the folly of many of the critics of public schooling.
71. Fiske (1989).
72. *The Economist* (1994, pp. 19–20, 26).
73. Marshall & Tucker (1992).
74. Rothstein (1993).
75. National Center for Education Statistics (1993c, Table 128 and Table 130, pp. 128 and 129).
76. Carson, Huelskamp, & Woodall (1991) and Sandia National Laboratories (1993).
77. Kerr (1983, p. 146).
78. Lanier (1986, pp. 527–569).
79. Darling-Hammond (1990a, p. 272).
80. See Evertson et al. (1985) or Roth & Pipho (1990). Note also that the SAT was not designed to do much more than predict freshman grades in college. Most assuredly, it should not be used to predict success on the job!
81. National Education Association (1992).
82. Kerr (1983).
83. Darling-Hammond (1990a).
84. Darling-Hammond (1990a). Darling-Hammond does not indicate that entry requirements have risen recently, but informal discussion with colleagues around the country suggests this is the case. On each of our two campuses *admission* to the College of Education requires a higher grade-point-average than does *completion* of a degree in the College of Arts and Sciences.
85. The results of the Harvard medical practice study were reported by Dye (1994).
86. Wolfe (1993).
87. See Baker (1979); Vitz (1986); & Nelsen (1987). Nelsen asserts that

today's textbooks have become so devoid of moral content that they are nearly useless!
88. Sharp & Wood (1992).
89. Sharp & Wood (1992, p. 147).
90. Sharp & Wood (1992, p. 151).
91. Sharp & Wood (1992, p. 153).
92. This quote from Mrs. Gabler is reported by Parker (1981).
93. Davis & Smith (1990).
94. See Kaplan (1992).
95. Elam, Rose, & Gallup (1993).
96. Bracey (1993).
97. Finn (1991).
98. Stevenson (1992).
99. Morgan (1981).
100. Coleman, Hoffer, & Kilgore (1981).
101. Coleman, Hoffer, & Kilgore (1982).
102. See, for example, Haertel, James, & Levin (1987).
103. See Coleman, Hoffer, & Kilgore (1982, p. 141).
104. Alexander (1987).
105. The original report was by Hoffer, Greeley, & Coleman (1985). The

critiques were by Alexander & Pallas (1987) and Willms (1987).
106. Willms (1987, p. 117).
107. Alexander & Pallas (1987, p. 108).
108. Willms (1987, p. 130).
109. Chubb & Moe (1990).
110. Chubb & Moe (1990, p. 67).
111. Glass (1993).
112. National Center for Education Statistics (1991b).
113. Shanker & Rosenberg (1992).
114. Shanker & Rosenberg (1992, pp. 128–145).
115. Quoted by Goldberg (1988, p. 1).
116. See, for example, Bryk, Lee, & Holland (1993).
117. Lewis & Wanner (1979).
118. Falsey & Heyns (1984); Hammack & Cookson (1980).
119. Alexander & Eckland (1977); Cookson (1981).
120. Farnum (1990, pp. 75–103).
121. See Armstrong (1990, pp. 3–24); Persell & Cookson (1990, pp. 25–52); Karen (1985); Kiltgaard (1985); and Persell (1977).

Chapter 4   **Why Now?**

1. Cremin (1990, pp. 10–11).
2. Recent right-wing political activities in America are discussed, for example, in Crawford (1980); Diamond (1989); and Bellant (1991).
3. Quoted in Pincus (1984, pp. 152–153).
4. Friedman (1962, p. 89).
5. Campbell (1994).
6. See Bell (1988).
7. Diamond (1989, p. 85).
8. Thoburn (1986, pp. 152–153).
9. Thoburn (1986, p. 159).
10. Again, as quoted in Pincus (1984, p. 155).
11. Pincus (1984, p. 56).
12. National Commission on Excellence in Education (1983, p. 5).
13. See Bell (1988, Chapter 10).
14. Adler (1982); Boyer (1983); Goodlad (1983); Task Force of the Business-Higher Education Forum (1983); Task Force on Education for Economic Growth (1983); Twentieth Century Fund Task Force on Federal Elementary and Secondary Education Policy (1983); Martin (1984); Sizer (1984); Committee for Economic Development (1985).
15. We distinguish here between these early critical reports and a second group of reform proposals that appeared toward the end of the 1980s including *A Nation Prepared: Teachers for the 21st Century* (Carnegie Forum on Education and the Economy,

1986); *Tomorrow's Teachers* (The Holmes Group, 1986); and *Time for Results* (National Governors' Association, 1986). By comparison, the latter were less critical and focused more on the teaching profession. We discuss their recommendations in Chapter 7.

16. See Spring (1985); or Martin (1984).

17. See, for example, Thurow (1982); Reich (1983); Committee for Economic Development (1983, 1984).

18. Shea (1989, p. 5).

19. See, for example, National Academy of Sciences (1983, 1984); National Science Board Commission on Precollegiate Education in Mathematics, Science, and Technology (1983); College Entrance Examination Board (1983); Lund & Hansen (1986); Servan-Schreiber & Crecine (1985).

20. See Schultz (1960); Denison (1962); Friedman (1962); Becker (1964); or Blaug (1970).

21. See Shaiken (1984); or Draper (1985).

22. Shaiken (1984, p. 157) and Draper (1985).

23. Timpane (1984).

24. Shapiro (1991).

25. Carson, Huelskamp, & Woodall (1991, p. 172).

26. See Cremin & Weiss (1952).

27. D'Aimée (1900, p. 263).

28. Orth (1909).

29. Lynch (1912, p. 5).

30. *Time Magazine* (1949).

31. Kent (1987, p. 142).

32. Bestor (1953); Lynd (1953); Rickover (1959).

33. Rickover (1959, p. 101).

34. Copperman (1978); Bloom (1987).

35. This apparent truism has often been confirmed by research—see Harvey & Weary (1984) or Ross & Fletcher (1985) for reviews.

36. Jellison & Green (1981).

37. Tetlock (1980).

38. Kozol (1992).

39. Pound & Stout (1991).

40. See de Tocqueville (1835); Huber & Form (1973); or Bellah et al. (1986).

41. Reich (1987, pp. 9–10).

42. Kluegel & Smith (1986).

43. Kluegel & Smith (1986, p. 91).

44. Fry & Ghosh (1980).

45. See Miller (1984); or Smith & Whitehead (1984).

46. Feagin (1972); Feather (1974).

47. Biddle & Marlin (submitted).

48. Colson & Eckerd (1991, p. 21).

49. Recent examples of the ritual citing of false evidentiary claims about education may be found in Colson & Eckerd (1991, Chapter 6) and Bennett (1992).

50. Carson, Huelskamp, & Woodall (1991, p. 172).

51. Chubb & Moe (1990).

52. Office of Educational Research and Improvement (1993, p. 1).

53. See Kaul (1993).

54. Coleman et al. (1966); Coleman, Hoffer, & Kilgore (1982).

55. For an account, see Herman (1990).

56. U.S. Department of Education (1986).

57. pp. iv–v.

58. p. 2.

59. p. 2.

60. See Glass (1987, p. 7).

61. Glass (1987, p. 8).

62. Carson et al. (1991); Sandia National Laboratories (1993).

63. Tanner (1993).

64. Huelskamp (1993, p. 719).

65. Tanner (1993, p. 292).

66. Zachary (1993).

67. Spielberger (in Penner et al., 1993, p. xi).

68. See Weiss & Singer (1988).

69. O'Neill (1994, p. 46).

70. National Council for Research on Women (1993).

71. See, for example, Bloom (1987); Sykes (1988); Kimball (1990); and D'Souza (1991).

72. National Council for Research on Women (1993, p. 9).

73. See El-Khawas (1991).

74. See, for example, Kaplan (1992).

Chapter 5 **Poor Ideas for Reform**

1. Friedman (1962).
2. See Catterall (1984).
3. Dougherty & Sostre (1992, p. 28).
4. See Pipho (1991).
5. See Cookson (1992); Raywid (1987); or Witte (1991).
6. See Levin (1988).
7. Blinder (1987).
8. Bernstein (1994).
9. Bernstein (1994, p. 79).
10. Wells & Biegel (1993, p. 229).
11. Cooley (1991).
12. Cooley (1991, pp. 5–6). Note: stress added.
13. See Moore & Davenport (1990).
14. Anderson (1992b).
15. Anderson (1991a).
16. Anderson (1992a).
17. Anderson (1992a, p. 8).
18. Fowler (1992, p. 433).
19. Fowler (1992, p. 441).
20. See Kirst (1988); Toch (1991); and Koppich & Guthrie (1993).
21. Angus & Mirel (1993) document the decline in numbers of students taking core academic courses.
22. Policy Information Center (1994).
23. Toch (1991, p. 102).
24. Toch (1991, Chapter 4).
25. National Commission on Excellence in Education (1983).
26. National Commission on Excellence in Education (1984).
27. Recent evidence suggests that the relation between teacher time-on-task and student learning is not as simple as was once thought (see Karweit, 1984), although the proper management of time in schools probably matters a good deal (see Berliner, 1990).
28. See Berger (1990); Norris (1990).
29. Wiley & Harnischfeger (1974); Karweit (1976).
30. Dahllöf (1971); Lundgren (1977).
31. See Barr & Dreeben (1983) or Dreeben (1987).
32. Further discussion of these issues may be found in Berliner (1987, 1990).
33. Cooper (1989).
34. Astuto et al. (1993, p. 66).
35. See Slavin (1983); Deci & Ryan (1985); or Cohen (1986).
36. Bruner (1962); Rogers (1969); Deci & Ryan (1985, p. 259).
37. Grolnick & Ryan (1985).
38. Benware & Deci (1984). Other studies confirming the negative effects of extrinsic motivation on intrinsic motivations among students are summarized by Deci & Ryan (1985, Chapter 9).
39. Deci & Ryan (1982); Deci et al. (1982); Smith (1991).
40. Darling-Hammond (1990b, p. 287).
41. National Council on Education Standards and Testing (1992).
42. Darling-Hammond (1990b, p. 287).
43. A good summary of major problems generated by national accountability systems appeared in testimony given by Daniel Koretz, George Madaus, Edward Haertel, and Albert Beaton before the Subcommittee on Elementary, Secondary, and Vocational Education, of the Committee on Education and Labor, U.S. House of Representatives, on February 19, 1992 (Koretz et al., 1992).
44. Gillman & Reynolds (1991); Smith (1991).
45. Smith (1991); Suárez & Gottovi (1992).
46. Gillman & Reynolds (1991); Suárez & Gottovi (1992); Wirth (1992).
47. Gilles et al. (1994, p. 1).
48. Madaus (1989, p. 644).
49. Wirth (1992, p. 79); National Commission on Testing and Public Policy (1990, p. 19).
50. See, particularly, Cannell (1987); and National Commission on Testing and Public Policy (1990).

51. Suárez & Gottovi (1992).
52. Wirth (1992, p. 81). See also Astuto et al. (1993) and Haney (1993).
53. A good discussion of this problem may be found in Cohen & Cohen (1983, pp. 413–422).
54. Expanded accounts of the history of bilingual education may be found in Casanova & Arias (1993) and Crawford (1992).
55. Crawford (1992).
56. Quoted in Crawford (1992, p. 151).
57. Crawford (1992).
58. United States General Accounting Office (1987, p. 47).
59. United States General Accounting Office (1987, p. 51).
60. United States General Accounting Office (1987, p. 44).
61. The shoddy report was by Baker and de Kanter (1983). For representative criticisms of this report consult Willig (1985) or Hakuta (1986).
62. United States General Accounting Office (1987, p. 4).
63. See, for example, Arias & Casanova (1993), Hakuta (1986), or Willig (1985). A major recent report on different models for bilingual education and immersion appears in Ramírez et al. (1991).
64. A good example of research confirming this result appears in Quinn & Kessler (1986). These authors showed that working-class, barrio, Hispanic children in bilingual programs outperformed upper-class, white children enrolled in monolingual programs in private schools, on a set of science tasks. Reviews of this literature may be found in Hakuta (1986) and Díaz (1990).
65. Fuentes (1989).
66. Wirth (1992, p. 82). A report of this event and its aftermath may be found in *From Gatekeeper to Gateway: Transforming Testing in America* (National Commission on Testing and Public Policy, 1990, pp. 9–10).
67. This effect has been reported in several studies, see for example Pegnato & Birch (1959).
68. Sapon-Shevin (1994) provides a persuasive discussion of this effect.
69. Silverman (1980).
70. See Siegler & Kotovsky (1986).
71. An example of this argument may be found in *Forbes Magazine*, see Brimclow (1994).
72. See Johnson (1994).
73. Office of Educational Research and Improvement (1993).

Chapter 6   **Real Problems of American Education**

1. Coder et al. (1989); also see Smeeding et al. (1990).
2. National Commission on Children (1991, p. 24); also see Bureau of the Census (1988).
3. Kozol (1991); also see Ellwood (1988).
4. National Commission on Children (1991, p. 182).
5. Phillips (1990).
6. Phillips (1990, p. 241); Hinds (1990).
7. Barlett & Steele (1994, pp. 17–18).
8. p. 46.
9. National Commission on Children (1991, p. 24).
10. Peterson (1993, Figure 2.7).
11. Thurow (1989). As we noted in Chapter 3, various methods have been proposed for comparing standards of living among nations,

none of them totally satisfactory. No recent study that we know of has placed the United States first, however, and it seems likely that our ranking would have fallen even further had researchers thought to factor in costs unique to our country such as our astounding medical care bills.

12. Caplan et al. (1992).
13. *The Economist* (1991).
14. Shulman (1990).
15. Meier et al. (1989).
16. Meier et al. (1989, p. 5).
17. Meier et al. (1989).
18. See, for example, results reported by Yinon Cohen & Andrea Tyree (1986).
19. Louis Harris and Associates (1993).
20. Robinson & Protheroe (1987).
21. See Porat (1977).
22. See Futrelle (1993) for a brief but effective summary of the problem.
23. See Aronowitz & DiFazio (1994).
24. Barr & Dreeben (1983).
25. Dreeben (1987, pp. 31–32).
26. See Hembree (1990).
27. Smith & Geoffrey (1968).
28. See, for example, work summarized by Elizabeth Cohen (1994).
29. Coleman (1990, p. 241).
30. Oakes (1989, pp. 176–177). Also see Oakes et al. (1992).
31. Oakes (1989, p. 178).
32. See Rosenbaum (1980a, b) for examples.
33. National Education Association (1992).
34. Norton (1980).
35. Elsbree (1939).
36. Spring (1986, p. 121).
37. See, for example, the review by Bank et al. (1980).
38. Carnegie Forum on Education and the Economy (1986, p. 98).
39. Spring (1986, p. 133).
40. DeYoung & Wynn (1972).
41. Callahan (1962, p. 247).

42. Altenbaugh (1989, pp. 170–171).
43. See Tyack (1974) or Spring (1986).
44. Taylor (1911).
45. National Center for Education Statistics (1989).
46. Spring (1986).
47. Bureau of the Census (1989a).
48. Cohen & Spillane (1992, p. 6).
49. Travers & Westbury (1989).
50. See Troen (1975).
51. Dewey (1902); Ross (1906); Ward (1913); and Curtis (1917).
52. Cremin (1961).
53. Goslin (1965, p. 4).
54. Tyack (1974).
55. Ferguson (1991, p. 492).
56. Kozol (1991, p. 237).
57. Educational Testing Service (1991b).
58. National Center for Education Statistics (1991).
59. Educational Testing Service (1991b, pp. 15–19).
60. Quoted in Kozol (1991, p. 89).
61. See Livingstone (1983, Chapter 1).
62. Organisation for Economic Co-operation and Development (1990).
63. Rasell & Mishel (1990).
64. National Center for Education Statistics (1991).
65. Applebee et al. (1988); Grissmer et al. (1994); Stedman et al. (1988).
66. Bureau of the Census (1989b).
67. See, for example, Milne et al. (1986) or Shinn (1978).
68. Grissmer et al. (1994) report that once controls are entered for poverty and other factors that truly affect achievement scores, one finds that students from broken homes do just about as well as those from two-parent homes.
69. Bureau of the Census (1988).
70. Applebee et al. (1988); Beaton (1986); Dossey et al. (1988).
71. Natriello, McDill & Pallas (1990, pp. 37–38).
72. Natriello et al. (1990).

Chapter 7   **Toward the Improvement of Education**

1. The federal government, in the Department of Education, has long promoted a National Diffusion Network (NDN), featuring many of these kinds of programs. A panel of knowledgeable people (the Joint Dissemination Review Panel—JDRP) have deemed a large number of programs worthy of dissemination. Anyone interested in school improvement should look over the NDN catalog of reasonably well-documented ideas for the improvement of education. The Regional Educational Laboratories, scattered throughout the nation, also have information on programs that have promise. They can usually provide information about sites where such programs are in operation.
2. Kozol (1991).
3. Bluestone & Harrison (1982).
4. See, for example, Thomas and Znaniecki (1918) who documented the cultural disintegration of the Polish immigrant families in America. The difficulties of the Puerto Rican immigration experience are described by Lewis (1966).
5. Steinberg (1989).
6. Drazen (1994).
7. See Biddle et al. (1981).
8. West (1993, pp. x–xi).
9. West (1993, p. 15).
10. Malcolm X (1973).
11. Gugliotta (1993).
12. Hinds (1993).
13. Ventures in Education (1992).
14. Zigler (1989); Zigler & Lang (1991); Comer (1988).
15. Comer (1988).
16. Holtzman (1992).
17. Natriello et al. (1990) provide a good review of the efforts of schools that serve at-risk students.
18. National Center for Education Statistics (1994).
19. Callahan (1962).
20. Conant (1959).
21. Barker & Gump (1964).
22. See Lee & Smith (1994).
23. Gregory & Smith (1987).
24. Finn (1989).
25. Hirsch (1987).
26. See, for example, Hirsch (1991) and Hirsch et al. (1993).
27. National Council on Education Standards and Testing (1992).
28. Adapted from Levin (1993) and Levin, Rumberger, & Finnan (1990).
29. Project 2061 (1989).
30. Project 2061 (1993).
31. National Council for the Social Studies (1994, p. 16).
32. National Council for the Social Studies (1993).
33. National Council of Teachers of Mathematics (1989).
34. Putnam, Lampert, & Peterson (1990, p. 138).
35. Presidential Task Force on Psychology in Education, American Psychological Association (1993).
36. See Driver et al. (1994).
37. See Cobb (1994).
38. Greeno (1994).
39. This discussion draws heavily from the chapter by Onosko & Newmann (1994) summarizing work in this field, particularly their own.
40. Onosko & Newmann (1994).
41. Onosko & Newmann (1994, p. 35).
42. See Levin (1988) for a description of the comprehensive restructuring needed to put into effect an accelerated school program. See McCarthy & Still (1993) for a successful case study of an accelerated school.
43. See, for example, Aaronson et al. (1978); Cohen (1982); Johnson & Johnson (1978); and Slavin (1983).
44. Cohen (1994b); Johnson & Johnson (1989); Slavin (1990).

45. Cohen (1994a); Educational Research Service (1990); Slavin (1990).
46. See Sapon-Shevin (1994, pp. 221ff).
47. Levin, Glass, & Meister (1984).
48. Blumenfeld et al. (1991).
49. Gardner (1963, pp. 21–22).
50. Newman (1988).
51. Newman (1988, p. 94).
52. Newman (1988, p. 240).
53. A good discussion of the way American industry has traditionally dealt with leisure may be found in Juliet Schor's *The Overworked American* (1991).
54. Smith (1991).
55. Wiggins (1989, p. 705).
56. Airasian (1991); Shepard & Bliem (1994).
57. Stiggins et al. (1985).
58. Good & Weinstein (1986); Good (1987); Haskins et al. (1983); Oakes (1985); Oakes et al. (1992); Peterson et al. (1984); Talbot (1990).
59. Useem (1992, p. 325).
60. See ASCD (1990). Mara Sapon-Shevin (1994, pp. 219ff) provides additional examples of responses to the threat of doing away with ability groups.
61. Oakes (1985, 1992, 1994); Wheelock (1992); Sapon-Shevin (1994).
62. Carroll (1963); Carroll (1985).
63. Holmes & Mathews (1984); Smith & Shepard (1988); Shepard & Smith (1989).
64. Oakes (1992); Wheelock (1992).
65. See Lareau (1989) and Epstein (1987).
66. Richardson et al. (1989).
67. Lareau (1989).
68. R. Clark (1983).
69. R. Clark (1983), Goldenberg (1985).
70. See Fruchter et al. (1993).
71. Moll & Greenberg (1990); Vélez-Ibáñez & Greenberg (1989).
72. This argument is made by Raywid (1989) and Nathan (1991). See also Harrington & Cookson (1992).
73. Driscoll (1993).
74. See particularly Cookson (1994, pp. 87ff).
75. Freedman (1993).
76. Heath (1994); Heath & McLoughlin (1994).
77. Holtzman (1992).
78. Popkewitz et al. (1982) provide an example and an analysis of why top-down reforms fail.
79. Giroux (1988, p. 9).
80. Good discussions of this principle may be found in various places, see, for example, Blase & Kirby (1992); Firestone & Bader (1992); and Romanish (1991).
81. Hollingsworth & Sockett (1994).
82. Little (1982).
83. Wasley (1991).
84. See Fantini (1986, Chapter 8).
85. Note particularly a (1985) speech by Albert Shanker, President of the American Federation of Teachers, before the National Press Club.
86. Schneider & Hood (1994).
87. Ashenden (1990, p. 11).
88. See, for example, Lane & Epps (1992).
89. Astuto & D. Clark (1992).
90. Sarason (1990, p. 7).
91. Astuto & D. Clark (1992, p. 99).
92. LeCompte & Dworkin (1991).

Chapter 8   **Fundamentals of School Improvement: Research and Compassion**

1. See, for example, Astuto et al. (1993), Cohen & Garet (1975), Cuban (1990), or Glickman (1993).
2. Biddle & Anderson (1991, p. 3).
3. Anderson & Biddle (1991) discuss this issue and provide a useful collection of articles concerned with the topic.

4. Misconceptions about social research are discussed by Biddle (1987).

5. See, for example, the hostile attack by then Assistant Secretary of Education Chester Finn (1988).

6. National Center for Education Statistics (1994).

7. Shavelson & Berliner (1988, p. 12).

8. Indeed, in November of 1990 the Bush administration's Office of Education assembled a conference of researchers who were asked to explain how the supposed "failures" of America's schools could be linked to the "inadequacies" of America's students and parents. This request was resisted by the more thoughtful people who attended the conference.

9. At one point the critics attempted to have ketchup declared a "vegetable" to reduce pressure for federal nutrition programs for poor students.

References

♦

Aaronson, Elliot, Blaney, Nancy, Stephan, Cookie, Sikes, Jev, & Snapp, Matthew (1978). *The jigsaw classroom.* Beverly Hills, CA: Sage.

Adams, John (1770). Argument in defense of the [British] soldiers in the Boston Massacre Trials. December.

Adams, John (1780). Letter to Abigail Adams, May 12.

Adler, Mortimore J. (1982). *The Paideia proposal.* New York: Macmillan.

Airasian, Peter W. (1991). *Classroom assessment.* New York: McGraw-Hill.

Alexander, Karl L. (1987). Cross-sectional comparisons of public and private school effectiveness: A review of evidence and issues. In Edward H. Haertel, Thomas James, & Henry M. Levin (Eds.), *Comparing public & private schools: Vol. 2. School achievement* (pp. 33–65). London: Falmer Press.

Alexander, Karl L. & Eckland, Bruce K. (1977). High school context and college selectivity: Institutional constraints in educational stratification. *Social Forces, 56,* 166–188.

Alexander, Karl L. & Pallas, Aaron M. (1987). School sector and cognitive performance: When is a little a little? In Edward H. Haertel, Thomas James, & Henry M. Levin (Eds.), *Comparing public & private schools: Vol. 2. School achievement* (pp. 89–111). London: Falmer Press.

Altenbaugh, Richard J. (1989). Teachers, their world, and their work: A review of the idea of "professional excellence" in school reform reports. In Christine M. Shea, Ernest Kahane, & Peter Sola (Eds.), *The new servants of power: A critique of the 1980s school reform movement* (pp. 167–175). New York: Praeger.

Anderson, Don S. (1991a). *Participation in public and private schools: Statistical local areas in major metropolitan regions, 1976 and 1986* (Resource document prepared for the Department of Employment, Education, and Training). Canberra: Australian National University, RSSS.

Anderson, Don S. (1991b). Is the privatisation of Australian schooling inevitable? In F. G. Castles (Ed.), *Australia compared: People, policies and politics* (pp. 140–167). Sydney: Allen & Unwin.

Anderson, Don S. (1992a). *The effect of private schools on the composition of higher education.* Seminar paper. Canberra: Australian National University, RSSS.

Anderson, Don S. (1992b). The interaction of public and private school systems. *Australian Journal of Education, 36,* 213–236.

Anderson, Don S. & Biddle, Bruce J. (1991). *Knowledge for policy: Improving education through research.* London: Falmer Press.

Angus, David & Mirel, Jeffrey (1993). High school course-taking and educational reform. *Education Week* (November 17), pp. 44, 36.

Applebee, Arthur N., Langer, Judith A., & Mullis, Ina V. S. (1988). *Who reads best? Factors related to reading achievement in Grades 3, 7, and 11.* Princeton, NJ: Educational Testing Service.

Arias, M. Beatriz & Casanova, Ursula (Eds.) (1993). *Bilingual education: Politics, practice, and research. Ninety-second yearbook of the National Society for the Study of Education, Part 2.* Chicago: University of Chicago Press.

Arizona Republic (1993). Immigrants' children choose English by big margin, study says (July 8), p. A3.

Armstrong, Christopher F. (1990). On the making of good men: Character-building in the New England boarding schools. In Paul William Kingston & Lionel S. Lewis (Eds.), *The high-status track: Studies of elite schools and stratification* (pp. 3–24). Albany: State University of New York Press.

Aronowitz, Stanley & DiFazio, William (1994). *The jobless future: sci-tech and the dogma of work.* Minneapolis, MN: University of Minnesota Press.

Ashenden, Dean (1990). *Professionalism of teaching in the next decade: A report of discussions by U.S. and Australian educators.* Wollongong, NSW, Australia: USA/Australia Education Policy Project.

Association of American Medical Colleges (1993). *Facts: Applicants, matriculants and graduates: 1987–1993.* Washington, DC: Author.

Association for Supervision and Curriculum Development (1990). Issue: Perspectives of Linda Silverman, Wilma Lund, John Feldhausen, and James Gallagher. *ASCD Curriculum Update* (October), p. 10.

Astin, Alexander W. (1993). College retention rates are often misleading. *The Chronicle of Higher Education, 40*(5), p. A48.

Astuto, Terry & Clark, David (1992). Challenging the limits of school restructuring and reform. In Ann Lieberman (Ed.), *The changing contexts of teaching. Ninety-first yearbook of the National Society for the Study of Education, Part 1* (pp. 90–109). Chicago: University of Chicago Press.

Astuto, Terry A., Clark, David L., Read, Anne-Marie, McGree, Kathleen, & Fernandez, deKoven Pelton (1993). *Challenges to dominant assumptions controlling educational reform.* Andover, MA: Regional Laboratory for Educational Improvement of the Northeast and Islands.

Averch, Harvey A., Carroll, Steven J., Donaldson, Theodore S., Kiesling, Herbert J., & Pincus, John (1972). *How effective is schooling? A critical review and synthesis of research findings.* Santa Monica, CA: The RAND Corporation.

Baker, Albert Aaron (1979). *The successful Christian school: Foundational principles for starting and operating a successful Christian school.* Pensacola, FL: A. Beka Book Publishers.

Baker, Keith A. & de Kanter, Adriana A. (1983). *Bilingual education: A reappraisal of federal policy.* Lexington, MA: D. C. Heath.

Bank, Barbara J., Biddle, Bruce J., & Good, Thomas L. (1980). Sex roles, classroom instruction, and reading achievement. *Journal of Educational Psychology, 72,* 119–132.

Barber, Benjamin R. (1993). A nation of dunces. *This World* (a supplement to the *San Francisco Chronicle, December 12)*, pp. 7, 10–12.

Barker, Roger G. & Gump, Paul V. (1964). *Big school–small school: High school size and student behavior.* Palo Alto, CA: Stanford University Press.

Barlett, Donald L. & Steele, James B. (1994). *America: Who really pays the taxes?* New York: Touchstone.

Barr, Rebecca & Dreeben, Robert (1983). *How schools work.* Chicago: University of Chicago Press.

Beaton, Albert E. (1986). *National assessment of educational progress 1983–84: A technical report.* Princeton, NJ: Educational Testing Service.

Becker, Gary (1964). *Human capital: A theoretical and empirical analysis with special reference to education.* New York: Columbia University Press.

Bell, Terrel (1988). *The thirteenth man: A Reagan cabinet memoir.* New York: The Free Press.

Bellah, Robert N., Madsen, Richard, Sullivan, William M., Swidler, Ann, & Tipton, Steven (1986). *Habits of the heart: Individualism and commitment in American life.* Berkeley: University of California Press.

Bellant, Russ (1991). *The Coors connection.* Boston: South End Press.

Bennett de Marrais, Kathleen P. & LeCompte, Margaret D. (1995). *The way schools work: A sociological analysis of education* (2nd ed.). New York: Longman.

Bennett, William L. (1984). *To reclaim a legacy: A report on humanities in higher education.* Washington, DC: National Endowment for the Humanities.

Bennett, William L. (1992). *The devaluing of America: The fight for our culture and our children.* New York: Summit Books.

Benware, Carl A. & Deci, Edward L. (1984). Quality of learning with an active versus passive motivational set. *American Educational Research Journal, 21,* 755–765.

Berger, Joseph (1990). Choosing $90 million in school cuts: Layoffs or attrition, it's class chaos. *New York Times* (November 21), p. B3.

Berliner, David C. (1987). Simple views of effective teaching and a simple theory of classroom instruction. In David C. Berliner & Barak Rosenshine (Eds.), *Talks to teachers* (pp. 93–110). New York: Random House.

Berliner, David C. (1990). What's all the fuss about instructional time? In Miriam Ben-Peretz & Rainer Brommer (Eds.), *The nature of time in school* (pp. 3–35). New York: Teachers College Press.

Berliner, Emanuel (1953). Personal communication.

Bernstein, Aaron (1994). Inequality: How the gap between the rich and the poor hurts the economy. *Business Week* (August 15), 78–83.

Berry, John M. (1993). Productivity growth at 20-year high in '92. *Washington Post* (February 5), p. F1.

Bestor, Arthur (1953). *Educational wastelands: The retreat from learning in our public schools.* Urbana, IL: University of Illinois Press.

Biddle, Bruce J. (1987). Social research and social policy: The theoretical connection. *The American Sociologist, 18,* 158–166.

Biddle, Bruce J. & Anderson, Don S. (1991). Social research and educational change. In Don S. Anderson & Bruce J. Biddle (Eds.), *Knowledge for policy: Improving education through research* (pp. 1–20). London: Falmer Press.

Biddle, Bruce J., Bank, Barbara J., Anderson, Don S., Keats, John A., & Keats, Daphne M. (1981). The structure of idleness: In-school and dropout adolescent activities in the United States and Australia. *Sociology of Education, 54,* 106–119.

Biddle, Bruce J. & Marlin, Marjorie M. (submitted). Self and other, topic, and the fundamental attribution error in Australia and America.

Binet, Alfred (1913). *Les idées modernes sur les enfants.* Paris: Flammarion.

Blase, Joseph & Kirby, Peggy C. (1992). *Bringing out the best in teachers: What effective principals do.* Newbury Park, CA: Corwin Press.

Blaug, Mark (1970). *An introduction to the economics of education.* London: Allen Lane.

Blinder, Alan (1987). *Hard heads, soft hearts: Tough-minded economics for a just society.* Reading, MA: Addison-Wesley.

Block, Alan (1983). *Effective schools: A summary of research.* Arlington, VA: Educational Research Service.

Bloom, Allan (1987). *The closing of the American mind: How higher education has failed democracy and impoverished the souls of today's students.* New York: Simon and Schuster.

Bloom, Benjamin (1964). *Stability and change in human characteristics.* New York: Wiley.

Bluestone, Barry & Harrison, Bennett (1982). *The deindustrialization of America.* New York: Basic Books.

Blumenfeld, Phyllis C., Soloway, Elliot, Marx, Ronald W., Krajck, Joseph S., Guzdial, Mark, & Palincsar, Annmarie (1991). Motivating project-based learning: Sustaining the doing, supporting the learning. *Educational Psychologist, 26*(3 & 4), 369–398.

Bok, Derek (1993). It's time to trim hefty paychecks. *New York Times* (December 5), p. F13.

Boyer, Ernest (1983). *High school: A report on secondary education in America.* Princeton, NJ: Carnegie Foundation for the Advancement of Teaching.

Bracey, Gerald W. (1991). Why can't they be like we were? *Phi Delta Kappan* (October), 104–117.

Bracey, Gerald W. (1992). The second Bracey report on the condition of public education. *Phi Delta Kappan* (October), 104–117.

Bracey, Gerald W. (1993). The third Bracey report on the condition of public education. *Phi Delta Kappan* (October), 104–117.

Bridge, R. Gary, Judd, Charles M., & Moock, Peter R. (1979). *The determinants of educational outcomes: The impact of families, peers, teachers, and schools.* Cambridge, MA: Ballinger.

Brimelow, Peter (1994). Disadvantaging the advantaged. *Forbes* (November 21), 52–57.

Broad, William J. (1992). Ridden with debt, U.S. companies cut funds for research. *New York Times* (June 30), pp. C1, C9.

Browne, Malcolm W. (1992). Amid "shortage," young physicists see few jobs. *New York Times* (March 10), pp. C1, C7.

Bruner, Jerome S. (1962). *On knowing: Essays for the left hand.* Cambridge, MA: Harvard University Press.

Bryk, Anthony S., Lee, Valerie E., & Holland, Peter B. (1993). *Catholic schools and the common good.* Cambridge, MA: Harvard University Press.

Bureau of the Census (various years). *Current population reports, Series P-20, Educational attainment in the United States.* Washington, DC: U.S. Government Printing Office.

Bureau of the Census (various years). *Statistical abstracts of the United States.* Washington, DC: U.S. Government Printing Office.

Bureau of the Census (1960). *1960 census of the population: Vol. 1, Part 1.* Washington, DC: U.S. Government Printing Office.

Bureau of the Census (1988). *Money income and poverty status in the United States: 1987 (Advance data from the March 1988 Current Population Survey).* Washington, DC: U.S. Government Printing Office.

Bureau of the Census (1989a). *Marital status and living arrangements: March 1988.* Washington, DC: U.S. Government Printing Office.

Bureau of the Census (1989b). *Projections of the population of the United States by age, sex, and race: 1988–2080.* Washington, DC: U.S. Government Printing Office.

Bureau of Labor Statistics (1985). *National survey of professional, administrative, and clerical pay, March, 1985.* Washington, DC: U.S. Government Printing Office.

Bureau of Labor Statistics (1991). *Employed persons by detailed industry and major occupations.* Unpublished data for year ending December, 1991.

Burroughs, John (1900). The modern skeptic. In *The light of day.* New York: Houghton-Mifflin.

Bush, George Herbert Walker (1989). White House transcript, Speech at the education summit. University of Virginia, September 28, 1989.

Cahen, Sorel & Cohen, Nora (1989). Age versus schooling effects on intelligence development. *Child Development, 60,* 1239–1249.

Callahan, Raymond E. (1962). *Education and the cult of efficiency: A study of the social forces that have shaped the administration of the public schools.* Chicago: University of Chicago Press.

Campbell, W. Glenn (1994). Personal communication.

Cannell, John J. (1987). *Nationally normed achievement testing in America's public schools: How all fifty states are above the national average* (2nd ed.). Daniels, WV: Friends for Education.

Caplan, Nathan, Choy, Marcella H., & Whitmore, John K. (1992). Indo-Chinese refugee families and academic achievement: The children of Southeast Asian boat people excel in the American school system. *Scientific American* (February), 36–42.

Card, David & Krueger, Alan B. (1992). Does school quality matter? Returns to education and the characteristics of public schools in the United States. *Journal of Political Economy, 100,* 1–40.

Carnegie Forum on Education and the Economy (1986). *A nation prepared: Teachers for the 21st century—The report of the Task Force on Teaching as a Profession.* New York: Author.

Carr, Robert (1994). Personal communication.

Carroll, John B. (1963). A model of school learning. *Teachers College Record, 64,* 723–733.

Carroll, John B. (1985). The model of school learning: Progress of an idea. In Charles W. Fisher & David C. Berliner (Eds.), *Perspectives on instructional time* (pp. 59–72). New York: Longman.

Carson, C. C., Huelskamp, R. M., & Woodall, T. D. (1991). *Perspectives on education in America: Annotated briefing—Third Draft.* Albuquerque, NM: Sandia National Laboratories, Systems Analysis Department.

Carter, James Earl, Jr. (1971). Inaugural address as governor of the state of Georgia (January 12). Atlanta.

Casady, Margie (1974). Insert box in Greene, David & Lepper, Mark R., How to turn play into work. *Psychology Today* (September), 49–53.

Casanova, Ursula & Arias, M. Beatriz (1993). Contextualizing bilingual education. In M. Beatriz Arias & Ursula Casanova (Eds.), *Bilingual education: Politics, practice, and research. Ninety-second yearbook of the National Society for the Study of Education, Part 1* (pp. 1–35). Chicago: University of Chicago Press.

Catterall, James S. (1984). *Education vouchers.* Bloomington, IN: Phi Delta Kappan Educational Foundation.

Ceci, Stephen J. (1991). How much does schooling influence general intelligence and its cognitive components? A reassessment of the evidence. *Developmental Psychology, 27,* 703–722.

Celis, William, III (1993). Study says half of adults in U.S. lack reading and math abilities. *New York Times* (September 9), p. A1.

Chira, Susan (1992). Study finds standardized tests may hurt education efforts. *New York Times* (October 16), p. A19.

Chubb, John E. & Moe, Terry M. (1990). *Politics, markets, and America's schools.* Washington, DC: The Brookings Institution.

Chubb, John E. & Moe, Terry M. (1992). Educational choice: Why it is needed and how it will work. In Chester E. Finn, Jr. & Theodor Rebarber (Eds.), *Education reform in the '90s* (pp. 36–52). New York: Macmillan.

Clark, Reginald M. (1983). *Family life and school achievement: Why poor black children succeed or fail.* Chicago: University of Chicago Press.

Cobb, Paul (1994). Where is the mind? Constructivist and sociocultural perspectives on mathematical development. *Educational Researcher, 23*(7), 13–20.

Coder, John, Rainwater, Lee, & Smeeding, Timothy (1989). Inequality among children and elderly in ten modern nations: The United States in an international context. *The American Economic Review, 79*(2), 320–324.

Cogan, John, Torney-Purta, Judith, & Anderson, Douglas (1988). Knowledge and attitudes toward global issues: Students in Japan and the United States. *Comparative Education Review, 32,* 282–297.

Cohen, David K. & Garet, Michael S. (1975). Reforming educational policy with applied social research. *Harvard Educational Review, 45*(1), 17–31.

Cohen, David K. & Spillane, James P. (1992). Policy and practice: The relationship between governance and instruction. In Gerald Grant (Ed.), *Review of research in education, Vol. 18* (pp. 3–49). Washington, DC: American Educational Research Association.

Cohen, Elizabeth G. (1984). Talking and working together: Status interaction and learning. In Penelope Peterson, Louise Cherry Wilkinson, & Maureen Hallinan (Eds.), *Instructional groups in the classroom: Organization and processes* (pp. 171–188). Orlando, FL: Academic Press.

Cohen, Elizabeth G. (1986). *Designing groupwork: Strategies for the heterogeneous classroom.* New York: Teachers College Press.

Cohen, Elizabeth G. (1994a). *Designing groupwork: Strategies for the heterogeneous classroom* (2nd ed.). New York: Teachers College Press.

Cohen, Elizabeth G. (1994b). Restructuring the classroom: Conditions for productive small groups. *Review of Educational Research, 64,* 1–35.

Cohen, Jacob & Cohen, Patricia (1983). *Applied multiple regression/correlation analysis for the behavioral sciences* (2nd ed.). Hillsdale, NJ: Lawrence Erlbaum.

Cohen, Yinon & Tyree, Andrea (1986). Escape from poverty: Determinants of intergenerational mobility of sons and daughters of the poor. *Social Science Quarterly, 67,* 803–813.

Coleman, James S. (1972). The evaluation of *Equality of educational opportunity.* In Frederick Mosteller & Daniel P. Moynihan (Eds.), *On equality of educational opportunity* (pp. 146–167). New York: Vintage Books.

Coleman, James S. (1990). *Equality and achievement in education.* Boulder, CO: Westview Press.

Coleman, James S., Campbell, Ernest Q., Hobson, Carol J., McPartland, James, Mood, Alexander M., Weinfeld, Frederic D., & York, Robert L. (1966). *Equality of educational opportunity.* Washington, DC: U.S. Government Printing Office.

Coleman, James S., Hoffer, Thomas, & Kilgore, Sally (1981). *Public and private schools* (Final report to the National Center for Education Statistics, Contract No. 300-78-0208). Chicago: National Opinion Research Center.

Coleman, James S., Hoffer, Thomas, & Kilgore, Sally (1982). *High school achievement: Public, private, and Catholic schools compared.* New York: Basic Books.

College Entrance Examination Board, The (various dates). *College bound seniors.* New York: Author.

College Entrance Examination Board, The (1983). *Academic preparation for the world of work.* New York: Author.

College Entrance Examination Board, The (1988). *Guidelines on the uses of College Board test scores and related data.* New York: Author.

College Entrance Examination Board, The (1993). *News from the College Board.* New York: Author.

Colson, Chuck & Eckerd, Jack (1991). *Why America doesn't work.* Dallas, TX: Word Publishing.

Comer, James P. (1988). Educating poor minority children. *Scientific American, 259,* 42–48.

Commission on the Skills of the American Workforce (1990). *America's choice: High skills or low wages.* Rochester, NY: National Center on Education and the Economy.

Committee for Economic Development (1983). *Productivity policy: Key to the nation's economic future.* New York: Author.

Committee for Economic Development (1984). *Strategy for U.S. industrial competitiveness.* New York: Author.

Committee for Economic Development (1985). *Investing in our children: Business and the public schools.* New York: Author.

Conant, James B. (1959). *The American high school today: A first report to interested citizens.* New York: McGraw-Hill.

Consumer Reports (1992). *Wasted health care dollars* (July), 435–448.

Cookson, Peter W., Jr. (1981). *Private secondary boarding school and public suburban high school graduation: An analysis of college attendance plans.* Unpublished doctoral dissertation, New York University, New York.

Cookson, Peter W., Jr. (1992). The ideology of consumership and the coming deregulation of the public school system. In Peter W. Cookson, Jr. (Ed.), *The choice controversy* (pp. 83–99). Newbury Park, CA: Corwin Press.

Cookson, Peter W., Jr. (1994). *School choice: The struggle for the soul of American education.* New Haven, CT: Yale University Press.

Cooley, William W. (1991). *School choice or school reform?* (Pennsylvania Educational Policy Studies, No. 12). Pittsburgh, PA: University of Pittsburgh, Learning Research and Development Center.

Cooper, Harris (1989). *Homework.* New York: Longman.

Copperman, Paul (1978). *The literacy hoax: The decline of reading, writing, and learning in the public schools and what we can do about it.* New York: Morrow.

Crawford, Alan (1980). *Thunder on the right.* New York: Pantheon.

Crawford, James (1992). *Hold your tongue: Bilingualism and the politics of "English only."* Reading, MA: Addison-Wesley.

Cremin, Lawrence (1961). *The transformation of the school: Progressivism in American education, 1876–1957.* New York: Knopf.

Cremin, Lawrence A. (1990). *Popular education and its discontents.* New York: HarperCollins.

Cremin, Lawrence A. & Weiss, Robert M. (1952). Yesterday's school critic. *Teachers College Record* (November), *54*, 77–82.

Crosswhite, F. Joe, Dossey, John A., Swafford, Jane O., McKnight, Curtis C., Cooney, Thomas J., Downs, Floyd L., Grouws, Douglas A., & Weinzweig, A. I. (1986). *Second international mathematics study: Detailed report for the United States.* Champaign, IL: Stipes.

Crouse, James & Trusheim, Dale (1988). *The case against the SAT.* Chicago: University of Chicago Press.

Cuban, Larry (1990). Reforming again, again, and again. *Educational Researcher, 19*(1), 3–13.

Curtis, Henry S. (1917). *The play movement and its significance.* New York: Macmillan.

d'Aimée, Lys (1900). The menace of present educational methods. *Gunton's Magazine* (September), *19*, 263.

D'Souza, Dinesh (1991). *Illiberal education: The politics of race and sex on campus.* New York: The Free Press.

Dahllöf, Urban (1971). *Ability grouping, content validity and curriculum process analysis.* New York: Teachers College Press.

Dannemayer, Rep. William E. (1991). Remarks to the U.S. House of Representatives. *Congressional Record,* May 1.

Darling-Hammond, Linda (1990a). Teachers and teaching: Signs of a changing profession. In W. Robert Houston (Ed.), *Handbook of research on teacher education* (pp. 267–290). New York: Macmillan.

Darling-Hammond, Linda (1990b). Achieving our goals: Superficial or structural reforms? *Phi Delta Kappan* (December), 286–295.

Davis, James A. & Smith, Tom W. (1990). *General social surveys, 1972–1990: Cumulative codebook.* Chicago: National Opinion Research Center.

de Tocqueville, Alexis (1835, 1840). *Democracy in America* (2 vols.). New York: Vintage Books [1960].

Deci, Edward L. & Ryan, Richard M. (1982). Intrinsic motivation to teach: Possibility and obstacles in our colleges and universities. In James L. Bess (Ed.), *New directions in teaching and learning* (pp. 27–35). San Francisco: Jossey-Bass.

Deci, Edward L., & Ryan, Richard M. (1985). *Intrinsic motivation and self-determination in human behavior.* New York: Plenum Press.

Deci, Edward L. Spiegel, Nancy H., Ryan, Richard M., Koestner, Richard, & Kauffman, Manette (1982). The effects of performance standards on teaching styles: The behavior of controlling teachers. *Journal of Educational Psychology, 74,* 852–859.

Denison, Edward Fulton (1962). *The sources of economic growth in the United States and the alternatives before us.* New York: Committee for Economic Development.

Dewey, John (1900). *The school and society.* Chicago: University of Chicago Press.

Dewey, John (1902). The school as a social center. *Proceedings of the National Education Association* (pp. 373–383).

DeWitt, Karen (1990). U.S. study shows pupil achievement at level of 1970. *New York Times* (October 1), p. 1.

DeYoung, Chris A. & Wynn, Richard (1972). *American education* (7th ed.). New York: McGraw-Hill.

Diamond, Sara (1989). *Spiritual warfare: The politics of the Christian right.* Boston: South End Press.

Díaz, Rafael M. (1990). Bilingualism and cognitive ability: Theory, research, and controversy. In Andrés Barona & Eugene E. Garcia (Eds.), *Children at risk: Poverty, minority status, and other issues of educational equity* (pp. 91–102). Washington, DC: National Association of School Psychologists.

Donlon, Thomas F. (1984). *The College Board technical handbook for the Scholastic Aptitude Test and achievement tests.* New York: College Entrance Examination Board.

Dossey, John A., Mullis, Ina V. S., Lindquist, Mary M., & Chambers, Donald L. (1988). *The mathematics report card: Are we measuring up? Trends and achievement based on the 1986 national assessment.* Princeton, NJ: Educational Testing Service.

Dougherty, Kevin J. & Sostre, Lizabeth (1992). Minerva and the market: The sources of the movement for school choice. In Peter W. Cookson, Jr. (Ed.), *The choice controversy* (pp. 24–45). Newbury Park, CA: Corwin Press.

Doyle, Denis P. (1991). The federal education role comes of age. In *Voices from the field: 30 expert opinions on "America 2000," the Bush administration strategy to "reinvent" America's schools* (p. 5). Washington, DC: William T. Grant Foundation Commission on Work, Family and Citizenship, and Institute for Educational Leadership.

Draper, Roger (1985). The golden ram. *New York Review of Books, 32* (October 24), 46–49.

Drazen, Shelly M. (1994). *Factors influencing student achievement from early to mid-adolescence.* Paper presented at the meeting of the American Psychological Association, Los Angeles, August.

Dreeben, Robert (1987). Closing the divide: What teachers and administrators can do to help black students reach their reading potential. *American Educator, 11*(4), 28–35.

Driscoll, Mary Erina (1993). Choice, achievement, and school community. In Edith Rasell & Richard Rothstein (Eds.), *School choice: Examining the evidence* (pp. 147–172). Washington, DC: Economic Policy Institute.

Driver, Rosalind, Asoko, Hilary, Leach, John, Mortimer, Eduardo, & Scott, Philip (1994). Constructing scientific knowledge in the classroom. *Educational Researcher, 23*(7), 5–12.

Dye, Michel (1994). Silent danger of medical malpractice. *Public Citizen, 14*(3), 10–13.

Economist, The (1991). America's blacks: A world apart (March 30), 17, 18, 21.

Economist, The (1994). O brave new world (March 12), 19–20, 26.

Educational Research Service (1990). *Cooperative learning.* Arlington, VA: Author.

Educational Testing Service (various dates). *PSAT/NMSQT summary report.* Princeton, NJ: Author.

Educational Testing Service (1990). *Accelerating academic achievement: A summary of findings from 20 years of the NAEP.* Princeton, NJ: National Assessment of Educational Progress.

Educational Testing Service (1991a). *Performance at the top: From elementary through graduate school.* Princeton, NJ: Author.

Educational Testing Service (1991b). *The state of inequality.* Princeton, NJ: Author.

Educational Testing Service (1993). *Adult literacy in America: A first look at the results of the National Adult Literacy Survey.* Washington, DC: U.S. Government Printing Office.

El-Khawas, Elaine (1991). *Campus trends, 1991.* Washington, DC: American Council on Education.

Elam, Stanley H., Rose, Lowell C., & Gallup, Alec M. (1993). The 25th annual Phi Delta Kappan Gallup poll of the public's attitude toward the public schools. *Phi Delta Kappan, 75*(October), 137–153.

Elley, Warwick B. (1992). *How in the world do students read?* Hamburg: International Association for the Evaluation of Educational Achievement.

Ellwood, David T. (1988). *Poor support: Poverty in the American family.* New York: Basic Books.

Elsbree, Willard (1939). *The American teacher: Evolution of a profession in a democracy.* New York: American Book Company.

Epstein, Joyce (1987). Parent involvement: What research says to administrators. *Education and Urban Society, 19*(2), 119–136.

Evertson, Carolyn M., Hawley, Willis D., & Zlotnik, M. (1985). Making a difference in educational quality through teacher education. *Journal of Teacher Education, 36*(3), 2–12.

Falsey, Barbara & Heyns, Barbara (1984). The college channel: Private and public schools reconsidered. *Sociology of Education, 57,* 111–122.

Fantini, Mario D. (1986). *Regaining excellence in education.* Columbus, OH: Merrill.

Farnum, Richard (1990). Prestige in the Ivy League: Democratization and discrimination at Penn and Columbia, 1890–1970. In Paul William Kingston & Lionel S. Lewis (Eds.), *The high-status track: Studies of elite schools and stratification* (pp. 75–103). Albany: State University of New York Press.

Feagin, Joe R. (1972). Poverty: We still believe that God helps those who help themselves. *Psychology Today, 6*(November), 101–129.

Feather, Norman T. (1974). Explanations of poverty in Australian and American samples. *Australian Journal of Psychology, 26,* 199–216.

Fenstermacher, Gary D. (1991). Assessment explained. *Briefs* (November 18, The Newsletter of the American Association of Colleges of Teacher Education).

Ferguson, Ronald F. (1991). Paying for public education: New evidence on how and why money matters. *Harvard Journal on Legislation, 28,* 465–498.

Fetterman, David M. (1988). *Excellence & equality: A qualitatively different perspective on gifted and talented education.* Albany: State University of New York Press.

Finn, Chester E., Jr. (1988). What ails education research. *Educational Researcher, 17*(1), 5–8.

Finn, Chester E., Jr. (1991). *We must take charge: Our schools and our future.* New York: The Free Press.

Finn, Chester E., Jr. & Rebarber, Theodor (1992). *Education reform in the '90s.* New York: Macmillan.

Finn, Jeremy D. (1989). Withdrawing from school. *Review of Educational Research, 59,* 117–142.

Firestone, William A. & Bader, Beth D. (1992). *Redesigning teaching: Professionalism or bureaucracy?* Albany: State University of New York Press.

Fiske, Edward B. (1989). Impending U.S. jobs "disaster": Work force unqualified to work. *New York Times* (September 29), p. A1.

Flynn, James R. (1987). Massive IQ gains in 14 nations: What IQ tests really measure. *Psychological Bulletin, 101,* 171–191.

Fowler, Frances C. (1992). School choice policy in France: Success and limitations. *Educational Policy, 6,* 429–443.

Freedman, Marc (1993). *The kindness of strangers: Adult mentors, urban youth, and the new voluntarism.* San Francisco: Jossey-Bass.

Friedman, John S. (1992). The Whittle-Alexander nexus: Big business goes to school. *The Nation* (February 17), pp. 188–192.

Friedman, Milton (1962). *Capitalism and freedom.* Chicago: University of Chicago Press.

Fruchter, Norm, Galletta, Anne, & White, J. Lynne (1993). New directions in parent involvement. *Equity and Choice, 9*(3), 33–43.

Fry, P. S. & Ghosh, Ratna (1980). Attributional differences in the life satisfactions of the elderly: A cross-cultural comparison of Asian and United States subjects. *International Journal of Psychology, 15,* 201–212.

Fuentes, Carlos (1989). *Centennial lecture.* Arizona State University, Honors College (September 9), Tempe, AZ.

Futrelle, David (1993). Suffer the children. *In These Times* (August 9), pp. 14–17.

Gardner, John W. (1963). *Self-renewal: The individual and the innovative society.* New York: Harper & Row.

Gilles, Jere L., Geletta, Simon, & Daniels, M. Cortney (1994). *What makes a good school? A methodological critique and reappraisal.* Paper presented at the annual meeting of the Midwest Sociological Society, St. Louis, March.

Gilman, David A. & Reynolds, Laura L. (1991). The side effects of statewide testing. *Contemporary Education, 62,* 273–278.

Giroux, Henry A. (1988). *Teachers as intellectuals: Toward a critical pedagogy of learning.* Granby, MA: Bergin and Garvey.

Glass, Gene V (1987). What works: Politics and research. *Educational Researcher, 16*(3), 5–10.

Glass, Sandra R. (1993). *Markets and myths: Autonomy of principals and teachers in public and private secondary schools.* Unpublished doctoral dissertation, Arizona State University, College of Education, Tempe, AZ.

Glickman, Carl D. (1993). *Renewing America's schools: A guide for school-based action.* San Francisco: Jossey-Bass.

Goldberg, Kirsten (1988). "Gravest threat" to private schools is better public ones, Finn warns. *Education Week, VII*(24), pp. 1–7.

Goldenberg, Claude (1985). *Low-income parents' contribution to the reading achievement of their first grade children.* Paper presented at the annual meeting of the American Educational Research Association, Chicago, April.

Good, Thomas L. (1987). Teacher expectations. In David C. Berliner & Barak Rosenshine (Eds.), *Talks to teachers* (pp. 159–200). New York: Random House.

Good, Thomas L. & Weinstein, Rhona (1986). Classroom expectations: One framework for exploring classrooms. In Karen Kepler Zumwalt (Ed.), *1986 ASCD yearbook: Improving teaching* (pp. 63–85). Alexandria, VA: Association for Supervision and Curriculum Development.

Goodlad, John I. (1983). *A place called school: Prospects for the future.* New York: McGraw-Hill.

Gordon, Jack (1990). Where the training goes. *Training: The Magazine of Human Resources Development* (October), 51–52.

Goslin, David A. (1965). *The school in contemporary society.* Glenview, IL: Scott, Foresman.

Gould, Stephen Jay (1981). *The mismeasure of man.* New York: Norton.

Graduate Management Admission Council (1993). *Graduate management admission test: Profile of candidates: March 1993.* Princeton, NJ: Author.

Greene, David & Lepper, Mark R. (1974). How to turn play into work. *Psychology Today* (September), 49–53.

Greeno, James (1994). *The situativity of learning.* Paper presented at the annual meeting of the American Psychological Association, Los Angeles, August.

Gregory, Thomas B. & Smith, Gerald R. (1987). *High schools as communities: The small school reconsidered.* Bloomington, IN: Phi Delta Kappa Educational Foundation.

Grissmer, David W., Kirby, Sheila Nataraj, Berends, Mark, & Williamson, Stephanie (1994). *Student achievement and the changing American family.* Santa Monica, CA: The RAND Corporation.

Grolnick, W. S. & Ryan, Richard M. (1985). Self-regulation and motivation in children's learning: An experimental investigation. Unpublished manuscript described in Deci & Ryan (1985), pp. 259–260.

Gugliotta, Guy (1993). An impromptu "dream" becomes a national model. *The Washington Post* (March 16), p. A6.

Hackett, Jack (1994). Personal communication.

Haertel, Edward H., James, Thomas, & Levin, Henry M. (Eds.) (1987). *Comparing public & private schools. Volume 2: School achievement.* London: Falmer Press.

Hakuta, Kenji (1986). *Mirror of language: The debate on bilingualism.* New York: Basic Books.

Hammack, Floyd M. & Cookson, Peter W., Jr. (1980). Colleges attended by graduates of elite secondary schools. *The Educational Forum, 44,* 483–490.

Haney, Walter (1993). Testing and minorities. In Lois Weis & Michelle Fine (Eds.), *Beyond silence voiced: Class, race, and gender in United States schools* (pp. 45–73). Albany: State University of New York Press.

Hanushek, Eric A. (1989). The impact of differential expenditures on school performance. *Educational Researcher, 18*(4), 45–62.

Harrington, Diane & Cookson, Peter W., Jr. (1992). School reform in East Harlem: Alternative schools vs. "Schools of Choice." In G. Alfred Hess (Ed.), *Empowering teachers and parents: School restructuring through the eyes of anthropologists* (pp. 177–186). Westport, CT: Bergin and Garvey.

Harvey, John H. & Weary, Gifford (1984). Current issues in attribution theory and research. *Annual Review of Psychology, 35,* 427–459.

Haskins, Ron, Lanier, Mark W., & MacRae, Duncan, Jr. (1988). Reforming the public schools: The commission reports and strategies of reform. In Don Haskins & Duncan MacRae (Eds.), *Policies for America's public schools: Teachers, equity, and indicators* (pp. 1–22). Norwood, NJ: Ablex.

Haskins, Ron, Walden, Tedra, & Ramey, Craig T. (1983). Teacher and student behavior in high- and low-ability groups. *Journal of Educational Psychology, 75,* 865–876.

Heath, Shirley Brice (1994). Play for identity: Where the mind is every day for inner city youth. In John N. Mangieri & Cathy Collins Block (Eds.), *Creating powerful thinking in teachers and students* (pp. 215–228). Fort Worth, TX: Harcourt Brace.

Heath, Shirley Brice & McLoughlin, Milbry W. (1994). *Possible selves: Achievement, ethnicity, and gender for inner-city youth.* New York: Teachers College Press.

Hedges, Larry V., Laine, Richard D., & Greenwald, Rob (1994). Does money matter? A meta-analysis of studies of the effects of differential school inputs on student outcomes. *Educational Researcher, 23*(3), 5–14.

Hembree, Ray (1990). The nature, effects, and relief of mathematics anxiety. *Journal for Research in Mathematics Education, 21,* 33–46.

Henslin, James M., Henslin, Linda K., & Keiser, Steven D. (1976). Schooling for social stability: Education in the corporate society. In James M. Henslin & Larry T. Reynolds (Eds.), *Social problems in American society* (2nd ed., pp. 302–314). Boston: Allyn and Bacon.

Herbert, Bob (1993). Listen to the children. *New York Times,* OP-ED (June 27), p. A24.

Heritage Foundation, The (1989). *Education Update, 12*(4).

Herman, Robin (1990). *Fusion: The search for endless energy.* Cambridge, England: Cambridge University Press.

Herrnstein, Richard J. & Murray, Charles (1994). *The bell curve: The reshaping of American life by differences in intelligence.* New York: The Free Press.

Hieronymus, A. N. & Hoover, H. D. (1986). *Iowa Tests of Basic Skills, Forms G/H: Manual for school administrator, Levels 5–14.* Chicago: Riverside Publishing.

Hillhouse, Barbara (1994). Personal communication.

Hinds, Michael deCourcy (1990). Reading the lips of the rich: Spending, not taxes, is the problem. *New York Times* (October 20), p. 8.

Hinds, Michael deCourcy (1993). A self-help offer of higher learning is extending to housing projects. *New York Times* (January 20), p. B7.

Hirsch, Eric D., Jr. (1987). *Cultural literacy: What every American needs to know.* Boston, MA: Houghton Mifflin.

Hirsch, Eric D., Jr. (Ed.) (1991). *What your first grader needs to know: Fundamentals of a good first grade education.* New York: Doubleday.

Hirsch, Eric D., Jr., Kett, Joseph F., & Trefil, James (1993). *Dictionary of cultural literacy* (2nd ed.). Boston, MA: Houghton Mifflin.

Hitler, Adolf (1933). *Mein Kampf,* Vol. 1. Munich: Deutschland Zentralverlag der NSDAP.

Hoffer, Thomas, Greeley, Andrew M., & Coleman, James S. (1985). Achievement growth in public and Catholic schools. *Sociology of Education, 58,* 74–97.

Hollingsworth, Sandra & Sockett, Hugh (Eds.) (1994). *Teacher research and educational reform. Ninety-third yearbook of the National Society for the Study of Education, Part 1.* Chicago: University of Chicago Press.

Holmes Group, The (1986). *Tomorrow's teachers.* Lansing, MI: Author.

Holmes, C. Thomas & Mathews, Kenneth M. (1984). The effects of nonpromotion on elementary and junior high school pupils: A meta-analysis. *Review of Educational Research, 54,* 225–236.

Holtzman, Wayne H. (Ed.) (1992). *School of the future.* Austin, TX: American Psychological Association and University of Texas, Hogg Foundation for Mental Health.

Huber, Joan & Form, William H. (1973). *Income and ideology.* New York: The Free Press.

Huelskamp, R. M. (1993). Perspectives on education in America. *Phi Delta Kappan,* *74*(9), 718–721.

Hunter, John E. (1986). Cognitive ability, cognitive aptitudes, job knowledge and job performance. *Journal of Vocational Behavior, 29,* 340–362.

Husén, Torsten (Ed.) (1967). *International study of achievement in mathematics: A comparison of twelve countries.* Stockholm: Almqvist & Wiksell; New York: Wiley.

Husén, Torsten & Tuijnman, Albert (1991). The contribution of formal schooling to the increase in intellectual capital. *Educational Researcher, 20*(7), 17–25.

Hutchins, Robert M. (1944). The THREAT to American education. *Colliers* (December 30), *114,* 20–21.

Jaeger, Richard M. (1992). World class standards, choice, and privatization: Weak measurement serving presumptive policy. *Phi Delta Kappan* (October), 118–128.

Japan Times (various dates).

Jefferson, Thomas (1821). Letter to John Adams (September 21).

Jellison, Jerald M. & Green, Jane (1981). A self-presentation approach to the fundamental attribution error: The norm of internality. *Journal of Personality and Social Psychology, 40,* 643–649.

Jencks, Christopher, Smith, Marshall, Acland, Henry, Bane, Mary Jo, Cohen, David, Gintis, Herbert, Heyns, Barbara, & Michelson, Stephen (1972). *Inequality: A reassessment of the effect of family and schooling in America.* New York: Basic Books.

Johnson, David (1994). Psychology in Washington: Education reform Clinton-style. *Psychological Science, 5,* 117–121.

Johnson, David W. & Johnson, Roger T. (1978). Cooperative, competitive, and individualistic learning. *Journal of Research and Development in Education, 12*(1), 3–15.

Johnson, David W. & Johnson, Roger T. (1989). *Cooperation and competition: Theory and research.* Edina, MN: Interactive Book Co.

Jordan, Mary (1993). Literacy of 90 million is deficient: U.S. survey sends alarms over skills in reading, arithmetic. *Washington Post* (September 9), p. 1.

Kamin, Leon (1981). Some historical facts about IQ testing. In Hans Jurgen Eysenck & Leon Kamin (Eds.), *The intelligence controversy* (pp. 90–97). New York: Wiley.

Kaplan, George R. (1992). *Images of education: The mass media's version of America's schools.* Washington, DC: National School Public Relations Association and the Institute for Educational Leadership.

Karen, David (1985). *Who gets into Harvard? Selection and exclusion.* Unpublished doctoral dissertation, Harvard University.

Karweit, Nancy (1976). Quantity of schooling: A major educational factor? *Educational Researcher, 5*(2), 15–17.

Karweit, Nancy (1984). Time-on-task reconsidered: Synthesis of research on time and learning. *Educational Leadership, 41*(8), 32–35.

Kaufman, Julie E. & Rosenbaum, James E. (1992). The education and employment of low-income black youth in white suburbs. *Educational Evaluation and Policy Analysis, 14,* 229–240.

Kaul, Donald (1993). Even our best students come up woefully short. *Des Moines Register* (November).

Kearns, David & Doyle, Denis P. (1988). *Winning the brain race: A bold plan to make our schools competitive.* San Francisco: The Institute for Contemporary Studies.

Kent, John D. (1987). A not too distant past: Echoes of the calls for reform. *The Educational Forum, 51,* 137–150.

Kerr, Clark (1991). Is education really all that guilty? *Education Week* (February 27), p. 30.

Kerr, Donna H. (1983). Teaching competence and teacher education in the United States. In Lee S. Shulman & Gary Sykes (Eds.), *Handbook of teaching and policy* (pp. 126–149). New York: Longman.

Kilborn, Peter T. (1993). New jobs lack the old security in time of "disposable workers." *New York Times* (March 15), pp. A1–A6.

Kilpatrick, James J. (1983). The crisis in our schools. *The Nation's Business* (July), p. 5.

Kiltgaard, Robert (1985). *Choosing elites.* New York: Basic Books.

Kimball, Roger (1990). *Tenured radicals: How politics corrupted our higher education.* New York: Harper & Row.

Kirst, Michael W. (1988). Recent state education reform in the United States: Looking backward and forward. *Educational Administration Quarterly, 24,* 319–328.

Kluegel, James R. & Smith, Eliot R. (1986). *Beliefs about inequality: Americans' views of what is and what ought to be.* New York: Aldine de Gruyter.

Koppich, Julia E. & Guthrie, James W. (1993). Examining contemporary education-reform efforts in the United States. In Hedley Beare & William Lowe Boyd (Eds.), *Restructuring schools: An international perspective on the movement to transform the control and performance of schools* (pp. 51–68). London: Falmer Press.

Koretz, Daniel M., Madaus, George F., Haertel, Edward, & Beaton, Albert E. (1992). *National educational standards and testing: A response to the recommendations of the National Council on Education Standards and Testing.* Santa Monica, CA: Institute on Education and Training, The RAND Corporation.

Kotkin, Joel (1991). Europe won't work. *Washington Post* (September 15), p. C-1.

Kozol, Jonathan (1991). *Savage inequalities: Children in America's schools.* New York: Crown.

Kozol, Jonathan (1992). Whittle and the privateers. *The Nation* (September 21), pp. 272–278.

Kramer, Rita (1991). Commentary: Reciting the sins of a "professional education industry." *Education Week* (October 23), p. 36.

Lane, John J. & Epps, Edgar G. (1992). *Restructuring the schools: Problems and prospects.* Berkeley, CA: McCutchan.

Lanier, Judith (1986). Research on teacher education. In Merlin C. Wittrock (Ed.), *Handbook of research on teaching* (3rd ed., pp. 527–569). New York: Macmillan.

Lapointe, Archie E. (1992). *Scientific sample but plenty of differences.* Princeton, NJ: Educational Testing Service.

Lareau, Annette (1989). *Home advantage.* Philadelphia, PA: Falmer Press.

LeCompte, Margaret D. & Dworkin, Anthony Gary (1991). *Giving up on school: Student dropouts and teacher burnouts.* Newbury Park, CA: Corwin Press.

Lee, Valerie E. & Smith, Julia B. (1994). *Effects of high school restructuring and size on gains in achievement and engagement for early secondary school students.* Paper presented at the annual meeting of the American Sociological Society, Los Angeles.

Levin, Henry M. (1988a). Accelerating elementary education for disadvantaged students. In Chief State School Officers (Ed.), *School success for children at risk* (pp. 209–225). Orlando, FL: Harcourt Brace Jovanovich.

Levin, Henry M. (1988b). Education as a public and private good. *Journal of Policy Analysis and Management, 6,* 628–641.

Levin, Henry M. (1993). *Education and jobs: A proactive view.* Paper presented at the Seventh Annual Conference on Education and Work, Ontario Institute for the Study of Education, Toronto, Canada, March.

Levin, Henry M., Glass, Gene V, & Meister, G. R. (1984). *Cost-effectiveness of four educational interventions* (Project Report No. 84-A11). Stanford, CA: Institute for Research on Educational Finance and Governance.

Levin, Henry M., Rumberger, R., & Finnan, C. (1990). *Escalating skill requirements or new skill requirements?* Paper presented at the Conference on Changing Occupational Skill Requirements: Gathering and Assessing the Evidence, Brown University, Providence, RI, June.

Levitan, Sar A. & Gallo, Frank (1991). *Got to learn to earn: Preparing Americans for work* (Occasional Paper 1991–3). Washington, DC: Center for Social Policy Studies.

Lewis, Lionel S. & Wanner, Richard A. (1979). Private schooling and the status attainment process. *Sociology of Education, 52,* 99–112.

Lewis, Oscar (1966). *La vida: A Puerto Rican family in the culture of poverty.* New York: Random House.

Linn, Robert L., Graue, M. Elizabeth, & Sanders, Nancy M. (1990). Comparing state and district test results to national norms: The validity of claims that "everyone is above average." *Educational Measurement: Issues and Practice, 10*(Fall), 5–14.

Little, Judith Warren (1982). Norms of collegiality and experimentation: Workplace conditions of school success. *American Educational Research Journal, 19,* 325–340.

Livingstone, David W. (1983). *Class ideologies and educational futures.* London: Falmer Press.

Louis Harris and Associates, Inc. (1985). *The Metropolitan Life survey of the American teacher 1985: Strengthening the profession.* New York: Author.

Louis Harris and Associates, Inc. (1993). *The Metropolitan Life survey of the American teacher 1993: Violence in America's public schools.* New York: Author.

Louisiana Coalition for Tax Justice (1993). *The great Louisiana tax giveaway.* Baton Rouge, LA: Author.

Lund, Robert T. & Hansen, John A. (1986). *Keeping America at work: Strategies for employing the new technologies.* New York: Wiley.

Lundgren, Ulf P. (1977). *Model analysis of pedagogical processes.* Lund, Sweden: CWK Gleerup.

Lynch, Ella Frances (1912). Is public school a failure? It is: The most momentous failure in our American life today. *Ladies Home Journal, 29,* 4–5.

Lynd, Albert (1953). *Quackery in the public schools.* Boston: Little, Brown.

Madaus, George (1989). New ways of thinking about testing: An interview with George Madaus. *Phi Delta Kappan* (April), *70,* 642–645.

Madison, James (1822). Letter to W. T. Barry (August 4).

Manno, Bruno V. (1993). Deliver us from Clinton's schools bill. *Wall Street Journal* (June 22), p. A14.

Manski, Charles F. (1987). Academic ability, earnings, and the decision to become a teacher: Evidence from the National Longitudinal Study of the High School class of 1972. In D. Wise (Ed.), *Public sector payrolls.* Chicago: University of Chicago Press.

Marshall, Ray & Tucker, Marc (1992). *Thinking for a living: Education and the wealth of nations.* New York: Basic Books.

Martin, Robert L. (1984). *Business and education: Partners for the future.* Washington, DC: National Chamber Foundation.

Mayer, Richard E., Tajika, Hidetsugu, & Stanley, Caryn (1991). Mathematical problem solving in Japan and the United States: A controlled comparison. *Journal of Educational Psychology, 83,* 69–72.

McCarthy, Jane & Still, Suzanne (1993). Holibrook accelerated elementary school. In Joseph Murphy & Philip Hallinger (Eds.), *Restructuring schooling: Learning from ongoing effects.* Newbury Park, CA: Corwin Press.

McKinsey Global Institute (1992). *Service sector productivity.* Washington, DC: Author.

Meier, Kenneth J., Stewart, Joseph, Jr., & England, Robert E. (1989). *Race, class and education: The politics of second-generation discrimination.* Madison, WI: The University of Wisconsin Press.

Meyer, John (1970). The charter: Conditions of diffuse socialization in school. In W. Richard Scott (Ed.), *Social processes and social structure* (pp. 564–578). New York: Holt.

Meyer, John (1977). Education as an institution. *American Journal of Sociology, 83,* 55–77.

Miller, Joan G. (1984). Culture and the development of everyday social explanation. *Journal of Personality and Social Psychology, 46,* 961–987.

Milne, Ann M., Myers, David E., Rosenthal, Alan S., & Ginsberg, Alan (1986). Single parents, working mothers, and the educational achievements of schoolchildren. *Sociology of Education, 59,* 125–139.

Mishel, Lawrence & Teixeira, Ruy A. (1991). *The myth of the coming labor shortage: Jobs, skills, and the incomes of America's workforce 2000.* Washington, DC: Economic Policy Institute.

Moll, Luis C. & Greenberg, Jim (1990). Creating zones of possibilities: Combining social contexts for instruction. In Luis C. Moll (Ed.), *Vygotsky and education* (pp. 319–348). Cambridge, England: Cambridge University Press.

Moore, Donald R. & Davenport, Suzanne (1990). School choice: The new sorting machine. In William L. Boyd & Herbert J. Walberg (Eds.), *Choice in education* (pp. 187–223). Berkeley, CA: McCutchan.

Morgan, Dan (1981). Private high schools are better than public, study concludes. *Washington Post* (April 3), pp. A1, A13.

Murphy, John & Schiller, Jeffry (1992). *Transforming America's schools: An administrator's call for action.* LaSalle, IL: Open Court Publishing Co.

Nathan, Joe (1991). *Free to teach: Achieving equity and excellence in schools.* New York: Pilgrim.

National Academy of Sciences (1983). *Education for tomorrow's jobs.* Washington, DC: National Academy Press.

National Academy of Sciences (1984). *High schools and the changing workplace: Employers' view.* Washington, DC: National Academy Press.

National Assessment of Educational Progress (1991). *The state of mathematics achievement: NAEP 1990 assessment of the nation and the trial assessment of the states.* Washington, DC: U.S. Department of Education, Office of Educational Research and Improvement, National Center for Education Statistics.

National Assessment of Educational Progress (1992). *The 1990 science report card: NAEP's assessment of fourth, eighth, and twelfth graders.* Washington, DC: U.S. Department of Education, Office of Educational Research and Improvement, National Center for Education Statistics.

National Center for Education Statistics (1988a). *Education statistics 1988.* Washington, DC: U.S. Department of Education, Office of Educational Research and Improvement.

National Center for Education Statistics (1988b). *Digest of education statistics 1988.* Washington, DC: U.S. Government Printing Office.

National Center for Education Statistics (1989). *Digest of education statistics 1989.* Washington, DC: U.S. Department of Education, Office of Educational Research and Improvement.

National Center for Education Statistics (1991a). *The condition of education, 1991, Vol. 1: Elementary and secondary education.* Washington, DC: U.S. Department of Education, Office of Educational Research and Improvement.

National Center for Education Statistics (1991b). *The state of mathematics achievement, Executive summary, NAEP's 1990 assessment of the nation and the trial assessment of the states.* Washington, DC: U.S. Department of Education, Office of Educational Research and Improvement.

National Center for Education Statistics (1992). *The condition of education, 1992.* Washington, DC: U.S. Department of Education, Office of Educational Research and Improvement.

National Center for Education Statistics (1993a). *Education in the states and nations: Indicators comparing U.S. states with the OECD countries in 1988.* Washington, DC: U.S. Department of Education, Office of Educational Research and Improvement.

National Center for Education Statistics (1993b). *The condition of education, 1993.* Washington, DC: U.S. Department of Education, Office of Educational Research and Improvement.

National Center for Education Statistics (1993c). *Youth indicators 1993.* Washington, DC: U.S. Department of Education, Office of Educational Research and Improvement.

National Center for Education Statistics (1993d). *The digest of education statistics, 1993.* Washington, DC: U.S. Department of Education, Office of Educational Research and Improvement.

National Center for Education Statistics (1994). *The condition of education, 1994.* Washington, DC: U.S. Department of Education, Office of Educational Research and Improvement.

National Commission on Children (1991). *Beyond rhetoric: A new American agenda for children and families.* Washington, DC: U.S. Government Printing Office.

National Commission on Excellence in Education (1983). *A nation at risk: The imperatives for educational reform.* Washington, DC: U.S. Department of Education.

National Commission on Excellence in Education (1984). *The nation responds.* Washington, DC: U.S. Department of Education.

National Commission on Testing and Public Policy (1990). *From gatekeeper to gateway: Transforming testing in America.* Chestnut Hill, MA: Boston College.

National Council on Education Standards and Testing (1992). *Raising standards for American education.* Washington, DC: U.S. Government Printing Office.

National Council for Research on Women (1993). *To reclaim a legacy of diversity: Analyzing the "Political Correctness" debates in higher education.* New York: Author.

National Council for the Social Studies (1993). A vision of powerful teaching and learning in the social studies: Building understanding and civic efficacy. *Social Education, 57*(5), 213–223.

National Council for the Social Studies (1994). *Curriculum standards for the social studies* (excerpted draft). Washington, DC: Author.

National Council of Teachers of Mathematics (1989). *Curriculum and evaluation standards for school mathematics.* Reston, VA: Author.

National Education Association, Research Division (1992). *Status of the American public school teacher 1990–1991.* Washington, DC: Author.

National Governors' Association (1986). *Time for results: The governors' 1991 report on education.* Washington, DC: Author.

National Science Board Commission on Precollegiate Education in Mathematics, Science and Technology (1983). *Educating Americans for the 21st century.* Washington, DC: National Science Foundation.

Natriello, Gary, McDill, Edward L., & Pallas, Aaron M. (1990). *Schooling disadvantaged children: Racing against catastrophe.* New York: Teachers College Press.

Nelsen, Frank C. (1987). *Public schools: An evangelical appraisal.* Old Tappan, NJ: F. H. Revell Co.

Newman, Katherine S. (1988). *Falling from grace: The experience of downward mobility in the American middle class.* New York: The Free Press.

Newsweek (1992). America's edge (June 8), pp. 40–43.

Norris, Bill (1990). School chief pitches for a longer day. *Times Education Supplement* (April 20), p. 395.

Norton, Mary Beth (1980). *Liberty's daughters: The revolutionary experience of American women, 1750–1800.* Boston: Little, Brown.

O'Neill, Barry (1994). The history of a hoax. *New York Times Magazine* (March 6), 46–49.

O'Reilly, Brian (1994). Personal communication.

Oakes, Jeannie (1985). *Keeping track: How schools structure inequality.* New Haven: Yale University Press.

Oakes, Jeannie (1989). Tracking in secondary schools: A contextual perspective. In Robert E. Slavin (Ed.), *School and classroom organization* (pp. 173–195). Hillsdale, NJ: Lawrence Erlbaum Associates.

Oakes, Jeannie (1992). Detracking schools: Early lessons from the field. *Phi Delta Kappan, 73,* 448–454.

Oakes, Jeannie (1994). One more thought. *Sociology of Education, 67,* 91.

Oakes, Jeannie, Gamoran, Adam, & Page, Reba N. (1992). Curriculum differentiation: Opportunities, outcomes, and meanings. In Philip W. Jackson (Ed.), *Handbook of research on curriculum* (pp. 570–608). New York: Macmillan.

Office of Educational Research and Improvement, U.S. Department of Education (1993). *National excellence: A case for developing America's talent.* Washington, DC: Author.

Onosko, Joseph J. & Newmann, Fred M. (1994). Creating more thoughtful learning environments. In John N. Mangieri & Cathy Collins Block (Eds.), *Creating powerful thinking in teachers and students* (pp. 27–50). Forth Worth, TX: Harcourt Brace.

Organisation for Economic Co-operation and Development (1989). *Education in OECD countries 1986–87: A compendium of statistical information.* Paris: Author.

Organisation for Economic Co-operation and Development (1990). *Education in OECD countries 1987–88. A compendium of statistical information.* Paris: Author.

Organisation for Economic Co-operation and Development (1992). *Education at a glance: OECD indicators.* Paris: Author.

Orth, Samuel P. (1909). Plain truth about public schools. *Atlantic Monthly, 102,* 419–432.

Parker, Barbara (1981). Target: Public schools. *Graduate Woman, 75* (September/October), 13.

Parkinson, Cyril Northcote (1957). *Parkinson's law: Or the pursuit of progress.* London: Sidgwick & Jackson [1986].

Partridge, Percy H. (1968). *Society, schools, and progress in Australia.* Oxford: Pergamon Press.

Pegnato, Carl W. & Birch, Jack W. (1959). Locating gifted children in junior high. *Exceptional Children, 26,* 300–304.

Penner, Louis A., Batsche, George M., Knoff, Howard M. & Nelson, Douglas L. (Eds.) (1993). *The challenge in mathematics and science education: Psychology's response.* Washington, D.C.: American Psychological Association.

Persell, Caroline Hodges (1977). *Education and inequality: The roots and results of stratification in America's schools.* New York: The Free Press.

Persell, Caroline Hodges & Cookson, Peter W., Jr. (1990). Chartering and bartering: Elite education and social reproduction. In Paul William Kingston & Lionel S. Lewis (Eds.), *The high-status track: Studies of elite schools and stratification* (pp. 25–52). Albany: State University of New York Press.

Peterson, Penelope P., Wilkinson, Louise Cherry, & Hallinan, Maureen (Eds.) (1984). *The social context of instruction.* Orlando, FL: Academic Press.

Peterson, Peter G. (1993). *Facing up: How to rescue the economy from crushing debt & restore the American dream.* New York: Simon & Schuster.

Phillips, Kevin (1990). *The politics of rich and poor.* New York: Random House.

Pincus, Fred L. (1984). From equity to excellence: The rebirth of educational conservatism. *Social Policy* (Winter), 50–56.

Pipho, Chris (1991). The vouchers are coming! *Phi Delta Kappan, 73,* 102–103.

Policy Information Center (1994). *What Americans study, revisited.* Princeton, NJ: Educational Testing Service.

Popkewitz, Thomas S., Tabachnick, B. Robert, & Wehlage, Gary (1982). *The myth of educational reform.* Madison, WI: University of Wisconsin Press.

Porat, Marc Uri (1977). *The information economy* (9 vols.). Washington, DC: U.S. Department of Commerce.

Postman, Neil (1993). Of Luddites, learning and life. *Technos, 2*(4), 24–26.

Pound, Edward T. & Stout, Hilary (1991). Bush nominee Alexander's investment successes have made senate investigators very inquisitive. *Wall Street Journal* (March 5), p. 16.

Presidential Task Force on Psychology in Education, American Psychological Association (1993). *Learner-centered psychological principles: Guidelines for school redesign and reform.* Washington, DC: Author.

Project 2061, American Association for the Advancement of Science (1989). *Science for all Americans: A Project 2061 report on literacy goals in science, mathematics, and technology.* Washington, DC: Author.

Project 2061, American Association for the Advancement of Science (1993). *Benchmarks for science literacy.* New York: Oxford University Press.

Putnam, Ralph T., Lampert, Magdelene, & Peterson, Penelope (1990). Alternative perspectives on knowing mathematics in elementary schools. In Courtney Cazden (Ed.), *Review of research in education* (pp. 57–150). Washington, DC: American Educational Research Association.

Quinn, Mary Ellen & Kessler, Carolyn (1986). Bilingual children's cognition and language in science learning. In James. J. Gallagher & G. Dawson (Eds.), *Science education and cultural environments in the Americas* (pp. 32–39). Washington, DC: National Science Teachers Association.

Ramírez, J. David, Yuer, Sandra D., & Ramey, Dena A. (1991). *Longitudinal study of structured English immersion strategy: Early-exit and late-exit transitional bilingual educational programs for language-minority children.* San Mateo, CA: Aquirre International.

Rasell, M. Edith & Mishel, Lawrence (1990). *Shortchanging education: How U.S. spending on grades K–12 lags behind other industrialized nations.* Washington, DC: Economic Policy Institute.

Ravitch, Diane (1993). Launching a revolution in standards and assessments. *Phi Delta Kappan, 74*(June), 767–772.

Ravitch, Diane & Finn, Chester (1987). *What do our 17-year-olds know?* New York: Harper and Row.

Ray, Carol Axtell & Mickelson, Roslyn Arlin (1993). Restructuring students for restructured work: The economy, school reform and non-college bound youths. *Sociology of Education, 66,* 1–20.

Raywid, Mary Anne (1987). Public choice, yes; vouchers, No! *Phi Delta Kappan,* 68(10), 762–769

Redovich, Dennis W. (1993). Personal communication.

Reese, Charley (1993). School choice overlooks our most needy students. *Orlando Sentinel* (October 30).

Reich, Robert B. (1983). *The next American frontier.* New York: Times Books.

Reich, Robert B. (1987). *Tales of a new America.* New York: Times Books.

Reich, Robert (1991a). Big biz cuts class: Firms talk loud, do little for schools. *Washington Post* (April 21), p. B1.

Reich, Robert (1991b). *The work of nations.* New York: Knopf.

Richardson, Virginia, Casanova, Ursula, Placier, Peggy, & Guilfoyle, Karen (1989). *School children at risk.* Philadelphia, PA: Falmer Press.

Richburg, Keith B. (1985). Japanese education: Admired but not easily imported. *Washington Post* (October 19), pp. A1, A4.

Rickover, Hyman G. (1959). *Education and freedom.* New York: Dutton.

Riddle, Wayne (1990). *Expenditures in public school districts: Why do they differ?* Washington, DC: Congressional Research Service.

Rippa, S. Alexander (1988). *Education in a free society* (6th ed.). White Plains, NY: Longman.

Robinson, Glen & Brandon, David (1992). *Perceptions about American education: Are they based on facts?* Arlington, VA: Educational Research Service.

Robinson, Glen E. & Protheroe, Nancy J. (1987). *Cost of education: An investment in America's future.* Arlington, VA: Educational Research Service.

Robitaille, David F. & Garden, Robert A. (1989). *The IEA study of mathematics, Vol. II: Contexts and outcomes of school mathematics.* Oxford, UK: Pergamon Press.

Rogers, Carl (1969). *Freedom to learn.* Columbus, OH: Merrill.

Romanish, Bruce (1991). *Empowering teachers: Restructuring schools for the 21st century.* Lanham, MD: University Press of America.

Rosenbaum, James E. (1980a). Social implications of educational grouping. In David C. Berliner (Ed.), *Review of research in education* (Vol. 8, pp. 361–401). Washington, DC: American Educational Research Association.

Rosenbaum, James E. (1980b). Track misperceptions and frustrated college plans: An analysis of the effects of tracks and track perceptions in the national longitudinal study. *Sociology of Education, 53,* 74–88.

Ross, Edward Alsworth (1906). *Social control: A survey of the foundations of order.* New York: Macmillan.

Ross, Michael & Fletcher, Garth J. O. (1985). Attribution and social perception. Gardner Lindzey & Eliot Aronson (Eds.), *Handbook of social psychology* (Vol. 2, 3rd ed., pp. 73–122). New York: Random House.

Rotberg, Iris C. (1990). I never promised you first place. *Phi Delta Kappan* (December), 296–303.

Roth, Robert A. & Pipho, Chris (1990). Teacher education standards. In W. Robert Houston (Ed.), *Handbook of research on teacher education* (pp. 119–135). New York: Macmillan.

Rothstein, Richard (1993). The myth of public school failure. *The American Prospect,* *13*(Spring), 20–34.

Rudman, Warren B. & Tsongas, Paul E. (1993). Foreword. In Peter G. Peterson, *Facing up: How to rescue the economy from crushing debt & restore the American dream* (pp. 13–16). New York: Simon & Schuster.

Sandia National Laboratories (1993). Perspectives on education in America: An annotated briefing. *Journal of Educational Research, 86*(5), 259–310.

Sapon-Shevin, Mara (1994). *Playing favorites: Gifted education and the disruption of community.* Albany: State University of New York Press.

Sarason, Seymour B. (1990). *The predictable failure of educational reform: Can we change course before it's too late?* San Francisco: Jossey-Bass.

Saxe, Geoffrey B. (1988). Candy selling and mathematics learning. *Educational Researcher, 17*(6), 14–21.

Schneider, Barbara & Hood, Stafford (1994). Pathways to institutional change: From the deans' network to the Holmes Group. In Kathryn M. Borman & Nancy P. Greenman (Eds.), *Changing American education: Recapturing the past or inventing the future?* (pp. 107–132). Albany: State University of New York Press.

Schneider, Joe & Houston, Paul (1993). *Exploding the myths: Another round in the education debate.* Washington, DC: American Association of Educational Service Agencies.

Schooland, Ken (1990). *Shogun's ghost: The dark side of Japanese education.* New York: Bergin and Garvey.

Schor, Juliet B. (1991). *The overworked American: The unexpected decline of leisure.* New York: Basic Books.

Schultz, Theodore W. (1960). Capital formation by education. *Journal of Political Economy, 68*, 571–583.

Servan-Schreiber, J. J. & Crecine, Barbara (1986). *The knowledge revolution.* Pittsburgh, PA: Carnegie Mellon Press.

Shaiken, Harley (1984). *Work transformed: Automation and labor in the computer age.* New York: Holt, Rinehart, and Winston.

Shanker, Albert (1985). *Speech before the National Press Club.* Washington, DC (January 29).

Shanker, Albert & Rosenberg, Bella (1992). Do private schools outperform public schools? In Peter W. Cookson, Jr. (Ed.), *The choice controversy* (pp. 128–145). Newbury Park, CA: Corwin Press.

Shapiro, Walter (1991). Can this man save our schools? *TIME* (September 16), 54–60.

Sharp, Patricia T. & Wood, Randy M. (1992). Moral values: A study of selected third- and fifth-grade reading and social studies textbooks. *Religion and Public Education, 19,* 143–153.

Shavelson, Richard J. & Berliner, David C. (1988). Erosion of the education research infrastructure: A reply to Finn. *Educational Researcher, 17*(1), 9–12.

Shea, Christine M. (1989). Pentagon vs. multinational capitalism: The political economy of the 1980s school reform movement. In Christine M. Shea, Ernest Kahane, & Peter Sola (Eds.), *The new servants of power: A critique of the 1980s school reform movement.* New York: Praeger.

Shepard, Lorrie A. & Bliem, C. L. (1994). *An analysis of parent opinions and opinion change about standardized tests and performance assessments (technical report).* Los Angeles, CA: University of California at Los Angeles, Center for Research on Evaluation, Standards and Student Testing.

Shepard, Lorrie A. & Smith, Mary Lee (Eds.) (1989). *Flunking grades: Research and policies on retention.* Philadelphia, PA: Falmer Press.

Shinn, Marybeth (1978). Father absence and children's cognitive development. *Psychological Bulletin, 85,* 294–324.

Shouse, Roger (1994). *Academic orientation within school society: The importance of academic press.* Paper presented at the annual meeting of the American Sociological Association, Los Angeles.

Shulman, Steven (1990). The causes of black poverty: Evidence and interpretation. *Journal of Economic Issues, 24,* 995–1016.

Sidel, Ruth (1990). *On her own: Growing up in the shadow of the American dream.* New York: Viking.

Siegler, Robert S. & Kotovsky, Kenneth (1986). Two levels of giftedness: Shall ever the twain meet? In Robert J. Sternberg & Janet E. Davidson (Eds.), *Conceptions of giftedness* (pp. 417–435). Cambridge, UK: Cambridge University Press.

Silverman, Linda K. (1980). *How are gifted teachers different from other teachers?* Paper presented at the annual meeting of the National Association for Gifted Children. Denver, CO (October–November).

Sizer, Theodore R. (1984). *Horace's compromise: The dilemma of the American high school.* Boston: Houghton Mifflin.

Slavin, Robert E. (1983). *Cooperative learning.* New York: Longman.

Slavin, Robert E. (1990). *Cooperative learning: Theory, research and practice.* Englewood Cliffs, NJ: Prentice-Hall.

Smeeding, Timothy M., Rainwater, Lee, Rein, Martin, Hauser, Richard, & Schaber, Gaston (1990). Income poverty in seven countries: Initial estimates from the LIS database. In Timothy M. Smeeding, Michael O'Higgins, & Lee Rainwater (Eds.), *Poverty, inequality and income distribution in comparative perspective* (pp. 57–76). Washington, DC: Urban Institute Press.

Smith, Gary (1994). Personal communication.

Smith, Louis M. & Geoffrey, William (1968). *The complexities of an urban classroom: An analysis toward a general theory of teaching.* New York: Holt, Rinehart and Winston.

Smith, Mary Lee & Shepard, Lorrie A. (1988). Kindergarten readiness and retention: A qualitative study of teachers' beliefs and practices. *American Educational Research Journal, 25,* 307–333.

Smith, Mary Lee (1991). Put to the test: The effects of external testing on teachers. *Educational Researcher, 20*(5), 8–11.

Smith, Stephanie H. & Whitehead, George I., 3rd (1984). Attributions for promotion and demotion in the United States and India. *Journal of Social Psychology, 124,* 27–34.

Smith-Morris, Miles (Ed.) (1990). *Book of world statistics.* New York: Times Books.

Solomon, Robert J. (1983). *Information concerning mean test scores for the Graduate Management Admission Test (GMAT); Graduate Record Examination (GRE); Law School Admission Test (LSAT); Preliminary Scholastic Aptitude Test (PSAT); and Scholastic Aptitude Test (SAT) for the National Commission on Excellence in Education.* Princeton, NJ: Educational Testing Service.

Spielberger, Charles (1993). Foreword. In Louis A. Penner, George M. Batsche, Howard M. Knoff, & Douglas L. Nelson (Eds.), *The challenge in mathematics and science education: Psychology's response.* Washington, DC: American Psychological Association.

Spring, Joel (1985). *American education.* New York: Longman.

Spring, Joel (1986). *The American school 1642–1985: Various historic interpretations of foundations and development of American education.* New York: Longman.

Stanglin, Doug (1985). Japan's blackboard jungle. *Newsweek: Atlantic Edition* (July 1), 5.

Stedman, James B., Salganik, Laura H., & Celebuski, Carin A. (1988). *Dropping out: The educational vulnerability of at-risk youth.* Washington, DC: Congressional Research Service.

Steinberg, Stephen (1989). *The ethnic myth: Race, ethnicity and class in America.* Boston: Beacon Press.

Stevenson, Harold W. (1992). Learning from Asian schools. *Scientific American* (December), 70–76.

Stiggins, Richard J., Backland, Phillip M., & Bridgeford, Nancy J. (1985). Avoiding bias in the assessment of communication skills. *Communication Education, 34,* 135–141.

Suárez, Tanya M. & Gottovi, Nancy C. (1992). The impact of high-stakes assessments on our schools. *NASSP Bulletin* (September), 82–88.

Sununu, John (1989). *Today show* (September 27). New York: National Broadcasting Company.

Sykes, Charles J. (1988). *Profscam: Professors and the demise of higher education.* Washington, DC: Regnery Gateway.

Talbot, Joan E. (1990). *Teacher tracking: Exacerbating inequalities in the high school.* Stanford, CA: Center for Research on the Context of Secondary Teaching, Stanford University.

Tanner, Daniel (1993). A nation "truly" at risk. *Phi Delta Kappan, 75*(4), 288–297.

Task Force of the Business-Higher Education Forum (1983). *America's competitive challenge: The need for a national response.* Washington, DC: Business-Higher Education Forum.

Task Force on Education for Economic Growth (1983). *Action for excellence: A comprehensive plan to improve our nation's schools.* Denver: Education Commission of the States.

Tauber, Robert T. (1992). Those who can't teach: Dispelling the myth. *NASSP Bulletin, 76*(54), 96–102.

Taylor, Frederick Winslow (1911). *The principles of scientific management.* New York: Norton [1967].

Terman, Lewis M. (1916). *The measurement of intelligence*. Boston: Houghton Mifflin.

Tetlock, Philip E. (1980). Explaining teacher explanations of public performance: A self-presentation interpretation. *Social Psychology Quarterly, 42*, 5–17.

Thoburn, Robert (1986). *The children trap*. Fort Worth, TX: Dominion Press.

Thomas, William Isaac & Znaniecki, Florian (1918–1920). *The Polish peasant in Europe and America* (Vols. 1–5). Boston: Gorham Press.

Thurow, Lester (1982). *The zero sum society: Distribution and the possibilities for economic change*. New York: Basic Books.

Thurow, Lester (1989). The great wall. *Alexander & Alexander World*, First Quarter.

Time Magazine (1949). Flapdoodle (September 19), 64.

Timpane, Michael (1984). Business has rediscovered the schools. *Phi Delta Kappan, 65*(6), 389–392.

Toch, Thomas (1991). *In the name of excellence: The struggle to reform the nation's schools, why it is failing, and what should be done*. New York: Oxford University Press.

Tooker, Gary L. (no date). Booklet sent to all employees and associates of the Motorola Corporation by its president and Chief Operating Officer.

Travers, Kenneth J. & Westbury, Ian (1989). *The IEA study of mathematics, Vol. I: Analysis of mathematics curriculum*. Oxford, UK: Pergamon Press.

Troen, Selwyn K. (1975). *The public and the schools: Shaping the St. Louis system, 1838–1920*. Columbia, MO: University of Missouri Press.

Twentieth Century Fund Task Force on Federal Elementary and Secondary Education Policy (1983). *Making the grade*. New York: Twentieth Century Fund.

Tyack, David (1974). *The one best system: A history of American urban education*. Cambridge, MA: Harvard University Press.

U.S. Department of Education (1986). *What works: Research about teaching and learning*. Washington, DC: Author.

UNESCO (1988). *Statistical yearbook*. Paris: Author.

UNESCO Division of Statistics on Education (1989). *Development of private enrollment first and second level education 1975–1985*. Paris: Author.

United States General Accounting Office (1987). *Bilingual education: A new look at the research evidence* (Report GAO/PEMD-87-12BR). Washington, DC: Author, March.

United States General Accounting Office (1993). *Educational achievement standards: NAGB's approach yields misleading interpretations*. Washington, DC: Author.

Useem, Elizabeth L. (1992). Getting on the fast track in mathematics: School organizational influences on math track assignment. *American Journal of Education, 100*, 325–353.

Vélez-Ibáñez, Carlos & Greenberg, Jim (1989). *Formation and transformation of funds of knowledge among U.S. Mexican households in the context of the borderlands*. Paper presented at the meeting of the American Anthropological Association, Washington, DC.

Ventures in Education (1992). *Expanding horizons: Success in high school and beyond*. New York: Author.

Verstegan, Deborah (1992). International comparisons of education spending: A review and analysis of reports. *Journal of Education Finance, 17*(4), 257–276.

Vitz, Paul C. (1986). *Censorship: Evidence of bias in our children's textbooks.* Ann Arbor, MI: Servant Books.

Wainer, Howard (1993). Does spending money on education help? *Educational Researcher, 22*(9), 22–24.

Ward, Edward J. (1913). *The social center.* New York: Appleton.

Wasley, Patricia (1992). Teacher leadership in a teacher-run school. In Ann Lieberman (Ed.), *The changing contexts of teaching. Ninety-first yearbook of the National Society for the Study of Education, Part 1.* (pp. 212–235). Chicago: University of Chicago Press.

Weiss, Carol H. & Singer, Eleanor, with Endreny, P. (1988). *Reporting social science in the national media.* New York: Russell Sage Foundation.

Wells, Amy S. & Biegel, Stuart (1993). Public funds for private schools: Political and First Amendment considerations. *American Journal of Education, 101,* 209–233.

West, Cornel (1993). *Race matters.* Boston: Beacon Press.

Westbury, Ian (1992). Comparing American and Japanese achievement: Is the United States really a low achiever? *Educational Researcher, 21*(5), 18–24.

Westbury, Ian (1994). Personal communication.

Wheelock, Anne (1992). *Crossing the tracks: How "untracking" can save America's schools.* New York: The New Press.

Whittingon, Dale (1991). What have 17-year-olds known in the past? *American Educational Research Journal, 28,* 759–780.

Wiggins, Grant (1989). A true test: Toward a more authentic and equitable assessment. *Phi Delta Kappan, 70,* 703–713.

Wiggins, Grant (1993). *Assessing student performance: Exploring the purpose and limits of testing.* San Francisco: Jossey-Bass.

Wiley, David E. & Harnischfeger, Annegret (1974). Explosion of a myth: Quantity of schooling and exposure to instruction, major educational vehicles. *Educational Researcher, 3*(4), 7–12.

Willig, Ann (1986). A meta-analysis of selected studies on the effectiveness of bilingual education. *Review of Educational Research, 55,* 269–317.

Willms, J. Douglas (1987). Patterns of academic achievement in public and private schools: Implication for public policy and future research. In Edward H. Haertel, Thomas James, & Henry M. Levin (Eds.), *Comparing public & private schools. Volume 2: School achievement* (pp. 113–134). London: Falmer Press.

Wingspread Group on Higher Education (1993). *An American imperative.* Racine, WI: The Johnson Fund.

Wirth, Arthur (1992). *Education and work for the year 2000: Choices we face.* San Francisco: Jossey-Bass.

Witte, John F. (1991). Choice in American education. *Educational Considerations, 19,* 12–19.

Wolfe, Sidney M. (Ed.) (1993). *Public Citizen Health Research Group Letter, 9*(11). Washington, DC: Public Citizen Health Research Group.

Wolpe, Howard (1992). *Projecting science and engineering personnel requirements for the 1990s: How good are the numbers?* (Opening statement made by its Chairman to a Hearing before The Subcommittee on Investigations and Oversight of the Committee on Science, Space, and Technology, U.S. House of Representatives, One Hundred Second Congress, Second Session). Washington, DC: U.S. Government Printing Office.

Wyllie, Irvin G. (1954). *The self-made man in America: The myth of rags to riches.* New Brunswick, NJ: Rutgers University Press.

X, Malcolm (1973). *The autobiography of Malcolm X.* New York: Ballantine.

Yates, Ronald E. (1985). Japanese twist bullying into a brutal art. *Chicago Tribune* (November 24), p. 5.

Zachary, G. Pascal (1993). Black hole opens in scientist job rolls. *Wall Street Journal* (April 14), p. B1.

Zigler, Edward (1989). Addressing the nation's child care crisis: The school of the 21st century. *American Journal of Orthopsychiatry, 59,* 485–491.

Zigler, Edward & Lang, Mary E. (1991). *Child care choices: Balancing the needs of children, family and society.* New York: The Free Press.

Zionek, Bob (1994). Personal communication.

Name Index

◆

Subject Index

◆

Grateful acknowledgment is made to the following for permission to reprint copyrighted material:

Chapter 2

Material reprinted with permission from *Guidelines on the Uses of College Board Test Scores and Related Data.* Copyright © 1988 by College Entrance Examination Board.

Material from Robert L. Linn, M. Elizabeth Graue, and Nancy M. Sanders, "Comparing State and District Test Results to National Norms: The Validity of Claims that 'Everyone Is Above Average'," *Educational Measurement: Issues and Practice*, Volume 10 (Fall): 5–14. Reprinted by permission of the National Council on Measurement in Education. Copyright © 1990 by the National Council on Measurement in Education.

Chapter 3

Material from Richard Rothstein, "The Myth of Public School Failure," is reprinted with permission from *The American Prospect* (Spring 1993). Copyright © New Prospect Inc.

Material from Glen Robinson and David Brandon, *Perceptions About American Education: Are They Based on Facts?"* Arlington, VA: Educational Research Service. Copyright © 1992. Reprinted with the permission of Educational Research Service.

Material from *Sector Productivity*. Washington, DC: McKinsey Global Institute. Copyright © 1992. Reprinted with the permission of the McKinsey Global Institute.

Excerpt from "Amid 'Shortage,' Young Physicists See Few Jobs" by Malcolm Browne, *New York Times*, March 10, 1992. Copyright © 1992 by The New York Times Company. Reprinted by permission.

Excerpt from "It's Time to Trim Hefty Paychecks" by Derek Bok, *New York Times,* December 5, 1993. Copyright © 1993 by The New York Times Company. Reprinted by permission.

Material from *Status of the American Public School Teacher 1990–1991*. Washington, DC: NEA. © 1992. Reprinted with the permission of the National Education Association.

Material from Albert Shanker and Bella Rosenberg, "Do Private Schools Outperform Public Schools?" in *The Choice Controversy*, Peter W. Cookson, ed. Washington, DC: Corwin Press. Copyright © 1992. Reprinted with the permission of Albert Shanker.

Chapter 4

Material from Lawrence A. Cremin, *Popular Education and Its Discontents*. New York: HarperCollins. Copyright © 1990 by Lawrence A. Cremin. Reprinted by permission of HarperCollins Publishers, Inc.

Excerpts from Fred L. Pincus, "From Equity to Excellence: The Rebirth of Educational Conservatism," *Social Policy* (Winter 1984). New York: Social Policy Corporation. Reprinted with the permission of the Social Policy Corporation.

Excerpt from Walter Shapiro, "Can This Man Save Our Schools?" *TIME* Magazine, September 16, 1991. Copyright © 1991 Time Inc. Reprinted by permission.

Excerpts from John S. Friedman, "The Whittle-Alexander Nexus: Big Business Goes to School," *The Nation* (February 17, 1992). New York: The Nation Company, Inc. Reprinted with the permission of The Nation Company, Inc.

Chapter 5

Excerpt from Charley Reese, "School Choice Overlooks Our Most Needy Students," *Orlando Sentinel*, October 30, 1993. Reprinted with the permission of Charles E. Reese.

Excerpt from Benjamin R. Barber, "America Skips School," *Harper's Magazine*. Copyright © 1993 by Harper's Magazine. All rights reserved. Reproduced from the November 1993 issue by special permission.

Insert box by Margie Casady from David Greene and Mark R. Lepper, "How to Turn Play into Work" *Psychology Today Magazine* (September 1974): 49–53. Reprinted with permission from *Psychology Today Magazine*, copyright © 1974 (Sussex Publishers, Inc.).

About the Authors

◆

David C. Berliner, Ph.D., is Regents' Professor in the College of Education of Arizona State University at Tempe. He has served as President of the American Education Research Association and of the Division of Educational Psychology of the American Psychological Association. He is also a Fellow of the Center for Advanced Study in the Behavioral Sciences, and has taught at the University of Massachusetts, Stanford University, and at universities in Australia and Spain. Professor Berliner's own schooling includes P.S. 79 and DeWitt Clinton High School in the Bronx, UCLA, and Stanford for his doctorate in educational psychology. Declared a *Friend of Education* by the National Education Association in 1994, Professor Berliner is also a grandfather of six.

Bruce J. Biddle, Ph.D., is Professor of both Psychology and Sociology at the University of Missouri in Columbia, where he also directs the Center for Research in Social Behavior. He is known as coauthor of the influential monograph *The Study of Teaching,* as well as many articles on the role of the teacher, classroom interaction, and education policy. He is also founding editor of the journal *Social Psychology of Education.* Professor Biddle was himself educated at Riverside High School in Milwaukee, Friends Central School in Philadelphia, Antioch College, the University of North Carolina, and the University of Michigan, from which he received his doctorate in social psychology. He has also held academic appointments at Columbia University's Teachers College, the University of Kentucky, the University of Michigan, and other colleges. He is a father of three and grandfather of three (so far).